AF712893

UNDERSTANDING PRIVATE LAW

This book engages with some of Stephen A Smith's most significant arguments, illustrating that he was a towering figure in the field of private law, with little of the field not impacted by his scholarship.

The contributors explore Professor Smith's most controversial thinking on private law. Interrogating questions of contract law, remedies, unjust enrichment, comparative law, and the legal theory underlying these fields, this is an important publication in the field.

Volume 52 in the series Hart Studies in Private Law

Hart Studies in Private Law

This monograph series brings together in one place two types of book: works which examine in-depth the fundamental doctrines and principles of private law, and works which engage with the theoretical underpinnings of private law. The series thus aims to contribute to ever-evolving debates about the nature of private law such as problems of classification and taxonomy, remedies, the relationship with public law and the boundaries of private law generally.

The series includes, but is not confined to, works on contract, tort, unjust enrichment, equity, property and the conflict of laws, welcoming work which intersects with other fields of study to enable a deeper understanding of private law theory and practice.

Understanding Private Law

Essays in Honour of Stephen A Smith

Edited by
Evan Fox-Decent
John CP Goldberg
and
Lionel Smith

•HART•
OXFORD • LONDON • NEW YORK • NEW DELHI • SYDNEY

HART PUBLISHING

Bloomsbury Publishing Plc

Kemp House, Chawley Park, Cumnor Hill, Oxford, OX2 9PH, UK

1385 Broadway, New York, NY 10018, USA

29 Earlsfort Terrace, Dublin 2, Ireland

HART PUBLISHING, the Hart/Stag logo, BLOOMSBURY and the Diana logo are trademarks of Bloomsbury Publishing Plc

First published in Great Britain 2025

Copyright © The editors and contributors severally 2025

The editors and contributors have asserted their right under the Copyright, Designs and Patents Act 1988 to be identified as Authors of this work.

All rights reserved. No part of this publication may be: i) reproduced or transmitted in any form, electronic or mechanical, including photocopying, recording or by means of any information storage or retrieval system without prior permission in writing from the publishers; or ii) used or reproduced in any way for the training, development or operation of artificial intelligence (AI) technologies, including generative AI technologies. The rights holders expressly reserve this publication from the text and data mining exception as per Article 4(3) of the Digital Single Market Directive (EU) 2019/790.

While every care has been taken to ensure the accuracy of this work, no responsibility for loss or damage occasioned to any person acting or refraining from action as a result of any statement in it can be accepted by the authors, editors or publishers.

All UK Government legislation and other public sector information used in the work is Crown Copyright ©. All House of Lords and House of Commons information used in the work is Parliamentary Copyright ©. This information is reused under the terms of the Open Government Licence v3.0 (http://www.nationalarchives.gov.uk/doc/open-government-licence/version/3) except where otherwise stated.

All Eur-lex material used in the work is © European Union, http://eur-lex.europa.eu/, 1998–2025.

A catalogue record for this book is available from the British Library.

A catalogue record for this book is available from the Library of Congress.

ISBN: HB: 978-1-50997-115-2
ePDF: 978-1-50997-117-6
ePub: 978-1-50997-116-9

Typeset by Compuscript Ltd, Shannon

To find out more about our authors and books visit www.hartpublishing.co.uk. Here you will find extracts, author information, details of forthcoming events and the option to sign up for our newsletters.

For our friend and colleague
Steve Smith

And for Steve's family:
Susan Law, Jamie Law-Smith,
Michael Law-Smith and Jennifer Law-Smith

Stephen Alexander Smith, 1958–2022
Photo credit: Lysanne Larose

FOREWORD

SHAUNA VAN PRAAGH

Steve Smith would have enjoyed this book. He would have liked the sustained attention given to his words and texts by colleagues and friends. He would have appreciated the critical engagement with ideas he had worked on over years as a teacher and scholar. And he would have loved responding to the arguments framed by these authors and participating in the endless conversations reflected in these pages.

As this collection of essays in his honour so clearly illustrates, Stephen A Smith was a remarkable contributor to thinking and practice in the private law of obligations and remedies. The title 'Understanding Private Law' is especially apt – not because of its reference to private law as the object of exploration but rather for its choice of 'understanding' as the first word. Steve had real confidence in the importance and dynamic character of understanding as a verb and process. Rather than a fixed destination towards which we should move or a comprehensive state for which we should strive, understanding can be a participatory and energetic activity. In a book created in his memory, we find thinkers and writers revelling, like he did, in the hard work associated with ongoing, demanding and deep understanding.

Three decades ago, I discovered how much Steve trusted me as a colleague when he asked me to read the manuscript of his Oxford doctoral dissertation prior to his submitting it. Although we had been law clerks together for the Chief Justice of Canada, that was the first time I read his careful, insightful and ambitious arguments related to contracts. It was a special opportunity to learn from his writing as a private law scholar and to offer editing suggestions as to how to make that writing even more compelling. In similar yet distinctive ways, the authors of the papers in this collection have benefited from meaningful and collegial interaction with Steve. All have learned from, reflected upon and reacted to his written work.

Readers should know that Stephen A Smith also had much to teach off the written page and outside the walls of any law school or university. Here I share two images taken from contexts that were just as central, important and comfortable for Steve. The first comes from his home kitchen, in which he was principal chef; the second from the outdoor adventures that marked his weekends and holidays.

First, I offer a picture of Steve's kitchen spice collection. Imagine pulling open a wide, shallow drawer just below the kitchen counter, in which dozens of herbs and spices are lined up from A to Z, each housed in a clear, oblong container. Steve was very proud of that drawer. He had worked out a theory for its organisation: the containers should not roll around, uniformity was crucial, use was most efficient if the order was alphabetical, and the creative work of cooking depended on easy and functional access to ingredients. Steve had lots of favourite dishes for which the herbs and spices were necessary. But he was also open to adaptation and discovery; the logic and dependability of his spice-drawer system offered a foundation for trying out and testing new recipes. In offering kitchen renovation advice to anyone who would listen, he argued persuasively that his spice-drawer concept and its implementation should be faithfully adopted. I now have a Steve Smith spice drawer in my own kitchen.

Second, I offer readers the image of Steve on a canoe trip. Here, as in the kitchen, preparation and organisation were crucial to success. Steve was extraordinarily good at listing and executing the pre-trip details, making sure that everything and everyone were ready by the time of departure. But he understood that the enjoyment and awe-inspiring beauty of any canoe trip could never be subject to complete control or reliant on comprehensive theory. There was always room for variation and surprise. An impressive sports enthusiast and an intrepid explorer, he was an in-the-moment participant and a high-energy adventurer, and he encouraged others to follow his example. Always happy to offer advice as to best watertight containers for canoe travel or to regale family or friends with stories from the latest voyage, Steve shared his weekend athlete self as openly and confidently as he did his weekday law professor self.

Cooking and outdoor adventure were constants in Steve's life, just as certain themes and questions in private law were constants in his scholarship. Human interactions and relationships, injuries and remedies, were ingredients to be organised, elements to pack in the baggage, pieces crucial to the big picture. He puzzled over promises, worried about the scope of the neighbour principle, considered the limits of loyalty, examined why and how we acknowledge and repair the harms we cause, and mapped out the ways in which connections could or should be traced throughout the universe of private law. He did all of that with the exacting care expected from a good chef or a trustworthy canoe-trip leader. The importance and integrity of classification, order and theory are underlined throughout this book collection just as they were throughout Steve's teaching and writing.

The metaphors of the spice drawer and the canoe trip can push us further than simply noting the importance of foundational structures in the complicated task of 'understanding' law. They challenge us to put aside the cookbook and turn off the GPS, to express with confidence our readiness for real adventure as jurists. Despite uncertainty as to outcome, Steve was always game to experiment in the kitchen. Despite extreme danger, he was keen to take on the risks of white-water canoeing. It might be safer to stick to tried-and-true recipes or choose calmer waterways, and it is true that a compass comes in handy, as does a system for herbs and spices. But Steve's example guides us to take real pleasure in navigating through uncharted, even wild, spots in the law of obligations. He reminds us to embrace the company of others also prepared for and excited about an inevitably bumpy ride.

This collection honours Steve Smith's memory. It cherishes his place and significance on the paths of its contributors as legal thinkers and brings its readers into the wide circle of people influenced by his ideas. Perhaps we honour him best, however, by leaving our desks from time to time and gazing up at the stars – not primarily to name the constellations or figure out direction, but rather to fill our souls with sheer joy and endless wonder.

CONTENTS

LIST OF CONTRIBUTORS

Peter Benson is Professor of Law at the University of Toronto, Faculty of Law.

Robert Chambers is Professor and Department Chair at Thompson Rivers University, Faculty of Law.

Hanoch Dagan is Distinguished Professor of Law and Founding Director, Berkeley Center for Private Law Theory, Berkeley Law School, and Stewart and Judy Colton Emeritus Professor of Legal Theory and Innovation, Tel-Aviv University.

Helge Dedek is Professor of Law and Wainwright Chair in Civil Law at McGill University, Faculty of Law.

Evan Fox-Decent is Professor and Canada Research Chair in Cosmopolitan Law and Justice, McGill University, Faculty of Law.

Mark P Gergen is Professor at the University of California, Berkeley School of Law.

Joshua Getzler is Professor of Law and Legal History at the University of Oxford, a Fellow of St Hugh's College, and Conjoint Professor of Law at UNSW Sydney.

Andrew S Gold is Professor of Law at University of California – Irvine School of Law.

John CP Goldberg is Interim Dean and Carter Professor of General Jurisprudence at Harvard Law School.

Rosalie Jukier is Professor of Law at McGill University, Faculty of Law.

Larissa Katz is Cecil A Wright Professor of Law, University of Toronto, Faculty of Law

Gregory Klass is the Frederick J Haas Chair in Law and Philosophy at Georgetown University Law Center.

Dennis Klimchuk is Associate Professor of Philosophy at Western University.

Adam Kramer is a Barrister at 3 Verulam Buildings, London, UK.

Nicholas J McBride is a Fellow of Pembroke College, Cambridge.

Paul B Miller is Robert and Marion Short Professor of Law and Associate Dean for International and Graduate Programs, Notre Dame Law School.

Jason W Neyers is Professor of Law at the University of Western Ontario.

James Penner is Kwa Geok Choo Professor of Property Law at the National University of Singapore.

Arthur Ripstein is University Professor in the Faculty of Law and the Department of Philosophy in the Faculty of Arts and Science at the University of Toronto.

Lionel Smith is the Professor of Comparative Law at the University of Oxford and a Fellow of Brasenose College.

Robert Stevens is Herbert Smith Freehills Professor of English Private Law at the University of Oxford and a Fellow of Lady Margaret Hall.

William Swadling is Professor of Law at the University of Oxford and a Fellow of Brasenose College.

Shauna Van Praagh is Professor of Law at McGill University and President of the Law Commission of Canada.

Frederick Wilmot-Smith is a Fellow of All Souls College, Oxford.

Benjamin C Zipursky is Professor and James H Quinn' 49 Chair in Legal Ethics at Fordham Law School.

Introduction

EVAN FOX-DECENT, JOHN CP GOLDBERG AND LIONEL SMITH

On Friday, 16 December 2022, the Moot Court Room of the Faculty of Law at McGill University was filled with friends and colleagues who had come through winter weather to share in a celebration of the life of Stephen Alexander Smith. The make-up of the crowd was a wonderful reflection of Steve's character, as speaker after speaker addressed the many aspects of his kaleidoscopic personality: husband, father, son, brother, carpenter, neighbour, athlete, outdoorsman, cook, intellectual, wit, and of course legal scholar and teacher of law.

Steve grew up mainly in Ontario, his youth a record of athletic and academic excellence that would presage his whole career. Following a BA in political science from Queen's University, he took his LLB from the University of Toronto and went on to doctoral study at Balliol College, under the supervision of Joseph Raz. In 1989–90, he was a law clerk to Brian Dickson, Chief Justice of the Supreme Court of Canada. During that year, he met Susan Law, and their marriage was almost contemporaneous with Steve's taking up his first academic post as a law fellow at St Anne's College in 1991. Their three children, Jamie, Michael and Jennifer, were all born in Oxford. The family moved to Montreal when Steve joined McGill's Faculty of Law in 1998, just as the Faculty was launching its innovative transsystemic undergraduate programme in which the common law and the civil law are studied in an integrated fashion from the very beginning of law school.

Many accolades came to Steve during his years at McGill. He was appointed James McGill Professor in 2009, and was awarded a Killam Research Fellowship during 2009–11. He held visiting appointments at both Cambridge and Oxford, as well as at the Universities of Queensland, Singapore and Toronto. In 2017 he was awarded the Law Foundation of New Zealand Distinguished Visiting Fellowship, in which the Fellow visits all of the law faculties in that country. In 2020 he was elected a fellow of the Royal Society of Canada.

His book *Contract Theory* (2004) includes an analytical discussion and typology of different accounts of private law, which is still widely cited by scholars in the field. Among a huge range of papers spanning all areas of private law and private law theory, 'Duties, Liabilities and Damages'[1] is regarded as seminal in debates about the nature of the law's responses to wrongdoing, and helped to lay the foundations of Steve's

[1] SA Smith, 'Duties, Liabilities and Damages' (2012) 125 *Harvard Law Review* 1727.

magnum opus *Rights, Wrongs and Injustices: The Structure of Remedial Law* (2019). This book was the culmination of over two decades of sustained, original scholarship on fundamental private law theory, touching especially on the articulation of the law of remedies as a distinct field of law with its own characteristic governing principles. The book and the scholarship that led to it have been influential all over the world. Steve also published *Atiyah's Introduction to the Law of Contract*, 6th edn (2005), making him a member of the very small group of authors with more than one title in the Clarendon Law Series.

Running through Steve's scholarship across his career are several distinctive characteristics that attest to his Oxford pedigree. If pushed, Steve likely would have said that he prized analytic rigour and clarity above all other scholarly virtues. He did not waste words, and sought always to make the grounds of disagreements with his interlocutors as perspicuous as possible. In one sense, some of his work is radically deflationary and iconoclastic, questioning as it does whether established fields such as comparative law and fiduciary law are in fact the distinct legal domains they purport to be. But at the same time, Steve was deeply committed to an interpretive approach to understanding law that took legal practice seriously. For Steve, a crucial test of both legal theories of doctrine and philosophical accounts of law was whether they could explain and illuminate the key aspects of the relevant legal practice or legal system *as legal practitioners presented and purported to understand the practice or system*. There was no view from nowhere.

True to his Razian roots, Steve was, jurisprudentially, a legal positivist. He recognised that this was a minority position among his North American private-law-theory peers, which seemed to make it all the more fun for him to so self-identify. Yet he had a highly moralised understanding of law, believing steadfastly that for a legal order to be a legal order, the law, through its practitioners, must implicitly or explicitly claim legitimate authority over its subjects. And so, over time, Steve developed a firmer and firmer distinction between, on the one hand, substantive rights and duties recognised in private law that govern relations between persons and, on the other, the public power of courts to issue remedial orders that, according to Steve, create new duties owed to courts. In one way or another, the contributors to this volume all engage with Steve's interpretivism and his work on method, his rich contributions to the substantive law of contract and remedies, and his subtle account of law's positive and normative dimensions.

There was much more to Steve than his outstanding academic achievements. He was devoted to his family. He was wise, thoughtful, generous, funny and fun. He was an extraordinary athlete and an outdoorsman who liked nothing better than to disappear into the wilderness for a few days in a canoe; the real wilderness, that is, beyond any shop, road or even cellphone signal. He was very gifted with his hands as well as with his mind, and over the years he singlehandedly renovated the family's large old house in Montreal West, including wiring, plumbing, and framing and finishing carpentry, from the basement to the third floor. He was full of recommendations for reading (fiction and non-fiction), for cooking and recipes, for the best way to organise a kitchen or a spice drawer or to pack a suitcase. Indeed, he seemed always to be in search of the best way to do anything. For example, he thought that when stopping for gas it was important to make the best use of one's time. The way to do that, for Steve, was to jar open the trigger of the gas pump nozzle with the car's gas cap, leave the nozzle running into the tank (it would shut off by itself if necessary) and then clean the car's windows with the available squeegee. If you were quick, you would just make it around the car before a once empty tank was full.

During several years of illness he was of good cheer, and continued to engage in scholarly debates. When some of his friends proposed this collection of essays in his honour, Steve wanted nothing more than that each contribution would engage with some argument that he had made in print, and he enthusiastically made a list of these arguments for the benefit of the contributors. He was not interested in *hommages*.

And so we present this collection of 23 essays written by 24 authors, all friends and admirers of Steve Smith, and all aiming – to put it bluntly – to disagree with Steve, just as Steve wanted, and in the academic spirit that disagreement is how we advance in our understanding of anything important. Like many of us, Steve was an admirer of Peter Birks, and he would surely have agreed with Peter's sentiment:

> University life has many blessings, never to be taken for granted. Of them, one of the greatest, perhaps the greatest, is that in a university disagreement, even serious disagreement about things which really matter, is never taken to be incompatible with admiration and affection. Many things are changing, but not that.[2]

By agreement among all of the contributors, any royalties from this book will be made over to McGill University's Paul-André Crépeau Centre for Private and Comparative Law, of which Steve was a member for many years. We thank our friend and colleague Shauna Van Praagh for writing the Foreword. We also thank Ms Elle Wintle for her assistance in preparing the list of Steve's publications in the Appendix to this volume; Lysanne Larose for her permission to use the photograph of Steve; and the people at Hart Publishing for their enthusiasm and professionalism.

It is not possible in the scope of this brief introduction to give even a conspectus of the arguments of the many scholars who here honour Steve's memory and his many contributions to our understanding of the law. The range of topics among the chapters reflects nothing so much as the range of Steve's interests, ambitions and mastery of private law. We all of us come together to give our thanks: our thanks to Steve, for everything he gave us; and our simple thanks that we were blessed with the good fortune to know him and to learn from him.

[2] P Birks, 'Rights, Wrongs, and Remedies' (2000) 20 *OJLS* 1, 37.

PART I

Methodology

1

Mapmaking and Law's Legitimacy

LARISSA KATZ

Over more than two decades, Stephen Smith championed the feasibility and the significance of legal maps, specifically, maps of the common law.[1] A legal map, according to Smith, sets out

> how the rules and decisions that are thought to make up the common law can be explained on the basis of a small number of abstract concepts. Ideally, each rule or decision is attached to a particular concept.[2]

Smith's conception of a legal map contains both vertical and horizontal dimensions.[3] On the vertical dimension, each area of law is (ideally) organised into a general part (the underlying concepts and principles appropriate to that sphere) and a special part (the doctrine and rules developing and extending these abstract concepts).[4] Along the horizontal dimension, each area of law is distinguished from and related to adjacent areas of law. Smith's conviction that the common law is mappable reflects his thinking about the nature of the common law itself as an internally coherent, rational legal order.

[1] While Smith did not see the traditional common law scholars as interested in mapmaking schemes, there were as he recognised a number of great mapmakers of English law. See SA Smith, 'Taking Law Seriously' (2000) 50(2) *University of Toronto Law Journal* 241, 241.

[2] SA Smith, 'A Map of the Common Law?' (2004) 40(3) *Canadian Business Law Journal* 364, 364.

[3] Smith took inspiration from the explicit distinction between general and special parts of criminal law. See SA Smith, 'The Limits of Contract' in J Neyers, R Bronaugh and S Pitel (eds), *Exploring Contract Law* (Oxford, Hart Publishing, 2009) 1, 24 ('In criminal law scholarship, the distinction between the special and the general parts of the law is well known. It has fostered the development of a sophisticated general criminal law of excuses, justifications … The parallel distinction is almost unknown in the law of obligations, at least in common law jurisdictions. Part of the explanation for this situation is no doubt the usual lack of attention that, historically, the common law has paid to classificatory undertakings generally. A more explicit reason is that the practical consequences of neglecting to distinguish between the general and the specific are less evident and certainly less immediate than those arising from neglecting the distinction between the different special parts of obligations law … But there are consequences. Failing to pay attention to contract law's vertical border can lead scholars, judges and lawyers to apply the wrong principles to understand legal rules, to draw the wrong inferences from those rules, and to fail to make appropriate generalisations.').

[4] At least this is the model of a map that Smith had in mind. See ibid.

Smith was absolutely firm that mapping the law is a prerequisite for legal knowledge. As he put it,

> to criticize classification per se amounts to criticizing the very possibility of increasing our knowledge about the object of our inquiry. Gaining knowledge of a subject is largely a matter of learning how to classify the subject and its constituent elements.[5]

A few years later, in 'A Map of The Common Law?' he wrote, in the same vein, that mapping was 'inseparable from the process of attaining knowledge'.[6] Smith did not just think that legal maps are useful things for lawyers, judges, and scholars to have around; he also thought that they are deeply connected to the common law's legitimacy. Judge-made law depends for its legitimacy on its rationality. Decisions that are not constrained by the appropriate forms of legal reasoning are arbitrary and violate rule of law values. Maps are in service of coherent, rational and stable judge-made law.

The idea of a legal map is of course not Smith's invention,[7] nor is the view that it is both possible and desirable (however difficult) to map the common law. Smith was influenced, as many have been, by Peter Birks' passionate advocacy for mapping the common law (although, as we will see, Smith had his own views about how to map and what the end product should look like).

In this chapter, I will sift through some core claims that Smith made about the very idea of a legal map as well as his views about why maps matter.[8] I will end by raising a question about whether Equity belongs on a map of private law.[9]

I. Legal Maps and Why they Matter

Maps of the common law organise decisions and rules in terms of more abstract concepts and principles and reveal how the parts relate. This idea of a legal map reflects a view of

[5] Smith, 'Taking Law Seriously' (n 1) 243.

[6] Smith (n 2) 365.

[7] The civilians of course are consummate mapmakers. See, eg, C Valcke, *Théorie des obligations*, 5th edn (Montréal, Thémis, 2023). On the civilian and common law mindsets, see L Smith, 'Civil and Common Law' in A Gold, J Goldberg and D Kelly (eds), *Oxford Handbook of the New Private Law* (Oxford, Oxford University Press, 2020) 227. See, eg, J Dietrich, 'What Is 'Lawyering'? The Challenge of Taxonomy' (2006) 65(3) *Cambridge Law Journal* 549. Common lawyers are of two minds. Some common lawyers insist that mapping (particularly in the Romanist or civilian style) is antithetical to the spirit of the common law. See P Matthews, 'Book Review of English Private Law, ed Peter Birks' (2002) 6 *Jersey Law Review* 115. In the North American context, legal realism provided a different but just as powerful basis for resisting classification projects. See, eg, A Gold and H Smith, 'Restatements and the Common Law' in AS Gold and RW Gordon (eds), *The American Law Institute: A Centennial History* 441 (describing the influence of conceptualists like Hohfeld within the Restatement movement and resistance by prominent realists like Myres McDougal). Compare, A Burrows, 'Understanding the Law of Restitution: A Map through the Thicket' (1995) 18:2 *University of Queensland Law Journal* 149 with R Stevens, *The Laws of Restitution* (Oxford, Oxford University Press; 2023) (insisting on the hodgepodge approach).

[8] On this connection see also P Birks, 'Introduction' in P Birks (ed), *English Private Law*, 1st edn (Oxford, Oxford University Press, 2000) xxxv.

[9] See A Popovici and L Smith, 'equity is not Equity' in B McFarlane and SB Elliott (eds), *Equity Today: 150 Years after the Judicature Reforms* (Oxford, Hart Publishing, 2023) 303. I follow Alexandra Popovici and Lionel Smith in using Equity to refer to the body of rules, principles and doctrine administered by Courts of Equity (and which, in my view, includes also an element of what Professors Popovici and Smith refer to as equity, the residual discretion to do justice in the particular case).

the common law as something capable of taking an internally coherent, rational shape. On Smith's view, the common law provides stable, rational and presumptively justified pathways for reasoning about legal problems.[10] As decisions proliferate, the pathways for legal reasoning may be harder to discern.[11] The job of the mapmaker is to thin out the thicket of decisions that conceals the concepts and principles underneath. This enables participants in a legal system – lawyers, judges, scholars and ordinary people generally – to navigate an area of law in order to see how rules or principles ought to apply in a particular case and whether (and in what way) they ought to be developed or changed.

A good legal map inevitably involves the exercise of judgement, informed by normative theory, about what concepts or principles ground and organise an area of legal rules and doctrine.[12] As a mapmaker, Smith thought it was important not to get 'bogged down in details'.[13] Indeed, a good map has to 'highlight certain features of the terrain, while flattening or ignoring others'.[14] Mapmaking of course requires a monumental amount of doctrinal work, pressing through the sprawl of common law doctrine in order to uncover its core organising principles. But Smith recognised the absurdity of insisting on a map of the common law that captures every bit of the legal terrain in all of its detail and complexity. Exactitude in mapmaking defeats its purpose as much in law as in geography. And the legal scholar who undertakes a life-sized 'map' of all the doctrine there is would end up producing a picture of the law that is of little use to anyone – like Borges' cartographers, who made an Empire-sized map of the Empire.[15]

While Smith recognised that people make maps, the law's structure, in his view – *what* we are attempting to map – inheres in the law itself. This is what Smith called law's self-organisation:

> Less studied by legal theorists than law's claim to authority, but more important for our present concerns, is a second aspect of law's self-understanding. This is that the law provides its own characteristic method of organizing legal rules and decisions. The law, and in particular legal

[10] Smith thought that judges, in their official capacity, must presume that legal rules are morally justified (that people *ought* to follow the law, as moral matter). See S Smith, 'Intermediate and Comprehensive Justifications for Legal Rules' in S Degeling, M Crawford and N Tiverios (eds), *Justifying Private Rights* (Oxford, Hart Publishing, 2020) 63.

[11] American Law Institute, Restatement of Property Law (III).

[12] Smith (n 2) 380. I will have more to say about the kind of normative theory that, on Smith's view, properly informs mapmaking – in short, not general comprehensive moral theories.

[13] SA Smith, *Contract Theory* (Oxford, Oxford University Press, 2004) 41. See also the Restatement of Law (Property law) about the purposes of a restatement.

[14] Smith (n 13) 42.

[15] Attributing to Suarez Miranda, *Viajes de varones prudentes*, Libro IV, Cap XLV (Lerida, 1658), Borges makes this point: 'In that Empire, the Art of Cartography attained such Perfection that the map of a single Province occupied the entirety of a City, and the map of the Empire, the entirety of a Province. In time, those Unconscionable Maps no longer satisfied, and the Cartographers Guilds struck a Map of the Empire whose size was that of the Empire, and which coincided point for point with it. The following Generations, who were not so fond of the Study of Cartography as their Forebears had been, saw that that vast Map was Useless, and not without some Pitilessness was it, that they delivered it up to the Inclemencies of Sun and Winters. In the Deserts of the West, still today, there are Tattered Ruins of that Map, inhabited by Animals and Beggars; in all the Land there is no other Relic of the Disciplines of Geography.' JL Borges, *Collected Fictions*, trans A Hurley (New York, Penguin Books, 1999) 325.

> decisions in the common law, divide[s] private law rules into the familiar legal categories of contract, tort, unjust enrichment, and so on. By doing this, legal decisions themselves tell us how they ought to be classified and categorized – whether they are tort cases, contract cases, or whatever. *Law thus possesses, as a part of its self-understanding, what I shall call a 'self-organization.'*[16]

A good map not only fits the data but also makes normative sense of it, probing the justifications we assume law to have and reorganising legal categories in light of the moral underpinnings of an area of law.[17] Indeed, without attention to the underlying questions of justification, we will likely remain in the dark about the meaning and organisation of the law. As Smith put it, 'deep taxonomic uncertainties in law usually indicate deep uncertainty about the existence or the distinctiveness of the assumed justification for the rules in question'.[18] Sorting out the justification for a rule is sometimes necessary to resolve mapmaking quandries. By no means did Smith mean that mapmakers require the services of a professional philosopher with a comprehensive moral or political theory.[19] Rather, as justification for a rule or doctrine, Smith had in mind the kind of intermediate principles that a judge might appeal to in clarifying, extending or refusing to extend a legal rule. These intermediate principles might include everyday moral principles, like fairness, honesty, reasonableness or proportionality, or rule of law principles, like stability, coherence, clarity. Smith was firm on this point: comprehensive and invariably contested moral theory (eg, utilitarianism) is not only unnecessary to make sense of the law; it can confound efforts to do so.[20] Smith thus flatly rejected purely functionalist approaches to understanding the law (he rejected on similar grounds the comprehensively Kantian accounts of private law). As he put it:

> Some scholarship, such as crude functionalist theories of law, simply ignores law's self-understanding: they impose an external order upon the legal materials that fails to take account in any way of law's organizational claims.[21]

For Smith, there is no good alternative to maps that organise the legal terrain in terms of its inner rationality. That is because judges need to understand not just what the rules are (a descriptive or what Kant might call 'historical' knowledge) but *why* a particular rule or principle is appropriate to one case and not another. Confronted with any given case, the judge needs to figure out the extent to which it is like or unlike other decided cases.[22] And in some small subset of new cases, the judge will be called on to extend the

[16] Smith (n 1) 250 (emphasis added).

[17] SA Smith, '"The Reliance Interest in Contract Damages" and the Morality of Contract Law' (2001) 1 *Issues in Legal Scholarship* 1, 5 ('A theory may fit the law, but still fail in its fundamental task of making sense of the law, of making the law intelligible.').

[18] SA Smith, 'Justifying the Law of Unjust Enrichment' (2001) 79(7) *Texas Law Review* 2177, 2179.

[19] SA Smith, *Rights, Wrongs, and Injustices: The Structure of Remedial Law* (Oxford, Oxford University Press, 2019) 27. 'Classificatory inquiries do not or at least should not require consideration of the kinds of comprehensive moral theories that are the focus of most contemporary normative scholarship. The law's effective day-to-day operation requires, therefore, that individuals be able to use it without taking a position on the kinds of comprehensive moral theories advanced in most normative scholarship.'

[20] See Smith (n 10) 63.

[21] Smith (n 1) 250.

[22] See P Jaffey, 'The Unjust Enrichment Fallacy and Private Law' (2013) 26(1) *The Canadian Journal of Law & Jurisprudence* 115, 116.

law in new ways – to act as a kind of lawmaker hemmed in by the constraints of legal reasoning.[23] That, in turn, requires the judge to understand the *grounds* on which she is to decide – the concepts and principles that account for a rule or doctrine.[24] As Kant recognised, a mere historical or descriptive knowledge of the law, without an understanding of law's conceptual and normative foundations, is inadequate to the demands of the judicial role:

> With some rational cognitions it is harmful to know them merely historically, while with others it makes no difference. Thus the sailor knows the rules of navigation historically from his tables, for example, and that is enough for him. But if the jurist knows jurisprudence merely historically, then he is fully ruined as a genuine judge, and still more so as a legislator.[25]

Smith's melding of intermediate normative theory and careful legal mapping is on display in his brilliant response to a moral objection that Professors Fuller and Purdue levied against traditional promise-based accounts of contract. The gist of the Fuller–Purdue challenge is that expectation interests give a plaintiff 'something he never had'[26] and so could not possibly be compensatory in nature.[27] Absent reliance, breach of contract is nonfeasance (the failure to confer a promised benefit) and not misfeasance (an interference with an interest that is already yours).[28] Expectation damages seem to be justifiable only on policy grounds and not on the basis of the harm principle.[29] Fuller and Purdue's moral objection to contract law threatened to destabilise the traditional common law thinking about contract law as organised around promise-keeping, with real implications for how courts decide cases.[30] In defence of the traditional view of contract as promise, Smith argued that we should understand promises as *creating* new rights – just as original rules of acquisition (eg, first possession) *created* new property rights that did not previously exist. This, he argued, was enough to establish that enforcing promises did not violate the harm principle because failing to keep a promise *does* violate a right the plaintiff already has – the newly created right arising from the promise itself. It would be an uncontroversial violation of the harm principle to fail to uphold property rights newly created through first possession. And in just

[23] RJ Sharpe, *Good Judgment* (Toronto, University of Toronto Press, 2018) 102 (distinguishing principles and policies: '[P]rinciples arise from considerations of justice and fairness and help us define and understand legal rights. Principles are used to explain and resolve the intricacies of the relationship between the parites and the just resplution of their dispute – matters that are the very stiff of adjudication.').

[24] See ibid 117.

[25] I Kant, *Lectures on Logic* (Pt IV: The Jaesche Logic, 9:22). Thanks to Arthur Ripstein for this reference.

[26] LL Fuller and WR Perdue Jr , 'Reliance Interest in Contract Damages: 1' (1936) 46(1) *Yale Law Journal* 52, 53. Their view has hardly any impact on substantive law of contract, see D Friedmann, 'A Comment on Fuller and Perdue, the Reliance Interest in Contract Damages' (2001) 1 *Issues in Legal Scholarship* 1.

[27] Fuller and Perdue (n 27) 52–53.

[28] P Benson, *Justice in Transactions: A Theory of Contract Law* (Cambridge, MA, The Belknap Press of Harvard University Press, 2019) 7. See also Peter Benson's fantastic article on the distinction between misfeasance/nonfeasance: P Benson, 'Misfeasance as an Organizing Normative Idea in Private Law' (2010) 60 *University of Toronto Law Journal* 740.

[29] Fuller and Perdue (n 27) 53, 60–65, 77; LL Fuller and WR Perdue Jr , 'The Reliance Interest in Contract Damages: 2' (1937) 46(3) *Yale Law Journal* 373, 417.

[30] For the traditional view, see RL Birmingham, 'Breach of Contract, Damage Measures, and Economic Efficiency' (1970) 24(2) *Rutgers Law Review* 273, 281–82.

the same way, Smith argued, it would violate the harm principle by failing to enforce promises, and the rights that these create. What came out of this inquiry into the moral foundations of contract law was a proposal to redraw the map of private law – placing rights-creating rules in contract adjacent to rights-creating rules in property law, and introducing a new category of transfer rules in private law, concerned with how pre-existing rights move from one person to the other without creating new rights.

Finally, for Smith, as for his colleague Peter Birks, common law maps are not just the product of reason. There is an artificiality to some of law's solutions to everyday problems because the law must provide closure in the context of a dispute. As Birks put it so memorably, 'while philosophers can debate and disagree, law must make up its mind … Hence, at a certain point, reason is controlled by authority, and the law makes its artificial choices.'[31]

The process of mapping, on Smith's account, is also never quite complete.[32] In part, that is because some parts of the legal terrain simply await exploration, requiring us over time to revise and refine our legal maps in light of new discoveries. For Smith, the very process of mapping meant bringing new meaning to legal phenomena, reforming law even as it restates it.[33] In part, it is because the legal terrain itself changes to adapt to new geographical, social and other circumstances.[34] Accretions to the terrain occur when judges add new forms of property rights (eg, intangible personal property rights to goodwill[35]) to the common law or resolve ad hoc equitable interventions into more stable, juridified forms (eg, restrictive covenants). So too do avulsions, when swathes of legal terrain come to be submerged by changes in society that effectively remove certain areas of law from the map (eg, old torts, like alienation of affection, are still technically law in some common law jurisdictions but have been largely overtaken by social norms and so do not appear in treatises or restatements classifying and making sense of tort law.) A good map, in Smith's view, might have to reorganise or break with traditional categories where these no longer (or perhaps never did) adequately make sense of legal rules, concepts and principles.[36]

In that sense mapping is in principle a completable task – at any given point in time the law is what it is – but in practice never complete, because the law continues to change and evolve, in part through the efforts of the mapmaker.[37]

[31] P Birks, 'Equity in the Modern Law: An Exercise in Taxonomy' (1996) 26:1 *University of Western Australia Law Review* 1, 5, 35.

[32] Smith (n 1) 245, 'The job of classifying law is … a neverending process in both common and civil law systems.'

[33] This view, that mapmakers are adding meaning rather than simply describing something static, is evident in the idea of a restatement approved by the American Law Institute. See ALI Council, *Revised Style Manual* (January 2015), defining a restatement as 'to state again or in a new form' and describing the 'two impulses at the heart of the restatement process … the impulse to recapitulate the law as it presently exists and the impulse to reformulate it, thereby rendering it clearer and more coherent while subtly transforming it in the process'.

[34] *Wastech Services Ltd v Greater Vancouver Sewerage and Drainage District*, 2021 SCC 7, para 51 ('the list of existing doctrines is not closed and may be developed incrementally where the existing law is found wanting'); *Nordenfelt v Maxim Nordenfelt Guns and Ammunition Co Ltd* [1894] AC 535, 558; [1891–94] All ER Rep 1 (UKHL), Lord Ashbourne: 'However it is accomplished, the law must work in harmony with the requirements of the times, and must advance and develop with the growth of our national life and institutions.'

[35] *Manitoba Fisheries Ltd v Canada* [1979] 1 SCR 101, 1978 CanLII 22 (SCC).

[36] Smith (n 17) (proposing a reorganising of transfer rules and rights-creating rules in private law).

[37] The criticism of 'legal maps' on the grounds that they presuppose a static or fixed landscape does not hit its mark in Smith's work. See, eg, H Dagan, 'Legal Realism and the Taxonomy of Private Law' in CEF

Why do legal maps matter – or why did they matter so much for Smith? Aesthetics play a role. The elegance and economy of a well-constructed legal map is a delight in itself. I suspect that Smith, who found the common law endlessly fascinating, might have agreed with Sir Fitzjames Stephen that 'the only thing which prevents English people from seeing that law is really one of the most interesting and instructive studies is that English lawyers have thrown it into a shape which can only be described as studiously repulsive.'[38] Smith liked to build beautiful things, legal maps included.[39]

But of course, Smith offered weightier reasons in support of mapmaking. Giving rational shape to the common law is required for its legitimacy. Smith, like Peter Birks, thought that the common law depends for its legitimacy on coherence and rationality in the way that legislation, as a mass, does not.[40] Quite simply, the legislation depends for its legitimacy on the legislator's right to govern and democratic accountability.[41] The output of a legislator reflects political choices and compromises that have no inherent self-organisation and so do not necessarily form a rational, coherent mass. The best we can do for legislation might be to arrange a list of statutes by name or topic, perhaps in alphabetical or chronological order. They need not have any deeper relationship with each other. We need to do better for the common law, on Smith's view because its legitimacy depends on it.[42]

Smith had a deep commitment to the rationality and mappability of common law on moral grounds – deeper even than the leading proponent of private law's mappability, Peter Birks. For Birks, exposing the rationality of the common law through maps is an instrument for addressing a rule of law concern that might be addressed otherwise.[43] Discretion, both Smith and Birks thought, is the enemy of the rule of law because it is antithetical to the clarity and stability that law required. Birks also thought

Rickett and R Grantham (eds), *Structure and Justification in Private Law: Essays for Peter Birks* (Oxford, Hart Publishing, 2008) 147, 155: 'This means that the analogy of legal taxonomy to cartography is mistaken and even misleading. Cartography assumes stability in the geographical features to be mapped; it implies that there is "a fixed and immutable topography 'out there' waiting to be accurately charted". But law is constantly changing.'

[38] CN Gregory, 'Bentham and the Codifiers' (1899–1900) 13(5) *Harvard Law Review* 344, 352, quoting Sir Fitzjames Stephen.

[39] I recall marvelling at how much attention and energy Smith put into revising the plans for McGill Law School's splendid renovation of New Chancellor Day Hall in 2009. He pointed out to me how the offices were clustered artfully so as to bring people working in different areas into conversation. I could see there was little he had not thought of in mapping out the best physical environment for scholarly life. See at www.worldarchitecturenews.com/article/1506433/new-chancellor-day-hall.

[40] Birks (n 31) 4, 97–98: 'The legitimacy of expert law-making in a sophisticated democracy depends on the truth of the assertion that the interpreters are and must be both the masters and the servants of a complex system of reasoning. Why are they not elected? The answer must be that they are doing something different from the legislator and something that cannot be done by just any commuter on the Clapham bus. They are restrained in their creativity by the system of reasoning which they serve, and they are qualified for the work which they do, not as chosen representatives, but by hard-won mastery of that specialised rationality.'

[41] See Smith (n 13) ch 1 (on the goals of interpretive theory).

[42] See SA Smith, 'The Reliance Interest in Contract Damages and the Morality of Contract Law' (2001) 1 *Issues in Legal Scholarship* 1, 5. For an impassioned defence of setting out the common law by topic in alphabetical order and the creative lawyering that common law chaos enables, see Matthews (n 7).

[43] According to Birks, earlier in its history, the common law had relied on 'crude mechanisms for producing stability and consistency'. These are no longer available: 'The list of forms of action has gone. The doctrine of precedent has lost much of its rigour. *The one hope now is to tighten up its reasoning, founding stability on a sophisticated rationality.*' Birks (n 31) 5 (emphasis added).

that the lack of systematicity in the common law is more of a threat to rule-of-law ideals now than during the period when there were other mechanisms for preventing rapid change and outcome-oriented decision-making in the absence of a 'network of reason … to imprison the judge'.[44]

Smith's view about the role of reason seems to run deeper than this. Like Birks, he thought a map of the common law as a rational order might constrain how courts reason in deciding how to apply or to extend the law, as well as whether to reform it (what new categories or organising concepts are required to make sense of the law).[45] Smith clearly had concerns about judicial discretion in substantive private law on legitimacy grounds. Indeed, his rejection of a 'bundle of factors' approach to judicial decision-making (like that Stephen Waddams championed) turned on his concerns about the discretion this would introduce into the common law. Waddams' approach, he thought, required that 'judges should regard themselves as having a significant amount of discretion. Discretion is central to bundle-of-factors reasoning. … Embracing his view thus requires us to lower our standards for what it means to decide.'[46]

Smith did not see legal maps just as a constraint on judicial decision-making, a mechanism for guarding against inconsistencies, duplications or inefficiencies in the law. Exposing the rationality of law is itself in service of a deeper source of private law's legitimacy: its reason-giving nature and its capacity to guide citizens' conduct. (One version of this claim, that law's legitimacy normally depends on giving us reason to do what morality requires of us anyway, derives from the work of philosophers like Joseph Raz, Smith's supervisor at Oxford.[47]) Arbitrary judge-made law cannot provide this service; only decisions that form a rational framework for action could. I do not think Smith would have thought that clarity and stability by other cruder means could serve to legitimise the common law, as Birks seems at times to have thought.[48]

A potential challenge to Smith's view that legal maps are importantly connected to rule-of-law ideals is that the common law has mostly done without explicit legal maps. The common law's history of largely avoiding legal maps may suggest either that the terrain is not mappable or, if it is, that judges and scholars know their way around without the kind of map or scheme that organises the law according to general abstract principles.[49] In that case, how important is it, really, to map the law?

One possible response is that these apparently mapless common law judges must have a map in their heads even if not in hand. And then the only question is whether there are additional reasons of legitimacy or efficiency for making *shared* maps – open to all to scrutinise, debate and refine. This is indeed what I believe Smith thought.

[44] ibid 98.

[45] Smith recognised that mapping can have a reformist objective.

[46] Smith (n 2) 382. See also Smith (n 19) 320: 'Judicial discretion is generally undesirable. The rule of law ideal requires that the law be clear and predictable.'

[47] J Raz, *The Morality of Freedom* (Oxford, Clarendon, 1988).

[48] Birks (n 31) 5.

[49] Smith recognises that the common law lacked a traditional practice of mapmaking. See SA Smith, 'A Map of the Common Law?' (2004) 40(3) *Canadian Business Law Journal* 364, 364: 'Lawyers in common law jurisdictions have traditionally had little interest in classification. The organic and piecemeal development of the common law, the late arrival of law as an academic discipline and the historical importance of procedural rules in shaping the law are just a few of the factors that have contributed to a way of thinking about law that is marked by practical, rather than scientific,concerns.'

The law, on his view, has its self-organisation. And courts might have had a good sense of what that is. But law's legitimacy is greatly enhanced when those maps are made public and shared. Indeed, even in the absence of an expressly shared map, we might say there is a duty on the part of judicial lawmakers to publish their inner maps so that others might understand – and contest – the grounds of their decision. As Birks put it, 'There is no agreed map. This does not exonerate each jurist from saying what map he has in mind and where he thinks his subject-matter fits into it.'[50]

II. Equity and Discretion

Smith was committed to the idea that all of private law – including Equity – was mappable, even if as yet unmapped. In this he remained adamantly opposed to the views of others (like the late Stephen Waddams) that 'large and significant parts of the law are based, not on single concepts, but on bundles of factors' and so are unmappable.[51] Experience, in Smith's view, reveals that the apparent disorder that characterises the common law is only contingent.[52] Its susceptibility to mapping is evident in the fact that large parts of it have over time been mapped: 'large parts of the law that once appeared a chaotic mess of sui generis rules and decisions have been explained and organized'.[53] Smith thought advances in mapping the law of contracts in the nineteenth century and unjust enrichment law in the twentieth century were particularly instructive. While the common law has never reduced the sprawl of doctrine and rules to the tight order of a civilian code, English mapmakers have succeeded in peeling back decisions to expose the more abstract concepts, principles and rules that organise legal reasoning in these areas.[54]

Smith extended the same optimism about mappability to other areas of private law. True, private law scholars have not (he thought) adequately mapped concepts like estoppel, abuse of rights, and good faith or much of Equity. And, in his view, the 'subject of property law, as presently understood, comprises a hodgepodge of rules whose strongest connection is often historical rather than conceptual'.[55] But Smith was convinced that this was simply work waiting to be done.

I have no doubt that Smith is right that there are many areas of private law – and property law in particular – that are mappable in the sense of being organised around abstract concepts (like ownership) and principles (like the principle that the law abhors

[50] Birks (n 31) 4: 'A sound taxonomy, together with a keen sense of its importance, constant suspicion of its possible inaccuracy and vigorous debate on its improvement, is an essential precondition of rationality. All these are wanting in common law systems. Until that is put right, the realists and the fundamentalists of the school of critical legal studies will continue to play from a winning hand.'

[51] Smith (n 2) 366, 372 et seq (describing Stephen Waddams' view of the limited value of mapping projects given Waddams' view of the nature of the common law).

[52] ibid 382.

[53] ibid 381.

[54] Always at risk, of course, of being broken back down into plurality. See R Stevens, *The Laws of Restitution* (Oxford, Oxford University Press, 2023).

[55] Smith (n 17) 31.

a vacancy).[56] But where if at all does Equity fit in a map of private law? Smith was, truth be told, something of an Equity sceptic, and I suspect would simply have brushed the question aside. As he saw it, Equity consists either in remedial law or just more private law waiting to be classified properly.[57] In a conversation some years ago, he told me that he had generally accepted the view of equity circulating at the University of Toronto's Faculty of Law while he was a law student, that Equity was a mere historical accident and not conceptually or normatively significant. He had apparently been taught as a law student that if he simply crossed out the word 'equitable' wherever it appeared in a case, no meaning would be lost.

Smith softened but largely maintained this view in his later work on remedies.[58] He wrote:

> [I]t appears to be assumed that it is impossible to understand contemporary remedies without understanding that they originated in different courts. Against this assumption, I argue … that the remedies that exist today and the rules governing their content and availability could easily have arisen in a unitary legal system. Moreover, I argue that it is possible to describe and explain both (so-called) Legal remedies and (so-called) Equitable remedies on the basis of the same principles.[59]

The discretionary nature of so many Equitable remedies simply reflected the scope for discretion at the remedial stage more generally.[60] That is because at the remedial stage, unlike in the adjudication of substantive private law rights, courts sometimes have to consider factors beyond the bilateral relationship between the parties (eg, the cost to the public of devoting judicial resources to supervising specific performance).[61]

[56] On the organising role of the principle that law abhors a vacancy in property law, see, eg, L Katz, 'The Moral Paradox of Adverse Possession: Sovereignty and Revolution in Property Law' (2010) 55 *McGill Law Journal* 47; L Katz, 'Ownership and offices: the Building Blocks of the Legal Order' (2020) 70 *University of Toronto Law Journal* 267.

[57] Smith (n 1) 245: 'The same could be said of equity, the black hole of the common law. Textbooks on "Equity" continue to be published in the common law world but it is unclear – and, unfortunately, usually left unclear – whether anything other than historical accident links the rules included therein. Maitland's adage about the forms of action continuing to rule us from their graves still has a discomfiting truth to it?' Birks thought the same thing: Birks (n 31) 22: 'One large-scale danger to the rationality of our law lies in the exaggeration of the historical mission of equity to do justice, as though it had some special licence to ignore the requirements of legal certainty.'

[58] Smith took account of the way that courts determine the appropriateness of specific relief and the adequacy of a damages award, although he considered this just a feature of a kind of remedy that has its place on a map of remedies alongside of others; see Smith (n 19) 320–21 ('[B]alance-of-factors reasoning is different in kind from the checklist process that courts go through when contemplating non-specific relief. There is no formula to balance "adequacy of damages" against "difficulty of supervision" or "cleanliness of the defendant's hands". The court must simply consider the relevant factors and make a global judgment.') He recognised, in other words, that courts have to exercise judgement in awarding such remedies – discretion – not required in other contexts. But he did not allow that some unifying idea of equity was behind this. PB Miller, 'Equity as Supplemental Law' in D Klimchuk, I Samet and HE Smith (eds), *Philosophical Foundations of the Law of Equity* (Oxford, Oxford University Press, 2020) 92 (arguing that accounts of equity should move beyond remedialism and be understood as *supplemental* law).

[59] Smith (n 19) 31.

[60] ibid. Smith may have been influenced by his exposure to civil law while at McGill Law School, where he would have noted that civilians have a much deeper commitment to specific relief in private law without the Equitable overlay.

[61] See Popovici and Smith (n 9) (noting that common law courts had, then lost then regained jurisdiction to award specific relief, leaving it to Courts of Equity to fill the gap in between).

Smith saw remedial law as largely a set of 'decision rules' addressed at judges rather than 'conduct rules' addressed at citizens.[62] The legitimacy of decision rules turns on institutional factors, including efficiency in the use of public resources, rather than on the clarity and predictability of conduct-guiding rules. Discretion in the context of decision rules is not as inimical to the rule of law as it is in the context of substantive private law rights, he thought. Smith in fact argued that vagueness in the context of decision rules might be an advantage, preventing citizens from behaving strategically with a view to decision rules directed at courts. Equitable remedies belong alongside of legal remedies on the map of the common law, even if they do not have quite as clear and fixed a form as substantive areas of private law do.

What, then, about the rest of Equity beyond remedies – core Equitable rights like the trust, where equity intervenes to protect someone on the pathway to acquiring legal property rights from interruption?[63] Smith's answer no doubt would be that Equitable rights are just part of property or contract law. But this misses the distinctive nature of Equitable rights as rights with respect to other people's property or contract rights.[64] The function of many of these rights, like the trust, the option to purchase, the equity of redemption or the restrictive covenant, is to protect someone on a completable but as yet incomplete path to acquire legal rights from interruption by someone with legal rights.[65] A beneficiary's interest constrains a trustee not to exercise her legal rights in ways that diverts the benefit to someone other than the beneficiary before the trust is executed and legal title in the beneficiary. The equity of redemption obligates the mortgagee to allow the mortgagor to complete the pathway to redeeming her legal title by repaying the mortgage loan after default. The option to purchase protects the pathway the optionee has to acquire legal rights by preventing the vendor from selling the property to a third party. The restrictive covenant prevents the owner of the servient tenement from exercising her property rights so as to obstruct the flow of the benefit of a covenant relating to land to the owner of the dominant tenemnt. And so on. Treating Equitable rights as just more law also downplays the inherently discretionary nature of Equity, which yields less predictability both in the application and in the development

[62] See M Dan-Cohen, 'Decision Rules and Conduct Rules: On Acoustic Separation in Criminal Law' (1984) 97 *Harvard Law Review* 624. See Smith (n 19) 320–21: '[However], a discretion to refuse specific relief is significantly less harmful to the rule of law ideal than a discretion to refuse to recognize a substantive right. Like other parts of remedial law, the rules governing remedial defences are directed primarily at judges, not citizens. Indeed, the vagueness of this part of the law might be thought useful insofar as it dissuades individuals from attempting to use remedial defences to guide their everyday behaviour.'

[63] *Popov v Hayashi* (2002) WL 31833731 (Cal) (reasoning as follows from an Equitable standpoint): '[W]here an actor takes significant but incomplete steps to achieve possession of a piece of abandoned property and the effort is interrupted by the unlawful acts of others, the actor has a cognizable pre-possessory interest in the property.'

[64] B McFarlane and R Stevens, 'The Nature of Equitable Property' (2010) 4 *Journal of Equity* 1 (rights against rights). See also G Williams (ed), *Salmond on Jurisprudence*, 11th edn (London, Sweet & Maxwell, 1957) 268–69 (describing a category of rights in respect of other rights, and including equitable rights arising by agreements of purchase and sale). Some equitable rights are rights in respect of equitable rights in respect of legal rights at the end of the chain.

[65] I develop this claim in L Katz, 'Equity: Pathways to Legal Rights' in Klimchuk, Samet and Smith (eds) (n 58) 168 (arguing for an idea of equity as a morally significant – indeed, a morally required – companion to a rights-based system of law). See also L Katz, 'Equitable Remedies and "What We Have Coming to Us"' (2020) 96 *Notre Dame Law Review* 1115.

of core Equitable rights (eg, the trust.)[66] Equity does not belong on the same map as the rest of substantive private law because Equity takes substantive private law as its object, constraining the execise of legal rights for purposes that are inconsistent with the purposes of a system of private rights as a whole.[67]

Rights in respect of other people's rights are not conventional private rights on the same plane as other private rights. If they were, it would lead to a contradiction of sorts, where one person's right cancels out another person's right. Rather, equitable rights convey the standing to petition courts to intervene in another's exercise of her private rights, the doing of which is never a matter of private right but rather always remains at the discretion of the courts.

Equity aims to preserve the integrity of private law, not by adding more of it but by ensuring that it lives up to its own fundamental commitments. The judicial power to do Equity is necessarily and inherently discretionary. It cannot be a matter of private right that a person not exercise her legal rights to their fullest extent. In this context, discretion does not raise the rule-of-law concerns that it might in the construction of the private law terrain itself (how things stand between us as a matter of right). That is because judicial discretion to intervene to constrain the arbitrary exercise of legal rights is just as important for the legitimacy of the common law as the absence of judicial discretion in the adjudication of substantive private law rights. Too much discretion in the application of rules that define private rights and we have a system of arbitrary (judicial) power. But too little discretion for courts to consider whether a particular exercise of private rights undermines the integrity of the system as a whole and we end up with a system of private power that is not appropriately constrained by the purposes for which it is conferred. That is a legitimacy problem too: a system of arbitrary (private) power.[68]

III. Conclusion

Smith did not just write about the importance of mapmaking, or about the maps that other scholars devised to explain the common law: he was himself a consummate mapmaker. Smith's approach to classifying the common law according to general principles has its detractors. Some thought that Smith's approach was a futile exercise in imposing one's favourite moral theory on a plurality of rules, principles and doctrines that defy unification.[69] Others had the opposite complaint, finding Smith's approach *too*

[66] See, eg, developments in the law of trusts that appear to jettison settled principles and concepts on pragmatic and institutional grounds, in a manner that would be alarming for core areas of private law (eg, the relaxation of the certainty of object standard for discretionary trusts). See discussion in Smith (n 7).

[67] See Katz (n 65). See also J CP Goldberg and BC Zipursky, 'From Riggs v Palmer to Shelley v Kraemer: Judicial Power and the Law–Equity Distinction' in Klimchuk, Samet and Smith (eds) (n 58) 291.

[68] Civilians may wish to object here that they lack a system of Equity but have nonetheless a perfectly legitimate system of private rights. But of course civilians have equitable principles of abuse of right and good faith even if not Equity in the common law sense. It is beyond the scope of this chapter to consider whether or not these principles do enough – or as much as Equity does – to constrain the arbitrary use of private rights.

[69] S Waddams, *Dimensions of Private Law: Categories and Concepts in Anglo-American Legal Reasoning* (Cambridge, Cambridge University Press, 2003) 366.

deferential to received legal categories, concepts and principles.[70] Smith placed himself in a middle ground, that of the philosophically oriented doctrinalist, concerned with understanding the law that we actually have while uncovering the law's own normative commitments. In his mapmaking, he rejected the cynicism of scholarship that treated traditional legal reasoning as in effect a sham, on the one hand, and the idealisation of law by scholars all too committed to an internal perspective on law, on the other.

[70] See, eg, Dagan (n 37).

2

The Elegance of Private Law

ANDREW S GOLD*

I. Introduction

Interpretive method is fundamentally important for private law theory, and Stephen Smith's work in this area is both ground-breaking and lasting in its significance. He seeks to render the law intelligible, and in particular to find theories that capture the law's 'self-understanding'. That in itself is not unusual, but this project requires a theorist to have some basis for assessing which theories are successful, and it is here that Smith's contribution is most noteworthy. He provides well-developed criteria to help us discern which theories best capture the internal point of view, and these criteria have deservedly become canonical.

On Smith's account, there are four primary interpretive criteria: fit, morality, coherence and transparency.[1] Fit is the most basic criterion: a theory of private law must match the law it seeks to explain. Under Smith's morality criterion, theorists should seek to show how legal actors could at least believe the principles of a private law field are moral, even if they are erroneous in that view.[2] A coherence criterion can be understood in various ways, but for Smith it means that, at the least, the law is shown to be non-contradictory.[3] It also means that the law is at least somewhat unified (a topic to which we shall return). Finally, his transparency criterion calls for explanations that use 'concepts that are recognizably "legal" … even if those concepts are not the same legal concepts that were employed by judges'.[4] A theory must use concepts that are at least 'in the right ball park'.[5]

A closer look at these criteria and their justifications shows a pattern; Smith's criteria fall short of the more stringent approaches in the literature. He does not call for a

* I am grateful to Steve Smith for his friendship, and for years of illuminating conversation about legal theory. I thank Hanoch Dagan, Chris Essert, Evan Fox-Decent, Greg Keating, Jamie MacLeod, Nick McBride, Paul Miller, Henry Smith, Lionel Smith and Ben Zipursky for helpful suggestions for this chapter. Any errors are my own.

[1] See SA Smith, *Contract Theory* (Oxford, Oxford University Press, 2004) 7–32.

[2] ibid 18–19.

[3] ibid 11.

[4] ibid 28–29.

[5] ibid 29.

fully unified private law; he does not require a successful theory to show that the law is actually justified; and he does not indicate that express judicial reasoning will always capture the concepts internal to private law. There is also a basic reason for this pattern: one of Smith's most significant contributions is his recognition that, in figuring out criteria that will match the law's self-understanding, we need also to be aware of the potential for judicial error. As he notes, it is a part of the law's self-understanding 'that the law may be mistaken in parts'.[6] A legal outcome might be less moral than judges realise, or the law's concepts might interrelate differently from what judges expect. Moderate criteria make room for such possibilities.

Smith's approach offers important insights for private law theory generally, but also for the New Private Law movement, which implicitly endorses moderate interpretive criteria. And yet even the most valuable contributions to private law theory can merit revision. I have argued elsewhere that the transparency criterion should be strengthened.[7] I will argue here that the coherence criterion should be weakened. Indeed, the coherence criterion should be supplemented with another, potentially more flexible, criterion: an elegance criterion. The goal, in each case, is to better comply with Smith's ultimate aim; it is to figure out the law's self-understanding.

II. The Coherence Criterion and its Justifications

A. Smith's Arguments

Coherence is a fundamental concern for private law theorists, including theorists concerned with the internal point of view. Yet while private law theorists characteristically seek coherence when they interpret private law fields, proponents offer more than one basis for adopting a coherence criterion. For example, a coherence criterion is commonly adopted because it will advance the theorist's objective of rendering the social practice of private law intelligible.[8] Alternatively, coherence is adopted as a criterion because, as Ernest Weinrib notes, 'those who think about private law in its own terms must include the law's pervasive impulse toward coherence within their purview'.[9] These are not identical reasons for caring about coherence, and agreement breaks down once we try to determine the type of coherence criterion that private law theorists should follow.

How much coherence a successful theory should demonstrate is a matter of debate. For some, it is enough for a legal theory to show the law to be non-contradictory.[10]

[6] ibid 17.

[7] See AS Gold, 'When Private Law Theory is Close Enough' in T Kuntz and PB Miller (eds), *Methodology in Private Law Theory: Between New Private Law and Rechtsdogmatik* (Oxford, Oxford University Press, 2024) 49.

[8] See Smith (n 1) 13–14 (suggesting a link between coherence and the intelligibility of the features of private law). See also ibid 11: 'A theory that reveals the law as inconsistent is less successful at achieving what was described earlier as the basic goal of interpretation: that of revealing an intelligible order in the law.'

[9] See EJ Weinrib, *The Idea of Private Law* (Cambridge, MA, Harvard University Press, 1995) 13–14.

[10] cf J Gardner, 'What Is Tort Law For? Part 2. The Place of Distributive Justice' in J Oberdiek (ed), *Philosophical Foundations of the Law of Torts* (Oxford, Oxford University Press, 2014) 338, fn 11: 'Any

Alternatively, a theorist might seek a theory that explains a legal field in terms of a single unifying principle.[11] This is a substantially more difficult standard to meet, and if we require a close fit between theory and doctrine, it may be impossible for any theory to attain this level of coherence.[12] Legal doctrines, taken seriously on their own terms, might embrace conflicting principles.

One could also take intermediate positions on coherence. In his work in contract theory, Smith suggests a moderate coherence criterion. In his view, 'a good theory must show that *most* of the core elements of contract law can be traced to, or are closely related to, a single principle'.[13] As Smith adds, 'Unless one assumes (as few people do) that all reasons for acting can, in the end, be reduced to a single master principle, it is accepted as perfectly intelligible, indeed appropriate, that people act for different reasons in different situations.'[14] Smith's perspective on the unity of private law will be a central concern of this chapter.

B. The Impulse Towards Coherence

In order to assess Smith's version of the coherence criterion, I will begin with Weinrib's argument, for it provides an important backdrop. Understanding the challenges for that argument will help us to discern the challenges for Smith's argument. Weinrib, recall, emphasises the law's impulse towards coherence. That impulse, while evident, is not enough to support a moderate coherence criterion.

Understood globally, the law's pervasive impulse toward coherence is recognisable, yet its effects are uncertain. As Joseph Raz's work indicates, there are several reasons why global coherence across the law may be doubtful, even if local coherence is common. For example, the law might begin from a premise of value pluralism, or the legal system may reflect the different viewpoints present in a given society.[15] Within limited domains, each view may be coherently instantiated in the law, but when our attention turns to private law as a whole the combination could be incoherent. Substantial shifts in legal philosophy are also a good reason to predict local coherence, particularly given that systems of precedent encourage piecemeal changes in legal doctrine rather than sea changes throughout a field.[16]

justification has to be coherent in the thin sense of intelligible. But Weinribian unity (or Dworkinian integrity) is not, in my eyes, any kind of plus. Reality, including moral reality, is fragmentary.'

[11] Smith (n 1) 11: 'According to the more demanding version [of the coherence criterion], mere consistency is not enough. This version states that theories should also be evaluated according to the extent that they show contract law as a unified system.'

[12] For example, if we are trying to theorise fiduciary law, the economic analysis common in Delaware corporate law may be impossible to fully reconcile with another jurisdiction's doctrine on the law of guardianship; a theory that fits both settings may need to recognise this tension. Note also that an abstract unifying principle may call for pluralism at the ground level of legal doctrine. See, eg, H Dagan, 'Pluralism and Perfectionism in Private Law' (2012) 112 *Columbia Law Review* 1409.

[13] Smith (n 1) 13.

[14] ibid 12.

[15] J Raz, 'The Relevance of Coherence' in J Raz, *Ethics in the Public Domain: Essays in the Morality of Law and Politics* (Oxford, Oxford University Press, 1994) 277, 315.

[16] cf J Waldron, '"Transcendental Nonsense" and System in the Law' (2000) 100 *Columbia Law Review* 16, 42 (describing a legislative process under which 'the law becomes a "checkerboard," incorporating

Furthermore, while the impulse itself is recognisable, it is not clear that this impulse is uniformly felt. There is plenty of doctrinal evidence – in the form of interstitial private law – that courts seek to preserve the modularity of private law subfields in settings of overlap (eg, contract and tort, tort and fiduciary law).[17] We accordingly cannot rely on this impulse to support a moderate coherence criterion for private law as a whole, let alone a strong criterion.

C. Private Law's Intelligibility

Raz's arguments clearly influenced Smith's own account.[18] Indeed, Smith diverges from Weinrib for broadly Razian reasons: he rejects Weinrib's strong version of coherence in part because of the possibility that the different values courts hold may be in tension. For Smith, the problem with the strong version is that it insists on a kind of unity that coherence does not require. And yet he still espouses a moderate coherence criterion, in light of the interpretivist's goal of rendering the law intelligible. This turn toward intelligibility is an interesting move, because it takes us away from the question of the law's self-understanding – could not the law's self-understanding be incoherent? – and turns us instead toward a distinct goal when doing interpretative work.

The challenge is that intelligibility does not seem to point in any obvious way to a criterion like the one Smith endorses. Having a majority of core doctrines explicable by a single principle might be a way of achieving intelligibility, but one could just as readily achieve intelligibility – and perhaps a greater degree of intelligibility – by means of theories that show that less than a majority of the field's core doctrines are explicable by a single principle. Indeed, efforts to unify across an entire field could actually create greater incoherence, as John Gardner hypothesised.[19]

Note furthermore that there are intelligible systems that are only loosely interconnected, and indeed some of these systems include contradictions. Smith expresses concern about a theory that reveals contract law to be 'a hodge-podge of entirely unconnected rules'.[20] But rather than entirely unconnected rules, there might be loosely connected rules that guide conduct and legal reasoning within certain parameters. For an example of a loosely connected system, consider the cultural system of 'common sense'. As Clifford Geertz recognises, the system of common sense is a 'loosely connected body of belief and judgment'.[21] As Geertz also indicates, '[c]ommon-sense wisdom is shamelessly and unapologetically ad hoc'.[22] The system of common sense operates through epigrams, witticisms, proverbs and the like – its content may even

half-measure upon half-measure in a way that defies any attempt to discern a single, coherent system'). As Waldron elaborates, similar issues can arise through judge-made law.

[17] AS Gold, 'Private Law's Choice of Private Law' in S Bray et al (eds), *Interstitial Private Law* (Oxford, Oxford University Press, 2024) 111.

[18] Smith (n 1) 11, fn 7 (citing Raz, 'The Relevance of Coherence' (n 15) 277–325).

[19] J Gardner, *Torts and Other Wrongs* (Oxford, Oxford University Press, 2020) 25.

[20] See Smith (n 1) 12.

[21] See C Geertz, 'Introduction' in C Geertz, *Local Knowledge: Further Essays in Interpretive Anthropology*, 3rd edn (New York, Basic Books, 2000) 10.

[22] C Geertz, 'Common Sense as a Cultural System' in Geertz (n 21) 90.

be inconsistent at times.[23] Whatever the strengths or weakness of a system of common sense, it is hard to say that such a system is not intelligible.[24]

One might respond that, notwithstanding these possibilities, a legal system is *more* intelligible if it meets Smith's criterion. I doubt that is true, but assuming it is, why is that something to aim for in interpreting private law? We are trying to figure out the law's self-understanding, not its platonic ideal; and to the extent courts might claim a high degree of intelligibility, they could also be in error. Gardner is right that our concern should be with intelligibility in a sense that allows for a 'fragmentary' moral reality.[25] With that limit as our standard, we do not need optimal levels of coherence – or unity – in order to meet the intelligibility test. Making sense of the law does not require us to make it sensible. It also does not require us to make it unified.

D. The Perspective of Legal Actors

Granted, there is another possibility. Perhaps an argument for unity can instead be grounded on evidence suggesting legal actors see a field in a comparatively unified way, as a single subject matter, in which case the real reason for our moderate coherence criterion is once again that it will help track the law's self-understanding. And indeed, Smith appears to make a form of this argument.[26] Notice, however, that this argument makes the basis for a moderate coherence criterion contingent on something other than intelligibility. The justification has now shifted to contextual evidence for the law's self-understanding with respect to unity. Once we make that methodological shift, our interpretive theory should be susceptible to contrary evidence regarding the internal point of view, such as express judicial reasoning and employment of concepts that do not readily support a more unified picture.

In addition, it is then also unclear why showing a mere majority of core components are explicable by a single principle would uniquely indicate that a field like contract law is a single subject matter. Could we not have a single subject matter, but with various explanatory principles in play, such that each principle explains a third of the core features of the relevant field? The requirement that a majority of core features be explicable by a single principle does not follow in any obvious way from the idea that contract law or tort law are understood by legal actors to be a single subject matter.

That is not to say that private law lacks unity; rather, the point is that we cannot support a moderate coherence criterion based on the arguments provided so far. If our goal is intelligibility, a coherence criterion should call for little more than a bare minimum of non-contradiction (and even then some contradiction may be anticipated within private law). And if we pin our hopes on the understandings of legal actors that

[23] ibid (describing these features).

[24] Note also that loosely connected systems may have major functional benefits. See AS Gold and HE Smith, 'Restatements and the Common Law' in AS Gold and RW Gordon (eds), *The American Law Institute: A Centennial History* (Oxford, Oxford University Press, 2023). The price for such loose connections may be a degree of contradiction within the system.

[25] Gardner (n 19) 82, fn 10. I say this without taking a position on whether this view of morality is accurate.

[26] Smith (n 1) 12 (emphasising the way that lawyers refer to 'contract law' as a field).

their field is a single subject matter, we again need to weaken our criterion considerably. I will suggest an alternative way to think about a moderate coherence criterion in the next section.

III. Towards an Elegance Criterion

A. Some Initial Thoughts on Elegance

There is another way to understand private law theorists' concerns with a unifying coherence. We might think of a coherence criterion as a subordinate criterion, as seeking coherence may be a way of respecting another criterion altogether: an elegance criterion. Expanding our list of criteria in this way ought not to trouble us. Various additional criteria are noted in the literature; notable examples include a simplicity criterion,[27] a consilience criterion,[28] a justice criterion[29] and a determinacy criterion.[30] Although elegance is less frequently discussed, its potential import is also recognised.[31] As the name suggests, such an account is concerned with the aesthetic qualities of the law (or of a theory of the law). Could an elegance criterion offer us a more fruitful perspective on the significance of coherence?

The possibility that one criterion (such as coherence) serves to advance another is also a well-recognised one. It is not unusual to think that the pursuit of one explanatory criterion is really a way of pursuing a more fundamental criterion. For example, well beyond the law, Quine tells us that simplicity may give us the more beautiful explanation, suggesting a basis in elegance for adopting a simplicity criterion.[32] And closer to home, Smith tells us that his morality criterion may be justified as a matter of coherence.[33] Indeed, he suggests that his morality and transparency criteria can both be subsumed within a fit criterion.[34] We should be open to the idea that a unifying coherence criterion is merely a way of capturing the elegance in private law.

But to assess that possibility, we must ask a further question. How does elegance fit in with the aim of capturing the law's self-understanding? In the realm of scientific explanation, it is a well-known challenge to explain why simplicity and elegance are desirable criteria for explanations, given that these features may not match the truth about the empirical world. As Brad Wendel notes, a version of this challenge also exists

[27] See AS Gold and HE Smith, 'Sizing Up Private Law' (2020) 70 *University of Toronto Law Journal* 489.

[28] J Coleman, *The Practice of Principle* (Oxford, Oxford University Press, 2001) 41.

[29] See AS Gold, 'Private Rights and Private Wrongs' (2017) 115 *Michigan Law Review* 1071, 1088.

[30] See JS Kraus, 'Transparency and Determinacy in Common Law Adjudication: A Philosophical Defense of Explanatory Economic Analysis' (2007) 93 *Virginia Law Review* 287.

[31] See WB Wendel, 'Explanation in Legal Scholarship: The Inferential Structure of Doctrinal Legal Analysis' (2011) 96 *Cornell Law Review* 1035, 1070–71 (discussing an elegance criterion for explanatory legal theories); Coleman (n 28) 38. See also Gold (n 7).

[32] See WVO Quine, 'On Simple Theories of a Complex World' in WVO Quine, *Quintessence* (Cambridge, MA, Harvard University Press, 2004) 210, 210.

[33] See Smith (n 1) 70, fn 29.

[34] ibid 7, fn 8.

for those who would apply an elegance criterion to the law.[35] That challenge should be front and centre if we want to capture the law's self-understanding.

We also need to know what it means to say something is 'elegant'. It is an aesthetic term, granted, and it is usually positive in connotation. Outside the law, the word has a range of overlapping meanings, including that something is beautiful, graceful, stylish or refined. While there is significant room for differences of opinion, however, not just anything is a likely candidate for elegance in the law. And while an elegance criterion could plausibly rule some theories out, how much is ruled out will depend on how the criterion is developed. In the present setting, I will suggest that elegance can refer to a range of such features, each of which shows an ordered patterning to the law that is plausibly taken to be elegant.

For example, if private law is elegant, this could mean that it is unified. But it could also mean other things, such as: that private law shows regular symmetries (as corrective justice theorists often indicate when they emphasise private law's correlative features); that it shows fractal patterns as we move from the micro-level to the macro-level;[36] that its doctrinal components fit together in a well-ordered way; or that it solves various problems through the use of simple, multi-functional legal structures. Viewed dynamically, we might also see an elegance to the way in which different legal subsystems (law and equity, for instance) interact with each other in private law contexts. An elegance criterion thus has the potential for considerably more flexibility than Smith's coherence criterion, depending on how it is developed.

I will take each of the above illustrations to be prima facie examples of elegance for purposes of assessing private law theories. These examples are nonetheless tentative, in part because elegance is so open to dispute. It is also because, just as with Smith's morality criterion (which is concerned with what judges could think is moral, whether or not they understand morality correctly), we may be concerned here with what legal actors could plausibly *perceive* as elegant rather than with elegance as such. What legal actors perceive to be elegant could sometimes differ from the above list, and it could change over time. Likewise, we could also be concerned with types of elegance that are byproducts unintended by legal actors, in which case the perceptions of legal actors may hold less significance. And we may be concerned with types of elegance that fall into both categories. I will develop these points further below, in the course of thinking through what an elegance criterion might look like.

B. Elegance as a Sign of the Internal Point of View

If the law's self-understanding is our ultimate goal, then a natural next step is to figure out if the common law is likely to be elegant in some way; if it is not, an elegance criterion will not assist in locating the internal point of view. One reason to think that

[35] See Wendel (n 31) 1074.

[36] cf E Fox-Decent, *Sovereignty's Promise: The State as Fiduciary* (Oxford, Oxford University Press, 2011) 113 (suggesting that both contract and fiduciary theories of state authority relations are fractal, retaining the same normative structure on any scale).

private law may have an elegance to it is that those who are steeped in the common law – including judges – have implicitly indicated that such an elegance exists. As Shivprasad Swaminathan notes, 'The common lawyers have, for a long time, been conscious of the centrality of tacit knowledge to their method, which is also sometimes described in the literature in terms of an "aesthetic feel".'[37] In theory, the aesthetics could diverge from elegance (compare the sublime), or from the types of elegance described above, but this 'aesthetic feel' is at least suggestive of elegance.

One might add that legal actors have a taste for a certain kind of elegance in the law.[38] If so, this suggests a potential practical challenge for would-be private law theorists. If private law theories pick up on whatever it is that gives the common law an aesthetic feel to its initiates, that should help us to capture the law's self-understanding. But this could mean in practice, however, that private law theorists have an advantage if they themselves are steeped in legal doctrine, or have experience as legal actors.[39] And even with that experience, not everyone will achieve the refined tastes of the common law expert; we are not all Cardozos. That possibility is real, but it can easily be overstated. It is not necessary to share in the precise tastes or aesthetic feel possessed by expert legal actors to identify the general patterns. It should be enough to discern the broad aesthetic sensibilities of those who share in private law practices, even if one is not an expert in the finer nuances.

A different kind of reason for thinking that an elegance criterion will help us match the law's self-understanding is that judges appear to aim at elegance (of a sort) when deciding cases. Consider Judge Cardozo's account of judges' pursuit of elegant law:

> A sentiment like in kind, though different in degree, is at the root of the tendency of precedent to extend itself along the lines of logical development. No doubt the sentiment is powerfully reinforced by what is often nothing but an intellectual passion for *elegantia juris*, for symmetry of form and substance.[40]

This is a picture of what judges do that suggests a pursuit of symmetry and order; a pursuit of a certain kind of elegance. Given that this pursuit will often succeed, it is a plausible reason to look for theories of law that incorporate such features.

Another reason to anticipate elegance – potentially of a different kind – is the judicial tendency to seek an eloquent expression for the court's legal reasoning. As Cardozo

[37] See S Swaminathan, 'What the Centipede Knows: Polycentricity and "Theory" for Common Lawyers' (2020) 40 *OJLS* 265, 275 (quoting K Gray and SF Gray, 'The Rhetoric of Realty' in J Getzler (ed), *Rationalizing Property, Equity and Trusts: Essays in Honour of Edward Burn* (London, Butterworths, 2003) 234). See also BN Cardozo, *The Growth of the Law* (New Haven, CT, Yale University Press, 1924) 88 (suggesting with respect to justice that '[a] trained sense of taste, approving or rejecting, will pass judgment on the whole'). Perhaps also there are connections between legal actors' taste and a legal system's 'style'. On the latter, see Y-C Chang and HE Smith, 'An Economic Analysis of Civil versus Common Law Property' (2012) 88 *Notre Dame Law Review* 1, 5 (suggesting that style 'has a certain reality from an internalist perspective').

[38] It is a separate question whether they ought to. cf Lord Goff, 'The Search for Principle', Maccabaean Lecture in Jurisprudence, Proceedings of the British Academy (5 May 1983) 174 (arguing against the 'temptation of elegance'). Of course, if there is a temptation of elegance, that may support an elegance criterion even if courts ought to avoid the temptation. I thank Nick McBride for noting this issue.

[39] For an excellent discussion of how tastes refine, see D Hume, 'Of the Standard of Taste' in D Hume, *Selected Essays* (Oxford, Oxford University Press, 1993) 133.

[40] See BN Cardozo, *The Nature of the Judicial Process* (New Haven, CT, Yale University Press, 1960) 34.

indicates, we can analogise the way courts look for the right path within the common law to the way poets seek the 'just word':

> The search is for the just word, the happy phrase, that will give expression to the thought, but somehow the thought itself is transfigured by the phrase when found. There is emancipation in our very bonds. The restraints of rhyme or metre, the exigencies of period or balance, liberate at times the thought which they confine, and in imprisoning release.[41]

Judges seek the just word when they craft opinions, and their word choice affects outcomes. It should not surprise us if the courts' search for eloquence produces aesthetic qualities in the law.

A third possibility is that there is something about private law decision making that is conducive to elegance, whether or not commentators perceive it, and whether or not judges intend it. Cardozo was on to something in emphasising how restraints like rhyme or metre can be productive. As Jon Elster notes, art and creativity may build on the constraints that govern the artist.[42] These constraints include restrictions that are intrinsic to the artist's medium (architects are limited by the available materials for building); constraints that are externally imposed (think of obscenity laws or other legal barriers); and constraints that are self-imposed (consider George Perec's novel written without the letter 'e').[43] One might think that the constraints of the judicial opinion writing mode are conducive to the development of a recognisable aesthetic. Such effects need not be intentional; they could be byproducts of the legal decision-making mode where that process is designed to advance other goals.

Some constraints involve the conventions of opinion writing. Judges are expected to describe the salient facts of a case, and they are also expected to candidly explain the legal reasoning that led them to a particular holding. While this is by no means a consistent feature, judges are often expected to focus on the case at hand, disregarding other, adjacent cases that could be hypothesised. There is also a pattern, albeit an imperfect one, of judges showing a 'reluctance to invoke ultimate values, or teleological aims'.[44] This fragmented vision gives common law reasoning a kind of modularity; it also makes judicial opinions resemble short stories (and, often, short stories with a moral to them). As with literary short stories, that can mean an aesthetic outcome.

A fourth possibility concerns the characteristic goal of adjudication: justice. In this regard, we might connect an elegance criterion to a justice criterion.[45] There are good reasons to think that courts attempt to do justice when resolving a case, and in particular that they attempt to do justice between the parties.[46] Doing justice is no ordinary

[41] See Cardozo (n 37) 89.

[42] See J Elster, *Ulysses Unbound* (Cambridge, Cambridge University Press, 2000) 191–200.

[43] See ibid (discussing G Perec, *La Disparition* (Paris, Gallimard, 1989) and other examples).

[44] See Swaminathan (n 37) 279.

[45] Note also that writing opinions that are legitimate exercises of power (or at least seem so) may require writing with a degree of transparency, clarity and coherence. The effects of doing so could also contribute to the law's elegance.

[46] This localised aspect may also be important for those who connect justice to beauty. See E Scarry, *On Beauty and Being Just* (Princeton, NJ, Princeton University Press, 2001). Scarry notes the importance of giving justice a doctrinal location as, in her view, 'justice itself is outside the compass of our sensory powers'. See ibid 102. I do not agree with the latter claim, but in any event the interpersonal justice in private law is well within our sensory powers.

constraint on judicial opinions, as it concerns a substantive feature of judicial reasoning. It is also likely to incline the law toward elegance.

Justice is often thought to have a 'fittingness' to it, and that fittingness can give justice a beautiful or at least aesthetically appealing quality.[47] Justice often also has a symmetry to it, at least as an aspiration. In saying this, I do not mean to suggest that the point of doing justice is aesthetic, nor that justice can best be understood in aesthetic terms. For present purposes, the significance of a connection between the just and the aesthetic is that it gives us additional reason to think an elegance criterion can help us in figuring out the law's self-understanding. Judges may care about the elegance of their judicial opinions; but even if they do not care, they are engaged in a practice that lends itself to the production of elegant legal doctrine. In other words, if courts are seeking to bring about a kind of justice, the results could have an aesthetic quality. Where that is sufficiently likely, an elegance criterion makes sense.

As noted, private law could be elegant in various ways – due to the way different doctrinal features neatly mesh together; due to its symmetry, including its bipolar remedial structures; due to its patterned complexity; and, notably, due to its unity. More needs to be said about which items on this list may best fit the arguments developed above. Once we settle on a view of what elegance means in private law settings, we will need to determine what our elegance criterion should be. We might, following Smith's practice, once again look for a moderate criterion. The goal then might be to find what judges and other legal actors could at least think is elegant, whether or not it is actually elegant. But, given the possibility that elegance is a byproduct and not a judicial goal, the criterion could need further weakening. For present purposes, it is enough to say the following: *a private law theory is better, all else equal, if it shows how private law is elegant in a way that is likely to result from the standard elaboration of private law cases.* I will adopt that criterion here, as a first cut at the problem.

C. The Pay-off of Adopting an Elegance Criterion

We can now see that an elegance criterion could have both content and justification, beyond advancing the aesthetic sensibilities of those who do private law theory. Meeting the aesthetic wishes of private law theorists is an unsatisfying pursuit given the usual goals of the field. Yet, in the right circumstances, by looking for the right kinds of elegance, we may better discern the internal point of view. Whether intentionally or unintentionally, there are reasons to think that judges decide cases in ways that will cause private law to at least tend toward elegance (of one kind or another), and the behaviours of other legal actors may encourage that.

May we then proceed with seeking a single principle that unifies all or at least a majority of components of a private law field? That could depend on context.

[47] For an example of the linkage, see R Hockett, 'Justice in Time' (2009) 77 *George Washington Law Review* 1135, 1150 (noting the connection between justice and 'fittingness' and tying justice to aesthetics). cf J Feinberg, 'Justice and Personal Desert' in J Feinberg, *Doing and Deserving: Essays on the Theory of Responsibility* (Princeton, NJ, Princeton University Press, 1970) 86 (discussing whether something is 'fitting' as a consideration for desert).

An impulse toward elegance is no more likely to give us unity in times of legal change or legal pluralism than an impulse toward coherence.[48] Indeed, the style of judicial opinion writing changes dramatically over time, and it is likely that aesthetic desiderata shift as well. Elegance could still matter in private law, however, and in a way that is discernible to the legal theorist.

Significantly, an elegance criterion may be more resilient than a moderate coherence criterion, for an elegance criterion can still be relevant even in the face of evidence that legal systems are confronted by significant legal change or pluralist tendencies. New legal content in private law is regularly absorbed into older conceptual structures (rights, duties, wrongs, remedies, private rights of action, etc). Even in contexts of reform, there is frequently a judicial effort to fit the existing legal architecture, and when an individual judge fails to make that effort, later judges will often do so.[49] What this means is that patterns of legal decision making (such as a deontological structure) remain in place even when legal content undergoes piecemeal changes and even when that content is explained by multiple, potentially conflicting principles. If this structure of private law also shows elegance, and if this structure is largely retained in times of legal change, there is room for an elegance criterion even where the law's coherence is local and not global.

There is also a notable further consequence if we subordinate coherence to elegance, with coherence as a means to elegance. A theory that can show how most of the core features of a private law field are explicable by a single principle will plausibly demonstrate private law's elegance (assuming unity is elegant). However, such a unifying theory may no longer have the advantage over rival theories that show less unity. Something that is elegant will not necessarily be unified in the way that the moderate coherence criterion calls for; it could be elegant for other reasons. Coherence thus advances elegance but not uniquely so. What would a less unified yet still elegant private law theory – or private law system – look like? I will turn to that question next.

IV. Towards Elegance as a Replacement

Given the variegation in types of elegance, and the depth of analysis required to show the likelihood of a given type of elegance within private law, these examples are just suggestions. That said, it is not difficult to find candidate theories, if we assume that private law is likely to show such things as: doctrinal symmetry; fractal patterns within legal doctrine; doctrinal components that fit together in a well-ordered way; the solution of problems through the use of simple, multi-functional structures; or a well-ordered interaction of the subsystems within private law.

Consider Greg Klass's account of contract law as both duty-imposing and power-conferring.[50] Contract law is about holding breaching parties accountable, yet it is also

[48] See Dagan, ch 4 in this volume.

[49] On the significance of architectural fit, see Gold and Smith (n 24).

[50] See G Klass, 'Three Pictures of Contract: Duty, Power, and Compound Rule' (2008) 83 *New York University Law Review* 1726.

about empowering private individuals to craft their legal relationships ex ante. Klass posits that contract law has compound rules: rules designed to serve both duty-imposing and power-conferring functions. With these premises in place, one could find the duty-imposing part to be more dominant than the power-conferring part, or vice versa, but it is not obvious how to do so. We thus have a sophisticated contract theory that could fail Smith's moderate coherence criterion due to its multiple overlapping principles. Yet the resulting picture that encapsulates duty-imposing and power-conferring features is compelling both doctrinally and in policy terms. It is also elegant how contract law's components then mesh together.

Alternatively, consider the account of private law that Henry Smith and I have offered. We suggest that both deontological theorists and functionalists should converge to a large degree, in light of the need for private law to keep complexity within manageable bounds, and in order to scale up successfully from micro to macro levels.[51] We further argue that both deontological and functional viewpoints should recognise the import of simple, deontological concepts for private law reasoning.[52] It is a short step from this view to the idea that private law is understandable in both deontological and functional terms, with each account potentially reinforcing the other. It is difficult to say that one principle then explains a majority of private law's core components, but the resulting picture of how legal principles and functions intersect – and how its legal structures are multi-functional – plausibly suggests the private law is elegant in its solutions to complexity.

Or consider John Goldberg and Ben Zipursky's account of how the principle of civil recourse links together a range of torts as a law of wrongs.[53] They readily allow that the wide diversity of wrongs tort law encompasses may be 'plural and irreducible'.[54] Yet they also suggest that their account would not lead to incoherence on that basis.[55] While I agree, note that their account nonetheless describes tort law in a way that could run afoul of Smith's version of the coherence criterion. We may have a hard time showing how a majority of the core components of tort law are explicable in terms of a single principle, assuming we see tort wrongs themselves as sufficiently plural. And yet the account Goldberg and Zipursky offer is no less elegant for that. Again, this is a theory that shows how law's components fit together in an ordered pattern, and it may well be a better fit with the legal doctrine than an account that tries for more unity.

None of these theories require the type of unification that Smith aims for; indeed, they may render that type of unification unlikely. Nevertheless, they plausibly each have an elegance to them, and they bring to light a kind of elegance within private law. It is also noteworthy that these are not the kinds of theories that pose a 'hodgepodge problem' or present a picture of ad hoc doctrine; rather, they are theories that show either how plural principles can justify multi-functional legal doctrine or, perhaps, how different components of a private law field can interact in a structured, well-ordered way. All of these theories take doctrinal fit and legal transparency seriously.

[51] See Gold and Smith (n 27).
[52] ibid.
[53] See JCP Goldberg and BC Zipursky, 'Torts as Wrongs' (2010) 88 *Texas Law Review* 917, 937–41.
[54] ibid 941.
[55] ibid.

To be sure, unification can also be elegant, and indeed this may be a good reason for seeking unifying theories; I am not arguing for elegance *contra* unification, or even for pluralism *contra* unification. But a coherence criterion that calls for unification around a single principle does not seem to achieve its stated goals, and an elegance criterion may be more successful at tracking the internal point of view. To the extent unifying theories are elegant, we should realise that a variety of other theories can likewise be elegant. An elegance criterion thus allows us to rule in unifying theories without ruling out some of the more compelling pluralist theories.[56] In each instance, a case can be made that this approach is consistent with the goal of capturing the internal point of view.

V. Conclusion

Interpretive criteria are a central yet oft neglected topic in private law theory, and no one has contributed more to this topic than Stephen Smith. His interpretive criteria will guide theorists for decades to come, and with good reason. The present chapter offers a proposal for replacing his coherence criterion in its current form, but, if it is worth making such adjustments, that is because Smith's achievement is so noteworthy. The proposed addition, an elegance criterion, is offered in the same spirit as Smith's original approach. I would simply add that Smith's theories are elegant in their own right: the best argument for his interpretive criteria is the exemplary work he produced while following them.

[56] Understood in this way, elegance plays a very different role in private law theory from the role it is sometimes thought to play. cf RL Rabin, 'Law for Law's Sake' (1996) 105 *Yale Law Journal* 2261, 2272 (suggesting that formalism 'as a nonsubstantive aesthetic principle is misplaced and unintelligible in a world of conflict resolution').

3

Comparative Legal Scholarship: Anything but Ordinary

ROSALIE JUKIER*

I. Introduction

It was June of 2011 when I first heard Steve Smith's contention that there is nothing distinctive about comparative law, that comparative legal scholarship is just ordinary legal scholarship and that all comparative law does is employ a 'broader range of data'.[1] Smith presented this argument at the Third International Congress of the World Society of Mixed Jurisdiction Jurists, a conference hosted by the Hebrew University of Jerusalem.

As I sat in the audience on that beautiful, balmy day, I vividly recall having two strong reactions to his presentation. The first was a visceral response to the very thesis itself. After all, Steve Smith was my colleague at McGill University's Faculty of Law, a faculty that offers a uniquely comparative legal curriculum, self-termed 'transsystemic'.[2] The distinctive feature of McGill's curriculum is that all law students learn the civil and the common law, and increasingly other legal traditions such as Indigenous legal traditions, in a deeply integrated and comparative way, right from the start, on a path to obtaining both the civil law BCL and the common law JD degrees. The programme is premised on the integrated and simultaneous (rather than sequential) comparison of legal traditions, across the entire curriculum. The program's goal is to strengthen students' understanding of each tradition and develop critical and creative thinkers who bring a broader set of resources to problem-solving than jurists trained in just one tradition.[3]

* The author wishes to thank McGill law student Joseph Ho for his invaluable research and editorial assistance, generously funded by the Law and You Fund of the McGill Faculty of Law.

[1] SA Smith, 'Comparative Legal Scholarship as Ordinary Legal Scholarship' (2011) 5 *Journal of Comparative Law* 331, 334.

[2] See, eg, J Bédard, 'Transsystemic Teaching of Law at McGill: "Radical Changes, Old and New Hats"' (2001) 27 *Queen's Law Journal* 237; Y-M Morissette, 'McGill's Integrated Civil and Common Law Program' (2002) 52 *Journal of Legal Education* 12; R Jukier, 'The Untapped Potential of Transsystemic Thinking' in Y Emerich and M-A Plante (eds), *Repenser les paradigmes: Approches transsystémiques du droit* (Cowansville, Éditions Yvons Blais, 2018) 6–10.

[3] R Jukier, 'The Impact of "Stateless Law" on Legal Pedagogy' in H Dedek and S Van Praagh (eds), *Stateless Law: Evolving Boundaries of a Discipline* (Farnham, Ashgate, 2015) 209.

Since its inauguration in 1999, McGill Law's Transsystemic Program has significantly recast our teaching and research. Both Steve Smith and I taught the first-year course of Contractual Obligations in this transsystemic programme: a blended course where, from day one, the students are immersed in the law and theory of contracts from a multi-systemic standpoint.[4] How could Smith make this claim about comparative law when we had spent countless hours in each other's offices debating and uncovering how the other legal tradition would view the topic we would soon be discussing in class? Usually, Smith, originally trained in the common law, would rely on me for the civil law and I on him for the common law. But as we both became more comfortable with the material in the respective traditions, sometimes it was the reverse. The debates were always stimulating, the insights profound. The important point is that our conversations yielded insights that would have eluded us but for our comparative exchange. How could this be just ordinary?

My second reaction was that, despite my reflexive disagreement with the very thesis itself, I could not help but find Smith's arguments oddly seductive! But that is because it was Steve Smith who was articulating these arguments. Smith had an uncanny ability to excel at the game of devil's advocate. He loved nothing more than conversation, engaging with legal, philosophical or theoretical arguments, and taking unorthodox or provocative positions, sometimes simply for the benefit of an enriching or fruitful debate. The article he wrote expounding this thesis, entitled 'Comparative Legal Scholarship as Ordinary Legal Scholarship',[5] presents a series of arguments that first lays out plausible reasons why comparative law may indeed be considered distinctive. It does not, however, take Smith long to shoot down each proposed argument in his typically compelling style. He proceeds to examine, in turn, whether comparative law is distinctive because of its method, subject matter, challenges or aims. In the end, as I summarise in the following paragraph, he discredits each of these potential reasons for its uniqueness.

In terms of method, he concludes that all legal scholars, even the most narrowly focused domestic scholars, are involved in some level of comparison, even if they are just 'compar[ing] domestic laws to moral rules, conventional rules or other domestic laws'.[6] As for subject matter, Smith asserts that while comparative law viewed as a study of legal transplantation and legal evolution, or as a study of the world's legal systems, might have distinctive characteristics, this is not how comparative law is traditionally understood.[7] Understood as merely the study of law from more than one jurisdiction,[8] it fails to live up to distinctiveness because 'the study of the laws of the world is indistinguishable from the study of law generally'.[9] Moving to challenges, he posits that 'comparative scholars must simultaneously adopt "insider" and

[4] See R Jukier, 'Where Law and Pedagogy Meet in the Transsystemic Contracts Classroom' (2005) 50 *McGill Law Journal* 789, 798–801. For an exposition of transsystemic teaching in the Torts classroom, see S Van Praagh, 'Palsgraf as "Transsystemic" Tort Law' (2011) 6 *Journal of Comparative Law* 243, 246–53.

[5] Smith (n 1).

[6] ibid 337.

[7] ibid 340.

[8] Smith defines comparative law and comparative legal scholarship as 'scholarship (of whatever kind) that examines the laws (however defined) of more than one jurisdiction.' ibid 336.

[9] ibid 343.

"outsider" perspectives'[10] and that they 'must simultaneously inhabit a legal system while standing apart from it'.[11] However, not even this makes comparative law distinctive. Smith proceeds to point out that 'domestic scholars regularly engage in the same kind of inside-outside perspectives' because they often 'compar[e] their law to a different normative order, such as morality, religion or conventional beliefs'.[12] Finally, with respect to aims, while the aim of studying law comparatively with a view to harmonising law may be somewhat distinctive, Smith argues that not only is this aim not uniformly accepted,[13] but that most legal study, even if related to domestic law, is ultimately aimed at improving and reforming the law.[14] As for the aim of studying law scientifically or academically, as opposed to pursuing it for primarily instrumental ends, again, Smith retorts that this aim is not unique to comparative law.[15]

Without meaning to oversimplify Smith's proposition, I think all his arguments lead to his conclusion that domestic legal scholars do pretty much the same thing as comparative legal scholars, and that the only difference with comparative legal scholarship is one of degree, not kind. For Smith, comparative law is just about a 'wider range of data'.[16] He illustrates this point with the example of the ornithologist. He states 'It is true that the scientific study of birds would be greatly diminished if all ornithologists focused exclusively on birds in their own gardens'.[17] Smith acknowledges, and lauds, the positive aspects of comparative study, saying that 'more data is better than less'.[18] He simply does not feel that its increased value leads to distinctiveness in any way.

In this chapter, I will engage with Smith's arguments and attempt to uncover the distinctiveness of comparative law, thereby demonstrating that it is anything but 'ordinary'.

II. The Concept of Distinctiveness

Smith asserts that 'comparative law is not, and never will be, a distinctive legal discipline. Scholars waiting for comparative law to develop into something that can take its place alongside subjects such as contract law, economic analysis of law, or feminist legal studies will wait forever'.[19] While Smith is adamant that comparative law is not distinct, and repeats this assertion throughout the paper, he never explains his definition of distinctiveness nor his conception of a distinctive legal discipline. In fact, he admits that he does 'not attempt this task'![20] Can one really claim something is *not* distinct without first defining or explaining what would make something distinct?

[10] ibid 348.
[11] ibid.
[12] ibid 348–49.
[13] In fact, as Steve Smith points out, this aim has many detractors, such as Pierre Legrand: ibid 352–53, fnn 89–91, 93–95.
[14] ibid 353.
[15] ibid 354.
[16] ibid 356.
[17] ibid 354.
[18] ibid 356.
[19] ibid 334. Steve Smith also describes these subjects as 'a free-standing discipline' in an earlier version of the same paper at ssrn.com/abstract=2159908 (accessed 15 July 2023).
[20] Smith (n 1) 335.

We learn from Rod Macdonald that the exercise of taxonomy – classifying things into distinct categories – is not only difficult but is, ultimately, illusory and artificial. For one, the exercise depends on how broadly you cast the net. At the broadest level, there may, in fact, be nothing distinctive about any area of law. Inspired by Lon Fuller, Macdonald's view of law, writ large, is that of 'a human project, a human accomplishment, and a human aspiration that emerges from ongoing patterns of human interaction and the reciprocal adjustment of human expectations'.[21] Put simply, for Macdonald, law is but one lens through which to analyse and solve human problems.[22] As for the study of law, Macdonald conceived it equally broadly as being, at its core, about learning how to 'attend to the complexities of human beings in interaction with each other'[23] and 'about finding social outcomes that help solve human problems'.[24]

Macdonald was not only critical about the attempt to classify law into distinct categories, he also bemoaned the traditional categorisation of legal subjects, stating 'Why, in heaven's name, do the labels put on subjects by practitioners and treatise-writers a century ago continue to drive the way we, as university law teachers, organize our curriculum?'[25] He argued that 'the connexions between and the limits of legal concepts' such as contracts are not necessarily 'easier to draw than other concepts'.[26] In his typically provocative style, he once wrote that he was not quite sure that teaching the law of contracts was preferable to teaching the law of bumble-bees, because it 'rests on a belief that the fact/concept contract is more legally meaningful as an organizing tool than the fact/concept bumblebee'.[27] He also posited that the first-year curriculum should be taught through the lens of cars rather than obligations and property.[28]

If we follow Macdonald's lead, we might be tempted to abandon entirely the debate about whether comparative law is distinctive. However, if we are to proceed with the exercise of classification, as Smith does, then, I submit, it needs to be done consistently. In what follows, I will question the consistency of Smith's position that certain areas of substantive law and various theoretical perspectives to law are 'distinct', all the while maintaining that comparative legal scholarship is not.

[21] RA Macdonald, 'Let Our Future Not Be Behind Us: The Legal Profession in Changing Times' (2001) 64 *Saskatchewan Law Review* 1, 16.

[22] RA Macdonald, *Lessons of Everyday Law* (Montreal, McGill-Queen's University Press, 2002) 7.

[23] RA Macdonald and TB McMorrow, 'Decolonizing Law School' (2014) 51 *Alberta Law Review* 717, 725.

[24] Macdonald (n 21) 26.

[25] RA Macdonald, 'Still "Law" and Still "Learning"?/Quel « droit » et « quel savoir ? »' (2003) 18 *Canadian Journal of Law & Society* 5, 15.

[26] R Macdonald, 'Legal Education on the Threshold of the 1980's: Whatever Happened to the Great Ideas of the 60's?' (1979) 44 *Saskatchewan Law Review* 39, 54.

[27] ibid.

[28] K Brooks, 'The World Needs More Rod Macdonald: The Potential of Big Ideas' (2014) 51 *Alberta Law Review* 871, 872, where the author recounts how Rod Macdonald told her 'I think we should teach all of first year through the lens of some regular object. Cars. Forget obligations and property. Imagine that we taught all of first year through something rooted in everyday life. Something that centred the real people for whom law is made.'

A. Sharing Similarities

Without providing a definition of distinctiveness, Smith argues that comparative law is not distinct because it shares similarities with domestic law in method, subject matter, challenges and aims. What he implies is that if two or more things share similarities, or at least enough similarities, then they are not distinct. However, the notion of sharing similarities requires further analysis. There exists a myriad of examples of areas of law or 'academic subject[s] in [their] own right'[29] that share many similarities, yet even Smith would admit that they are distinct. Let us take an example that he describes as a distinct and free-standing discipline: contract law.[30] He asserts explicitly that contract law is distinct from tort law.[31] This, of course, would not be surprising to any common law student or professor. As Nathalie Vézina writes, '[t]he common law … still regards tort law and contract law as essentially separate areas'.[32] As a result, we see common law faculties mounting separate courses in Contracts and Torts, and common law authors publishing separate books on each subject.[33]

The question of whether contract and tort law should be treated as separate areas highlights the challenge of the exercise of taxonomy that Rod Macdonald raised. While Smith would classify them distinctly, I would argue that they share the same methods, subject matter, challenges and aims. At a basic level, both are fundamentally about regulating the relationships between people and setting out the normative boundaries of these inter-personal dealings. Both are concerned with redressing wrongs and the responsibility to repair damage to the victim of a breach.

In fact, a comparative approach with the civil law in this area is quite revealing. The civil law views contracts and civil responsibility[34] as two sides of the same 'obligations' coin.[35] The obligation between the parties may arise involuntarily, such as through the commission of a wrong, or voluntarily, through a juridical act such as a contract. But, regardless of its origin or source, the major aspects of all obligations share significant overlaps. Rather than giving rise to a distinctive regime, civilian scholars generally 'view all sources of obligations as being variations on a single theme – that of

[29] M Reimann, 'The Progress and Failure of Comparative Law in the Second Half of the Twentieth Century' (2002) 50 *American Journal of Comparative Law* 671, 684.

[30] Smith (n 19) 5.

[31] Smith (n 1) 339.

[32] N Vézina, 'Part One: Preliminary Notions, Duality of Regimes, and Factual Basis of Liability' in A Grenon and L Bélanger-Hardy (eds), *Elements of Quebec Civil Law: A Comparison with the Common Law of Canada* (Toronto, Thomson Carswell, 2008) 327.

[33] See, eg, E Chamberlain and S Pitel (eds), *Fridman's The Law of Torts in Canada*, 4th edn (Toronto, Thomson Carswell, 2020); SM Waddams, *The Law of Contracts*, 8th edn (Toronto, Thomson Reuters, 2022).

[34] The term 'Torts' does not exist, per se, in the civil law.

[35] Book Five of the Civil Code of Québec begins, in Title One, by dealing with 'Obligations in General' before dividing the subject of obligations into more specific rules applicable to Contracts and Civil Liability. See, in particular, Arts 1371–1373, which lay out the constituent elements of all obligations as well as their sources (namely, 'a contract or from any act or fact to which the effects of an obligation are attached by law', Art 1372 CCQ (Can)). As a result, instead of there being separate treatises on Contractual Obligations and Extra-Contractual Obligations, there are often texts on Obligations writ large. See, eg, J Carbonnier, *Droit civil*. Tome 4: *Les obligations*, 22nd edn (Paris, Presses universitaires de France, 2000); MA Tancelin, *Théorie du droit des obligations* (Québec, Les Presses de l'Université Laval, 1975).

the obligation'.[36] As Brierley and Macdonald go on to explain, the 'basic architecture [of the Code] signals what jurists in both Quebec and France have come to label the "conceptual" unity of the law of obligations'.[37] There is 'structural symmetry' between all obligations, regardless of their source, and the entire law of obligations 'can be understood as a unified whole'.[38]

Given the unitary theory of obligations in the civil law, which recognises the common core of private law relationships, it is undeniable that the subjects of contracts and torts share significant similarities. Nonetheless, Smith recognises these as distinct areas of law. Are they more distinct than domestic and comparative law? I would argue that it is inconsistent to assert that there is nothing distinctive about comparative law (because domestic law is also involved in comparison), all the while maintaining that contract and tort law are distinct.

B. Lenses Through which We Analyse Law

Contracts and torts are subjects that most would refer to as substantive areas of law, areas which deal with the 'what' of the law, namely: What are the rules that govern the relationship between persons when there is a juridical link between them, imposed either contractually or extra-contractually? What makes obligations come into being and what remedies are available for their breach? We can contrast these 'what' subjects with those that are not substantive but, rather, seek to offer a specific lens through which to analyse, interpret, critique or understand substantive law. The latter includes areas of study such as feminist legal studies, critical race theory and economic analysis of law. I use these three specific examples of lenses that seek to explain or critique substantive legal outcomes because Smith recognises them as distinct in his paper. He asserts that not only are these 'free-standing disciplines'[39] and 'well-recognized fields',[40] but that they are so recognised because of their distinctive aims.

Indeed, these three fields do have distinctive aims. Feminist legal theory, to the extent one can generalise, 'is designed to expose how the substance of law may silently and without justification submerge the perspectives of women and other excluded groups'.[41] It also 'challenges the legitimacy of the norms of those who claim to speak, through rules, for the community',[42] thus 'reveal[ing] insights about gender exclusion within existing legal rules and principles'.[43] And it 'offers a means of testing the validity of accepted legal principles through the lens of the personal experience of those directly affected by those principles'.[44]

[36] JEC Brierley and RA Macdonald, *Quebec Civil Law: An Introduction to Quebec Private Law* (Toronto, Emond Montgomery Publications Limited, 1993) para 403.

[37] ibid. See also J-L Baudouin, P Deslauriers and B Moore, *La responsabilité civile*, 9th edn (Cowansville, Éditions Yvon Blais, 2020) vol 1, 1–48, where they say, 'sur le plan ontologique et de la théorie juridique, il existe une *unité conceptuelle* des concepts de base de la responsibilité civile' (emphasis added).

[38] Brierley and Macdonald (n 36).

[39] Smith (n 19) 5.

[40] Smith (n 1) 351.

[41] KT Bartlett, 'Feminist Legal Methods' (1990) 103 *Harvard Law Review* 829, 836.

[42] ibid 855.

[43] ibid 858.

[44] ibid 837.

Critical race theory (CRT) is 'an analytical toolset for interrogating the relationship between law and racial inequality'.[45] It is based on the premise that race is 'socially and legally constructed',[46] and that racism is embedded in legal systems and policies.[47] It is 'engaged in studying and transforming the relationship among race, racism, and power'[48] and critically confronting 'the historical centrality and complicity of law in upholding white supremacy'.[49] As is the case with feminist legal theory, personal narrative is a prominent methodology of CRT.

Economic analysis of law uses 'economic models to evaluate legal rules'.[50] The theory posits that our understanding of law 'can be enhanced … by economic concepts, including the criterion of economic efficiency'.[51] Assuming that '[p]eople act as rational maximizers of their satisfactions',[52] it 'looks at cost-justified precautions the defendant might have taken to prevent the harm and asks, how can the law encourage the defendant and others to take these precautions in future'.[53]

What feminist legal studies, CRT and economic analysis of law all have in common is that they are not areas of substantive law that ask the question 'What?'. They are all specific lenses, toolsets or theoretical perspectives used to analyse and explain substantive legal outcomes in defined areas of law. Rather than being substantive, seeking to uncover the 'outcome', they are process-driven, seeking to examine the 'how' and the 'why' of the law, rather than the 'what'.

The article co-authored by Richard Devlin, Anthony Duggan and Louise Langevin, 'Doing Theory in First Year Contracts: The Iceberg Method', illustrates how these and similar theoretical perspectives on law are lenses through which to analyse substantive law.[54] In that publication, the authors demonstrate how they 'introduce [first-year Contracts] students to a range of theoretical perspectives by comparing and contrasting the application of competing legal theories to a particular legal problem'.[55] The authors chose, for purposes of illustration, the spousal guarantee cases in contract law[56] as their reference point, and critical legal studies, law and economics, and feminist theory as their perspectives.

[45] KM Bridges, *Critical Race Theory: A Primer* (St Paul, Foundation Press, 2019) 7.

[46] B Capers, 'Critical Race Theory' in MD Dubber and T Hörnle (eds), *The Oxford Handbook of Criminal Law* (Oxford, Oxford University Press, 2014) 26.

[47] Bridges (n 45) 11–12.

[48] R Delgado and J Stefancic, *Critical Race Theory: An Introduction*, 3rd edn (New York, NYU Press, 2017) 3.

[49] C West, 'Foreword' in K Crenshaw et al (eds), *Critical Race Theory: The Key Writings That Formed the Movement* (New York, New Press, 1995) xi.

[50] TJ Miceli, 'Economic Models of Law' in F Parisi (ed), *The Oxford Handbook of Law and Economics*, vol 1 (Oxford, Oxford University Press, 2017) 13.

[51] N Mercuro and SG Medema, *Economics and the Law: From Posner to Postmodernism and Beyond*, 2nd edn Princeton, NJ, Princeton University Press, 2006) 20.

[52] RA Posner, 'The Law and Economics Movement' (1987) 77 *American Economic Review* 1, 5. Posner, former law professor and former US judge, is one of the more well-known proponents of the law and economics movement.

[53] R Devlin, A Duggan and L Langevin, 'Doing Theory in First Year Contracts: The Iceberg Method' (2007) 1 *Canadian Legal Education Annual Review* 1, 19.

[54] ibid 35.

[55] ibid 1.

[56] *Barclays Bank plc v O'Brien* [1993] UKHL 6, [1994] 1 AC 180; *Royal Bank of Scotland plc v Etridge (No 2)* [2001] UKHL 44, [2002] 2 AC 773.

Similarly, comparative law may be seen as a lens through which we can learn about substantive law, critique and better understand it, and even perhaps be inspired by it.[57] A comparative lens on spousal guarantee cases in contract law would have yielded equally interesting perspectives to those uncovered by Devlin, Duggan and Langevin.[58] In my Contractual Obligations class, I use these identical cases as a launch pad for a discussion of how the civil law might have approached the same issue (given that the doctrine of undue influence does not, per se, exist in the civil law). This analysis yields compelling possibilities and different ways of conceiving of the problem, as I explain in section III.[59]

Viewed in this light, it seems inconsistent for Smith to assert that feminist legal studies, CRT and economic analysis of law are distinct categories of legal analysis and scholarship while maintaining that comparative law is not. In McGill's integrated courses,[60] the purpose of comparing multiple sources, from different legal systems and different legal traditions, is not so students will get to know more substantive law. The goal is merely to provide different lenses, multiple hypotheses of solutions and additional potential approaches to any given legal issue or human problem, so that aspiring jurists can learn the crucial lesson that there is not necessarily one right answer or one way of building or understanding a legal framework. As Harry Arthurs has written, this approach 'challenges the notion that law's logic is bounded, its values fixed, its processes ascertainable, and its outcomes predictable'.[61]

Comparative law is thus used for analysis and 'as a framework',[62] making it as distinct a lens as feminist legal studies, CRT and economic analysis of law. If Smith admits that various theoretical lenses used to explain, understand and critique law are distinct, then it behoves him to add comparative law to that list.

III. Rethinking the Axes of Analysis

Smith organises his paper around four headings – method, subject matter, challenges and aims – and analyses the potential distinctiveness of comparative law through the prism of these four self-imposed categories. Why, however, are these the headings that define exhaustively whether law is distinct or ordinary? If we rethink the axes of analysis, we might we reach a different conclusion than he does.

I propose that if we were to focus on the results or effects of a comparative analysis, we would conclude that it is indeed distinct from a domestic, or mono-jural, approach. Comparative legal analysis necessitates the consideration of multiple perspectives that compel us to look at issues through different lenses. It thereby forces us to transcend

[57] See text to nn 83–85 in section IV, where I discuss how comparative law may inspire judges in their judicial reasonings.

[58] Devlin, Duggan and Langevin (n 53).

[59] See text to nn 65–69 in section III, where I discuss undue influence as an example.

[60] It is acknowledged that there is no singular conception of comparative law or comparative method. The comparative method I will use as an illustration in this chapter is that inspired by McGill's Transsystemic Program, outlined in section I.

[61] HW Arthurs, 'Law and Learning in an Era of Globalization' (2009) 10 *German Law Journal* 629, 637.

[62] *CM Callow Inc v Zollinger*, 2020 SCC 45 [73] (Kasirer J).

and challenge orthodoxy, to focus upon the questions we need to ask rather than on the answers we want to learn and, as such, it leads to different results than would a mono-jural analysis. Daniel Jutras has written that a multisystemic perspective leads to a 'thicker' understanding of law.[63] He used the term 'thicker' not as a synonym for 'more', but rather to indicate that a deeper understanding results from a 'cross-cultural dialogue in law', what Nicholas Kasirer has termed 'métissage' in describing McGill's transsystemic focus.[64]

The McGill experience of teaching law has shown us that the simultaneous comparison of different legal systems and traditions not only results in a greater understanding of others but, in the process, also teaches us more about ourselves. This is because understanding the difference in another mode of thinking (such as a legal tradition) causes one to question the approach in one's own mode of thinking (or legal tradition), which ultimately invites opportunity for greater insight and more sophisticated contemplation of both. A comparative approach invites us to question assumptions, daring us to challenge existing orthodoxy and, in particular, to renounce a given legal tradition's doctrinal reality as orthodox wisdom. I have often used the common law doctrine of consideration in contract law as a simple illustration of this assertion. In the common law, the lack of consideration will impede the formation of an enforceable contract. Yet studying contract law comparatively teaches us that consideration, oft-considered part of common law contract gospel, has no direct equivalent in the civil law tradition. When confronted with this absence in the civil law, and therefore the multitude of civil law jurisdictions that survive well without this concept, it becomes easier to question the wisdom of the doctrine's very existence and the possibility of serious alternatives to this orthodox doctrinal reality of the common law.

A comparative approach also enables us to uncover hidden assumptions, and to explore the veiled reasons and justifications underlying a legal doctrine or outcome. To illustrate this, I often turn to the common law doctrine of undue influence.[65] As with consideration, a comparative approach again shows the lack of direct equivalent comparators in the civil law tradition. This compels us to ask how the civil law persists – and continues to aspire to fairness – without the benefit of the tool of undue influence. Moreover, this question obliges us to confront why the doctrine exists in the common law in the first place.

Somewhat ironically, it is by turning to something written by Smith himself, namely the sixth edition of Atiyah's treatise on the *Introduction to the Law of Contract*, that helps answer this question.[66] Here Smith includes a lengthy discussion of the basis for relief under the doctrine. He posits that 'presumed undue influence is a particular kind of impaired consent … most closely related to the defence of incapacity'.[67]

[63] D Jutras, 'Two Arguments for Cross-Cultural Legal Education' in H-D Assmann, G Brüggemeier and R Sethe (eds), *Different Legal Cultures – Convergence of Legal Reasoning / Unterschiedliche Rechtskulturen – Konvergenz des Rechtsdenkens* (Baden-Baden, Nomos Verlagsgesellschaft, 2001) 86.

[64] N Kasirer, 'Legal Education as *Métissage*' (2003) 78 *Tulane Law Review* 481, 483–84.

[65] Undue influence is an equitable doctrine unique to the common law, which enables a party to ask for relief from a contract into which they entered due to an abuse of a relationship of trust and confidence, presumed or proven, enabling the stronger party to take unfair advantage of the contracting party.

[66] SA Smith, *Atiyah's Introduction to the Law of Contract*, 6th edn (Oxford, Oxford University Press, 2006) 288–91.

[67] ibid 290.

Not only is this explanation of undue influence interesting and unconventional, it is also one inspired by Smith's understanding of the civil law of contractual obligations in which the integrity of contracting parties' consent is of critical importance.[68] Indeed, Smith was directly influenced by a comparative approach to this issue, because it was one of the subjects of, and insights from, our pre-class office discussions to which I referred earlier in this chapter! In writing about Smith's novel understanding of undue influence, I stated that '[i]t is perhaps no accident that Smith teaches at McGill and has accordingly been examining common law undue influence in *métissage* with the civil law, rather than in isolation'.[69] The very lack of civilian counterparts, discovered as part of the comparative examination of the doctrine, is what opens one up to questioning, and uncovering, the underlying assumptions of the doctrine itself. Smith learned this himself from comparative analysis. It is, therefore, surprising that he adamantly maintains the lack of distinctiveness of the comparative method.

Finally, teaching and learning law comparatively can be a useful vehicle for instilling creative, critical and flexible thinking skills. A comparative approach can help develop skills of imaginative insight instrumental in creating independent and innovative, rather than mechanistic, thinkers. The emphasis in this approach is placed on the process, not the result; on the question, not the answer; on 'the particular shape of the law (why is the law this way?) over the particulars of the law (what is the law?)'.[70] Comparison invites curiosity and scepticism, and its purpose is not to know more law but, rather, to help us conceive of law as a potential response to common human problems, and think creatively of how law may be used in this way. This, in turn, can help us solve novel problems,[71] and improve our skills in novel problem-solving methods, such as those that come under the large umbrella known as alternative dispute resolution (ADR).[72] Rather than the expert application of domestic legal principles combined with clever argumentation, ADR encourages jurists to brainstorm innovative solutions. Thus, it requires an aptitude for envisaging a multiplicity of creative ways to solve the parties' problems, one 'that no court has jurisdiction to provide'.[73] A comparative perspective is instrumental in honing that skill.

Comparative law is, therefore, not about more 'what' but more about 'how' and 'why'. As Catherine Valcke has stated, '[t]he emphasis is on the *how* things are done rather than *what* is being done'.[74] This is echoed by Justice Kasirer of the Supreme Court of Canada, who has written that, '[t]his exercise of comparison between legal

[68] Other common law authors, such as McCamus, do not venture to uncover the hidden purpose of the doctrine of undue influence as does Smith. They define it and comment on leading cases that apply it. J McCamus, *The Law of Contracts*, 3rd edn (Toronto, Irwin Law Inc, 2020) 428.

[69] Jukier (n 3) 208.

[70] H Whalen-Bridge, 'A Common Law Fly on the Transsystemic Wall: Observing the Integrated Method at McGill Faculty of Law' (2017) 51 *The Law Teacher* 188, 190.

[71] A concept I develop in Jukier, 'The Untapped Potential of Transsystemic Thinking' (n 2) 17–20.

[72] ibid 20–24.

[73] J Reno, 'Lawyers as Problem-Solvers: Keynote Address to the AALS' (1999) 49 *Journal of Legal Education* 5, 8. See also M Keet and TB Salamone, 'From Litigation to Mediation: Using Advocacy Skills for Success in Mandatory or Court-Connected Mediation' (2001) 64 *Saskatchewan Law Review* 57, 72.

[74] C Valcke, 'Comparing Legal Style' (2019) 15 *International Journal of Law in Context* 274, 275. See also M Van Hoecke, 'Deep Level Comparative Law' in M Van Hoecke (ed), *Epistemology and Methodology of Comparative Law* (Oxford, Hart Publishing, 2004).

traditions [is] for the purposes of "explanation" and "illustration"'[75] and not for the purpose of relying on 'specific rules that would govern a similar claim'[76] in another legal jurisdiction.

Before concluding this section, I will return to Smith's example of the ornithologist and the collection of more birds for their study. With respect, I think the question is not merely whether one has collected more birds but, rather, what one does with those extra birds. If all the birds are from the ornithologist's own garden, the insights gleaned may be useful, but they will not be as interesting or fruitful as those collected from beyond when compared to the local birds. Like comparisons in law, the outcome of a comparative examination of these foreign birds is likely to change our perceptions about birds, may disrupt conventional wisdom about them or may reveal hidden assumptions of avian anatomy that were, hitherto, undiscovered. Rather than the collection of more birds, it is the exercise of comparison, or *métissage*, that brings about the exponential learning that allows us to look at birds, law and life differently.

IV. Examining the Thesis in the Judicial Arena

Smith asserts that '*[a]ll* legal scholars are involved in "bringing together" different materials, that is to say, in comparison'.[77] He also states that '*anyone* interested in the academic study of law should, in principle, be interested in law from other jurisdictions'.[78] It is interesting to examine these assertions, and the corollary thesis that, as a result, there is nothing distinctive about comparative law, by looking at the judicial arena, and in particular the Supreme Court of Canada. Although Smith is referring to legal scholars and academics, and judges do not fit neatly into these categories, Supreme Court justices are, arguably, the most academic and scholarly of their genre, and many of the contemporary judges sitting on the Canadian Supreme Court are former academics.[79]

To assert that there is nothing special or unique about comparative law, since everyone does it in one way or another, ignores a heated debate that has been going on in the Supreme Court of Canada almost since its very inception in 1875. Over its nearly 150-year history, Supreme Court justices have articulated multiple conceptions of the role that comparative law plays in the Court's decisions. More precisely, there have often been spirited discussions between the justices regarding the interrelationship between the civil law and common law legal traditions and their mutual influence, or lack thereof, in the Court's decisions.[80]

[75] *Callow* (n 62) [60] (Kasirer J).

[76] ibid [73].

[77] Smith (n 1) 337 (emphasis added).

[78] ibid 356 (emphasis added).

[79] eg, Justice Nicholas Kasirer, Justice Sheilah Martin, Justice Russell Brown (who stepped down from the Court in June 2023).

[80] One of the earliest examples of an explicit conversation, and disagreement, about the role of comparative law is the 1885 decision in *Sweeny v Bank of Montreal* (1885) 12 SCR 661, a case from Québec dealing with the interpretation of the trust, a quintessential common law construct. There is an interesting dialogue between the majority judge, Justice Ritchie, who simply applies common law precedent because the legal principle in

Of particular interest is the exchange surrounding the use (or usefulness) of comparative law in two contemporary Supreme Court decisions: *Callow v Zollinger*[81] and *Wastech Services Ltd v Greater Vancouver Sewerage and Drainage District*.[82] Both cases deal with the controversial doctrine of good faith in the performance of contractual promises in the common law, and both contain heated debates between the majority judge, Justice Kasirer, and the minority judge, Justice Brown. Justice Brown concurs in the substantive outcome of both cases. His only disagreement with the majority is the role that comparative law should play in arriving at the Court's decisions. Justice Kasirer promotes the comparison between the common law and civil law as 'a particularly useful and familiar exercise for this Court', one that 'has been described as "worthwhile", "useful" and "helpful"'.[83] Justice Kasirer subscribes to what may be described as the inspiration theory of comparative law,[84] namely that 'principles from the common law or the civil law may serve as a "source of inspiration" for the other'.[85]

Justice Brown, on the other hand, feels that there is no place for such comparative exercise on the Court. He labels the majority's dialogue between the civil and common law as a 'digression' that 'will only inject uncertainty and confusion into the law'.[86] He discredits the majority's inspiration-based use of comparative law, calling it 'inappropriate'[87] as well as risky and confusing,[88] and one that would even serve to erect 'barriers that impede access to justice'.[89] His admonition is even stronger in the *Wastech* decision, where he states that Justice Kasirer's 'reliance on the civil law of Quebec is unnecessary, ill-advised and wholly misplaced … [leading to] complication, uncertainty and confusion'.[90]

Justice Brown is not, of course, the first justice on the Supreme Court of Canada to react negatively to a comparative law approach. Justice Pierre-Basile Mignault, who served on the Court from 1918 to 1929, is perhaps the most well-known judge to do so. Mignault emphasised the distinctiveness of the civil law and argued that it needed to be developed autonomously from common law influences in order to preserve its

question was borrowed from the common law, and the dissent, Justice Strong, who disagrees asserting that 'the decision … must depend entirely upon the law of the Province of Quebec' and that 'the English law of trusts … [is] entirely inapplicable and cannot be resorted to': ibid 670.

[81] *Callow* (n 62).

[82] *Wastech Services Ltd v Greater Vancouver Sewerage and Drainage District*, 2021 SCC 7.

[83] *Callow* (n 62) [60] (Kasirer J).

[84] The inspiration theory is exemplified by Justice Stevenson's statements in *Canadian National Railway Co v Norsk Pacific Steamship Co* [1992] 1 SCR 1021, 1174, [1992] ACS no 40, 'This Court has the benefit of being the final court of appeal in a country that has two legal traditions: the English common law and the French civil law. Our two legal traditions are independent and should not be confused. Concepts and solutions found in one tradition should not be imposed on the other tradition. But this does not mean that there is no place for comparative law on this Court.' See also R Jukier, 'Canada's Legal Traditions: Sources of Unification, Diversification or Inspiration?' (2018) 11 *Journal of Civil Law Studies* 75.

[85] *Callow* (n 62) [60] (Kasirer J).

[86] ibid [122] (Brown J).

[87] ibid [154] (Brown J).

[88] ibid [156] (Brown J).

[89] ibid [170] (Brown J).

[90] *Wastech* (n 82) [115] (Brown J). To be fair, Justice Brown does not entirely exclude a comparative approach, but he does limit it to rare instances where it might be needed 'to fill a 'gap' in the law or to provide 'reassurance that posited concerns are unfounded or overstated'. *Callow* (n 62) [123] (Brown J).

identity, originality and integrity.[91] Like Justice Brown, he argued that using one legal system to inform the other would not only render each system less coherent but would be illogical.[92]

Given the debate throughout the Supreme Court's history as to whether, to what extent and for what purpose comparative law should be used in court decisions, it is hard to agree with Smith's assertion that everyone is 'interested in law from other jurisdictions'.[93] Justice Mignault, from the civilian jurisdiction of Quebec, and Justice Brown, from the common law jurisdiction of Alberta, were equally uninterested in law from the other legal tradition and, in fact, reacted vehemently to the use of comparative law on the Court. If comparative law were indeed as ordinary as Smith suggests, then its use should not have elicited such strong reactions amongst Supreme Court justices. That domestic law is relevant in judicial reasoning is obvious. No justices would dispute this assertion. The fact that they contest comparative law's relevance demonstrates that there is indeed a distinction between the two.

V. Conclusion

In one of our heated exchanges about his thesis following the conference in Jerusalem, Steve Smith turned to me and said, 'Look Rosalie, it's not complicated. Comparative law is simply about more dogs.' While not as eloquent as the image of the field ornithologist he uses in the paper, that was how he expressed the essence of his view. From that day forward, Steve and I shared this as an inside joke, often turning to one another, saying 'It's just about more dogs!' This would always generate a warm smile and even a little chuckle. The 'more dogs' phrase will forever be a fond remembrance of our academic collaboration and, especially, our friendship. When Steve Smith passed away in November of 2022, the world lost an incredible legal scholar, a brilliant legal mind, and a devoted law professor and mentor. On a personal level, I lost a dear colleague and friend, and I am extremely sad that I will no longer have an opportunity to share our private joke. I am, however, grateful and deeply honoured to have been able to engage with his thesis about 'more dogs' in this collection and to articulate why, without discrediting the value that Steve Smith attaches to comparative law, I simply cannot agree that there is nothing distinctive about it.

[91] See, eg, *Magann v Auger* [1901] SCJ No 12, 31 SCR 186, 193; *The Mile End Milling Co v Peterborough Cereal Co* [1924] SCR 120, 129, [1924] 4 DLR 716; P-B Mignault, 'L'avenir de notre droit civil: L'exemple de l'Afrique du Sud et de la Louisiane' (1922) 1 *Revue du Droit* 104, 116.

[92] P-B Mignault, 'Les rapports entre le droit civil et la "common law" au Canada, spécialement dans la province de Québec' (1932) 11 *Revue du Droit* 201, 205–06. Justice Brown describes the common law and civil law as 'two massive jigsaw puzzles' whose 'pieces are cut differently so that pieces from one cannot fit (or at least fit easily) into the other', *Callow* (n 62) [162].

[93] Smith (n 1) 356.

4

Two Genres of Interpretive Legal Theories

HANOCH DAGAN*

I. Introduction

Reading and re-reading Steve Smith's important work on private law theory is always challenging to me, just like the conversations we have had, in which we so often disagreed. Great minds, like Steve's, offer compelling theses; ones you do not need to embrace but cannot ignore. This is why I have chosen to focus in this chapter on Smith's answer to the question 'What is Contract Theory?', to which he dedicated the first chapter of his seminal book on contract theory.[1] Knowing how different our approaches to this crucial question are, I thought that engaging Steve's answer would be illuminating for me, even if our disagreement persists. I end up with a much more limited disagreement than I would have suspected; indeed, with what may be read as a plea to join forces.

Smith developed a 'theory about contract theory'[2] or, more precisely, a theory about an interpretive contract theory, which he defines as one that 'helps us to better understand the law by illuminating the significance of, and connections between, its different parts'.[3] His theory about contract theory, which can apply *mutatis mutandis* to another field of private law (or indeed law), is subtle and sophisticated. It is also important and compelling in so far as what I will (metaphorically) describe as the normal science of the law is concerned.[4] An interpretive theory that can helpfully serve judges, lawyers and other students of contract law in understanding the law in its daily operation should indeed reveal, as Smith writes, 'an *intelligible* order in the law, so far as such an order exists',[5] and should thus follow his account of a contract theory, which I sketch in section II.

* Thanks to Brian Bix, Evan Fox-Decent, Andrew Gold, Greg Klass, Paul Miller, Roy Kreitner and Fred Wilmot-Smith for their helpful comments.

[1] SA Smith, *Contract Theory* (Oxford, Oxford University Press, 2004).

[2] ibid 3.

[3] ibid 36.

[4] My reference here to 'normal science', and later to 'paradigm shift', evokes of course Thomas Kuhn's distinction in TS Kuhn, *The Structure of Scientific Revolutions* (Chicago, IL, University of Chicago Press, 1962).

[5] Smith (n 1) 5.

The reason for this is not, however, that theories, which substitute the adjective 'intelligible' with a more normatively-demanding adjective (say 'just'), are – as Smith ultimately treats them – not properly interpretive. Rather, Smith's theory of contract theory is important, as I claim in section III, because the rule of law requires lawyers to be able to rely on interpretations that take on board some conventional wisdoms, and Smith's meta-theory helpfully identifies the more specific role of these wisdoms. But these conventional wisdoms, as I further argue, are contingent; they necessarily rely on (oftentimes implicit) presuppositions that cannot credibly find support in the doctrine itself. This means that the cogency of Smith's theory of contract theory is limited to interpretive theories that seek to guide the daily operation of the law under the normal science of law.

Smith is correct in criticising the interpretive credentials of theories that are overly normative in so far as these theories purport to apply on a par with those that properly adhere to the presuppositions that are necessary for the rule of law. But, as I contend in section IV, the rule of law does not imply that the life of the law *qua* law is exhausted by its normal science. Indeed, the contingency of these presuppositions implies that no credible conception of the rule of law can allow exclusive dominion to theories that willingly rely on them. A credible conception of law – and, indeed, of the rule of law – requires some openings, certain moments in the path of the law, for doubting the conventional wisdoms prevailing in the pertinent legal community as interpretive guides.

At these times, which (again metaphorically) may be termed law's 'paradigm shifts', lawyers can – and sometimes do – resort to external, non-legal considerations; and in so far as they do that, they rely on normative theories. But alongside such (implicit or explicit) external claims, paradigm shifts are also times in which lawyers invoke, as they should, *legal* claims: critical arguments that were hitherto 'off the wall' but nonetheless rely on an understanding of the law that illuminates its deep normative meaning and significance, as well as the proper connections between its different parts.

Thus, whereas Smith's theory of contract theory is valuable for law's normal science, it cannot account for legal theories for law's paradigm shifts; theories that offer lawyers an *internal* critical reflection on the law. This inadequacy is particularly unfortunate, since it might push interpretive legal theorists away from reconstruction with the possible unintended consequence of rendering legal theory overly quietist.

Furthermore, because Smith's theory excludes *all* the theoretical arguments about law that aim at reconstruction from the promised land of interpretive legal theories, it must treat claims that present themselves as interpretive (say, those that rely on a proper understanding of 'contract') as a sham. But this means that Smith ends up, somewhat paradoxically, not sufficiently loyal to law's self-understanding on which his own theory heavily – and appropriately – relies.

These pitfalls, however, need not be devastating; they only imply that while Smith's theory properly characterises one genre of interpretive theories of contract, it must not claim exclusivity on the species as a whole. Alongside Smith's fine theory for law's normal science, we need to develop a sister meta-theory, which properly captures the criteria for evaluating interpretive theories for law's paradigm shifts. That meta-theory is different from Smith's. But it can, as we shall see, helpfully build on the same analytical framework he developed.

II. Normal Science Interpretive Theories

Smith's most general proposition is that interpretive contract theories are assessed according to four criteria:

(a) 'how well they fit the rules and decisions that make up contract law';
(b) 'how coherent they are';
(c) how well they explain 'law's claim to authority', namely, 'the claim that law is a legitimate or morally justified authority'; and
(d) how well they explain 'law's claim to transparency', namely, 'the claim that legal reasoning is meaningful'.[6]

His more specific thesis adds important observations regarding all four criteria, as shown below.

A. Fit

An interpretive theory of contract should obviously 'be consistent with, and supported by, the relevant facts', which here means 'a group of legislative or precedent based legal rules and a set of decisions'.[7] This surely requires a prior decision as to 'What qualifies as *contract* law?', and Smith acknowledges that disputes as to the 'parameters of contract law', as well as 'what is central and what is peripheral to contract law', abound. But he argues that an interpretive theory does not require 'perfect agreement'; that its viability only requires a 'reasonable consensus' among 'those familiar with the law' on 'the core elements of the subject' as well as on 'what counts as "core"'.[8]

Smith realises that a credible interpretive theory should necessarily allow for the possibility that 'what is commonly understood as contract law' is actually better characterised as an exception or even as foreign to contact law; and similarly – I assume – that what is commonly understood as an exception of, or as foreign to, contract law is actually better viewed as part of its core. But he claims that 'we have little choice but to adopt again the consensus approach', namely, 'rely on the experience of lawyers and others familiar with contract law to tell us when we have gone too far'.[9]

B. Coherence

For a contract theory to be coherent, Smith argues, it is not enough that it is 'consistent or non-contradictory', which is 'a basic requirement of intelligibility'. It must also show 'that *most* of the core elements of contract law can be traced to, or are closely related to, a single principle'.[10] This careful formulation of the coherence criterion

[6] ibid 36.
[7] ibid 7.
[8] ibid 8–9.
[9] ibid 10.
[10] ibid 11, 13.

is important for two reasons. First, as Smith writes, a sound understanding of the coherence criterion should distance itself from a notion of 'perfect unity', which is 'not only unattainable in practice, but also inappropriate in theory'.[11] Moreover, a proper conceptualisation of this criterion regarding contract theory should allow for a theory that recognises – even celebrates – 'mid-level multiplicity'. This refinement accommodates theories that take seriously the profound heterogeneity of law's repertoire of contract types as long as they offer a coherent foundation for such a structurally pluralist edifice (such as its service of people's self-determination[12]).

C. Morality

To understand a legal practice like law, Smith writes, we need to follow its participants' self-understanding. And because 'law is understood internally as a *legitimate* authority', this means that 'legal theory must somehow take account of law's claim to authority', namely, to be 'a morally justified authority'.[13] Smith insists, however, that this requirement must not be understood in its strong version, in which law must be 'actually morally justified', but rather in a moderate version, requiring only that law's 'normative justification … is recognizably "moral"'.[14]

Smith rejects the strong version, which 'must engage with substantive moral argument', since 'although intelligibility and truth must be related, they are, fundamentally, distinct concepts'.[15] This means that the strong version 'conflates accounts of what the law *should be* (the goal of a *prescriptive* theory) with accounts of what the law *is* (the goal of an *interpretive* theory)'.[16] By contrast, the moderate version, in which it is enough for a legal theory to show 'how the law *might be thought to be* justified even if it is not justified', is appropriate, since it can 'show how legal actors could sincerely, though perhaps erroneously, claim that the law is morally justified'.[17]

For this to be the case, the theory must show 'that the law is – or might plausibly be thought to be – supported by recognizably "moral" principles'.[18] Thus, the proper test for the third criterion 'is not whether the proposed [moral] principle is a good one, but whether it is the kind of principle that someone could intelligibly adopt in defense of law's claim to authority'.[19] Smith recognises that this test necessarily relies on the answer to the question of 'What qualifies as "moral" principle?' His way of facing this difficulty is by now familiar: 'a moral principle is one that is regarded as moral by the consensus of those familiar with the practice of making moral principles'.[20]

[11] ibid 13.
[12] See H Dagan and M Heller, *The Choice Theory of Contracts* (Cambridge, Cambridge University Press, 2017).
[13] Smith (n 1) 13–15.
[14] ibid 36.
[15] ibid 17.
[16] ibid 18.
[17] ibid.
[18] ibid 20.
[19] ibid 21.
[20] ibid 22.

D. Transparency

This fourth criterion is rarely mentioned by legal theorists, but for Smith 'it is equally, if not more important, in assessing contract law theories'.[21] Because an interpretive theory must account for the self-understanding of legal officials, he argues, 'a good theory must explain the law in a way that shows how legal officials could sincerely, even if erroneously, believe' that 'the reasons they give for deciding as they do are their real reasons'.[22] Therefore, a good legal theory must *not* 'be based on concepts that are external to legal reasoning', namely, concepts which 'are not just different from those [legal officials] use but from those [they] *might* have used'.[23]

This means that the transparency criterion necessarily relies on a notion of 'recognizably legal'. And Smith is again well aware of the difficulty: after all, 'Ideas that were once discussed only in law schools often eventually find their way into legal judgments.'[24] But he has a ready answer, which nicely coheres not only with his response to the difficulty of defining what is recognisably moral, but also with his formula for identifying what is included in contract law and which elements count as its core. As with these two focal questions of criteria (a) and (c), the test of 'recognizably legal' resorts to 'the consensus of those familiar with law'.[25]

In other words, what makes explanations *legal* in a way that qualifies them to present themselves as interpretive is that they are 'the kind of explanations raised in legal arguments', so that 'once translated into concrete concepts, [they] could be accepted by a court, even if no court has yet done so'.[26] This criterion requires interpretive theories to remain close for the daily practice of law, and Smith is clear about the verdict it implies – that 'a large amount of contemporary legal scholarship scores poorly'[27] in the interpretive front. But this does not make it valueless. The idea that law should promote gender equality – to use one of his examples – may well play 'a crucial role in evaluating the law and in considering legal reforms'.[28] It is important, however, to remember that this is 'a different project from that of interpreting the law'.[29]

III. Their Limits and Significance

The title I have chosen for section II, which summarises Smith's theory of contract theory – 'Normal Science Interpretive Theories' – incorporates a conclusion that has yet to be defended. Smith's theory, I argue, cannot plausibly exhaust the field of interpretive theories; it is necessarily limited to a subset of such theories. But its failure where it overreaches does not render it useless, since it nicely captures the essence of this important subset.

[21] ibid 24.
[22] ibid 25, 28.
[23] ibid 29.
[24] ibid 30.
[25] ibid.
[26] ibid.
[27] ibid 32.
[28] ibid.
[29] ibid.

A. Turning Contingency into Necessity

To clarify: the blind spot in Smith's account is *not* its limitation to theories that elucidate the practice 'internally'. *That* conclusion is appropriate: as Smith claims, interpretive theories cannot ignore legal actors' self-understanding, because a 'complete account' of a human practice like law must elucidate 'what the participants in the practice think they are doing'.[30] But Smith takes this proposition a step further. As we have seen, his account fully subordinates the concept of an interpretive legal theory to the conventional dominant views within the pertinent communities in a given time and place as to (i) what is included in contract law; (ii) what is deemed part of its doctrinal core; (iii) what qualifies as a moral principle; and (iv) what qualifies as a legal principle. The subordination of interpretive legal theory to these conventional understandings is unjustified since they are necessarily contingent.

This contingency, which Smith himself recognises (recall his acknowledgement of the way legal education informs legal discourse), is not only a sociological observation. The difficulty is much deeper. Smith's idea that interpretive theories must *always* take as a given the conventional answers to the four questions mentioned above unacceptably marginalises, if not dismisses, the dynamics of legal evolution, which imply that what may seem obviously an implausible ('off-the-wall') understanding at one time, may become perfectly plausible ('on-the-wall') at another (and vice versa). Because trained lawyers are familiar with this dynamic – think, for example, of tort law before and after *Donoghue v Stevenson*[31] – it is necessarily part of how they experience the law, and thus of law's self-understanding, which interpretive theories should illuminate.[32]

Many years ago, Roscoe Pound described this core feature of the practice of law in terms of a pattern of repeated shifts (or structural circularity) between periods of fixity and periods of innovation and change. In former times, '[p]erfection of scientific system and exposition tends to … stifle independent consideration of new problems and of new phases of old problems, and to impose the ideas of one generation upon another'.[33] These are the periods in which law's consequences and purposes are not explicitly considered. Then, at some point (which I have dubbed law's paradigm shift), discontent with the distance between doctrinal discourse (lawyers' normal science) and law's ends reaches levels that will only be mollified by breaking this inertia and explicitly engaging with law's ends. But after a while, such more open-ended legal discourse stabilises on new conventional understandings, which now become canonised and treated as law's 'on-the-wall' interpretations; it is entrenched, in other words, as lawyers' *new* normal science.[34]

Pound's analysis captures the significance of the prevalent understandings within any given legal community. The implicit sense of obviousness shared by insiders regarding

[30] ibid 14. See also J Dickson, *Elucidating Law* (Oxford, Oxford University Press, 2022) 103–34.

[31] *Donoghue v Stevenson* [1932] AC 562.

[32] In other words, Smith's theory adopts a static understanding of law to the detriment of a dynamic understanding that incorporates the ways and processes through which law evolves.

[33] R Pound, 'Mechanical Jurisprudence' (1908) 8 *Columbia Law Review* 605, 606–08.

[34] ibid 611–12.

law's 'on-the-wall' interpretations[35] offers exactly the relatively stable foundation for the type of theories Smith accounts for. Smith is thus correct in recognising the key role the conventional understandings of the pertinent legal community play in securing law's perceived determinacy; these understandings provide the indispensable foundation of law's predictability and stability given the profound and irreducible indeterminacy of the 'naked' pedigreed sources of law.[36]

But Pound also highlights the inevitable fragility of this foundation. Implicit understandings are by definition contingent: they can, and at times do, change even when law's pedigreed sources themselves remain intact. The possibilities of reconstruction and transformation, in other words, are *not* necessarily external to the law. At times – maybe even more often than not? – reconstruction relies on a doctrine's off-the-wall understanding, namely, on demarginalising a pedigreed source or an understanding of a legal concept that was hitherto conventionally perceived as peripheral.[37]

A complete theory of legal theory must also account for this dynamic dimension of the law. Therefore, it cannot fully rely, as Smith's theory does, on lawyers' on-the-wall understandings of law's pedigreed sources and concepts (or, for that matter, of what are recognisably legal or moral claims).[38] This is why section IV turns to typify interpretive theories for law's paradigm shifts, which question these conventional wisdoms. But before exploring what Smith's theory omits, it is important to appreciate its significance for the type of theories it properly governs.

B. Normal Science Interpretive Theories and the Rule of Law

The value of normal science interpretive theories is captured in Smith's own work – this time in *Rights, Wrongs, and Injustices*,[39] where he explains why his remedies theory takes the moderate (as opposed to the strong) version of the morality criterion. 'For the law to operate effectively,' he writes, 'lawyers, judges, legal officials, scholars, and ordinary citizens must be able to understand it without excessive effort.'[40] Moreover, 'law's effective day-to-day operation requires' that people 'who may have radically different comprehensive moral views' are able to use it without taking a position in the normative debates underlying their disagreements.[41]

[35] See JM Balkin, '"Wrong the Day It Was Decided": *Lochner* and Constitutional Historicism' (2005) 85 *Boston University Law Review* 677, 711–25.

[36] This is of course a major jurisprudential proposition, which I cannot defend here. See H Dagan, *Reconstructing American Legal Realism and Rethinking Private Law Theory* (Oxford University Press, 2013) 18–22, 25–26. *Contra* PB Miller, 'Juridical Justification of Private Rights' in S Degeling et al (eds), *Justifying Private Law Rights* (Oxford, Hart Publishing, 2021) 105, 111, 113–14, which implies otherwise.

[37] H Dagan, 'The Real Legacy of American Legal Realism' (2018) 38 *OJLS* 123, 128, 130–31. For some examples, see H Dagan, *Property: Values and Institutions* (Oxford, Oxford University Press, 2011) 30–31.

[38] cf A Gold, 'Interpreting Fiduciary Law' in DG Smith and AS Gold (eds), *Research Handbook on Fiduciary Law* (Cheltenham, Edward Elgar, 2018) 15.

[39] SA Smith, *Rights, Wrongs, and Injustices: The Structure of Remedial Law* (Oxford, Oxford University Press, 2019).

[40] ibid 26.

[41] ibid 27. See also, eg, Miller (n 36) 126.

Smith implicitly invokes here a crucial aspect of the rule of law, famously described by Joseph Raz as the requirement that law provide people with effective guidance.[42] Normal science interpretive theories facilitate law's day-to-day operation. They improve our understanding of the law as it is exactly because they rely on, but also clarify and solidify, the implicit background understandings of the pertinent legal actors that significantly affect their daily decisions. In that, this genre of theories serves law's role as a 'safe basis for individual planning', which is a prerequisite to people's 'ability to choose styles and forms of life, to fix long-term goals and effectively direct one's life towards them'.[43]

Sustaining law's predictability and stability, which are indispensable for the rule of law, indeed requires that, for the purposes of the daily practice of law, legal actors accept as a given, no questions asked, the conventional answers to the four questions posed at the beginning of section II. Normal science interpretive theories follow this requirement and thus also – one may hope – clarify the distinction between what the law is and what it should be. In that they also hopefully entrench an 'attitude of due wariness', as Julie Dickson puts it, towards existing law, facilitating a 'staged inquiry', in which 'a clear, cool-headed and unromanticized' study leads the way to the investigation of law's 'moral value, justifiability, and obligatoriness'.[44] By insisting on some 'cognitive breathing space' between the 'is' and the 'ought' of the law, Smith's theory of legal theory can – if properly understood as a guide for law's daily operation – push back against law's powerful claim to authority, which is always there but not always justified.[45]

IV. Interpretive Legal Theories for Paradigm Shifts

Valuable as they are for the normal science of legal discourse, normal science interpretive theories are, on their own terms, useless for times of paradigm shifts, in which the on-the-wall understandings of the pertinent legal community are challenged. Because the signature of a paradigm shift is the questioning of these consensual views,[46] Smith's theory implies that the idea of interpretive legal theories for paradigm shifts – the title of this section – is confused. But it is not.

[42] J Raz, *The Authority of Law: Essays on Law and Morality*, 2nd edn (Oxford, Oxford University Press, 2009) 213. On the connection between law (and thus legal theory) and the rule of law, see also J Waldron, 'The Concept and the Rule of Law' (2008) 43 *Georgia Law Review* 1. To clarify: notwithstanding the quotations reproduced in the previous paragraph, I acknowledge that the virtues of normal science interpretive theories this subsection addresses may go beyond Smith's own ambition for his theory.

[43] J Raz, *The Morality of Freedom* (Oxford, Oxford University Press, 1986) 220, 222. See also J Raz, 'The Law's Own Virtue' (2019) 39 *OJLS* 1, 2.

[44] Dickson (n 30) 94–103, 176.

[45] ibid 96. See also Dagan, *Real Legacy* (n 37) 136–38; Miller (n 36) 127.

[46] The astute reader may question this characterisation, invoking the common law story in which what starts as a set of minor exceptions becomes regularised until the exceptions end up so numerous that they become the rule. This is probably true, and it suggests – as I argue in the very last paragraph of this chapter – that the reconstructive theories I address in this section are even more important than I currently argue.

A. Legal Arguments for Law Reform

Smith, to be sure, is correct to imply that the on-the-wall understandings of any given legal community of core legal concepts such as contract are typically quite resilient. Yet these understandings – exactly because they are simply taken for granted – nonetheless can be, and have been, successfully challenged. In fact, such challenges typify some of the happier episodes of legal evolution, often triggered by either public-interest lawyering or legal scholarship and legal education. Crucially, because they only demand to reconsider the sense of obviousness that grounds such conventional wisdoms, these episodes often do not (at least not necessarily) require any changes in law's pedigreed sources.

When reformers claim that a section in a statute or a case, hitherto considered by law's insiders to be marginal, deserves to be taken more seriously in order for the doctrine to comply with a more defensible account of contract, for example, they – and the courts that accept their innovative claims – rightly perceive themselves as offering a *legal* argument. They build on law's self-understanding that its relative stability is not, and should not be, equated with stagnation. Indeed, law's claim to authority, which grounds the significance of the internal point of view Smith (following HLA Hart) rightly emphasises,[47] also requires that '*some* legal actors, such as legislators and judges of appellate courts, should occasionally use new social developments and cases as triggers for the law's ongoing refinement, that is, as opportunities for revisiting the normative viability of the legal doctrine's existing understandings'.[48]

To see why, recall Smith's starting point in which law's self-understanding must necessarily be such that it can be sincerely held as one that *justifies* law's authority. Because law is always, indeed necessarily, a product of human agency, the rule of law requires – alongside the stability noted earlier – that the power of law's architects will always be 'kept within their due bounds'.[49] This facet of the rule of law as aimed at constraining the exercise of political power responds to 'the specter of the usurpation of power by an unaccountable elite', misrepresenting political decisions 'as if they were matters of law' and thus making 'the rule of law ideal … a fraud'.[50]

Law's self-understanding accordingly requires that the conservative starting point that appropriately guides legal reasoning in its day-to-day operation would not obscure law's intrinsic dynamism, which 'invites challenges to the on-the-wall interpretations of law's pedigreed sources, pushing law's carriers to intermittently rethink what otherwise tends to be treated as obvious'.[51] These challenges are not part of the normal science of the law – they are not welcomed in law's day-to-day operation. But they are sincerely presented and treated as *legal* reasons, and rightly so: they

[47] Smith (n 1) 15.
[48] Dagan, *Real Legacy* (n 37) 135.
[49] J Locke, *The Second Treatise of Government*, ed P Laslett (Cambridge, Cambridge University Press, 1988) 378.
[50] BZ Tamahana, *On the Rule of Law: History, Politics, Theory* (Cambridge, Cambridge University Press, 2004) 125; BZ Tamahana, 'How an Instrumental View of Law Corrodes The Rule of Law' (2006) 56 *DePaul Law Review* 469, 493.
[51] Dagan, *Real Legacy* (n 37) 131.

expose the contingency of the implicit background understandings that ruled the day thus far; explain why they are mistaken – why they render the existing law normatively indefensible; and offer a different understanding of the very same pedigreed sources and concepts (say, by marginalising what was implicitly deemed core and demarginalising what was unjustifiably treated as peripheral) so as to avoid this predicament.

A mature conception of law appreciates the significance – indeed, inevitability – of *both* dimensions of the rule of law, which is why the division of labour Pound highlighted, between law's normal science and its paradigm shifts, is part of the self-understanding of the participants in the practice of law. Legal actors know (at least implicitly) that law's stability is valuable, and thus accept the important role of the contingently dominant background understandings of concepts like contract in the type of legal reasoning pertinent to law's day-to-day operation. They must therefore recognise the contribution of normal science interpretive theories, which facilitate law's daily operation.

But at the same time, trained lawyers often identify the fragility of legal reasoning that so heavily relies on the dominant views of law's insiders. They can accept its legitimacy if, but only if, it implies that the rule of the incumbents is potentially in check; that arguments that defy such accepted wisdoms by offering more normatively charitable readings of law's pedigreed sources and concepts would not be summarily dismissed. These *legal* arguments cannot resort to Smithian interpretive theories. For them to flourish, lawyers must be able to consult with interpretive theories that are able to – maybe even aimed at – identify and defend possible off-the-wall understandings of the law that would push it closer to becoming the legitimate authority that it claims to be.

B. The Character of Reconstructive Theories

Reconstructive theories are not, *pace* Smith, illegitimate members in the family of interpretive theories. They also do not repudiate – in fact, they follow – his most general proposition, in which the four criteria of fit, coherence, morality and transparency help adjudicate among competing theories. Moreover, in so far as their ambition of coherence and the evaluation of this criterion are concerned, reconstructive theories are no different from normal science theories. But because reconstructive theories aim at assisting legal actors in devising and assessing legal arguments for times of paradigm shifts, they take a very different strategy when it comes to the other three criteria. Let me explain why and what this strategy entails.

To start with, law's self-understanding as per the division of labour between its normal science and paradigm shifts implies that these different genres of interpretive theories have different approaches to the evaluation of the two aspects of a given theory's account of 'the way that legal actors themselves explain what they are doing' – namely, morality and transparency.[52] Normal science interpretive theories take very seriously, as Smith insists, judges' express reasoning, while being agnostic as to the

[52] Smith (n 1) 36.

question whether the way these judges understand the law (that is, their reading of its pedigreed sources and concepts with the implicit conventional understandings in mind) is in fact morally justified (as long as it purports to be just). Both stances are out of place for reconstructive legal theories.

In so far as transparency is concerned, reconstructive theories appreciate how the distinct role played by a purely doctrinal discourse in the run-of-the-mill operation of a vibrant system of contract inevitably collapses in times of paradigm shifts. Therefore, in line with lawyers' and judges' self-understanding, they assign law's more doctrinal language to the back seat in so far as the more self-reflective stages of law's evolution are concerned. In law's day-to-day operation, these types of legal reasoning are justifiably much more significant than abstract normative reasons like justice or autonomy. But paradigm shifts are typified by a reversal of this ordering: law's technical terms no longer provide a stable premise once the implicit understandings that sustained them are effectively challenged; and what remains – and properly becomes focal – is the other types of legal reasons, which purport to offer normative justifications for (or challenges to) the way law's pedigreed sources and concepts are currently read.[53]

With Smith, reconstructive legal theories may accept the fact that even in times of paradigm shifts legal actors do not – at least not typically – follow economic justifications.[54] But, *pace* Smith, they are unmoved by the fact that a proposed line of legal argument for a paradigm shift, which relies heavily on a normative account, such as ensuring or promoting gender equality, is not recognisably legal in the day-to-day operations of the law. The division of labour between normal science and paradigm shifts implies a corresponding division of types of legal arguments exactly along these lines.

This brings us to the difference between the way normal science theories and reconstructive theories approach the morality criterion. The former take, as noted, the moderate version, and should, as discussed, approach law's proud claims of its pursuit of justice cautiously. Reconstructive interpretive theories reject this version of the morality criterion and adopt in its stead the strong one, in which 'a good theory of law ought to show that the law *is*, in fact, morally justified'.[55] This shift is unsurprising. Reconstructive interpretive theories seek to challenge the existing understanding of the law and are thus not concerned with the risk that this understanding would be unduly romanticised. By the same token, since reconstructive theories are supposed to serve a moment of law's self-reflection and reconstitution, they are justifiably untroubled by the way they upset the pre-existing status quo.

This normative side of legal reasoning for paradigm shifts is continuous with external – non-legal – moral reasoning about the dilemmas at hand. But it is nonetheless distinctive. The difference between legal reasoning at paradigm shifts and nakedly moral arguments lies in the criterion of fit: unlike external critique of the law, reconstructive legal reasoning relies on a re-reading of law's pedigreed sources – of the statutes, cases and concepts that were there to begin with. Indeed, the main contribution of

[53] See, eg, H Dagan, *A Liberal Theory of Property* (Cambridge, Cambridge University Press, 2021) 163–65, 170–72.

[54] Smith (n 1) 26.

[55] ibid 17.

reconstructive legal theories is exactly in the marriage they offer between the pedigreed materials and an attractive normative foundation, which allows legal actors to apply these materials in a way that is morally justified, or at least more morally justified than they were hitherto understood to be.[56]

In order to be able to achieve that, reconstructive legal theories should approach the questions of what qualifies as, say, contract law and what counts as its core in a diametrically different way from normal science interpretive theories. Rather than embracing a legal community's conventional views, they must question them; indeed, the very same 'attitude of due wariness' towards law that grounds its cool-headed study by normal science theories, demands that reconstructive theories would be suspicious towards these implicit understandings and push for more justified ones.

For reconstructive theories to perform their role, they must *not* rely on the implicit dominant wisdoms in the given legal communities regarding the proper understandings of law's pedigreed sources and concepts. Rather, they should imagine competing organisations of the pertinent statutory materials and case law, which demarginalise what was deemed peripheral and marginalise what was deemed core, in order to examine whether such a re-ordering makes the doctrine more normatively justified. They should likewise question the prevalent implicit understandings of key legal concepts and look for competing conceptions to the hegemonic ones, examining whether a reconceptualisation – assuming it can fit the (re-ordered) pedigreed sources – would allow the law to be more normatively justified.[57]

C. The Significance of Reconstructive Theories

Reconstructive legal theories, exactly like normal science theories, offer understandings of the doctrine that serve legal actors in the practice of law. But these two genres are distinct in the *modus operandi* they anticipate. While the latter help participants to navigate their way in the day-to-day operation of the law, the former facilitate their reasoning when developing or assessing *legal* claims that question implicit assumptions and advance *heterodox* ways of reading law's pedigreed sources and concepts.

Reconstructive contract theories – to use the same area of law on which Smith's meta-theory focuses – are important for at least two reasons. First, the conventional understandings of the basic concepts of private law in general, and of contract more specifically, play a significant, albeit often unarticulated, role in legal reasoning. Second, although every legal area necessarily privileges arguments that are deemed internal to it over external ones, the resistance to external considerations is especially conspicuous in private law generally and contract law more particularly.[58]

[56] The text is reminiscent of Dworkin's theory of law. For some important differences, see Dagan, *Real Legacy* (n 37) 136–38.

[57] I cannot hope to properly demonstrate in this short chapter this idea of reconstructive theory, but I hope to have practices what I preach for. See, eg, Dagan (n 53) 136–38; H Dagan and A Dorfman, *Relational Justice: A Theory of Private Law* (Oxford, Oxford University Press, 2024).

[58] For a parallel analysis of the significance of reconstructive theories of property, see H Dagan, 'Liberal Property and The Power of Law' (2023) 36 *Canadian Journal of Law & Jurisprudence* 281, 285–89. The degree of permeability follows – or at least should follow – the animating principles of the pertinent legal area.

Consider how much the way we interpret doctrines of contract law turns on what we understand to be internal or external to the idea of contract and the concomitant commitment to 'freedom of contract'. To be sure, legal actors nowadays cannot deny that contemporary law no longer corresponds to contract's (real or imagined) laissez-faire incarnation in years past. There are just too many rules that go well beyond what can be credibly attributed to the parties' presumed intent, as well as too many rules that set up what I describe elsewhere as the *limit* to people's jurisdiction to commit their future selves (as in non-competes) and the *floor* of relational justice (as in unconscionability).[59] Yet the prevalent understanding of freedom of contract still echoes contract's dominant theories, in which law should enforce whatever private deals individuals agree to and otherwise get out of the way.[60]

This strictly voluntaristic understanding of contract implies that while at times law may legitimately cut down on the parties' agreement in the name of overriding exogenous commitments, these curtailments are – and in a liberal system should be treated as – external to contract, and thus require a separate doctrinal pedigree.[61] Where no such reliable doctrinal source is available, contract law has, in this understanding, no internal resources to address any concern regarding the parties' future self; and it must be blind to their respective predicaments.

Indeed, the distinction between contract's internal commitments and the possible – even if treated as legitimate – 'interventions' in contract is crucial in the way we think about contract law and reason in contract cases. A liberal polity justifiably takes freedom of contract seriously, and thus carves out any external exception to it with care: fully subjecting contract to a society-wide all-things-considered rigorous normative audit risks the outright elimination of private ordering. If the core of contract is understood in strictly voluntaristic terms, denigrating existing gap-filling rules and those that prescribe contract's limit and floor to the margins seems inescapable from the legal point of law. This conclusion is consequential in numerous legal contexts affecting, for example, workers' rights, tenants' rights and consumers' rights.[62]

But since contract need not follow a strictly voluntaristic rendition, this normatively disturbing stance is not inevitable. I do not deny that legal insiders (still) think of freedom of contract in these terms, and that a normal science interpretive theory should reflect the (often implicit) core-margin structure of their reasoning that presupposes a limited realm for rules responsible for relational justice or for the autonomy of the parties' future self. But these are, as Smith acknowledges, *background* understandings of the *incumbents*. Therefore, appreciating their hidden work opens up possibilities for a different reading of the very same pedigreed sources and concepts, and thus a different theory that can then serve as a loadstar for legal reconstruction. On this theory, which

[59] See H Dagan, *Two Visions of Contract* (2021) 119 *Michigan Law Review* 1247.

[60] eg, S Williston, 'Freedom of Contract' (1921) 6 *Cornell Law Quarterly* 365, 368–69, 373; R Craswell, 'Freedom of Contract' in EA Posner (ed) *Chicago Lectures in Law and Economics* (Goleta, CA, Foundation Press, 2000) 81; Smith (n 1) 59, 139.

[61] A Ripstein, 'The Contracting Theory of Choices' (2021) 40 *Law & Philosophy* 185, 206–11; RS Scott, 'A Joint Maximization Theory of Contract and Regulation' in H Dagan and B Zipursky (eds), *Research Handbook on Private Law Theory* (Cheltenham, Edward Elgar Publishing, 2020) 22.

[62] H Dagan, 'The Liberal Promise of Contract' in H Psarras and S Steel (eds), *Private Law and Practical Reason: Essays on John Gardner's Private Law Theory* (Oxford, Oxford University Press, 2022) 315; cf H Dagan, 'Between Regulatory and Autonomy-Based Private Law' (2016) 22 *European Law Journal* 644.

I develop in some detail elsewhere, the commitments to both relational justice (namely, reciprocal respect for self-determination) and the autonomy of the future self, as well as to proactively facilitate people's cooperation efforts, are the three animating principles of a genuinely liberal – that is autonomy-enhancing – contract law.[63] This means that, properly understood, the right to freedom of contract is the right to tailor a joint plan within the (broad) boundaries of legitimate arrangements sanctioned and facilitated by an autonomy-based contract law.[64]

Such a reconstructive theory, if accepted, can avail lawyers with legal reasoning that shows that certain existing interpretations of the rules, while coherent with the currently dominant contract theories, are in fact *legal mistakes*. Contract's relational-justice floor, as well as its concern for the future-self limit, do not rely, in this account, on any consideration external to contract. Rather, these constraints on contractual choice follow the very same rationale that justifies enforcing contracts in the first place. They are internal to contract or, more precisely, preconditions for the legitimate use of contract as a legal instrument. As such, they should be *liberally*, rather than cautiously, interpreted: a liberal polity must be vigilant in ensuring that contracts do not undermine their own autonomy-enhancing *telos*.

While the previous paragraphs sketch one possible reconstructive contract theory, their lesson for our purposes is general. Law's architects are understandably more responsive to legal (as opposed to non-legal) arguments. Trained lawyers recognise moments in which off-the-wall interpretations of law's concepts and pedigreed sources can be introduced. Reconstructive interpretive theories may play a key role in facilitating these moments by rethinking dominant preconceptions, thus serving both the rule of law and law's continuous legitimacy. This is why reconstructive theories are often part of what we teach in law schools; and it may also explain why, as Smith notes, many (he says most) contract theorists develop reconstructive theories, and are accordingly 'very concerned to show not just that their theory fits the law, but also that it justifies the law *and* that it justifies the law better than the alternatives'.[65]

V. Peaceable Cohabitation

In her recent account of the philosophy of legal philosophy, Julie Dickson states that because law 'exists both as institutional practice and social fact, and as a normative, reason-giving, and value-aspiring phenomenon' a successful theory of law must do

[63] H Dagan and M Heller, 'Choice Theory: A Restatement' in Dagan and Zipursky (eds) (n 61) 112; H Dagan and M Heller, 'Can Contract Emancipate? Contract Theory and The Law of Work' (2023) 24 *Theoretical Inquiries in Law* 49. See also H Dagan and A Dorfman, 'Precontractual Justice' (2022) 28 *Legal Theory* 89; H Dagan and A Dorfman, 'Justice in Contracts' (2022) 67 *American Journal of Jurisprudence* 1; H Dagan and O Somech, 'When Contract's Basic Assumptions Fail' (2021) 34 *Canadian Journal of Law & Jurisprudence* 297; H Dagan and M Heller, 'Specific Performance: On Freedom and Commitment in Contract Law' (2023) 98 *Notre Dame Law Review* 1323; H Dagan and MP Gergen, 'Autonomy and Form' (2024) 53 *Hofstra Law Review* 1; H Dagan and MP Gergen 'Autonomy, Implication, and Interpretation' (unpublished manuscript), https://papers.ssrn.com/sol3/papers.cfm?abstract_id=4928208.

[64] H Dagan, 'Freedom of Contract, Properly Understood: The 2024 Maastricht Private Law Lecture' (unpublished manuscript) at https://papers.ssrn.com/sol3/papers.cfm?abstract_id=4809815.

[65] Smith (n 1) 18.

'adequate justice to each aspect of this key duality, and to the relations between them'.[66] She also notes that since 'law is a multi-faceted and complex phenomenon', its different aspects 'can be illuminated from different theoretical directions, at different times, and for different reasons'.[67] Part of this diversity derives from the fact that 'the importance of some aspects of law's character, and the importance of some of the puzzles concerning them, may only come to light at certain points in time, or in response to particular interests and concerns'.[68]

The schism between normal science and reconstructive interpretive theories may offer one particularly significant example – that Dickson does not consider – for her important proposition regarding the value of diversity in legal theory. In many respects, these genres of interpretive theories are opposed to each other; indeed, their respective emphases on the institutional practice and social facts of the law and on its normative, reason-giving and value-aspiring facet mirror each other. But appreciating the division of labour between law's normal science and its paradigm shifts implies that our understanding of the complex phenomenon of law cannot be complete without their peaceable cohabitation.

In fact, as some of the preceding examples suggest, the relationship between these two genres of interpretive theories is probably more complicated than that since the life of the law is not so neatly divided. Pound's account is more charitably read as referring to two 'ideal types' of what is actually more of a spectrum of categories of moments in the evolution of law. Thus, alongside instances that clearly fall at the normal science or the paradigm shift poles, there are others that are situated in between these poles, where law's background understandings are more or less resilient. This may mean that the two genres of interpretive theories discussed in this chapter are also ideal types, which arguably implies that there are more than two genres, and that reconstruction affects not only clear paradigm shifts.[69]

[66] Dickson (n 30) 87. See similarly H Dagan and R Kreitner, 'The Character of Legal Theory' (2011) 96 *Cornell Law Review* 671.

[67] Dickson (n 30) 2.

[68] ibid.

[69] *Contra* Miller (n 36) 112, fn 20, who implies that they may play a role only in 'periods of social, cultural, religious, or political tumult'.

5

'Comparative Law' as an Academic Discipline

HELGE DEDEK

I. Why a Piece on Comparative Law?

One thing that makes this collection in memory of Stephen Smith so special is that he himself had a hand in planning it, in selecting topics and articles he had penned that he wished colleagues to discuss. Steve and I talked about possible themes for my contribution, and we agreed on an article by him entitled 'Comparative Legal Scholarship as Ordinary Legal Scholarship', published in 2010.[1] Steve's abstract summarised the article's argument thus:

> This essay argues that comparative law is not and never will be a distinctive academic discipline. … The essay concludes by arguing that comparative scholars should embrace the ordinariness of their scholarship. To the extent that comparative law is associated with a particular subject-matter, method, challenge, or aim its value will always be a matter for debate. By contrast, if comparative scholarship is just ordinary scholarship with more data (as I argue), its value is undeniable.

In other words: sure, comparing stuff can be helpful when doing what legal scholars are supposed to be doing (which is what, by the way?). Yet 'comparativists' and 'comparative scholars' (ie scholars who are working with this enlarged data pool but mistakenly believe that this makes them adherents of a distinctive discipline) should embrace the ordinariness of the activity, to wit: let go of feeling special and just generally get on with it.

A chapter engaging Steve's claim about comparative law's status as a non-discipline might not be the most obvious choice in a volume that is heavily focused on private law. I am fortunate to have had Steve as a colleague, and grateful for our many exchanges, sometimes literally at the watercooler. Typically, these focused on private law theory and history; when I had the opportunity to comment on Steve's ideas in a formal

[1] SA Smith, 'Comparative legal scholarship as ordinary legal scholarship' (2010) 5 *Journal of Comparative Law* 331.

setting, it had been in the context of discussions in private law theory.[2] Why not choose a topic relevant to the field to which Steve dedicated most of his work, and to which he probably left his greatest intellectual legacy?

Indeed, Steve was (and much more so than many other hard-nosed common lawyers I have met) exceedingly curious and open-minded about non-common law perspectives, and surely also found inspiration in them. Many if not most of our exchanges revolved around differences between common and civil law approaches to questions of legal theory. However, Steve simply never assumed this curiosity would, should or could make him a 'comparative law scholar'. I believe that he thought of such comparative inquiries just as a natural element of reflecting on a theoretical problem thoroughly from all possible angles before putting pen to paper. And I surmise that it is against the backdrop of this personal lived practice of 'comparative law' that his idea for his article took shape: for him, a healthy dose of comparative groundwork was simply an 'ordinary' part of the job.

Steve told me that he would value a response to his essay on the (lacking) disciplinarity of comparative law in this volume, also since he felt that the piece might not have had a significant impact in comparative law circles. Of course, it is unsurprising that 'comparative law scholars' would not be particularly receptive to Steve's message – who likes to be told that they are mistaken as to their 'specialisation' amounting to a proper discipline? I thought it only appropriate to honour this wish, especially since I, unlike Steve, have been openly identifying as belonging to this troubled community of 'comparativists'. Due to this choice, and the fundamental nature of Steve's criticism, the article resonated with me on a personal level as well: was I not guilty myself of contributing to the navel-gazing discourse on what it means to do 'comparative law'? And had I not, for 10 long years, served as the editor-in-chief of a journal in comparative law (CL) – and thus perhaps invested uncounted hours of reading and reviewing into publishing a *Journal of Nothing Special*? Well, it is always healthy and edifying to reflect on the futility of our modest earthly endeavours.

When looking at the countless contributions to the discourse on the 'proper' disciplinary definition of CL and its 'proper' methodology, one cannot help but feel that many contributors would concede that Steve indeed has a point. I, for one, am certainly a bit tired of the discipline's 'febrile introspection', as William Twining[3] has called it; and, therefore, not without sympathy for Steve's exhortation to let it go and move on. Indeed, I have explicitly expressed the hope that we – as in 'we comparatists' – might be able to do so, at least with respect to some particularly worn-out aspects of the discussion.[4]

[2] See, eg, H Dedek, 'Border Control: Some Comparative Remarks on the Cartography of Obligations' in R Bronaugh et al (eds), *Exploring Contract Law* (Oxford, Hart Publishing, 2009) 25 – reacting to SA Smith, 'The Limits of Contract', ibid 1. Our exchanges also significantly impacted on my 'remedial imagination', which also happened to be the title of a panel, comprising Steve and myself, that gave us the opportunity to discuss differences between common and civil law conceptualisations of remedies: see H Dedek, 'The Relationship between Rights and Remedies in Private Law: A Comparison between the Common and the Civil Law Tradition' in R Sharpe and K Roach (eds), *Taking Remedies Seriously* (Montreal, Canadian Institute for the Administration of Justice, 2009) 63, 64, fn 1; SA Smith, 'Rights and Remedies: A Complex Relationship' in Sharpe and Roach (eds) ibid 31; and, for further detail, H Dedek 'From Norms to Facts: The Realization of Rights in Common and Civil Private Law' (2010) 56 *McGill Law Journal* 1.

[3] W Twining, 'Glenn on Tradition: An Overview' (2006) 1.1 *Journal of Comparative Law* 107.

[4] H Dedek, 'Preface' in H Dedek and F Werro (eds), 'What We Write About When We Write About Comparative Law' (2017) 65 *American Journal of Comparative Law – Supplement* ix.

I shall therefore refrain from staging anything resembling a spirited defence of the well-known positions put forth in the debate among comparatists on the disciplinarity of comparative law – that is, the positions that Steve sets out to refute, one by one. Rather, I shall reflect on Steve's core concern: that CL somehow fails to understand its own nature, that it wrongly *classifies* itself as a discipline while a *proper* classification reveals that it is not.

It is this idea that connects this piece to my own earlier encounters with Steve's work on taxonomy – a connection that becomes even clearer if we understand 'discipline' to be a concept that 'demarcate[s] areas of academic territory'[5] and the scholarship in which a discipline reflects on its disciplinarity as 'boundary work'.[6] This concern with ordering, drawing borders and demarcation lines was what had animated our earlier exchange on Steve's 'The Limits of Contracts', with my response entitled 'Border Control'.[7] Back then, Steve advocated a new system of classificatory boundaries in the area of contract law, whereas I voiced concern. With respect to the disciplinarity of CL, Steve wants to redraw the map as well, this time erasing disciplinary boundaries.

II. The Prantocox

Reflecting on Steve's approach to the allegedly misconceived disciplinarity of CL triggered for me an unlikely association – the recollection of a children's story that has stuck with me since my kindergarten days: the story of the Prantocox, by German children's book author Ursula Wölfel, first published 1974 in a small volume entitled *Twenty-nine Crazy Stories*.[8]

One of the reasons why my train of thought took this direction might be that Steve, besides being a renowned legal scholar (and so many other things, such as an accomplished athlete, chef and carpenter), was a dedicated family man. This trait was not just obvious to those who knew him well, it also found its expression in Steve's academic work: he loved to illustrate, in his teaching as well as in his scholarship, the normative conundrums of private law with instructive scenarios from his home life, pondering, for example, the remedial options in case of a child breaking a promise to their parents. Vice versa, I am sure, he taught his children many an important life lesson developed from the inherent morality of (private) law.

This context encouraged me to follow my stream of consciousness (and I would kindly ask the reader to bear with me for a moment). Thus indulging my impulse, I found that the collection of 'Crazy Stories' had been reviewed by well-known

[5] cf, eg, RE Kohler, *From Medical Chemistry to Biochemistry. The Making of a Biomedical Discipline* (Cambridge, Cambridge University Press, 1982) 1; RE Kohler, *sv* 'Discipline History' in WF Bynum et al (eds), *Dictionary of the History of Science* (Princeton, NJ, Princeton University Press, 1991) 104.

[6] TF Gieryn, 'Boundary-Work and the Demarcation of Science from Non-Science: Strains and Interests in Professional Ideologies of Scientists' (1983) 48 *American Sociological Review* 781; DR Shumway and E Messer-Davidow, 'Disciplinarity: An Introduction' (1991) 12 *Poetics Today* 201, 208. See also section IV.

[7] See Dedek (n 2).

[8] U Wölfel, 'Die Geschichte vom Prantocox' in U Wölfel, *Neunundzwanzig verrückte Geschichten* (Düsseldorf, Hoch-Verlag, 1974) 62.

American philosopher, Gareth B Matthews, who specialised in philosophising with children, an activity he thought not only beneficial for children in developing critical thinking skills but also genuinely helpful for the adult philosopher engaged in the conversation.[9] In a way, what Steve used to do intuitively, Matthews made a focal point of his scholarship.

Matthews gave the following summary and assessment of Wölfel's story:

> The last tale in the collection, 'The Story of Prantocox,' ('prantocox' is a made-up word), is perhaps the most philosophical. It concerns a chimera, Prantocox, that thinks itself up, but then, when assured by an official, 'You're impossible!' obediently disappears, on the grounds that what is impossible doesn't exist. (The thoughtful reader will note another asteismus here.) The story of Prantocox raises questions central to philosophy, among them, questions about possibility and existence. But it also makes fun, gentle fun, of the pretensions of officialdom.[10]

The story had indeed stuck with me because of the word play on the Prantocox's being impossible, to which Matthews refers as 'asteismus', and the paradox of its being there despite being impossible. I would add to Matthews's able summary that the scene of the story is a German registry office, something like the heart of darkness of German bureaucracy and formality. When the Prantocox, having invented itself that very day, gives 'today' as its day of birth, and also otherwise does not behave in the way expected of a respectable citizen, the official thinks he is being pranked; exasperated, he reprimands the Prantocox that it is 'being impossible', in the sense of expressing displeasure with certain conduct.[11] Yet the Prantocox takes his words literally as a statement regarding the possibility of its very existence, and whispers, crestfallen, 'Absolutely and entirely impossible? What a shame.' And dissolves into thin air.

By now you have figured out where I am going with this little tale of 'philosophical whimsy',[12] as Matthews put it. Here, *Is* and *Ought* are irreconcilably at odds. The Prantocox is a figment of its own imagination. It is *impossible* and thus cannot and should not be in existence – *and yet, there it is.* Not unlike, one might venture, the 'discipline' of CL.

III. The Paradox

Let me explain – and let us together take a closer look at Steve's argument. Steve's article takes aim at what he calls a 'paradox': the popularity of comparative law as a label, being one expression of the fashionable fascination (in 2010) with everything global, trans- or international. The paradox, then, supposedly lies in the fact that despite the

[9] cf MR Gregory and MJ Laverty, 'Gareth B Matthews: A Philosopher's Life with Children' in MR Gregory and MJ Laverty (eds), *Gareth B Matthews, The Child's Philosopher* (London, Routledge, 2022) 1.

[10] GB Matthews, 'Thinking in Stories. Neunundzwanzig verrueckte Geschichten. Twenty-Nine Crazy Stories, by Ursula Woelfel' (1985) 6:4 *Thinking: The Journal of Philosophy for Children* 1.

[11] cf the definitions of 'impossible' at https://dictionary.cambridge.org/dictionary/english/impossible, as 'An impossible person behaves very badly or is extremely difficult to deal with.'

[12] Matthews (n 10).

apparent omnipresence of the 'comparative' label, 'the status and even the existence of comparative law as an academic discipline continue to be questioned'.[13]

After recounting some staples of the discourse on the famous 'malaise of comparative law',[14] including the well-known calls for interdisciplinarity and increased theoretical sophistication, Steve offers a striking diagnosis: 'The paradox exists because comparative law is not, and never will be, a distinctive legal discipline.'[15] Comparative scholarship is 'ordinary' legal scholarship, expanding what legal scholars usually do beyond national borders: comparatists simply work with a larger pool of data. That, Steve finds, is a generally a good thing, and he therefore emphasises that, while the article is 'critical of many of the claims and assumptions of comparativists about the nature of the activity in which they are engaged, it is, ultimately, a defence of this activity'. But, 'to the extent that scholars believe that comparative law is or should be a distinctive discipline, its status will rightly continue to be questioned'.[16]

This is Steve's cue – he is going to lend his hand to this enterprise, bringing some order to this line of questioning:

> The existence and distinctiveness of comparative law have been questioned by other scholars, including some comparative scholars, but the case for its 'non-distinctiveness' has never been made in a systematic fashion. This is the primary aim of this article.[17]

I am not sure the 'comparative' label is, factually, as popular as Steve makes it out to be in order to set up his 'paradox'. Nor am I entirely convinced that the perceived tension between this popularity and the existence of an ongoing discourse on disciplinarity among comparatists can be described as a 'paradox', at least in the technical sense of the word.

Things become more interesting, however, when we pay closer attention to the fact that the participants in this discourse on the disciplinarity of CL almost exclusively identify as 'comparativists' (etc), and that the venue for this discourse is treatises on CL, CL journals, and conferences and workshops held by and for 'comparativists'.

In other words, the 'malaise' of comparative law turns out to be a *self-diagnosis* – a fact evidenced by the sources that Steve cites, which reference all the usual suspects of the CL canon. And while he states that '[t]he existence and distinctiveness of comparative law have been questioned by other scholars, including some comparative law scholars', I was not able to spot a single reference in the footnotes to a text dealing with the disciplinarity of CL that was not penned by an author who is known as a 'comparative law scholar'. Steve and his article are the sole (or rare) exceptions.

Now, a proposition along the lines of 'scholars of comparative law state that comparative law does not exist' might come closer to resembling familiar paradoxes – just think of Epimenides, the Cretan, stating that all Cretans are liars. At the very least, it might appear somewhat strange. Why engage in a seemingly self-sabotaging activity? I therefore suggest that we take a closer look.

[13] Smith (n 1) 332.
[14] cf W Ewald, 'Comparative Jurisprudence: What Was it Like to Try a Rat?' (1995) 142 *University of Pennsylvania Law Review* 1898.
[15] Smith (n 1) 334.
[16] ibid.
[17] ibid.

In particular, I suggest that paying attention to the fact that the activity of questioning disciplinarity of CL is an activity carried out as an *exercise in self-critique* will remind us of the function performed by the distinction between insider and outsider for disciplinarity in general, which will also allow us, incidentally, to see the disciplinarity of CL – even understood in a *substantive* sense – in a different light.

As I shall try to explain in more detail, the self-referentiality of the language games surrounding CL's disciplinarity is at the core of a self-affirming ritual that – maybe *paradoxically* – stabilises and even constitutes an epistemic community exactly by contributing to the canon that also amounts, substantively, to the 'body of knowledge' that ultimately defines it. The display of concern about the state of one's own discipline – the 'handwringing', as Teemu Ruskola has called it[18] – thus functions as a performative gesture that signals belonging, *membership*. The gesture is also performative in that it situates the speaker, depending on the concrete position assumed in the debate, in a certain camp or school, as conservative, progressive or critical; yet, importantly, even 'heretical' positions are understood as being presented by fellow comparatists, by *colleagues*, from *within* the discipline.[19]

By contrast, to Steve – who did not see himself as a member of this community – the inside/outside distinction bears no significance. Without accepting border-drawing as the major function of disciplinarity, the meaning of the paradoxical ritual of self-avowed comparative law scholars questioning the existence of their own discipline is lost. Instead of asking what purpose the ritual serves, he takes it at face value and tells the comparatists that they have been asking the right questions but simply have not thought it through.

Of course, there is a certain contradictory tension inherent in the fact that those people who are thus most likely to question the existence of CL identify as 'comparativists' or 'comparative law scholars'. It is at this point that the paradoxical becomes prantocoxical: if we follow Steve's reasoning, scholars believing themselves participants in an academic discipline called 'comparative law' are, in reality, collectively mistaken as to their own existing in a capacity as 'comparativists' simply because CL, *in reality*, cannot and will never be a discipline.

IV. 'Discipline'

A. What is a 'Discipline'?

Naturally, Steve does pick up on the fact that, while he rejects the notion of CL's being a discipline, he himself constantly refers to 'comparativists' and 'comparative law scholars'. Since CL does not exist as a discipline, and the tension inherent in the ritualistic self-loathing therefore bears no significance from Steve's theoretical vantage point, it can

[18] T Ruskola, 'Legal Orientalism' (2002) 101 *Michigan Law Review* 179, 180.

[19] For a comparison with the discipline of Comparative Literature and the phenomenon of its diagnosing and bemoaning its own permanent state of crisis, see now H Dedek, 'The Tradition of Comparative Law: Comparison and its Colonial Legacies' in M Siems and PJ Yap (eds), *The Cambridge Handbook of Comparative Law* (Cambridge, Cambridge University Press, 2024) 387, 392ff.

be resolved with an adjustment of definition: 'In practice, CL and "comparative legal scholarship" are widely understood to mean scholarship (of whatever kind) that examines the laws (however defined) of more than one jurisdiction.'[20] Understood in this way, CL is not a discipline but an activity – 'ordinary legal scholarship with a larger data pool'. Therefore, it is not contradictory (despite the non-existence of CL as a discipline) to refer to scholars engaged in this activity as 'comparativists' or 'comparative law scholars'.

To this definition, the popular preoccupation with reflecting on one's own disciplinarity is useless, is just noise; it is an unnecessary concern that only distracts from that which 'comparative law scholars do', the activity that Steve, we remember, set out to 'defend': dealing with legal stuff, broadly defined, beyond one's own jurisdiction. I believe, however, that, in turning a blind eye to what might be *the* crucial (albeit only apparent) paradox of CL's disciplinarity, Steve misses exactly what sets aside CL scholarship from 'ordinary legal scholarship' and what, ultimately, *makes* CL an academic discipline.

One of the reasons why this aspect remains in the blind spot lies in Steve's definition of 'discipline' – or, rather, the lack thereof. Nowhere in his article does the reader find any definition or description of 'discipline', nor any explanation as to the theoretical (or disciplinary) perspective whence the author approaches the complex concept of 'discipline'. Instead, from the first diagnosis of the 'paradox' (ie, that despite its alleged popularity, the 'status and existence of CL as an academic discipline continue to be questioned') to the subsequent restatement of the 'paradox' ('[t]he paradox exists because CL is not, and never will be, a distinctive legal discipline'), the focus begins to shift from 'discipline' to 'distinctive discipline'. At that point, however, 'distinctiveness' replaces 'discipline', as Steve posits four criteria of 'distinctiveness' that guide his further inquiry.[21] While now the focus seems to be on 'distinctiveness' alone, the quality of scholarship being distinctive is then, throughout the text, treated as synonymous with scholarship amounting to a 'discipline'.[22]

This conceptual vagueness is very un-Steve-like: the hallmark of his scholarship has always been to develop his arguments with the rigour and strictness of the Oxford-trained analytic. Such a style of reasoning requires, in particular, a fulcrum that is rock-solid – especially if the aim is to unhinge an entire discipline. Yet at no point do we learn what a 'discipline' *is*, and how the concept relates to 'distinctiveness'. Is 'distinctiveness of scholarship' indeed synonymous with 'disciplinarity of scholarship'? If so, what is a 'distinctive discipline' – is this statement tautological or are there disciplines that are non-distinctive?

None of these questions can be answered based on intuition alone. It is not self-evident what a 'discipline' is. Nor is it a fact that can be assessed in a 'I-know-it-when-I-see-it' manner; 'discipline' is not unlike the 'legal words' that, according to Hart, have 'no simple equivalent in the real world'.[23] When approaching this topic, we cannot rely on our assumed mastery of legal theory or 'ordinary legal scholarship' in general to

[20] Smith (n 1) 336.
[21] ibid 334.
[22] ibid 339, 351.
[23] HLA Hart, 'Definition and Theory in Jurisprudence' in HLA Hart, *Essays in Jurisprudence and Philosophy* (Oxford, Oxford University Press, 1983) 21, 22.

provide any help. 'Discipline' is instead a highly complex concept with a complex history that an abundance of complex scholarship has focused on, from the respective vantage points of several (you guessed it) academic disciplines, such as the sociology and history of science, and the sociology of knowledge.

B. Scholarly Approaches to Disciplinarity

Scholars in these fields mostly agree that 'discipline' – in the sense of 'scientific discipline' or 'university discipline' – describes 'units of structure' (Rudolf Stichweh)[24] or 'units for teaching, research, and professional organization' (Johan Heilbron),[25] specifically in the context of professionalised academia, and particularly the institutional environment of the modern (Western) university institution.[26] There appears to be broad consensus that the development of disciplinarity in a 'modern sense' is a historical process that begins in the eighteenth century and picks up momentum in the nineteenth century, when the university in the Western world came into its modern form.[27] Scholars have also shed light on the earlier history of 'discipline' and the etymology of *disciplina*: the Latin terms *disciplina*, *doctrina* and *scientia* all belong to a semantic field related to the process, substance and result of transmitting knowledge.[28] While in this triad *disciplina* seems to emphasise the perspective of the student (the *discipulus*), in medieval Latin the word was used in an academic context as synonymous with the established subjects of learning themselves, particularly the liberal arts, and even as synonymous with knowledge/science as such.[29] Intellectual historian Donald R Kelley, in particular, has worked on the significance of this 'mathetic' disciplinarity – the passing on of knowledge from a master to a 'disciple' – for the epistemological tradition in Western thought concerned with the mapping and ordering of knowledge, mainly focusing on early modern philosophy.[30]

What emerges from this brief survey is that Steve's article does not situate itself in any of these contemporary literatures on disciplinarity. Rather, his project appears closer to that pursued by pre- and early modern authors whom Kelley especially has

[24] R Stichweh, *sv* 'Scientific Disciplines, History Of' in NJ Smelser and PB Baltes (eds), *International Encyclopedia of the Social & Behavioral Sciences* (Amsterdam, Elsevier, 2001) 13727.

[25] J Heilbron, 'A regime of disciplines: toward a historical sociology of disciplinary knowledge' in C Camic and H Joas (eds), *The Dialogical Turn: New Roles for Sociology in the Postdisciplinary Age* (Lanham, MD, Rowman & Littlefield, 2003) 23, 30.

[26] On this, with further references, H Dedek, 'Stating Boundaries: The Law, Disciplined' in H Dedek and S Van Praagh (eds), *Stateless Law. Evolving Boundaries of a Discipline* (Farnham, Ashgate, 2015) 9, 11.

[27] cf R Stichweh, *Zur Entstehung des modernen Systems wissenschaftlicher Disziplinen* (Frankfurt aM, Suhrkamp, 1984); Heilbron (n 25) 31.

[28] JJ Kockelmans, 'Science and Discipline: Some Historical and Critical Reflections' in JJ Kockelmans (ed), *Interdisciplinarity and Higher Education* (University Park, PA, Penn State University Press, 1979) 11, 12ff; S Meier-Oeser, *sv* 'Wissenschaft' in J Ritter (ed), *Historisches Wörterbuch der Philosophie* (Basel, Schwabe, 2005) vol 12, col 51190, 51191 et seq; G Jüssen and G Schrimpf, *sv* 'disciplina', 'doctrina' in ibid, vol 2, col 257.

[29] For details, see Jüssen and Schrimpf, 'disciplina' (n 28), col 258.

[30] DE Kelley, 'The Problem of Knowledge and the Concept of a Discipline' in DE Kelley, *History and the Disciplines. The Reclassification of Knowledge in Early Modern Europe* (Rochester, NY, University of Rochester Press, 1997) 13, 14.

studied: the project of ordering knowledge according to substantive criteria – although we note, from the outset, that Steve draws all his criteria from the internal discourse of 'CL' scholars, instead of adopting a 'metalanguage',[31] as Kelley calls it, that transcends disciplinary particulars. However, Steve's concern with 'distinctness' of a field of knowledge, based on *substantive* criteria, does resonate with classic themes in this tradition.[32]

The quest for substantive criteria that help in ordering and classifying knowledge is indeed a time-honoured endeavour, which inspired, for example, some of the great encyclopedic works on the categorisation of sciences in the Enlightenment.[33] I do not wish to dismiss Steve's project out of hand simply because he chooses to discuss it under the label of 'disciplinarity' without any reference to the current scholarship that focuses on the concept. Rather, I believe that, even if we assume Steve's perspective and posit that the inquiry into substantive criteria of 'distinctness' (I shall refer to it as 'epistemological/cognitive' approach) is a worthwhile undertaking, by completely setting aside this intellectual context and the surrounding scholarship, he creates a blind spot that prevents him from seeing what he is looking for. To understand why this is the case, we have to first connect CL to the concept of 'academic discipline' in the sense it is used in contemporary scholarship.

C. The 'Modern Concept' of an 'Academic Discipline'

As we have seen, the emergence of 'academic disciplines' in the modern, technical sense is generally understood to be historical process starting in the eighteenth century and gaining more dynamism in the nineteenth century.[34] Scholars agree on the *institutional* aspect of the definition and function of disciplines thus understood. The definition initially devised by historian of science Robert E Kohler, and since then often repeated and expanded upon,[35] exemplifies these aspects of historicity and institutionality:

> Disciplines are political institutions that demarcate areas of academic territory, allocate the privileges and responsibilities of expertise, and structure claims on resources. They are the infrastructure of science, embodied in university departments, professional societies, and informal market relationships between the producers and consumers of knowledge. They are creatures of history and reflect human habits and preferences, not a fixed order of nature.[36]

Similarly, Stichweh emphasises the role of disciplines as communication systems, and highlights the institutional mechanisms that enable and stabilise a delineation from other systems: journals, conferences, academies, professorial chairs, and generally a

[31] ibid 13.

[32] ibid 16.

[33] eg, as a maybe lesser-known example, WT Krug, *Versuch einer systematischen Enzyklopädie der Wissenschaften*, 2 vols (Winkelmann, 1797); and also I Kant, *Der Streit der Facultäten in drey Abschnitten* (Nicolovius, 1798).

[34] See Stichweh (n 27).

[35] See, eg, T Lenoir, *Instituting Science. The Cultural Production of Scientific Disciplines* (Stanford, CA, Stanford University Press, 1997) 58.

[36] Kohler, *From Medical Chemistry to Biochemistry* (n 5) 8.

professionalisation and specialisation that make possible entire professional careers within a discipline.[37]

The small sample already indicates that research on disciplines has focused on disciplinarity in the natural sciences, and also in sociology (due to the interest of sociologists in the development of their own field):[38] thus mostly on 'young' disciplines that trace their origins to the neuralgic period of accelerated change in the eighteenth and nineteenth centuries. Johan Heilbron has suggested that the formation of these disciplines typically follows a pattern of increasing institutionalisation in three stages:

> the formation of a new intellectual practice accompanied by some sort of disciplinary ambition (chemistry, sociology), the formation of a university discipline (marked by the founding of chairs, disciplinary journals, and professional associations), and the establishment of a fully fledged discipline of which autonomous degrees are the key element.[39]

Again, the recognition through the formalisation of institutional structures is the very hallmark of modern disciplinarity.[40] Heilbron adds 'Only the oldest branches of knowledge – primarily law, medicine, and theology – followed a different course, since they were officially taught well before the rise of the modern university.'[41]

Of course, this does not mean that the disciplines with roots in the pre-modern university are not disciplines. It means instead that the sequentiality of the three-stage pattern does not apply to them. Rather than asserting their place as newcomers in the university curriculum, the traditional 'higher faculties' had to position themselves in the changing university environment and defend their turf under a new paradigm of 'science' replacing medieval habitual notions of scholarship. I have tried to show elsewhere how the 'law' has responded to this challenge, in an attempt to explain the positivistic turn in law in the nineteenth century, when the consolidating discipline ceded the area of legal philosophy – that is, reflections on 'natural law' – in an act of self-disciplining to the rising discipline of philosophy.[42]

The subdiscipline of CL thus emerged *as a (sub)disciplinary structure* only in the context of a broader disciplinary re-formulation of 'law' in the nineteenth century. Scholars of CL often stipulate an even later point of origin, around 1900.[43] Regardless of whether this origin story is the right one,[44] what matters for our inquiry is that the manner in which a *subdiscipline* develops mirrors the process of increasingly formalised

[37] R Stichweh, 'The Sociology of Scientific Disciplines: On the Genesis and Stability of the Disciplinary Structure of Modern Science' (1992) 5 *Science in Context* 3, 8ff.

[38] See, eg, H Joas, 'A Postdisciplinary History of Disciplines: Two Recent Publications in the History of Sociology' (1999) 2 *European Journal of Social Theory* 109. On disciplinarity in the Humanities, see Shumway and Messer-Davidow (n 6) 201ff.

[39] Heilbron (n 25) 31.

[40] cf also the strong focus on institutionality in Eastern European social theory; eg, M Guntau and H Laitko, 'On the Origin and Nature of Scientific Disciplines' in WR Woodward and RS Cohen (eds), *World Views and Scientific Discipline Formation. Science studies in the German Democratic Republic* (Dordrecht, Springer, 1991) 17, 20.

[41] ibid.

[42] Dedek (n 5) 13ff; in more detail, H Dedek, 'Ernstes Spiel: Theoretische und akademische Befassung mit Recht' in L Kähler and G Calliess (eds), *Theorien im Recht und über das Recht* (Stuttgart, Franz Steiner Verlag, 2018) 135, 140ff.

[43] G Frankenberg, *Comparative Law as Critique* (Cheltenham, Edward Elgar, 2016) 42. See also ibid 8.

[44] For some doubts, see Dedek, 'Tradition of Comparative Law' (n 19) 387.

institutionalisation that we have observed in the formation of disciplines. Within the larger unit of an academic discipline, further differentiation occurs and a sub-community emerges, whose discourse crystallises into a disciplinary structure through gradual institutional recognition: the establishment of specialised journals, associations that hold conferences, named chairs, institutes; courses and degree programmes.

From this perspective, there can be little doubt that CL is a discipline – to be precise: a subdiscipline under the large disciplinary umbrella of 'law' – as it bears all the hallmarks of institutionalisation as '"coagulated" social recognition'.[45] The 1900 Paris Congress may not have been the mythical point of origin at which the discipline was conjured out of thin air, but as a first major international scholarly meeting in the 'field' it was undoubtedly a milestone in the process of institutionalisation; as was, from the nineteenth century onwards, the foundation of the many national and international scholarly associations, of journals, of specialised chairs, research institutes and even degree programmes.[46]

The degree to which social recognition of CL has crystallised in formal structures might vary from jurisdiction to jurisdiction; this depends to a large extent on the larger academic culture in which the subdiscipline is embedded. On the Continent, the entire academic curriculum in law is more closely tied to subdisciplinary division, beginning with the public–private divide. Concomitantly, academic careers in law are closely tied to a subdisciplinary identity, and the qualifications candidates for teaching positions must obtain are often granted for specific subdisciplines, 'comparative law' being one of them. For someone coming up in such a system, specialising in CL means, among other things: working under the supervision of scholars who identify as comparatists, who had, in turn, studied under comparatists (thus establishing a 'school'); producing a dissertation in what is understood to be the field of CL, then being appointed professor of CL; teaching (possibly exclusively) courses on CL, and regularly celebrating the cohesion of the discipline and meeting likeminded colleagues during the ritualised gathering of their scholarly societies. For someone thusly socialised, Steve's advice to let go of CL's ambitions to disciplinarity would be nothing but puzzling, given that this disciplinarity is a lived experience that creates a habitus of 'being' a comparatist.

By comparison, to a law professor in the United States (US), the idea of 'comparative law' as a 'discipline' might be more suspect. The set-up of socialising and habitus-creating factors is simply arranged differently in US academia – starting with the fact that a PhD in law is still a rarity in the US legal professoriate (not to mention a PhD in 'comparative law') and specialised disciplinary socialisation occurs mainly outside of the law school (through graduate degrees in, say, history or economics). Additionally, there are few institutional structures that cement sub-disciplinary affiliations at the level of the institution where law is taught itself, beyond teaching assignments (which can change over the years) and specialised chairs and research centres.

[45] Guntau and Laitko (n 40) 20.

[46] At McGill, students can obtain an 'LL.M. in Comparative Law': see at www.mcgill.ca/law/grad-studies/masters-programs/llm-comparative-law. Furthermore, at McGill, for decades the *Institute of Comparative Law* was the locus of *all* graduate degree study in law, outside of air and space law studies (the Institute of Air and Space Law was founded in 1951) – JEC Brierley, 'Developments in Legal Education at McGill, 1970–1980' (1982–83) 7 *Dalhousie Law Journal* 364, 369f.

It is therefore unsurprising that the critical discourse on CL's disciplinarity first arose and, arguably, has been the most vibrant in the US, where the institutional recognition of CL is much less entrenched, especially as compared to Continental Europe. From a sociological perspective, then, this particular discourse of disciplinary self-reflection appears as 'boundary work'. In line with an understanding of disciplines of structural units, debates on substantive criteria of demarcation are seen, following a suggestion by Thomas Gieryn, as ideological and rhetorical strategies and gestures that either protect or claim academic turf.[47] This also makes more obvious why there is, unless animated by the conquest of academic territory and its resources, so little boundary work from outside the discipline: there is simply very little at stake beyond being right.

D. An Epistemological/Cognitive Approach

As we have already seen, it is the substantive question of what characterises the intellectual activity and its cohesion underlying the institutional structures of a discipline that is what Steve is interested in. The scholarly view on disciplinarity thus far presented accounts for this aspect only in that the stages of institutional entrenchment assume the formation of professionalised discourse with an epistemic community that shares research interests, substantive focus and/or methodologies.[48] However, it is of course legitimate to go beyond simply labelling discourses focused on such questions as 'boundary work' and inquire into their substantive content.

We do not need to rehash the arguments exchanged in the discourse on the 'malaise' to conclude that the case for a substantive or methodological coherence of the CL is underwhelming. And Steve undoubtedly makes some good points – as I said before, I do not wish to defend any of the particular positions Steve sets out to refute. My issue is rather that by only targeting certain arguments exchanged in internal discourse on disciplinarity, he not only misses the institutional background and context of this discourse.

He also misses that – and this is more significant for his own epistemological interest in *substantive* cohesion – the *substantive knowledge* amassed by the 'boundary work' also could itself be a major factor in what substantively constitutes the epistemic community of CL. This becomes particularly obvious if we are connecting Steve's project to the classical tradition of Western thought on the classification of knowledge, and to the concomitant longstanding meaning of *disciplina* that pre-dates the 'academic discipline in the modern sense': as teachings that are traditionally being handed down from master to student, the 'teaching of an established body of knowledge, its transmission, and the learning process it implied'.[49]

In CL, the proceeds of the 'boundary work' now amount to a considerable canon, and thus to what one might call a 'body of knowledge'. Entire careers have been built on contributing to the self-critique of CL, and this literature has, in all its ritualistic

[47] Gieryn (n 6) 781ff; on the use of the concept with respect to disciplinary delineation specifically, see ibid 792; and Shumway and Messer-Davidow (n 6) 208.

[48] Heilbron (n 25) 31ff.

[49] Heilbron (n 25) 27; DE Kelley, 'Introduction' in Kelley, *History* (n 30) 1.

rehashing of certain positions – for example, the unending and tiresome reflections on 'functionalism' – injected CL discourse with theoretical and interdisciplinary innovation. And it provides the epistemic common ground when not much else is there to hold on to. No course, no introductory treatise on CL, would do without a reference to this discourse. The reference to the debate is 'boundary work' also in the sense that it serves to identify the speaker and their disciplinary credibility: who is writing as an insider, who as an outsider? This signal has to be carried out with subtlety: a too-dutiful rehashing, for example, would mark one as a beginner or newcomer. It is important to understand the performative value of authors ironically distancing themselves from the 'handwringing' and the 'navel-gazing' – it is a means of participating in the ritual by pretending not to participate, and thus signalling insider-ship in a particularly sophisticated fashion.

This discourse, the literary canon that keeps growing out of it and the rituals that surround it are, even though other legal subdisciplines may have similar concerns regarding their disciplinarity, without exact analogue; it is what sets CL aside, what makes it distinct from 'ordinary legal scholarship' or better, since there is no such thing, from the other legal subdisciplines. Substantively, it is an expertise, a highly specific 'body of knowledge', focusing on the difficulties of engaging with otherness in law and the possible failure to try within the boundaries of a discipline.

Comparative law's vexatious self-critique of its lacking disciplinarity is exactly the body of knowledge or 'doxa' that amounts to the epistemic glue for the discipline. This might seem the ultimate paradox. Yet CL is not the only discipline that finds itself in this situation. I am taking my cues here especially from Comparative Literature. Just like CL and other 'comparative' disciplines, Comparative Literature was initially born in the nineteenth century out of a fascination with the 'Comparative Method',[50] which had its origins in Comparative Philology and which promised 'scientificity' in fields outside the hard sciences:[51] 'the great glory of the nineteenth century',[52] as Hutcheson Macauley Posnett, a pioneer of Comparative Literature, put it in 1886. Since the middle of the twentieth century, CompLit has – remarkably also to different degrees on both sides of the Atlantic – reflected on being 'saddled with an obsolete methodology' and on its own failure to define a 'distinct subject matter and specific methodology', as René Wellek wrote in his famous 'The Crisis in Comparative Literature'.[53] The diagnosis of 'crisis' resembles that of a 'malaise' in CL – a sense of crisis that has become permanent in CompLit.[54] But, at the same time, as especially Haun Saussy has stated more than once, nothing defines CompLit so well as the search for its own definition, and this constant crisis, 'the crisis we make for ourselves … is our greatest resource'.[55]

[50] See H Saussy, 'Exquisite Corpses Stitched from Fresh Nightmares: Of Memes, Hives and Selfish Genes' in H Saussy (ed), *Comparative Law in an Age of Globalization* (Baltimore, MD, Johns Hopkins University Press, 2006), 3, 5.

[51] E Rothacker, 'Die vergleichende Methode in den Geisteswissenschaften' (1957) 60 *Zeitschrift für vergleichende Rechtswissenschaft* 13.

[52] HM Posnett, *Comparative Literature* (London, Kegan Paul, Trench & Co, 1886) 76.

[53] R Wellek, 'The Crisis in Comparative Literature' in S Nichols (ed), *Concepts of Criticism* (New Haven, CT, Yale University Press, 1963) 282.

[54] H Saussy, 'Comparative Literature[.] The next ten years' in UK Heise (ed), *Futures of Comparative Literature: ACLA State of the Discipline Report* (London, Taylor & Francis, 2017) 24.

[55] ibid 28.

Practitioners of CL have been more hesitant to see crisis as opportunity, and to embrace explicitly the possibility that it might indeed be the creative critical thinking emerging from the incessant self-searching that is, crystallised into a 'body of knowledge', what defines the 'discipline'.[56] Because Steve's perspective was focused on a limited canon of arguments exchanged within this discourse, this lack of distance made it difficult for him to consider this possibility.

Yet even where the internal CL discourse itself opened the door to considering a specific disciplinary canon as making CL distinct, Steve immediately closed it. Steve makes short work in a footnote of CL scholar Mathias Reimann's suggestion that CL could indeed be defined by a 'body of knowledge'. The possibility that a 'body of knowledge' could be considered in addition to the four criteria that Steve stipulates – (i) distinct method, (ii) subject matter, (iii) challenges, (iv) aims – he dismisses as follows:

> A fifth possibility is that comparative law is distinctive because it is a 'body of knowledge'. … But the existence of a body of knowledge, no matter how valuable, does not show that the object of that knowledge is an academic subject in its own right … If a body of knowledge reveals a distinct field, it is because that literature employs a distinctive method, concerns a distinctive subject-matter, arises from distinctive challenges, or pursues distinctive aims.[57]

V. Conclusion

This reasoning is so dizzyingly circular and thus, once more, so un-Steve-like that I am wondering whether his project might have been animated by a different concern altogether: he may have thought that the distinctive discourse CL has developed is indeed not valuable at all and that, ultimately, CL does not *deserve* the distinction of being its own 'discipline'. This would be a value judgement and leads to a normative question: *should* a discipline be recognised as worthy of this distinction? A university administrator might ask this question, for example, for practical reasons when considering cutting funding to a programme (very real threats like that have contributed significantly to the sense of crisis in CompLit). Of course, especially the case that *Law* itself does not necessarily deserve its place among the modern university disciplines – just because it had been traditionally taught in Western universities – has been frequently made, by no lesser thinkers like Kant[58] and JS Mill.[59]

Considering this larger context, the question whether CL deserves disciplinary recognition is too weighty to be considered here; suffice it to say that I do believe that 'ordinary scholarship' (understood as those subdisciplines that are more easily defined by the criteria Steve enumerates) benefits from having a designated space for asking about how we confront 'otherness' in law, how we relate to legal traditions and cultures

[56] Dedek, 'Tradition of Comparative law' (n 19) 393.
[57] Smith (n 1) 334f, fn 20.
[58] cf Kant (n 33).
[59] JS Mill, 'Inaugural Address at St Andrews' in FA Cavenagh (ed), *James and John Stuart Mill on Education* (Cambridge, Cambridge University Press, 1931) 133.

other than our own. And I believe this to be true even though the boundaries of this space are 'permeable boundaries', which are typically 'associated with loosely knit, divergent academic groups and signal a more fragmented, less stable and comparatively open-ended epistemological structure'.[60] It is exactly this eclecticism that makes it possible to sometimes gain perspectives beyond the restrictions of disciplinarity strictly defined by subject matter or methodology.

Comparative law is, to be sure, a weird creature. Initially grown out of the fascination with the methodology that had its heyday in the nineteenth century but has lost lustre since,[61] it owes its existence to a contingent historical development in a rapidly changing academic environment. This development is a very unlikely story that might not be repeated in a different age and setting. And yet, paradoxically, the insecurity resulting from this apparent randomness has triggered the constant self-searching that might be said to be the unifying epistemic concern to which the discipline owes its canon, its substantive core.

But no matter how unlikely or paradoxical (or even 'crazy') the story sounds, the strange beast is alive, even though some might think it ought not to be. Just as the 'impossible' Prantocox frustrates the poor official in our story when it challenges the quiet normalcy of his daily process, CL, unsurprisingly, may, in all its weirdness and insecurity, frustrate serious practitioners of 'ordinary legal scholarship' who have grown accustomed to the security this very ordinariness brings. However, unlike the Prantocox, CL is here to stay. It will not vanish into thin air when told that it is impossible – even when the one conveying the message is an extraordinary legal scholar like the much-missed Stephen Smith.

[60] T Becher and PR Trowler, *Academic Tribes and Territories. Intellectual enquiry and the culture of disciplines*, 2nd edn (Buckingham, Open University Press, 2001) 60.

[61] On the disenchantment with the 19th-century 'Comparative Method', see most recently G Resta, 'The Comparative Method at the Roots of Comparative Law' in H Dedek (ed), *A Cosmopolitan Jurisprudence* (Cambridge, Cambridge University Press, 2022) 44; and Dedek, 'Tradition of Comparative law' (n 19) 402ff.

PART II

Remedies

6

Continuity and Creativity in the Law of Remedies

ARTHUR RIPSTEIN*

I. Introduction

In his groundbreaking book *Rights, Wrongs, and Injustices*,[1] Stephen Smith distinguishes between what he calls 'creative' and 'replicative' orders. He deploys the distinction in order to explain why exemplary damages cannot be understood as anything other than creative. Smith goes further however, also arguing that 'all damages awards (as well as most restitutionary awards) are similar to exemplary damages in that they direct defendants to do things that are not appropriate subject matter for substantive rules'.[2]

In drawing out the implications of this distinction, Smith rejects what he characterises as the 'continuity thesis' – the idea that the basis of a private law remedy is the continuation of a right. Different writers frame the continuity thesis in different ways: Peter Birks describes the remedy as 'the same things as the right, looked at from the other end';[3] John Gardner talks about reasons continuing, and so the need to do the next best thing;[4] Ernest Weinrib describes normative continuity; my own work represents what might be the most extreme view, insisting that the remedy follows from the fact that a right survives its own violation.

Smith raises a number of objections to the continuity thesis. These fall into two broad categories. The first line of objection is conceptual, focusing on the differences between the duty to perform a contract or avoid breaking someone's window, which tells the defendant what to do, and the very different situation of being ordered by a court to pay a certain sum of money. The second line of objection is doctrinal, pointing

* I am grateful to Steve Smith for many decades of illuminating conversation, and to Larissa Katz for comments on an earlier draft of this chapter.

[1] SA Smith, *Rights, Wrongs, and Injustices: The Structure of Remedial Law* (Oxford, Oxford University Press, 2019).

[2] ibid 127.

[3] P Birks, 'Definition and Division: A Meditation on Institutes 3. 13' in P Birks (ed), *The Classification of Obligations* (Oxford, Oxford University Press, 1998) 1, 24.

[4] J Gardner 'What is Tort Law For. Part 1: The Place of Corrective Justice' (2011) 30 *Law and Philosophy* 1.

to differences between the way in which the law regards an order as being satisfied and the way in which Smith contends the continuity thesis must understand the duty to pay damages.

In this chapter I examine these objections and argue that, properly understood, the continuity thesis is not vulnerable to them. The theoretical objection faces doctrinal as well as theoretical difficulties; the doctrinal objection faces theoretical as well as doctrinal ones. I conclude by showing that by reconciling Smith's distinction between replicative and creative orders with the continuity thesis, the distinction becomes sharper and even more illuminating, because it explains the sense in which orders can be fundamentally creative without departing from the antecedent rights of the parties. My focus will be on remedies for wrongs; I believe that the same general perspective provides an answer to some of Smith's arguments about unjust enrichment, but I defer that task to another occasion.

II. Continuity

I will develop my argument though an account of the irreducibly interpersonal and relational nature of private law duties, rights and remedies. Properly understood, the continuity thesis reflects this relational structure: the specific defendant owes it to the specific claimant to avoid (or perform) some particular action with respect to that very claimant. The claimant has a right against the defendant, where a right is an entitlement to constrain the defendant's conduct with respect to the object of that right. The objects of rights in private law include the claimant's own person (including both their body and their reputation), land or chattel, contractual performances or the defendant's loyalty. In each of these cases, the object of the right is not a state of affairs or aspect of the claimant's well-being, even though the protection of the right will frequently maintain some state of affairs or prevent a negative impact on the claimant's well-being. Nor is the object of the right the entitlement that others provide a favourable context for its exercise.

The relational version of the continuity thesis insists that rights survive their own violation because someone who is entitled to stand in a certain relation to others continues to be so entitled; the particular acts that those relations require may well be different in different circumstances: my duty to avoid injuring you through my careless cycling will sometimes require me to slow down, at other times perhaps to speed up, sometimes to move left, at other times right, and so on. So too, my contractual duty to deliver goods to you might require me to do different things in different circumstances to procure those goods and arrange their delivery. When courts talk of a duty of care, they are not talking of an aggregate of separate things I must do on separate potential occasions, but rather a duty that your right to bodily security governs the way in which I manage my bicycle. So too with my duty to perform a contract: it requires that we stand in a certain relation (of completed performance) and your right to performance constrains my conduct even though it does not spell out the particular steps I must take. As Peter Birks puts it in introducing the Roman legal idea of an obligation:

> An obligation is a rope … by which we are tied … Dwell on that image. Here am I with a rope around my neck. We must allow for the other end of the rope. You are holding that.

> I am under an obligation to you: the picture is of this rope between us, and you in control; the rope is round my neck but in your hand.[5]

As Birks goes on to emphasise, the rope is juridical, not physical or moral. The transactional interpretation of the continuity thesis does not need to take a position on whether private rights are coextensive with moral obligations, or on the structure of practical reason more generally. It therefore takes no position on whether there is a non-legal reason to pay damages. It says instead only that, to continue with Birks' evocative image, if I sever the rope, I commit a wrong for which the remedy is to reattach it, because I am still bound to you. The organising structure of the idea of obligation is a relation between one person and another with respect to some object or performance. The subject matter of the continuity thesis is the rightholder's ongoing entitlement to compel the wrongdoer, even if the wrongdoer has violated the right by destroying the object of the right. Your right that I not break your window – your right to constrain me – survives even if I have broken the window.

On this understanding, the point of the remedy is to uphold the right. The correlative structure of the liability – the defendant is liable to pay the claimant – expresses the correlative structure of the wrong, which is nothing more than violation of the claimant's right to constrain the defendant. The continuity of right and remedy depends on the relation between the parties, not on any claim that the action of refraining from breaking a window or performing a contract is the same as the action of paying damages. Smith's objections to the continuity thesis focus on the contrast between norms of conduct, which people are supposed to accept, and court orders, which people are supposed to obey. He makes the striking claim that 'In most (but not all) such cases, the wrong is at most a condition, not the reason, for awarding the remedy.'[6] For Smith, once the rope is severed, its ends cannot be rejoined; any new connection between the parties must be creative in a strong sense.

It is worth distinguishing three ways in which the idea of creativity might be understood:

(a) dependence on an affirmative act by the court;
(b) a different action is demanded by it than the primary duty; and
(c) a different normative basis.

The first two are unremarkable features of the law of remedies: until the court has ordered something, the claimant normally cannot call on the state's assistance in, for example, seizing the defendant's assets; on the first point, the court's order is creative because empowering for the claimant, enabling the claimant to do something that could not have lawfully been done before. Second, in cases in which a court orders damages to address property damage such as a broken window, it calls on the defendant to perform a different act; this, too, is creative in a clear sense, because the court is exercising judgement about what would count as a remedy appropriate to the wrong, even if in so doing it is significantly constrained in its discretion. These first two points are among the things to be explained by an account of remedies, whether Smith's account or some

[5] P Birks, *The Roman Law of Obligations* (Oxford, Oxford University Press, 2014) 5.
[6] Smith (n 1) 178.

version of the continuity thesis. I will say more about the second than the first, because the first is common to replicative and creative duties. The third is the striking one: for the continuity thesis, the wrong is the reason for the remedy, whereas for Smith it is 'at most a condition'. Deciding between these competing accounts requires considering Smith's arguments, but no less significantly, considering the origin, domain and validity of judicial creativity.

Smith introduces a number of doctrinal examples that are supposed to show that the duty-confirming view could not be correct. In some of these examples, the action that the duty requires must be understood as insufficient; a second set examples is supposed to show that an order to pay damages could not replicate a duty because, until the order is given, the defendant is not in a position to know what is required, and so not in a position to perform the duty because of the duty itself. At most, the defendant could turn out to satisfy the duty. But this, Smith plausibly contends, deprives the concept of a duty to pay damages of a feature required for it to count as a duty (or indeed anything legal) at all, that is, its capacity to guide conduct. Call the first of these the 'wrong transaction' objection, the second 'the lack of guidance objection'.

A. 'The Wrong Transaction Objection'

> An action for damages cannot be avoided on the ground that the defendant offered to pay the damages prior to judgment. Indeed, even prior payment of damages does not extinguish the claimant's right to an award of damages (other than where the claimant accepts payment as part of a settlement). If you sue me because I threw a rock through your window, it is no defence that my next act was to place £100 in your mailbox, which you then deposited in your bank account. Even if the judge assesses your damages at £100, your suit will succeed (though I may be able to recover my £100 in a counter-claim for restitution). Except where pre-payment is part of a settlement, it is legally irrelevant in a claim for damages.[7]

The continuity thesis demands exactly this result: it focuses exclusively on the transaction between the parties. Its unwavering focus on relations and transactions requires that only the right transaction can count as a remedy. The fact that there could be an outcome or an action with consequences, measured either in terms of accountancy or well-being, that is the same as the remedial transaction does not show that it is equivalent to it, precisely because rights, duties and remedies are individuated by relations and transactions, and never by results. Smith contrasts this with the case in which the action is for an agreed sum; in that case, proof of payment of the amount in question provides a complete answer.

The fact that I gave you money in a separate transaction does nothing with respect to the wrong I committed against you by throwing a rock through your window. (Conversely, if I mistakenly overpay you £100 in some other transaction, I cannot even things out between us by breaking your window.) Parties in ongoing interactions are often in this situation, having multiple transactions taking place between them. The transactions are individuated on the basis of the rights of the parties, not by the overall balance of

[7] Smith (n 1) 196.

benefits and burdens as between them. That is why my payment does not discharge my liability but could potentially ground a counterclaim in restitution. It does not discharge my liability because it is a separate transaction; that same separateness engages the analytical apparatus of restitution because I placed the money in your mailbox without donative intent. It therefore differs from the action for the payment of an agreed sum because in that case the two sides of the transaction – a requirement that the sum be paid and a requirement that the claimant receive it – are perfectly matched as transactions, rather than merely in their quantum.

Indeed, this is a point that Weinrib made to introduce the transactional rather than distributive or advantage-based structure of wrongdoing. He developed an example from Peaslee, involving a claimant who missed a flight as a result of a collision caused by the defendant's negligence.[8] The missed flight crashed, leaving no survivors. The claimant plainly benefited from the defendant's wrong, but that is, as Weinrib remarks, no answer to an action for damages, and has no bearing on the quantum of damages owed. The benefit conferred is irrelevant, not because the continuity thesis is false but precisely because of its truth. The thesis is focused exclusively on the particular transaction; as such, any other transactions between the same parties require separate analysis, such as the counterclaim for restitution that Smith contemplates. It might well be eminently sensible for the parties to tally up their accounts and figure out the final amount owing as between them, rather than each of them standing on their rights and going back and forth, with Smith claiming his money back from the person whose window he broke, and that person repaying it while demanding a quantitatively identical payment for the cost of repair.

The difference between the multiple disputes presupposes the continuity thesis because it supposes that the transactions, and the actions to which they give rise, are individuated by the rights of the parties. That is, both duties of conduct and duties to pay damages are not simply a matter of what one party is supposed to do or what each party is supposed to have. Instead, the subject matter of both primary and remedial duties is always a transaction: a contractual duty to engage in a particular transaction based on the terms of a previous transaction of contract formation; in the case of tort duties, a duty to avoid interfering with some right of the claimant. In both tort and contract, remedial duties refer to the wrongful transactions that they are meant to remedy, rather than being duties to bring about a result considered in isolation from the wrongful transaction.

Weinrib uses the example of the missed flight to illustrate the Aristotelian idea of the unity of doing and suffering, that is, that the wrong that the defendant commits and the wrong that the claimant suffers are the same act. It is not that two things take place, namely misconduct on the part of the defendant and injury on the part of the claimant; they are the same thing. This same unity applies to the remedial stage: the requirement is not that the defendant pay £100 and that the claimant receive £100; it is a requirement that the defendant pay £100 to the claimant, who receives it as a remedy for the wrong.

[8] E Weinrib, 'Right and Advantage in Private Law' (1989) 10 *Cardozo Law Review* 1283, citing R Peaslee, 'Multiple Causation and Damage' (1934) 47 *Harvard Law Review* 1127, 1139–41.

The unity is imposed by the transaction itself only if the payment is itself remedial, that is, either offered and accepted in settlement or awarded by a court.

If the wrong is the reason, rather than 'at most a condition' for the payment, the payment must be in response to the wrong. I break your window, you sue me, and the court orders me to pay you £100. On my way home from court, I leave £100 in your mailbox. It is not difficult to describe a context in which this would not count as complying with the judicial order; most significantly, if you have not received and accepted the money, I have not complied with the order to pay it to you. As a general matter, the claimant must participate in any remedial satisfaction of a claim. The continuity thesis says that a tortious wrong is a transaction, something that the defendant wrongfully does to the claimant. It says that a remedy is a transaction that is addressed to the initial wrongful transaction because of that transaction's wrongfulness. Leaving money in someone else's mailbox is not, on its own, a transaction at all.

As Smith notes, in the contrasting case in which pre-payment is part of a settlement, it is legally relevant in a claim for damages. The continuity thesis provides a clear explanation of how this could be so, in a way that its denial is unable to explain. What (legally) am I doing when I offer you £100 in settlement of your claim for the window that I broke? Perhaps I make the offer right after the window breaks, or after you have filed your claim against me, or partway through our litigation of it. In each of these cases, the fact that I am offering to settle your claim takes your claim against me as its subject matter. I have not yet been ordered to pay you, and so I cannot be complying in advance with an order that has not been given, and indeed may never be given (perhaps you will decide against suing me or make a mistake in your pleadings or fail to file in a timely fashion). Even if an order would have been given, its contours are not yet determinate, because as Smith rightly emphasises, orders are in some respects creative. That makes it difficult to suppose that the hypothetical order is somehow the subject matter of the settlement. Nor am I doing something that has no bearing on your claim; your claim is something, and, indeed, if I offer you £100 in settlement of it, and you accept the £100 payment as a settlement of the claim you have based on the wrongful transaction between us, we have entered into a transaction, as a result of which I will have thereby discharged something. That transaction takes our first transaction – my breaking your window – as its subject matter. Have I discharged a duty to pay you damages? Have I discharged my remedial obligation to you? Or have I merely pre-empted the operation of the court? The naive answer here is the best one: we have settled your claim against me, because you had a claim against me.

Your claim may have been in some ways uncertain. But, provided that my payment to you takes your claim against me as its subject matter, and you accept that the payment takes your claim as its subject matter, we have settled the claim. We have settled it even if my offer to settle is carefully worded in the ways in which settlements frequently are, saying that I do not concede any liability but that you have agreed to accept my payment in settlement of your claim because both of us recognise that litigating it is not prudent in light of our other overall priorities. I have not made a gift to you; instead, I have paid you the sum of £100 in relation to your potential claim against me. Smith is right to note the aspect of creativity in the court's crafting of a precise remedy (issue (b) in section II). As we negotiate the settlement, we, too, engage in some joint creativity, even though each of us perhaps is thinking strategically about the costs and likely outcomes of litigating the matter. We also might be more creative than a court is entitled to be; in particular, someone might assert a claim without merit, and the person against whom it is asserted might settle it anyway, just to save some bother. Nonetheless, both creative exercises, that of the court and the one in which we engage while negotiating a settlement, have a common subject matter: your claim against me for having broken your window. Your claim is personal to you and to me based on what I have done to you. The existence and continuity of claims rests on the continuity of rights and transactions. Settlements and remedies are different in one fundamental respect; the remedy rests on the court's finding that there was a wrong in a way in which a claim can be settled in the absence of any such finding. The acceptance of payment in settlement of a claim does, however, mean that it is relevant to a claim for damages.

This idea of continuity of wrongs is familiar as a matter of legal doctrine. In *Moses v Macferlan*,[9] arguably the founding case for the English law of unjust enrichment, the claimant sued to recover a payment to the defendant that he made in error. The payment was made in satisfaction of a debt; the claimant's error consisted in failing to note that the limitation period had expired, and so the debt was no longer enforceable. Lord Mansfield held that although the defendant could not bring an action to enforce the debt, the unenforceable debt was nonetheless a juristic reason for holding that the mistaken payment did not need to be returned. The debt could not be the subject of a judicial order because no proceeding could be brought that would generate such an order, but there was, one might say, the ground of a legal duty. That ground survived even though the duty was not the possible object of judicial order.[10]

B. 'The Lack of Guidance Objection'

Smith also argues that until the defendant has been ordered to pay, a duty to pay would be unknowable, and so violate one of the existence conditions for any duty:

> To begin, wrongdoers will often be unaware that they have even committed a wrong. Vendors who sell defective goods may not know that their goods are defective. Similarly, manufacturers will often be unaware that their products have caused an injury. Further, even when wrongdoers are aware that they have committed a wrong, they will rarely know the extent of damage that it caused. By definition, the facts on which such claims are based are in the victim's hands. The extent of a victim's losses depends on the victim's income, business prospects, leisure activities, medical expenses, pain and suffering, insurance, pre-existing medical condition, living arrangements, life expectancy, and so forth. Even a simple claim for the value of goods that were destroyed, damaged, or lost, depends on the goods' characteristics and condition. All of these facts are in the victim's hands (though in some cases even the victim cannot ascertain them).[11]

[9] *Moses v Macferlan* (1760), 2 Burr 1005, 97 Eng Rep 676.

[10] Further doctrinal counterexamples to Smith's claim are developed in detail in S Steel and R Stevens, 'The Secondary Legal Duty to Pay Damages' (2020) 136 *LQR* 283. They discuss, among other things, the prepayment rule, the claim that no damages are due for failure to pay damages in advance, rules governing the payment of pre-trial interest for non-pecuniary injury, as well as the right to detain property that has damaged the claimant's land until damages are paid, in advance of any kind of order from the court.

[11] Smith (n 1) 197.

The idea that duties must be knowable admits of two quite different interpretations, both of which are consistent with Joseph Raz's widely endorsed claim that 'the law must be capable of guiding the behaviour of its subjects'.[12] On the first, what might be called the 'wide' interpretation, to be under a duty you must be able to bring your conduct into conformity with it, and you could (in some extended sense of that elastic modal term) have considered what the duty required in deciding what to do. On the wide interpretation, a duty that did not tell you what to do at all would be no duty, but a duty that told you the kinds of things you had to do, even if you were not in a position to ascertain its application to particulars, would still be a duty. On the second, 'narrow' interpretation, to be under a duty you must know the specific action that the duty requires of you, such as paying £100 to the claimant.

The difficulty with the narrow interpretation is that if it is accepted, significant features of the common law of obligations turn out to involve no duties at all. To pick up on Smith's examples, the duties that are breached have the same structure as the remedies that are eventually ordered: vendors have a duty to deliver non-defective goods even if they do not know that they are defective, and manufacturers a duty to not injure others with their products, even if they do not know whether a particular product could or will cause, or has caused, an injury. Again, the basic rule governing trespass against land and conversion provides a clear case of a first-order legal duty that may in the particular case be entirely unknowable to a person subject to it. Smith has misgivings about strict duties, but if his distinction between duties and orders for remedies is to fit uncontroversial legal doctrine, it must apply to them as well. The boundary between your land and mine may be unmarked, or perhaps a forest fire destroyed the markers that we had set out. If I wander onto your land, I commit a trespass. Yet the law still insists that I have a duty not to trespass. I also have a duty to perform my contracts, even if circumstances are so unfortunate (but short of frustration) that I am factually unable to perform. Again, the duty not to defame another person is strict; you could be liable in defamation even though you had no way of knowing that the claim you made about the claimant was false.

You can avoid trespassing by never going anywhere, avoid defamation by always keeping silent and avoid contractual breach by never making any contracts. Such hypervigilant possibilities do not somehow show that such duties are knowable after all. To avoid going anywhere, saying anything or entering into contractual arrangements is not a way of complying with duties but rather of avoiding the situations in which they impose demands, and the duties themselves do not tell you to stay put and keep quiet. The rules of contract and the rules of trespass are action-guiding in general, even though you do not always know exactly how they will apply in particular circumstances.

Smith has in the past expressed normative discomfort about strict duties,[13] but the point is not specific to them; it applies to cases in which the law imposes duties via standards, the application of which is adjudicated by a court. My duty of care in the tort

[12] J Raz, *The Authority of Law* (Oxford, Clarendon Press, 1979) 214.

[13] SA Smith, 'Strict Duties and the Rule of Law' in LM Austin and D Klimchuk (eds), *Private Law and the Rule of Law* (Oxford, Oxford University Press, 2014) 189.

of negligence tells me to be careful. Whether I was careful enough is determined by the court, and so in fact I may be unable to know what the law requires of me in the particular case. Although Smith's stone was deliberately thrown through the window, nothing in his argument turns on that feature of the example. Suppose that I negligently kick up a stone with my lawnmower. Was I being careful enough? The law tells me to be careful: that much I know. But it does not tell me what I must do with respect to stones on the road, except to exercise reasonable care, or to behave as careful people do when they are being careful or some other such platitude. When the window breaks, the judge or jury, rather than either of us, will determine whether I exercised appropriate care. Some of the facts are in your hands; others are in mine. But the answer is the court's, and if our case makes it to trial, we might well both have precedents to cite and analogies to settled cases to draw, none of which are conclusive until the court issues its judgment. Does that mean that I do not have a duty to be careful as I mow my lawn? If it does, there are no rights or duties in law, only liabilities. The same point applies to the interpretation of contractual terms. Goods must be delivered in good condition, but whether you have delivered them in good condition is not a matter of what you or the recipient think but rather the decision of a court.

On the wide interpretation, however, your liability if you commit a wrong is no less knowable than whether you have committed a wrong. You may not know what steps you have to take in order to satisfy that duty, but the duty can nonetheless to be an action-guiding norm, even if you need to wait for a court's determination to know what it requires of you, and even if you do no wrong by not actively seeking out the aggrieved party and offering to settle (although the duty to make it up could provide an incentive to settle and a rough idea of what to offer in settlement). On this wide interpretation, then, the duty to pay damages before they are determined by a court is knowable, however incompletely.

Second, with respect to the magnitude of the loss occasioned by the breach of duty, the fact that the defendant does not know the magnitude of the claimant's losses does not make the duty objectionably unknowable on the wide interpretation. Perhaps it does on the narrow interpretation but, if so, that shows a problem for the narrow interpretation. Again, as a landowner you might have a legal duty to abate a nuisance on your land, even if you are unaware that the emanations from it constitute a nuisance or you are on some remote wilderness expedition and did not realise that the items stored on your land had begun to decompose. On Smith's classification, an injunction is merely replicative, but application of the thing that it replicates – the duty to avoid interfering with your neighbour's use and enjoyment of their land – to the specific circumstances may be unknowable to the defendant on the narrow interpretation.

Anticipating this form of response, Smith characterises it as the view that the duty is inchoate, remarking that 'a substantive duty that is inchoate until confirmed by a court seems indistinguishable from the duty that is simply created by a court'.[14] Yet the exact same knowability requirement, narrowly construed, would seem to make the duty to abate your nuisance, my duty to be careful as I operate my lawnmower, my duty to avoid saying something false about you or entering your land without authorisation also be

[14] Smith (n 1) 199.

duties that are simply created by a court. This kind of retroactivity is at odds with the way in which Smith presents the rule of law, an example of what Bentham disparaged as dog law.[15]

III. Creativity

I have argued that neither the doctrinal argument nor the theoretical argument from the requirement that someone subject to a duty be able to know what the duty requires is successful. I now turn to the issue of creativity. As I said at the outset, Smith's deeply illuminating distinction between replicative and creative orders is more rather than less illuminating if understood in terms of the continuity thesis.

The court is charged with determining what wrongdoers should do for their victims; its task is creative in one sense, but passive in another. Smith contends that the idea that the remedy is the right looked at from the other end must suppose that a court takes an active interest in seeing to it that the wrongdoer provides the requested remedy, on the grounds that that is the way in which courts respond to wrongdoing. The observation that courts do no such thing leads Smith to conclude that the role of the court is to create a new duty, and that the wrong is merely the condition but not the reason for doing so. Once more, this way of framing things reflects an assumption about what it is to be subject to a duty. For Smith, you are subject to the duty if the law has instructed you to perform some specific act.

The continuity thesis does not contend that courts take an interest in every wrongful transaction; even the case of replicative orders makes it clear that courts do not act every time a wrong has been committed or a right is in jeopardy. Instead, they are passive: they leave it to claimants who believe that they have been wronged, or that their rights are in jeopardy, to initiate a claim. But although they are passive with respect to the initiation of a claim, they are creative in processing one. But that creativity is, as I shall explain, bounded by the role of a court as a court.

The burden of establishing that the wrong took place lies with the claimant. If the claimant fails to initiate proceedings, the defendant is not subject to any sanction for failing to take the initiative; the court does not care.

Instead, the continuity thesis explains what a court does when a claimant establishes that a wrong has been committed. In cases of wrongdoing, Birks' juridical rope remains intact even when the defendant has sundered it; that is why the claimant is entitled to demand satisfaction. Far from making the wrongdoing irrelevant, the continuity thesis explains its relevance: the wrong converts initial obligation into a claim. The claim is (staying with the rope image) in the claimant's hands; if the claimant does not make a claim in court, the court will do nothing, because of the way in which courts are passive;

[15] As Ben Zipursky once observed, tort law scores poorly against conventionally accepted rule-of-law norms highlighted by Dicey, Fuller and Hayek: 'particularized, non-explicit, retroactive, and unclear'. BC Zipursky, 'Torts and the Rule of Law' in Austin and Klimchuk (eds) (n 13) 139. Smith's understanding of the requirements of the rule of law seems to lead to the conclusion that it does not impose duties. But Zipursky's point is that the conclusion that there are no duties in tort law casts doubt on the premises of which it is an implication, not on its status as law.

they operate on disputes that are brought to them by the parties, they do not go seeking them out. As Smith notes, courts do not exercise initiative, because whether there is a dispute between private parties is left to the parties. They may or may not be in a privileged position for finding out such things; juridically, however, they are in a unique position, because they are the holders of the rights that are potentially in dispute. That is why courts are passive even with respect to replicative orders; as Smith correctly points out, courts do not order people to pay an agreed sum or perform their contracts until the party to whom such performance is owed establishes that they will not.

This passivity is combined with the court's creativity. The court's task is to make a determination both of whether the wrong took place as alleged and of the suitable remedy. This is not, however, the inchoate duty view. Instead, it might be understood as the rule-of-law view: you do not have an affirmative legal duty unless the law tells you to do something. In the case of wrongdoing, however, the burden lies with the claimant of convincing the court that you have done wrong. So the creativity is genuine but works on the material of the claimant's complaint. And indeed, as Smith makes clear in his discussion of defences, normally when a claimant has established the wrong has taken place, the specifics of the remedy may vary but the court continues to look at how things stood between the parties. Its assessment of the remedy, including damages for injuries that are consequential on the wrong rather than included in the antecedent duty breached by the defendant, depends on that relationship. If I owe you a duty not to break your window, in breaching the duty and breaking the window I deprive you of something that may have had an important role in enabling you to do other things in your life, and so your entitlement to constrain my conduct in relation to the window can only be properly upheld if, for example, I also pay for the water damage caused by the rain that entered through the broken window.

That a court should combine activity and passivity in this way is not surprising. Judges are public officials; like other public officials they have mandates. The mandate of a court is to resolve a dispute on its merits; as Smith concedes, the way in which a court processes a private legal dispute draws on what transpired between the parties. If the defendant is found liable, the court then turns to determining the remedy, exercising its creativity in a way different from the way in which the parties crafting a settlement might engage in joint creativity by means of bargaining.

By contrast, parties seeking to settle a dispute do not have a mandate; it is up to them to find terms acceptable to both, and if they do not find such terms, to litigate instead. The possibility of litigation may provide incentives that influence the ways in which the parties exercise their creativity in negotiating a settlement, because each will have a view about the likely outcome and cost of litigation, and, if they are prudent, each will take account of the other's position and strategise accordingly.

A court charged with crafting a remedy is in a very different position, because it has a mandate: to resolve the dispute before it in accordance with the law. As such, it does not engage in bargaining; nor does it ask itself about the terms on which the parties would have settled, or on which they would have bargained in the absence of transaction costs. Instead, it looks at the transaction, focusing on the claimant's right that was violated by the defendant, and asks itself what it would take to put the claimant back in some semblance of the same position that the claimant would have been in if not for the defendant's wrong. Its creativity is genuine, because it has to determine an adequate substitute or, more often, which among a plethora of inadequate substitutes would put the claimant into something at least loosely resembling the prior position. It is creative because it also has to make projections about the subsequent course of events, so that what the claimant receives is not only what the claimant had at the time but also what the claimant would have had if, in the absence of the wrong, the claimant had continued to have the use of the object of the right. It therefore needs to quantify things that are not readily quantifiable, another aspect of creativity. This type of creativity depends entirely on the fact of the wrong. Creativity in crafting a remedy is particular to wrongs precisely because the fact of the wrong must be addressed in light of the right that was violated. By contrast, merely replicative remedies respond to what Smith characterises as rights-threats; the point of a replicative order is to prevent the threat from being realised. Sometimes a court will do both, as when it grants the claimant an injunction and also damages for the past effects of the defendant's nuisance.

The output of the court's creativity is also itself creative, because it empowers the claimant to call on the state to enforce the terms of the judgment, should the defendant not comply with the court's remedial order. There is therefore a new legal relationship, a new liability to the use of force by the state against the defendant, a liability to which the defendant was not subject until so ordered. But that liability is a standard feature of all orders; an order to pay an agreed sum places the defendant under such a liability, even though the defendant was already under a fully developed duty to pay that sum.

A court engages in all of these forms of creativity because the object of the claimant's right, the claimant's entitlement not to be interfered with by the defendant, is not merely the condition of the remedy but the reason for it, because its subject matter is always the continuing relation between the claimant and the defendant.

IV. Conclusion

I have argued that Smith's arguments against the continuity thesis are not successful: instead, the continuity thesis helps to explain why his distinction between creative and replicative orders is so illuminating; it explains the sense in which orders can be fundamentally creative without departing from the rights of the parties.

7

The Moral Authority of Rulings

EVAN FOX-DECENT*

I. Introduction

Stephen Smith's passing is felt deeply by all who knew him. I was immensely fortunate to have had an office just a few steps down the hall from Steve for the better part of 15 years. We first met at McGill while I was on a post-doctoral fellowship. From the outset, before I was appointed to faculty, he treated me warmly and generously, as a colleague, with time always to discuss and sharpen, or help me discard, one fuzzy idea after another. Over time we would become close friends, and shared a love of legal theory and jurisprudence.

In this essay I attempt to build on the potentially paradigm-shifting claim in Smith's most recent opus, *Rights, Wrongs, and Injustices*, that judicial rulings or orders are a distinctive normative form through which the law imposes itself on its subjects.[1] Ultimately, I suggest that Smith may have significantly understated the contribution of his analysis to jurisprudence. If Smith is roughly correct in his assessment of judicial rulings, then they are a necessary feature of law for law to be able to claim or possess legitimate authority. Put slightly differently, an implication of Smith's view is that for law to claim legitimate authority, as Joseph Raz says all legal systems must,[2] or for law to possess legitimate authority (in addition to claiming it), as non-positivist theorists say all legal orders must,[3] then legal systems – to be legal systems – must include rulings (or their equivalents) within them. Or so I shall argue in section II.

In section III, I suggest that Smith may not have drawn out this implication expressly because he adopts a justification of rulings that is external to law's self-understanding of them. His argument begins with the observation that it would be costly to use sanctions

* I thank Andrew Gold, John Goldberg and James Penner for valuable comments, and the Social Science and Humanities Research Council, Canada Research Chair programme, for financial assistance that helped make this chapter possible.

[1] SA Smith, *Rights, Wrongs, and Injustices: The Structure of Remedial Law* (Oxford, Oxford University Press, 2019). I will generally refer to judicial remedial orders indiscriminately as rulings or orders.

[2] J Raz, *Ethics in the Public Domain: Essays in the Morality of Law and Politics* (Oxford, Oxford University Press, 1994).

[3] D Dyzenhaus, *The Long Arc of Legality: Hobbes, Kelsen, Hart* (Cambridge, Cambridge University Press, 2022).

to right every judicially recognised private wrong, since sanctions require public institutions to take coercive action. Decent societies are concerned with public goods such as hospitals and schools, as well as with the administration of justice. So, Smith says, for practical reasons having to do with limited resources, judges who wish to impose a remedy in a given case ordinarily issue rulings that command defendants to do or not do something voluntarily.

I will present a complementary and moralised justification of rulings that is internal to law's self-understanding of them. This internal account helps Smith's insights on rulings contribute to the jurisprudential idea that it is in the nature of law that it must either claim or possess legitimate authority. And importantly, the internal account can provide a bulwark to defend the practice of remedial orders against arguments from efficiency that would curtail orders in favour of sanctions. On the moralised account, even if the practice of issuing judicial orders were shown to be more costly than direct sanctions, there would still be reason, however defeasible, to maintain the practice. First, however, we need to have in view the main elements of Smith's account of rulings, as well as an outline of the significance of authority to jurisprudential inquiry into the nature of law.

II. Rulings and Authority

Smith begins *Rights, Wrongs, and Injustices* asserting that the law addresses its subjects through three distinctive modes. The first consists of substantive legal rules enacted by lawmakers. These rules tell subjects such things as the general duties they owe to one another (eg, 'everyone has a duty to perform one's contractual promises', 'no one is entitled to use another's property without permission') and the legal powers individuals possess and how to exercise them (eg, the legal powers to make contracts and wills). The second mode comprises judicial rulings by which courts command individuals to do or not do certain things (eg, 'It is ordered that the defendant pay the claimant $1,000'). Unlike substantive rules that are general in that they typically apply to all individuals or a class of individuals in a given legal order, remedial orders are directed at particular individuals. And, crucially, rulings are addressed to defendants with the expectation that their addressees will comply voluntarily. The third principal way in which the law imposes itself on its subjects, Smith claims, is through sanctions. In the domain of sanctions, legal officials impose measures forcibly to execute a judicial order. For example, officials may fine or imprison the defendant to induce compliance, or officials may seize and sell the defendant's property in order to satisfy a judgment for damages.

Smith rightly notes that that legal scholars working on questions related to the nature of law have generally focused on the first and third modes – substantive legal rules and sanctions – leaving rulings undertheorised.[4] For Austin, law consisted in the commands of a sovereign who Austin framed as uncommanded commander. The sovereign's commands were habitually obeyed and backed by sanctions.[5] For Austin's successor,

[4] Smith (n 1) 4, 11–13.

[5] J Austin, *The Province of Jurisprudence Determined* (1832).

Hart, law consisted in the union of primary rules and secondary rules, where primary rules are essentially Smith's substantive legal rules and secondary rules are norms governing the production, change, adjudication and recognition of primary rules.[6] And for sceptics such as Holmes, who doubted law's normativity, substantive legal rules were to be understood in terms reducible to (and so not conceptually distinct from) orders backed by sanctions. On the Holmesian view, all substantive legal duties, such as 'everyone has a duty to perform their contractual promises', were really disjunctive statements of the kind 'perform your contractual promises or be liable to pay damages'. Smith seeks to fill the lacuna left by jurisprudence scholars while answering Holmesian sceptics in part by showing that the form, legal effects and function of rulings are distinct from the form, legal effects and functions of substantive rules and sanctions.

The form of rulings is typically laconic, imperative, and particularised to a specific defendant. Smith gives the following as examples:[7]

> 'It is ordered that the defendant: pay the claimant the sum of £ …'
>
> '[T]he Court orders that: the defendant give the claimant the possession of … on or before …'
>
> 'It is ordered that the contract dated … referred to in the Particulars of Claim … be specifically performed.'
>
> 'The Court ordered that [the defendant] is forbidden to …'

In sum, rulings take an imperative form in which courts, upon proof of a cause of action by a claimant, tell defendants to do or not do something that is intended to serve as a remedy responsive to the cause of action. Substantive legal rules ordinarily assume a general form and declare general duties, whereas sanctions are characterised by the forcible implementation of rulings rather than by their imperative expression per se. Sanctions are actions carried out by legal officials, whereas, for Smith, '[o]rders are just words'.[8]

Smith likewise identifies several distinctive legal effects of rulings.[9] First, court orders impose duties on defendants to do as they command (eg, pay damages to the claimant), and importantly, these duties are owed to the court, not the claimant. Second, rulings give claimants a conditional legal power: if the defendant fails to comply with the order, the claimant can call on the state's coercive machinery to enforce the order. Sometimes the enforcement is direct, such as when a bailiff seizes and sells the defendant's property to execute an order for damages in the claimant's favour. In other cases, enforcement is indirect, such as when officials imprison or fine a defendant to induce compliance.

The basic function of rulings, Smith says, is to do justice between the claimant and defendant where the claimant has proved a cause of action. Smith sets out and distinguishes three causes of action: rights-threats, wrongs and injustices.[10] A rights-threat arises when a claimant's substantive rights are likely to be infringed in the future if

[6] HLA Hart, *The Concept of Law*, 3rd edn (Oxford, Oxford University Press, 2012) 92–99.
[7] Smith (n 1) 49.
[8] ibid 66.
[9] ibid 58–87.
[10] ibid 132–272.

a defendant's actions or plans do not change. The usual remedy is an order that the defendant respect the claimant's substantive right by complying with the defendant's correlative substantive duty or by complying with a monetary substitute for that duty.

A wrong is a breach of a substantive duty owed to another individual. Smith's innovation here is his suggestion that the core damages award (compensatory damages) is a response to an injustice rather than a wrong, and that damages awards for specific relief (substitutionary damages) are responses to rights-threats rather than wrongs. For Smith, wrong-based damages are limited to those falling under nominal damages, exemplary damages, pain and suffering damages, and damages he calls 'vindicatory damages' (user damages, waiver damages, market-price damages, non-pecuniary damages and gain-based damages). These for Smith are part of remedial law rather than substantive law; on his view, damages orders create new duties rather than confirm substantive duties.

An injustice in Smith's catalogue of causes of action is an unfair loss or gain that has arisen from a transaction between the defendant and claimant. For Smith, this is the cause of action following defective transfers such as mistaken payments (restitutionary orders) and orders to pay damages for consequential losses (compensatory orders). As with wrong-based damages, Smith argues that restitutionary and compensatory orders are duty-creating and therefore are governed by remedial rather than substantive law. But restitutionary and compensatory orders, he claims, are injustice-responding orders rather than wrong- or rights-threat-responding. These are bold and important claims, and even bolder is the idea that restitutionary and compensatory orders belong in the same remedial category. I will not assess these arresting views here. Rather, I will take Smith's account of remedies as provisionally sound, and will use the foregoing sketch to show how Smith's conception of rulings may connect to jurisprudential concerns regarding law's claim to or possession of authority.

On Smith's view, rulings, and rulings alone, have the requisite form through which law can claim or possess legitimate authority, in the relevant sense. The relevant sense is, roughly, law's claim or possession of a moral power to direct its subjects, with the expectation that its subjects will obey and comply voluntarily with the law's commands. Correlatively, legal subjects are under a standing liability to become subject to judicial orders should a claimant prove a cause of action against them. The kind of authority on which courts rely when they issue orders, Smith says, is the authority to command obedience. This form of authority arises, on Smith's account, from the presumption that legal subjects are under a general duty to do as courts order. Smith describes this as 'directive authority' because 'it is an authority to direct actions'.[11] The question facing defendants subject to court orders is whether to obey them or risk facing sanctions.

Smith explicitly denies that substantive legal rules claim or possess directive authority. He insists that because substantive lawmaking merely declares general rules, 'the question of whether to obey [general rules] does not arise ... [i]t is not possible to obey or disobey a statement that something exists'.[12] While acknowledging that substantive

[11] ibid 117.
[12] ibid 116.

rules are duty-imposing, Smith nonetheless claims that 'the question they raise is … whether to accept that they do what they purport to do, namely, to create or affirm a valid duty'.[13] The issue here, Smith says, is not simply whether the legislature, court or other lawmaker enacts a valid legal duty, but 'whether it is an "all-things-considered" (or "moral" or "unqualified") duty'.[14] In other words, the question 'is whether to view legal rules as the law presents them, namely, as unqualified standards for behaviour. It is not possible to obey a standard; a standard is either accepted or not accepted.'[15]

Smith does think that lawmakers enjoy a certain kind of authority when they enact substantive rules, and that their rules partake in this authority. He characterises this authority as 'declarative' or 'declarative-constitutive', because 'the statement of a duty-imposing rule by an appropriate court or other lawmaker both authoritatively affirms, or declares, the existence of a legal duty and, at the same time, is constitutive of the duty's existence'.[16] But, to reiterate, whereas '[o]rders call for obedience, not acceptance', legal rules, according to Smith, call merely for acceptance of the duties they affirm. Smith emphasises that although a duty-imposing general rule does give its addressees a reason for action, 'it does not direct its addressees to do anything. Rather, it affirms that they have a duty to do something.'[17] Orders, on the other hand, express directive authority precisely because they direct their addressees to do as they say.

Some may object that the distinction Smith is drawing between obedience and acceptance is too fine, or a distinction without a difference. The objector might query whether there is not some good sense in which the performance of one's contractual promises should count as abiding by a legal standard and therefore performance is a kind of obedience of the law. Smith can reply, however, that conformity with a legal standard is not obedience in the relevant sense. In the case of orders, the call for obedience is individualised and unavoidable. In the case of general rules, they can be avoided by not participating in the regulated activity or by avoiding the circumstances that trigger application of the relevant rules. In principle, the contract rule demanding performance can be avoided by not entering contracts, and trespassing can be avoided by not leaving one's property or otherwise interfering with another's. With rulings, however, in the standard case the defendant subject to a court order is under an unavoidable duty to comply, at least to the extent the defendant is within the court's jurisdiction.[18]

Furthermore, in contrast to substantive legal duties owed to private parties, such as the contractual duty to perform, the duty to obey a court order, on Smith's theory, is owed to the court. It is counterintuitive to think that private contracting parties might

[13] ibid.

[14] ibid. Citing J Raz, *The Authority of Law: Essays on Law and Morality*, 2nd edn (Oxford, Oxford University Press, 2009) and Raz (n 2), Smith underlines that law generally, from an internal point of view, understands its substantive duties as unqualified and morally justified; Smith (n 1) 116, fn 19.

[15] Smith (n 1) 116.

[16] ibid.

[17] ibid fn 20.

[18] This conclusion cannot be avoided by stipulating that defendants can avoid rulings by not breaching substantive legal rules. To compare apples and apples, we need to compare rules as we find them in law with rulings as we find them in law, and it is partially definitive of rulings as we find them in law that they are particularised to defendants.

owe each other a general duty to obey the law that is somehow generated from their bilateral duties to perform. We can explain the contractual relationship and its legal effects without making any reference to a general duty to obey the law, or at least one that is in any way distinguishable from the ordinary duty to perform.

I appreciate that the obedience/acceptance aspect of Smith's rulings/rules distinction may be controversial. I do not expect the short reply I have given on Smith's behalf to satisfy all sceptics. Nonetheless, I do think his account is more than plausible enough to warrant consideration of its connection to wider jurisprudential questions concerning the relationship between law and authority. To see this connection, we need first to see in outline how the question of law's authority has risen to the fore of jurisprudential debates over the past century.

Hart famously criticised Austin's command theory of law for confusing law with 'the gunman situation writ large'.[19] The individual subject to the gunman's threat could be coerced to hand her money over, but, Hart said, 'we should misdescribe the situation if we said … that [the individual] "had an obligation" or a "duty" to hand over the money'.[20] In these and other ways, Hart argued, Austin's theory failed to take into account the normative and authoritative perspective adopted by legal officials who apprehend law from an internal point of view, which is roughly the point of view of officials enmeshed in legal practices (eg, legislators enacting substantive rules, judges writing decisions and issuing rulings).

Hart's solution was a theory of law premised on the union of primary and secondary rules.[21] However, he did not think legal subjects generally had to accept or even have knowledge of 'the legal structure or of its criteria of validity [ie, its rule of recognition]'.[22] For officials, 'there should be a unified or shared acceptance of the rule of recognition,' whereas the 'ordinary citizen' could obey the law 'out of fear of consequences, or from inertia, without thinking of himself or others as having an obligation to do so and without being disposed to criticize either himself or others for deviations'.[23]

Importantly, for the Hartian subject who accepts a legal rule or obeys a judicial ruling purely 'out of fear of consequences', the rule or ruling's claim to be law would not be undermined simply because they arose from a sanction-driven system that ruled its subjects through terror while making no claim to possess legitimate authority. Although Hart's theory does not embody 'the gunman situation writ large' in anything like the way the command theory does, it nonetheless does not disqualify a terror regime from counting as a legal order merely on the grounds that the regime is in fact a gunman writ large. Arguably, however, a terror regime would find its legal credentials under stress for the very reasons Hart invoked to discredit the command theory: unmediated coercion of the gunman variety is inconsistent with legal obligation.

Smith's doctoral supervisor, Joseph Raz, offers a way forward by linking authority to law at the conceptual level, but in a way that lets illegitimate regimes with merely de

[19] Hart (n 6) 5.
[20] ibid 82.
[21] ibid 92–99.
[22] ibid 114.
[23] ibid 114–15.

facto authority count as legal systems so long as in principle it is possible for them to possess legitimate authority. The lynchpin of Raz's positivist strategy is his separation of the law's *claim* to legitimate authority, on the one hand, from the question of whether the law *is* a legitimate authority, on the other. Regarding the law's claim to authority, Raz argues that the claim

> is manifested by the fact that legal institutions are officially designated as 'authorities,' by the fact that they regard themselves as having the right to impose obligations on their subjects, by the claims that their subjects owe them allegiance, and that their subjects ought to obey the law as it requires to be obeyed.[24]

Not only, however, does Raz's conceptual claim stipulate an existence condition on which the designation 'legal' depends. The content of the claim is such that it applies comprehensively to the relationship of ruler and ruled, official and subject.

Implicit to the law's claim to authority is the idea that the law's officials and institutions are in a relationship of authority with their legal subjects, since claims to authority presuppose relations of authority. Whereas for Hart a legal system can exist without concerning itself with the legal subject beyond ensuring that its primary rules are obeyed on any grounds by 'the bulk of the population', for Raz a constitutive element of a legal system is that it must claim that its coercive framework of rules helps its subjects comply with reason.[25] In this sense, Raz's conceptual claim is comprehensive in scope across officials and subjects, because it implies that law claims to frame and inform an authority relationship between ruler and ruled, a relationship whose justification lies in its service to the ruled. While Raz denies that actual legitimate authority is an existence condition of legal order, he acknowledges that a corollary of his view is that law 'must be capable of possessing authority'.[26] It follows that a regime incapable of possessing authority would find its legal credentials in doubt.[27]

In a recent monograph dedicated to showing that law, properly understood, must possess as well as claim authority, David Dyzenhaus argues that 'What makes law authoritative is that the officials who speak in its name can answer satisfactorily the legal subject's question "But, how can that be law for me?"'[28] Dyzenhaus argues that the best reading of Hobbes, Kelsen and Hart is one that takes seriously their acknowledgement – at times incomplete – that law is not 'the gunman situation writ large'. On Dyzenhaus's non-positivist interpretation of these theorists, they each recognise that law asserts authority (not mere coercive force) through an internal normative vocabulary of rights, duties, powers, liberties and so on that permit the judge or official to answer in

[24] Raz (n 2) 215–16.

[25] There is a burgeoning literature on Raz's 'service conception' of authority. For my contribution, see E Fox-Decent, 'Fiduciary Authority and the Service Conception' in AS Gold and PB Miller (eds), *Philosophical Foundations of Fiduciary Law* (Oxford, Oxford University Press, 2014) 363.

[26] Raz (n 2) 215.

[27] For discussion of slavery as a test case for legality, see E Fox-Decent, 'Is the Rule of Law Really Indifferent to Human Rights' (2008) 27 *Law & Philosophy* 533; E Fox-Decent, *Sovereignty's Promise: The State As Fiduciary* (Oxford, Oxford University Press, 2011); E Fox-Decent, 'Jurisprudential Reflections on Cosmopolitan Law' in J Bomhoff, D Dyzenhaus and T Poole (eds), *The Double-Facing Constitution* (Cambridge, Cambridge University Press, 2019); K Rundle, 'Form and Agency in Raz's Legal Positivism' (2013) 32 *Law & Philosophy* 767.

[28] Dyzenhaus (n 3) 2.

a principled way the subject's question 'But, how can that be law for me?' Dyzenhaus, in other words, agrees with Hart and Raz that to understand law, one must recognise that, from an internal point of view, law sees itself as authoritative. His principal disagreement is that he thinks law must not only claim authority but must also, in some measure, possess it, and that its authority must be transparent and intelligible to the legal subject.

Now, while Smith considered himself a legal positivist,[29] his theory of rulings is jurisprudentially ecumenical in that it could be amended readily to be brought into conformity with a non-positivist theory of law such as Dyzenhaus's. To the question from the legal subject 'But, how can that be law for me?', Smith's reply with respect to rulings would be that they are law for their addressees because there is 'a presumed duty to obey court orders'.[30] The only difference from Smith's stated positivist theory would be that the 'presumed duty' would be actual rather than simply a presumption of judicial practice or a claim that courts implicitly make when they issue rulings. On this rendering, Smith's view would become Kelsenian in the sense that it would posit a presumed *grundnorm* of authority, but the account would be non-positivist in as much as the *grundnorm* would be treated as actual rather than merely asserted.[31]

The main point I wish to make, however, is that whether one adopts Smith's positivist account of rulings or a non-positivist variant, the implication of his theory for theoretical inquiry into the nature of law is that rulings must be recognised as the focal or core instance of authority that law either claims or possesses. Rulings occupy this hallowed ground because, on Smith's telling, rulings alone categorically direct individuals to do things on the grounds that they have a general duty to obey the law by doing what courts say. The significance of this can hardly be overstated, because the legal power to impose duties and direct legal subjects in this way is conventionally what theorists since Plato have been referring to when they discuss law's claim to or possession of authority. If Smith is right, western legal theorists, by missing the distinction between declarative and directive authority, have overlooked the centrality of rulings to law's authority, and have mistakenly viewed rules or sanctions as law's fundamental organising elements.

In section III, I set out Smith's justification of rulings. This justification, I suggest, may explain why Smith did not develop significantly the momentous jurisprudential implications of his view. I also offer a complementary moralised justification of rulings that allows Smith's understanding of rulings to illuminate the centrality of authority to the nature of law.

[29] So, not surprisingly, in *Rights, Remedies, and Injustices*, Smith deploys a sources-based method to identify legal rules: 'If the Supreme Court says that "everyone has a duty to perform their contractual promises," then it is automatically the case that everyone has such a duty.' Smith (n 1) 114. Smith also clarifies (ibid 117, fn 22) that he refers 'to the courts' "claims" to declaratory and directive authority to make clear that [he does] not assume that courts actually possess either kind of authority … [T]o explain the practice of issuing orders … it is sufficient to show … that the practice might plausibly be thought to be justified. It is not necessary that the practice actually be justified.'

[30] ibid 117.

[31] See L Vinx, *Hans Kelsen's Pure Theory of Law: Legality and Legitimacy* (Oxford, Oxford University Press, 2007) and Dyzenhaus (n 3) for sustained defence of the idea that there is a compelling non-positivist interpretation of Kelsen's legal theory.

III. The Justification of Rulings

A puzzle raised by remedial orders is why courts bother with them at all, since it seems they could simply attend a rights-threat, a wrong or an injustice by skipping directly to a sanction when the relevant legal rule has failed to motivate the defendant. In principle, instead of ordering the duty-breaching defendant to pay damages to the wronged claimant, courts could simply order a sheriff to seize and sell the defendant's property so as to transfer the relevant sum to the claimant. Smith claims that orders are usually 'means to the ends they contemplate', and so if those ends could be achieved 'by a judge physically removing money from a defendant's pockets' then 'orders would be unnecessary'.[32]

Smith suggests practical considerations resolve the puzzle. His argument is that decent societies are concerned with a multitude of public goods in addition to the administration of justice, and it would be too costly to use public institutions to transfer property or take other action to right every judicially recognised private wrong. Courts' use of rulings is therefore justified because they save society resources that can be deployed elsewhere. In the case of non-monetary orders, such as an injunction to restrain a trespass or an order to remove a building from the defendant's property, third parties cannot bring about the outcome save through incarceration or other invasive or costly forms of inducement. In the case of monetary orders, Smith says the explanation is simply 'convenience' and that 'In principle, there is no reason to order a defendant who owes money to make payment if third parties can obtain the money as easily for the claimant.'[33] The reason for using orders rather than sanctions is that 'defendants are often willing to pay voluntarily once courts order them to pay' and so 'there is an obvious practical advantage to issuing orders prior to resorting to sanctions'.[34] This explanation of rulings, however, has a number of weaknesses.

First, courts do not explain or appear to understand the justification of rulings this way. If they did, one would expect to see reasons sometimes weighing the practical benefits and possible costs of issuing orders rather than sanctions. Courts generally do not do so, even though they do sometimes tailor orders with practical considerations in mind; for example, when they order damages for breach of contract rather than specific performance. Smith's justification of rulings appears to be external to the practice.

A consequence of Smith's account is that were the direct imposition of sanctions costless (or of negligible cost), remedial orders would appear anachronistic and undermotivated. Certainly, as Smith makes clear, they would be unnecessary. In our world they happen to serve a practical function of reducing the cost of the administration of justice, but on Smith's theory there is no reason to order the defendant to do anything if officials could bring about the remedy at negligible cost. Again, this approach seems to treat orders as optional in a way that most judges would likely find alien to their understanding of orders.

Let us imagine that in some future world all judicial orders are monetary orders, and they are all eliminated and replaced by sanctions. Officials or other third parties simply transfer the defendants' money or other assets to the claimant to execute the remedy.

[32] Smith (n 1) 56.
[33] ibid 124.
[34] ibid 125.

Defendants are not asked to comply with rulings; they play no role other than serving passively as repositories of resources that officials seize to execute judicial orders. If we adopt Smith's theory of rulings, a dramatic implication in a legal order such as this one is that there would be no directive authority, since the practice to which directive authority attaches – judicial rulings – has been eliminated. It follows that that law could not claim or possess authority as it is conventionally understood to do. And if law cannot do that, then Smith's account is at risk of collapsing into an Austinian sanction theory, despite his emphasis throughout on the importance of directive authority to understanding rulings and law more generally.

Finally, there is, in my view, something unattractive about a legal order that would deny defendants the opportunity to obey a ruling voluntarily and simply subject them directly to a sanction. This is the thought underlying the moralised account of the justification of rulings I will now sketch briefly. The account I provide is consistent with the idea that rulings either claim or possess directive authority. This alternative view, however, stands in tension with Smith's claim that rulings are mere means to outcomes that could be brought about at no loss by sanctions alone.

Consider the position of defendants in unjust enrichment cases involving mistaken payments. Typically, these defendants are subject to restitutionary orders that, Smith rightly observes, 'are clearly not responses to wrongs'.[35] In the standard case, the defective transfer involves an innocent mistake on the part of the claimant and no wrongdoing on the part of the defendant. Consider also the morally innocent position of defendants who have a good faith and reasonable disagreement with the claimant over the location of a property line, or over a contractual term, such as whether delivery on a weekend counts as delivery within the week stipulated under the contract for delivery. In these and scores of other cases, defendants are morally innocent notwithstanding their being potentially liable to court orders in favour of the claimant.

In cases that impose legal liability on a defendant who is morally innocent and who would willingly comply with a remedial ruling, for a court to order a sheriff to seize assets or impose some other sanction without giving the defendant an opportunity to comply would be for that court to engage in, by hypothesis, an unnecessary use of force. In a modern age such as ours with advanced technology, assets may be seized with a few keystrokes, and so with minimal (if any) use of physical force.[36] But the relevant sense of force in this context refers not to physical seizure of assets per se but to the non-consensual appropriation by an official of assets to which the defendant would otherwise be entitled (the appropriation is non-consensual in the sense that defendant's consent is irrelevant; the official will appropriate for the purpose of imposing a sanction with or without the defendant's consent). Now, of course, there could be arguments in favour of a private law regime of sanctions without rulings (eg, under certain assumptions the regime might be more efficient and fairer to claimants). However, strong reasons suggest that the moral cost of imposing force or sanctions unnecessarily is too high for a sanctions-without-rulings regime to be justified on the balance of relevant considerations.

[35] ibid 225. See, eg, *Kelly v Solari* (1841) 9 M & W 54.

[36] I thank James Penner for this point. See J Penner and KL Quek, 'The Law's Remedial Norms' (2016) 28 *Singapore Academy of Law Journal* 768 (arguing *inter alia* that the defendant owes the claimant a moral duty of repair subsequent to breach).

States that use force or sanctions unnecessarily against their subjects make it much harder for their officials to answer Dyzenhaus's question 'But, how can that be law for me?' Indeed, it is difficult to imagine how officials deploying unnecessary force could even *claim* to possess legitimate authority to do so, because in this context they need not use force to obtain the desired end; they could instead use rulings. There is, then, a real question of whether it is even possible for a legal system to possess legitimate authority to use force against its subjects unnecessarily. At the very least, we are perilously close to failing to satisfy an existence condition Raz sets out to connect authority to law – that it must be possible for law to claim legitimate authority – so as to avoid law's conceptualisation as 'a gunman situation writ large'.

Moreover, in a liberal legal regime, the state is generally expected to use the least restrictive means available when it seeks to advance policy. For example, constitutions in Commonwealth and European countries allow states to infringe enshrined constitutional rights, but subject to a proportionality requirement that requires the state to show that its chosen means to advance its end minimally impair constitutional rights.[37] Private law rulings, by favouring voluntary compliance over the use of force, may be understood as private law's analogue to public law's least-restrive-means requirement. Relatedly, because private law supplies civil recourse for wrongs committed between private parties, the use of rulings limits the direct power the successful claimant has over the defendant. The prevalence of rulings means a claimant cannot file a suit that, if successful, concludes with an automatic withdrawal of funds from the defendant's bank account. The claimant can call on the coercive machinery of the state only if the defendant refuses to comply with the court's ruling.[38]

By using rulings backed by sanctions rather than sanctions alone, courts can avoid unnecessary uses of force that, in at least some cases, would place their claim to authority in doubt. Indeed, rulings make it possible for the legal system to use sanctions authoritatively. Force is used only as strictly necessary and only as a last resort to meet the demands of justice. In short, rulings make a limited and last-resort use of sanctions possible. Arguably, by doing so, rulings thereby make the law's limited and last-resort use of sanctions legitimate, or at least the claim to legitimacy is made plausible. Rulings therefore take their justification from within the wider practice of private law, and in a way that lets private law claim and possibly possess legitimate authority.

An Aristotelean or Kantian sceptic might object that if the argument above is persuasive, it is persuasive only in relation to morally innocent but legally liable defendants. Wrongdoers, our sceptic might press, have no standing to resist forcible sanctions the only purpose of which is to restore the rightful normative equality between the claimant and defendant that the defendant's wrong has disturbed.[39] The objection misses the mark for several reasons.

[37] See, eg, *R* v *Oakes* [1986] 1 SCR 103 (the leading case in Canada that sets out a proportionality test rights-infringing legislation must meet to survive judicial review).

[38] I thank John Goldberg for comments that inspired this paragraph.

[39] See, eg, Aristotle, *Nicomachean Ethics*, Book Five, tr Terence Irwin (Indianapolis, IN, Hackett 1985) (affirming bilateral equality as the lodestar of corrective justice); EJ Weinrib, 'The Gains and Losses of Corrective Justice' (1994) 44 *Duke Law Journal* 277 (distinguishing normative from factual gains and losses using Kantian right and duty so as to explain Aristotle's allegiance to equality as an organising idea of private

First, there is no necessary connection between the purported lack of standing of wrongdoers to resist forcible sanctions, on the one hand, and the question of whether the use of sanctions without a prior ruling ('unnecessary sanctions') is consistent with law's capacity to claim or possess legitimate authority, on the other. The question of standing is ultimately justified by one's view of the consequences of wrongdoing (ie, whether the liability produced by wrongdoing includes a certain kind of disability). The question of the legitimacy of unnecessary sanctions is answered by reflection on the nature of authority and its connection to law. There is no necessary inconsistency between wrongdoers' lack of standing to resist unnecessary sanctions and the legal system's inability to claim or possess legitimate authority to use unnecessary sanctions against wrongdoers. It is possible for wrongdoers to lack standing to make certain claims all the while the remedial authority of their legal order is in question because it relies on unnecessary sanctions.

Second, there is an additional and more substantive moral reason linked to equality that supports the practice of rulings. As noted above, some theorists have looked to Aristotle's understanding of equality to explain private law, but have updated Aristotle's conception of equality so that the normative loss of the claimant and the normative gain of the defendant are understood in Kantian terms of right and duty. Other scholars understand private law as a regime of equal freedom and reciprocal limits that prevent one individual from being in charge of another.[40] In Hobbes' case, unilateral assertions of private power lack authority precisely because they implicitly deny the equality of legal subjects that legal institutions make possible.[41] Across these views there is general agreement that when a court orders a remedy to address a wrong, part of what it does is restore a normative equality that the wrong compromised. The beneficiary of the restoration is the claimant, whose standing as a moral equal is affirmed by the court's ruling.

Private law scholars have not given similar attention to developing a positive account of how the defendant's blighted moral status might be restored through remedial law, other than to assume that by ordering the defendant to provide a remedy, the defendant is appropriately stripped of a wrongful or unjust gain.[42] I tentatively suggest that a further reason to support rulings independently of practical considerations has to do with the opportunity for redemption they offer defendants. Remedial orders can be understood as courts' attempt to allow wrongdoers to redeem themselves and reassert their moral standing as equals. Orders allow wrongdoers to acknowledge their transgressions publicly by participating in the remedy that cures them. With the issuance of an order to remedy wrongdoing, the court invites the defendant to repair the normative breach in the claimant–defendant relationship caused by the wrong.

law). To be clear, neither Aristotle nor Weinrib condemns rulings in favour of a sanctions-only approach to private law. But it is conceivable that a sceptic might deploy selectively some of their premises, in the way suggested in the text, to resist the account of rulings on offer.

[40] A Ripstein, *Private Wrongs* (Cambridge, MA, Harvard University Press, 2016).

[41] E Fox-Decent, 'Unseating Unilateralism' in L Austin and D Klimchuk (eds), *Private Law and the Rule of Law* (Oxford, Oxford University Press, 2014) 116.

[42] Important exceptions include E Encarnacion, 'Corrective Justice as Making Amends' (2014) 62 *Buffalo Law Review* 451; L Radzik, 'Tort Processes and Relational Repair' in J Oberdiek (ed), *Philosophical Foundtions of the Law of Torts* (Oxford, Oxford University Press, 2014) 231.

As James Penner suggests in his contribution to this volume, usually the morally appropriate first thing for a good-faith wrongdoer to do after committing a wrong, independently of the law, is apologise.[43] Of course, morally and legally, much more than an apology may be appropriate to properly acknowledge and take responsibility for the wrong. But a genuine apology at least puts the good-faith wrongdoer on the path to redemption by admitting responsibility and demonstrating willingness to repair the injury as well as the relationship with the sufferer of the wrong. Of course, complying with a ruling is not necessarily intended by the wrongdoer as an apology aimed at normative repair. For some litigants, complying with a ruling may be regarded as simply the cost of doing business. Many defendants will comply with the relevant order simply because they know they are liable to sanction if they do not. Nonetheless, as Smith notes, orders give defendants new reasons for action.

For good-faith defendants who wish to repair their relationship with the claimant and restore their standing in the community, voluntary compliance with a court order can serve much the same function as an apology, or it may supplement and reinforce an actual apology. Compliance demonstrates solicitude toward the claimant and a willingness to be held accountable publicly for one's default. For good-faith wrongdoers, it is important that the order is determined publicly and by a court of law, since this gives them an objectively fair and transparent means of making amends. This may be true of garden-variety individual wrongdoers who, through a moment's inadvertence, cause harm they deeply regret. And, in more dramatic cases, such as those involving religious or other organisations whose members have been found liable for historical abuses, the public aspect of court rulings and subsequent compliance offers them the opportunity to repair relations with their victims and wider communities. Good-faith wrongdoers would not be so served by a legal regime that imposed sanctions without rulings.

Even in the case of recalcitrant wrongdoers who comply for at best mixed motives of duty and interest, there is reason to think their compliance has value. While the defendant's motives may be mixed, their compliance can still be interpreted as a voluntary act, and to that extent it may have redemptive value. Our moral duties commonly align with our self-interest (eg, duties of friendship), but that does not bar them from being moral duties. Because compliance is voluntary notwithstanding the prospect of sanction, the defendant's agency is engaged. By respecting the authority of the court and obeying its ruling, the defendant voluntarily participates in a public process that aims at justice through normative repair, and therefore the defendant may be credited for their contribution to the justice private law makes possible.

The potentially redemptive quality of rulings arguably contributes to the authority courts may claim or possess when they issue orders. By providing wrongdoers with a public and institutional vehicle for making amends, rulings let wrongdoers demonstrate both fidelity to law and a substantive concern for the wrong or injustice they caused. Through this demonstration, wrongdoers can rehabilitate, or begin to rehabilitate, their standing in the community. To the wrongdoing legal subject who faces a ruling and asks 'But, how can this be law for me?' there is an evident reply: 'The ruling

[43] Penner, ch 8 in this volume.

is law for you because it both remedies a harmful wrong you produced and because it lets you take authorship of the rehabilitation of your character and standing in our community.'

IV. Conclusion

If Smith is right that rulings, and rulings alone, possess directive authority, this idea will provide a wellspring for jurisprudential reflection for decades to come. A possible reason Smith soft-pedals the jurisprudential implications of his account is that his justification of rulings is 'normatively inert', in that rulings are viewed as mere means that can be replaced by sanctions at no moral cost.[44] As a consequence, Smith's justification of rulings is in tension with the legitimate authority law claims or possesses, since this justification is consistent with legal systems' elimination of rulings and using force or sanctions unnecessarily against defendants.

I also sketched an internal and moralised account of rulings that resists replacing rulings with sanctions, even if doing so were practicable. The moralised theory takes on board Smith's view of rulings as an instance of directive authority, but it adds a justification that helps rulings to actually have legitimate authority as well as claim it. This account of orders sits congenially with Smith's otherwise moralised conception of private law, one that takes seriously law's self-understanding of its practices. And, if the reader will forgive me for ending with what may be cheating, in his last email to me, where he responded to my abstract, Steve quipped with his characteristic blend of encouragement and enthusiasm, 'I like it!'

[44] John Gardner famously described legal positivism as 'normatively inert': J Gardner, 'Legal Positivism: 5½ Myths' (2001) 46 *American Journal of Jurisprudence* 199, 202.

8

The Continuity Thesis: The Gift that Fails to Keep on Giving

JAMES PENNER*

I. Introduction

My current impression, doubtless underinformed, is that there are as many versions of the 'continuity thesis' as there are scholars who purport to endorse it.[1] Stephen Smith's assault on the thesis, at least in so far as it aims to explicate remedies for wrongs, aka breaches of duty, is tantalising in part because his suggestion is that we not only could do without the continuity thesis but that its embrace will almost certainly lead us astray. My aim here is neither Linnaean, to sketch a genera and species overview of the varieties of the thesis that we find, nor to endorse my own version of it so as to displace others. My aim is to consider Smith's objections to it and also to bring into relief a central tension in the thesis, which I have discussed before,[2] which is how the law should respond to three different aspects of any breach of duty: its results, its normal effects and its consequences.[3] To my mind, much of the difficulty in applying the continuity thesis so as to specify a remedy for a breach of duty results from a failure to distinguish these three. I will argue that Smith's consideration of the thesis helps to bring these distinctions into sharp relief. In particular, Smith's work shows how indeterminate the thesis is regarding duties to compensate for consequential loss. With regret, I find myself believing that the most prominent exponent of the continuity thesis, John Gardner,[4] wrongly held that the thesis was primarily concerned with damages for consequential loss.

* Thanks to Mala Chaterjee, Mark Crawford, Evan Fox-Decent, David Froomkin, Duncan Horne, Arthur Lau, Barbara MacDonald, Daniel Markovitz, Ketan Ramakrishnan, Sandy Steel and Rob Stevens for very helpful comments and suggestions.

[1] See, eg, S Steel,'Compensation and Continuity' (2020) 26 *Legal Theory* 250, for a discussion of some of the versions.

[2] J Penner, 'Don't Crash into Mick Jagger when He is Driving his Rolls Royce: Liability in Damages for Economic Loss Consequent upon a Personal Injury' in PB Miller and J Oberdiek (eds), *Civil Wrongs and Justice in Private Law* (Oxford, Oxford University Press, 2020) 253, 261–66.

[3] A modification of von Wright's famous distinction between results and consequences; see section V of this chapter.

[4] First set out in J Gardner, 'What is Tort Law For? Part 1. The Place of Corrective Justice' (2011) 30 *Law and Philosophy* 1, and reprinted with modifications in J Gardner, *Torts and Other Wrongs* (Oxford, Oxford University Press, 2019) ch 2. It is the latter reprinted text that will be cited hereinafter.

II. The Continuity Thesis

Such a simple idea. My reasons not to smash your vase do not lose their significance for me when I happen to smash it. I was wrong to smash it because it was yours. Those same reasons, not to deprive you of your vase, are also reasons for me to replace it. We could state the general form of the continuity thesis as follows:

> My reasons for not violating your rights are also reasons to make the world going forward, following that violation, most compatible with the world in which the rights were not violated in the first place.

In the smashed vase example, that is the world in which you have a replacement vase. This simple idea is even more obviously applicable to obligations voluntarily undertaken. If I agree to meet you in the pub at 5pm, but am delayed for some reason so that I cannot get there until 5:15pm, I should show up at 5:15pm, as that is the next best thing to showing up on time. Doing so brings the world going forward as close as it can be to the world where I showed up at 5pm.

Framed in terms of rights,[5] my obligation to replace the vase or show up at 5:15pm simply reflects the same right that you had that I not smash the vase in the first place, or your right that I turn up on time. The breach of the right–duty relationship between us does not cause that right–duty relationship to evaporate; rather, it continues but with a variation in content.[6] As Ripstein frames the point,[7] a right is a constraint on the behaviour of others. That constraint binds a person both prior to and after his wrong, although that constraint manifests itself differently following the wrong.

What is there not to like? For Stephen Smith, quite a lot.

III. Smith's Objections to the Continuity Thesis

The main thrust of Smith's magisterial *Rights, Wrongs, and Injustices*,[8] is that paying attention to remedial law, in particular the distinctions between different kinds of causes of action and the orders courts will make in response to their successful proof, is essential for understanding the structure of private law more generally. These orders respond to what he calls 'rights-threats', 'wrongs' and 'injustices'. In the case of rights-threats, the claimant will, in general, be awarded specific relief. 'Rights-threats' are cases where the law enforces the primary right–duty relationship between the parties, requiring the fulfilment of the defendant's duty. The classic examples are an order to the defendant to pay a sum due, specific performance of the duty to convey land under a contract for the

[5] A Ripstein, *Private Wrongs* (Cambridge MA, Harvard University Press, 2016) chs 8, 9; A Ripstein, 'Kantian Perspectives on Private Law' in AS Gold et al (eds), *The Oxford Handbook of the New Private Law* (Oxford, Oxford University Press, 2020) 69.

[6] Some of the *sturm und drang* in this area largely turns on questions concerning the individuation of reasons, rights and duties, which I address in section IV.

[7] Ripstein, *Private Wrongs* (n 5) 4, 11, 33–34.

[8] SA Smith, *Rights, Wrongs, and Injustices: The Structure of Remedial Law* (Oxford, Oxford University Press, 2019).

sale of land, an order that the claimant shall recover land from an unlawful occupier and an injunction requiring the defendant to cease committing a nuisance.[9] In this category Smith also includes 'substitutionary' awards, which provide the claimant with a money sum allowing her to purchase substitute performance.[10]

Remedies that address wrongs are, according to Smith, a subset of awards of damages. These include nominal damages, exemplary damages, pain and suffering damages, and others not all of which have agreed labels.[11] Excluded from this category of wrong-responsive remedies is an award of damages for consequential loss, which falls into the third category, 'injustices'.[12] Wrong-responsive damage awards are 'creative', in the sense that a wrongdoer has no substantive duty to pay any damages to the person she has wronged prior to any court order. She is merely *liable*, upon proof of the claimant's claim before a judge, to be ordered to pay a sum in damages to the claimant she has wronged. The court's order creates the duty to pay damages.[13] These awards are also 'creative' in a second sense. They are necessarily creative in virtue of the fact that the amounts of these awards cannot arithmetically be determined by the type and seriousness of the wrong outside rules and conventions framed as guidelines to judges. These damages awards are necessarily 'unliquidated' prior to judgment. In this sense wrong-responsive awards have the same structure as criminal punishments.[14] Prior to conviction, a criminal wrongdoer has no duty to punish himself, and the sentence he receives will be determined by a judge according to sentencing guidelines. Similarly, a civil wrongdoer has no duty to pay damages prior to a final court order following judgment; and in the same way that the seriousness of a crime does not tell us exactly what sort of punishment should ensue, wrong-responsive damages awards cannot be 'read off' some natural tariff – the amount of a damages award for a severed arm, for example, is necessarily conventional.[15]

As regards the distinction between rights-threats and wrongs, Smith points out that it is firmly established as a matter of English legal history:

> [Prior to] the abolition of the writs in the nineteenth century, the most important distinction within the English law of obligations [was] the distinction between actions to enforce existing rights (eg an action for a sum due) and actions to obtain redress for wrongs, that is, actions for damages (eg an action for damages for physical injury) – in short the distinction between rights and wrongs. The praecipe writs that initiated claims to enforce rights demanded that the defendants fulfill the asserted right or come to court to explain themselves. Thus, where defendants were sued for a sum due they could avoid going to court by paying the sum to

[9] ibid, ch 6. Smith carefully explains the differences in form of 'orders', traditionally given by courts of equity, and 'judgments' given by common law courts; see ibid 17–21. I will not seek to distinguish them here.

[10] Smith does not discuss remedies that trace their origins to what is known as Chancery's 'exclusive' jurisdiction, in particular remedies for breach of trust or breach of fiduciary duty: ibid, 14, fn 23. However, I would suggest that in the case of breach of trust, the orthodox 'accounting' principles enforce the primary rights of the beneficiaries to the trustee's performance, and so would fall within this first category of remedies addressing 'rights-threats': JE Penner, *The Law of Trusts*, 12th edn (Oxford, Oxford University Press, 2022) paras 13.10–13.25.

[11] Smith (n 8) 178–79, 206.

[12] ibid.

[13] ibid 191–202.

[14] Ibid 202–06.

[15] ibid 193–94, 198, 203–04, 207–08, 219–20.

> the 'demandant' (as the claimants in such actions were described). In contrast, the trespass writs that initiated claims for damages left defendants no option: they had to come to court. The defendant could not avoid court by paying damages because the 'complainant' (as they were called) had no right to damages. There was no demand that the defendant could satisfy because the complainant was not seeking to enforce a right, but, instead to obtain redress for a wrong.[16]

Smith's third category of awards respond to what he calls 'injustices', which include awards to reverse unjust enrichments, such as mistaken payments, and damages for consequential loss. In unjust enrichment cases, the injustice lies in the mistaken payee's gain at the payor's expense; in damages cases, the injustice arises because the loss suffered by the claimant is one for which the defendant is *responsible*. The latter cases turn on, or are explained in light of, our general theoretical views about the nature of responsibility,[17] and this covers cases outside cases of blameworthy conduct, for example 'necessity' cases such as *Vincent v Lake Erie Transportation Co*,[18] where a shipowner was liable to compensate a dock owner for damage to the dock to which the ship was tied without permission in order to avoid its destruction in a storm.

Smith is happy to agree that the continuity thesis

> easily explains orders to perform already breached contractual duties. My duty to pay you a contractually promised sum of money survives my failure to pay that sum on time. However, the reason that the continuity thesis easily explains such orders is that there is an obvious and straightforward sense in which it is possible for me to comply with my duty to pay you a sum of money notwithstanding that the payment may be late. Paying late is still paying.[19]

So the continuity thesis seems apt to deal with cases of rights-threats. For example, in the case of substitutionary damages, the defendant remains under the primary duty to perform, but is denied specific relief only for 'remedial law' reasons, such as because an order for specific relief would be difficult to monitor, would enforce a contract of personal service and so on. In this case, the order to pay damages is a kind of 'continuation' of the defendant's primary liability, because the duty to pay damages is intended to allow the claimant to obtain substitute performance, *funded* by the defendant but not *performed* by him.

Where, in Smith's view, the continuity thesis heads into trouble is when we get to wrongs and injustices. In addressing Smith's view, I shall put the injustice addressed in restitution cases to one side and focus on wrongs and the 'injustice' claim for damages for consequential loss. In these cases, Smith's primary complaint about the continuity thesis is that it fails to explain why a defendant is only *liable* to pay damages, subject to the court's making a damages award, rather than having a substantive post-wrong duty to pay the claimant a sum of money, aka a substantive duty to pay damages. So the crux of the matter appears to be Smith's claim that the continuity thesis would require there to be substantive legal duties to pay damages prior to any court order, and this is not, according to Smith, the positive law. Moreover, it would be an inferior positive law

[16] ibid 196–97 (footnotes omitted).
[17] ibid 265–69.
[18] *Vincent v Lake Erie Transportation Co*, 124 NW 221 (1910), discussed in Smith (n 8) 261.
[19] Smith (n 8) 184.

if it were in fact instantiated. In most cases, but especially in the case of damages for consequential loss, it would be, practically speaking, difficult if not impossible for the defendant to determine the amount he should pay. Second, it would almost certainly require the cooperation of the claimant, and that cooperation in many cases would not be forthcoming. If the law adopts a principle of 'ought implies can', imposing a legal duty to pay damages on the defendant would unfairly burden him with a task impossible to discharge, at least in those cases where the defendant could not know the content of the duty because he could not know in advance the consequential loss resulting from his action.

As to the positive law point, I find Smith's views here persuasive. I will deal with only two counterarguments, one from Sandy Steel and Robert Stevens, and one that derives from a point made by Arthur Ripstein.[20]

Steel and Stevens point out that many positive law duties require the participation of another for their discharge.[21] A payee has to accept payment, which is why an intending payor has a defence of tender. But as Smith points out,[22] there is no equivalent defence of tender or payment in the case of the supposed legal duty to pay damages, and if the cases of the need for another's cooperation stood on the same footing, one would expect there to be such a defence. But I agree, with one qualification, with this statement by Steel and Stevens: '[E]ven if the liability view is correct as a matter of the positive law, it does not follow that moral duties of corrective justice play no role in justifying awards of compensatory damages.'[23] The qualification is that 'compensatory damages' includes for Steel and Stevens damages for *consequential* loss, and, as I will go on to argue,[24] in agreement with Smith,[25] these damages are generally not, *pace* Gardner, justified by the continuity thesis. I do, however, agree with Steel and Stevens that the continuity thesis reflects a *moral* obligation of repair.[26]

In any case, it is perfectly allowable for the law to draw distinctions between cases of cooperation, providing a defence of tender in the case of contractual payments, whilst not providing such a defence in the case of payment of damages (although the rules of costs, which take into account offers of settlement or payment into court prior to judgment, have the same basic motivation). The more problematic aspect of the payment of damages case is the 'duty to enter into an agreement', that is, a duty to enter into a contract of settlement. As I wrote long ago,[27] in the moral realm, duties to enter into

[20] It seems to me to be a strength of Ripstein's account of the continuity thesis that it does not hold that a defendant comes under an immediate post-wrong duty to pay the claimant damages; rather, the defendant comes under a liability to pay damages if the claimant chooses to pursue the claim. See Ripstein, *Private Wrongs* (n 5) 271–75.

[21] S Steel and R Stevens, 'The secondary legal duty to pay damages.' (2020) 136 *LQR* 283, 285–86.

[22] Smith (n 8) 196.

[23] Steel and Stevens (n 21) 284.

[24] See section V.

[25] Smith (n 8) 189–91.

[26] It is unclear to me what Smith's ultimate view was in relation to a continuity thesis-minded *moral* obligation of repair, concerned as he was to establish the view that there was no legal duty of repair in 'wrongs' claims and consequential loss claims prior to a court's order. For discussion of some of Smith's earlier views on this, see J Penner and K Quek (2016). 'The Law's Remedial Norms' (2016) 28 *Singapore Academy of Law Journal* 768, 786–93. As far as I can tell, Smith did not revisit this issue in *Rights, Wrongs and Injustices*.

[27] JE Penner, 'Voluntary Obligations and the Scope of the Law of Contract' (1996) 2 *Legal Theory* 325.

agreements are common, in particular in families. The parents have a duty to coordinate their behaviour and agree who is going to collect the kids from school, who is making dinner this evening and so on. Where the defendant injures the claimant, both the claimant and the defendant have a moral obligation to enter into an agreement; and where this fails, both can be said to be at fault in the sense that they failed to fulfil their obligations, though one side may be more to blame for the failure than the other. But as far as I know, no one claims that either the claimant or the defendant has a *legal* obligation to enter into a contract of settlement; surely this tells against the claim that the defendant has a legal duty to pay damages, since the only way of complying with that duty is to enter into a contract of settlement. This thought is bolstered by the fact that a contract of settlement provides a complete defence to the claimant's claim, but the court's recognition of it *as a defence* does not amount to something like the court's declaration that the defendant paid the right, or even reasonably close to the right, amount of damages had the claim proceeded to judgment. I would argue that the law's refusing to recognise a duty to pay damages, or what is essentially the same thing, a duty to settle, and its imposing a liability structure instead, just is, on the continuity thesis, the next best thing given the nature of how the court process best works to vindicate the claimant's rights.[28]

Turning to Ripstein's objection, Ripstein asks rhetorically 'How can you settle a claim if you have no claim until a court orders a remedy?'[29] All I want to say about this is to point out that a claim is not itself a right, in particular not a right with a correlative duty. A legal claim in this context, what I have elsewhere called an 'action right',[30] is the power to initiate and pursue a legal action leading to a judgment and an award. A 'claim' can be settled in the sense that a contract of settlement will provide the defendant with a complete defence against the claimant's legal claim or right of action. It provides no support for the view that a defendant has a duty to pay damages.

There is a second feature of the continuity thesis to which Smith objects, which is that it makes irrelevant that in tort and breach of contract cases the defendant has committed a wrong. As Smith puts the point:

> [T]he wrongdoer's wrong is irrelevant to the continuity thesis' explanation of the substantive duty to pay damages. According to the thesis, the legal question facing wrongdoers after they have committed a wrong is the same question they faced before the wrong: What is the best way to comply with my substantive duty? The fact that they previously failed to comply with this duty changes the context, but normatively their situation is unchanged. A wrong is no different from any other action or change of circumstance that affects a substantive duty's content. … [Wrongs] may be part of the causal explanation for why the wrongdoer's duty takes the particular form that it takes (namely, to pay damages), but its wrongfulness is irrelevant. In Arthur Ripstein's words, a wrong 'is a datable event in the history of the world, but one that is entirely without normative significance'.[31]

At least part of Smith's objection here is, if I have understood him correctly, that the array of awards available in the case of wrongs, nominal damages, aggravated damages,

[28] See Ripstein, *Private Wrongs* (n 5) chs 8 and 9 for a Kantian explanation along these lines.
[29] ibid 280.
[30] Penner and Quek (n 26) 783.
[31] Smith (n 8) 183–84.

exemplary damages, pain and suffering damages, and so on, indicates that there is no sufficient 'continuity' between the nature of the duty breached and the nature of the court award.[32] To my mind, the same 'continuity' worry arises with his 'injustice' case of damages for consequential loss. This will be the subject of section V.

IV. The Individuation of Reasons, Duties and Rights

One source of 'noise' in the continuity thesis literature is the vexed issue of the individuation of reasons, duties and rights. Each is individuated by its content. If the content of a reason, duty or right A is distinguishable from the content of another reason, duty or right B, then the latter are different, or separate, reasons, duties or rights from the former. So much, so obvious. But reasons, rights and duties can be framed more or less generally. They can be specified in context, as when a reason to eat dinner can indicate a reason to go to this restaurant or to pick up the ingredients necessary for cooking at home. Duties may be discharged in different ways. If I have a duty to do X, I have a duty to choose the only way or one out of a range of possible ways of discharging the duty – for example, paying you the £10 I owe you with one £10 note or two £5 notes. It also does not follow from the fact that an obligation is disjunctive[33] that there is no priority between the disjuncts, for one disjunct may be unconditional while the other is not. So, if one has a disjunctive duty not to injure you or pay damages upon injuring you, the first disjunct is unconditional (which is not to say absolute) while the second disjunct is conditional on my failing to comply with the first. Similarly, I cannot pay you damages for breach until I have breached. Rights are even more problematic. A will theorist believes each right–duty relationship is coupled with a power–liability relationship (the right-holder having a power to waive the right), where an interest theorist does not. Moreover, some have contended[34] that rights should be individuated one-by-one with their correlative duties; while others, Raz most famously,[35] have contended that rights, being protected interests, can correlate with a range of duties.

So, as regards the continuity thesis, it is a matter of controversy what actually 'continues' to make the remedy the continuation of the breached duty. Is it the reason for the duty, the duty itself, or the right itself? I now do not believe there is a 'right' answer to

[32] John Oberdiek argues (J Oberdiek, 'Wrongs, Remedies, and the Persistence of Reasons: Re-Examining the Continuity Thesis' in H Psarras and S Steel (eds), *Private Law and Practical Reason: Essays on John Gardner's Private Law Theory* (Oxford, Oxford University Press, 2023) 161) that Smith's objection here, which is close or identical to ones made by others, can be countered by focusing upon the relationality between the injurer and the sufferer. His notion of relationality is that of Gardner's 'loose relationality', as described in J Gardner, *From Personal Life to Private Law* (Oxford, Oxford University Press, 2018). I have discussed this notion of Gardner's elsewhere: JE Penner, (2019). 'BOOK REVIEW: From personal life to private law, by John Gardner, Oxford, Oxford University Press, 2018' (2019) 10 *Jurisprudence* 300, 303–05. It is beyond the scope of this chapter to discuss the matter here, but I would maintain that this notion of relationality is insufficiently robust to explain the nature of the wrongdoer–victim relationship in such a way as to meet Smith's objection.

[33] 'Disjunctive' in the broad sense that the word 'or' can be employed in describing the situation. A person faced with whether or not he should or must breach a contractual duty then falls, if he does breach, under a duty to compensate.

[34] Me, once upon a time: JE Penner, 'The Analysis of Rights' (1997) 10 *Ratio Juris* 300.

[35] J Raz, 'Legal Rights' (1984) 4 *Oxford Journal of Legal Studies* 1.

this question, for the question of individuation here is always relative to context and the purpose of the explanation being sought. Very generally, one might say, as does Ripstein, that what is being sought is the 'rationale'[36] for regarding the remedy as an appropriate response to the wrong. The explanation of this rationale would perhaps have been best expressed without thinking about 'continuity' at all, since that seems to require we identify some thing, a right or reason or duty, that continues throughout. Framing the remedy as the 'next best thing' to do in the circumstances avoids this problem, for 'next best' concerns comparative equivalence, not identity. In other words 'continuity' means just what it says, that something continues, maintains its identity. Whereas 'next best' plainly states that next best is not best, so we are in the realm of comparative equivalence.

V. Results, Effects and Consequences

Smith distinguishes damages for pain and suffering, mental distress and other intangible harms, which fall into his second category of wrong-responsive remedies, on the basis that though they flow from the defendant's wrong, they are not 'losses' or losses of the kind addressed by compensatory awards, that is awards that compensate consequential losses.[37] In the interests of brevity I will use 'compensation' and 'compensatory' to refer to awards that respond to consequential loss. Whilst agreeing with Smith that the former are wrong-responsive and the latter injustice-responsive, I would frame the reason for this slightly differently, which turns on von Wright's famous distinction between results and consequences.[38] It is a result of my killing you that you die. If you do not die, I have not killed you. It may be a consequence of my killing you that I frustrate a contract of personal service you have with X. But this will obviously depend upon further facts – some such consequence, unlike the result, is not 'internal' to the concept of killing the way death is. But we should notice a third category, which I will call a 'normal effect', or just an 'effect', which is distinct from both a result and a consequence. It is not a result. So, for example, it is normally an effect of my killing you that your body loses temperature and rigor mortis sets in. But this is not inevitable: I might kill you by throwing you into an active volcano. But an effect normally arises upon the act without proof of further facts. Another way of putting this is to say that in the case of an effect, there is a 'natural' but *defeasible* connection of the effect to the result in question.

To draw upon an example I have used before,[39] imagine I negligently injure Mick Jagger, breaking his leg, so that he is prevented from going on tour with the Rolling Stones. The *result* of my failing to take care is Mick's broken leg. To make out his claim, Mick needs to establish that he was within my duty of care, and that my failure to take care led to the result that his leg was broken. No broken leg, no claim. Now, as a matter of corrective justice as understood in light of the continuity thesis, my first obligation

[36] Ripstein, *Private Wrongs* (n 5) 278–79.
[37] Smith (n 8) 249.
[38] GH von Wright, *Norm and Action: A Logical Inquiry* (New York, The Humanities Press, 1963) 39–41.
[39] Penner (n 2).

must be to address the broken leg itself. That is where my primary 'duty to repair' must lie. I must then attend to the normal effects of this wrong, and here this would be Mick's pain and suffering. Only thirdly should I attend, if I should attend at all, to Mick's consequential losses.

John Gardner and Joseph Raz disagree with this approach. Gardner argues that the continuity thesis *does not* explain 'general damages', such as damages for pain and suffering, for these are 'not reparative in the strict sense'.[40] Because of this they are not a direct reflection of the continuity thesis: their rationale is rather 'mainly to assuage frustration, resentment' and so on, so as to take 'the heat out of claimant-defendant conflicts'.[41] So, for Gardner:

> It matters that the payment of general damages takes a quasi-reparative form, being paid by or on behalf of the tortfeasor, being pegged to results or consequences of the tort, being quantifed (notionally) according to the severity of the result or consequence in question, and so on. It matters, in other words, that some of the implications of the continuity thesis are preserved in the norms regulating general damages even though the continuity thesis does not strictly apply. Thereby some of the placatory social meaning of effecting reparation according to the continuity thesis spills over; general damages bask in the reflected glory of special damages.[42]

Raz takes a similar line.[43] He claims that many cases where the law awards damages are not justified by the continuity thesis, which Raz calls the 'conformity principle'. To make the point Raz provides the following example:

> Suppose I undertook to make it possible for you to get to Australia for your mother's wedding (I may be your employer, and I promised timely leave and the cost of the ticket). Having failed to do that, I offer you a week's holiday in Brighton as compensation. This may be a sensible way to mollify hurt feelings, but it does nothing to bring you closer to sharing in your mother's great day, and therefore nothing to get me closer to fulfilling my undertaking. It may be justified, and something like it may be required, but it is not required or justified by the conformity principle.[44]

A number of things can be said about these views. First, Gardner and Raz would seem to agree with Smith that the continuity thesis does not justify what Smith calls 'wrong-responsive' damages awards, such as nominal damages, aggravated damages, exemplary damages, pain and suffering damages, and so on, damages which is some sense measure the defendant's wrongdoing. Second, the duty of repair on these accounts, doing the next best thing, seems to encompass only what might be called 'material restoration' awards, such as money to replace destroyed property, money for medical bills that go to restoring the claimant's body, money to replace lost earnings, and so on. Other damages awards are not 'reparative in the strictest sense', as Gardner puts it. Third, I do not see how the basking of non-reparative damages such as general damages in the glory of special damages is supposed to work, or is justifiable. I take it one of the central planks

[40] Gardner, *Torts and Other Wrongs* (n 4) 74.
[41] ibid 74–75.
[42] Ibid 75.
[43] J Raz, 'Personal Practical Conflicts' in P Baumann and M Betzler (eds), *Practical Conflicts: New Philosophical Essays* (Cambridge, Cambridge University Press, 2009) 172, 192–93.
[44] ibid 192.

of Smith's objection to the applicability of the continuity thesis is this way of presenting non-reparative damages, damages which are not 'material restoration' awards, as something like reparative awards, which causes us to misunderstand their nature. Fourth, in the realm of compensation, Gardner's and Raz's versions of the continuity thesis seem not to distinguish between compensatory awards that more or less work to reverse the result of the wrong (the replacement vase, the mended broken leg) and those that compensate for consequential loss (the lost earnings). Finally, it is worth remembering Gardner's paradigm case of the continuity thesis, the 'beach case': I promise to take the kids to the beach today but an emergency intervenes so that I cannot do so. My 'next best' duty on the continuity thesis is, say, to take them to the beach tomorrow. This is not a compensatory, consequential loss-based next-best duty at all. It is a *substitute performance* next-best duty. So it is unclear why Gardner wants to narrow the continuity thesis's range primarily to compensatory damages.

It seems to me that Smith's *Rights, Wrongs, and Injustices* is mostly important for our understanding of the continuity thesis because it allows us to distinguish awards that reflect the results and effects of our wrongs from those that are compensatory.

The continuity thesis has the bite that it has because it is regarded first and foremost as a *moral* principle, a principle we can discern apart from whatever the law is doing. Its relevance to the law is that it can serve as a justificatory principle for the awards the courts make in response to at least some of the cases that come before it. Any such justification will therefore be hostage to what we understand our moral duties of repair to be.

Let me propose an alternative way of pursuing the nature of the continuity thesis. As a matter of raw morality apart from the law, we first acknowledge ourselves as having what Gardner calls 'basic responsibility':

> Basic responsibility is what it sounds like. It is an ability. More fully, it is the ability and propensity to have and to give self-explanations in the currency of reasons. The ability and the propensity are but two sides of the same coin. As beings who are able to respond to reasons we cannot avoid being disposed to respond to them. There is nowhere to hide from them.[45]

It seems to me that the continuity thesis is an outworking, in part, of our basic responsibility. As such it requires us to respond appropriately to our wrongdoings. And, as I have suggested, this requires us to distinguish between the results, effects and consequences of our wrongdoing. So, returning to the Mick Jagger example, as a matter of morality apart from the law, it would seem to me that my first obligation to Mick is to acknowledge my carelessness and apologise to him. This has nothing to do with mollifying Mick's hurt feelings or assuaging any frustration, resentment or other kinds of ill-feeling that afflict him. Or rather, thinking so gets the matter the wrong way round. An apology can and often does, as a matter of commonsense morality apart from the law, effect a restoration or repair of the normative relationship between wrongdoer and the one who suffers the wrong, without further ado. Compensating the sufferer is often not even necessary, or would be counterproductive. This is also very much a part of our commonsense morality. To the extent that an apology does this, then it *follows* that only a sufferer who fails in their moral basic responsibility would continue harbouring feelings of resentment and

[45] J Gardner, 'The Negligence Standard: Political Not Metaphysical' (2017) 80 *Modern Law Review* 1, 7. See also J Gardner, 'Nearly Natural Law' (2007) 52 *American Journal of Jurisprudence* 1.

so on. So if the goal of a wrongdoer is to repair first and foremost the *normative* breach in his relationship with the sufferer, as opposed to addressing its material results, effects and consequences, an apology makes the world going forward, *normatively speaking*, one that is least incompatible with the world where the wrong never happened.

Of course a wrongdoer ought in many cases to do more than simply apologise. There are those material results, effects and consequences of his wrong, after all. The primary continuity thesis response must be to restore the normative breach by way of apology, and this may properly be accompanied by, and in some cases must be accompanied by, the wrongdoer's attending to those material results, effects and consequences. Mick's broken leg should come first, as that was the result of the wrong. If that can be restored, in a sense the wrong is fully repaired.[46] As to pain and suffering, this natural effect so consistently coincides with the result that this must be attended to as well. As to the other awards that Smith identifies as 'wrong-responsive', they are in one sense symbolic, but this does not deprive them of any continuity thesis grounding. As Smith puts it, these are in some sense measures, in money, of the defendant's wrongdoing. In repairing the normative breach, they serve much like an apology; but unlike an apology, they do so indirectly by way of a court order. This is why the court's judgment and setting of the amount of the award is so important in such cases. A good-faith defendant seeking to do the right thing morally, to show that he takes his wrong seriously and wishes to do something appropriately material to signify that he does so, is served by the law when it makes such an award.[47]

Finally, damages for consequential losses. Unlike Gardner, and with Smith, I think damages for consequential loss are very difficult to justify on any version of the continuity thesis. As Gardner argues, one cannot determine what the continuity thesis requires as a matter of repair unless one understands the nature of the primary obligation that was breached.[48] To put the point in my own terms, one cannot apply the continuity thesis unless one understands the interest or value that the primary obligation was there to serve or protect. On this view, understanding a claim for consequential loss requires understanding that these claims are almost always a matter of a 'contractual' or 'market' connection, in the sense that they are secondary economic losses arising as a consequence of the breach of the primary obligation. In the Mick Jagger case, these are the losses arising from the frustration of his contract to go on tour with the Rolling Stones. To compensate him for these losses is to tie his legal interest in his contractual performance (but not of those of his fans under that contract) to his legal interest in his leg. It is a policy choice the law makes. Notice that if the continuity thesis is capaciously construed, it could equally tie Mick's fans' interests in Mick's performance to Mick's leg, via their contract with him. This is just the problem of pure economic loss. In principle, the continuity thesis supports liability for pure economic loss. Another way to put this point is that results and effects are localised by the nature of the wrong itself to the holder of the right not to be wronged, but consequences are by their very nature not so localised. This point is brought out exceptionally clearly by Smith, with his claim that

[46] I find it suggestive that in explaining the continuity thesis, Steel takes as his stock example of repair the replacement of a lost limb with an artificial one. See Steel (n 1) 251.

[47] See Fox-Decent, ch 7 in this volume, for an extended elaboration of this thought.

[48] Gardner, *Torts and Other Wrongs* (n 4) 66–68.

liability for consequential loss is a matter of attributing *responsibility* for a loss occasioned by a wrong. In my view, whereas liabilities to repair the results and effects of a wrong flow pretty much automatically on the continuity thesis when an apology alone will not fulfil the task of healing the normative breach, it is always a tricky question, a tricky question of responsibility, to determine what further interests, in terms of consequential losses, any right protects.

Gardner himself addresses the Mick Jagger example, but I do not think his response is entirely adequate. He frames it in terms of a 'distributive' question. He says:

> And yet the Jagger example also shows how quickly things can get out of hand … It is one question what duties I might have towards Jagger. It is another question what help others, including the law, should give me in upholding those duties. The second (distributive) question immediately raises problems of proportionality. 'Full' recovery of losses, as John Goldberg puts it, may sometimes exceed 'fair' recovery. The law already acknowledges this fact in remoteness of damage, mitigation, and contributory negligence cases. It would take only modest changes in the law's remoteness-of-damage doctrine to acknowledge the same fact in the Jagger case. The doctrine at the moment assigns the risk of an unforeseeably high-value accident victim to the defendant. By contrast, it assigns to the claimant the risk of an unforeseeably high-value accident type. These are ordinary choices of local legal policy. They clearly could have been otherwise, and are otherwise in some legal systems.[49]

Whilst I agree with the spirit of this, I do not think that '[i]t would take only modest changes in the law's remoteness-of-damage doctrine' to deal with the Mick Jagger case. Being put out of action for a while is a clearly foreseeable consequence of a personal injury like a broken leg, and losing wages or the equivalent is a clearly foreseeable consequence of being put out of action for a while. Nor is this an especially lucrative contract *for Mick*;[50] that is not the implication of the example. The upshot is that the problem here is the continuity thesis itself, and how we choose to understand and apply it. And so I agree with Smith that here, individual renderings of the continuity thesis must reflect underlying ideas of responsibility, that is must tell us why, for example, the law of negligence makes us responsible for the market position of defendants in a society where those market positions are in many cases at least very arguably a matter of luck and social inequality, rather than owing to desert or merit. I should add that, in any case, market value is only a very inadequate proxy measure of the true or 'objective' value of things. Markets do not establish the 'objective' value of anything. What markets do, amongst other things, is aggregate the subjective preferences of those in the market; the market is not concerned with objective value, otherwise there would be many fewer things on the market that manifest execrable taste.

VI. Conclusion

I hoped to have given good reasons for supporting Smith's claim that in cases of wrongs and injustices giving rise to claims for consequential loss, the continuity thesis should

[49] ibid 99–100 (footnotes omitted).
[50] As was the case in *The Naxos* [1972] 1 Lloyd's Rep 149.

not be read so as to generate a secondary *legal* duty to pay damages prior to a court award. At the same time, very much drawing upon what I take to be the intuitions underlying his incisive distinctions between the various different grounds for damages awards for wrongs and for consequential losses, I hope also to have shown that the continuity thesis is, one might say, a fairly clear moral principle, whose guidance is reasonably determinate in addressing the result and effects of a breach of an obligation, where what the law awards can be seen to track our moral duties of repair reasonably closely. But I have also contended that the continuity thesis is largely indeterminate when we address damages for consequential loss. That is not a tragedy for the law of course, for one of the main things the law does is to make determinate, or crystallise into rules, what morality counsels us to do. But in doing so we must always acknowledge the very many moral choices the law makes in so doing, a point I have emphasised.

9

Monstrans de droit, Petition of Right, and Liability for Crown Debt

JOSHUA GETZLER*

This chapter in memory of my friend and colleague Stephen Smith investigates the history of common law remedies for the assertion of debt obligations, notably against the Crown as a subjective person as well as before the Crown as an objective adjudicator and enforcer.

Smith understood a court order to pay a debt generally as replicating a primary contractual duty to pay a specified sum of money. A court might transform a breached duty to pay a sum certain into an adapted duty to pay as best possible after the due date, as a continuation of the original duty. The final curial order to pay then replicated that second, transformed duty. Such a replicative order might be conjoined to a substitutionary order, creating a further liability to pay, for example in damages estimated by the court. A sum awarded to compensate consequential loss following on breach was a stereotypical creative liability, which might be called a 'judgment debt' but really was quite different from a substantive debt set up by the parties as primary duty prior to any court order. In all cases, it made sense to see the issuance of remedies as the exercise of a power by the court, acting on a liability of the obligor, the party subject to the original obligation, on the motion of the obligee.[1]

The elegant Smithian theory, bringing the remedial powers of the court to the fore, has captured the imagination of fellow scholars of private law.[2] I can proudly claim to have been present at or near the theory's genesis. On a perfect Oxford spring day over a decade ago, Steve took the afternoon with me to discuss the historical shape of law judgments and equitable orders, and to think through how those remedies interacted. Steve wanted his models to rest on sound evidence, and he had read carefully into the historical sources.[3] It was a delight to hear his arguments unfold that day, and then to

* My warm thanks to John Baker, Will Bateman, Mitchell Cleaver, Lionel Smith, and David Winterton, for invaluable help and advice.

[1] SA Smith, 'Duties, Liabilities and Damages' (2012) 125 *Harvard Law Review* 2012; SA Smith, *Rights, Wrongs, and Injustices: The Structure of Remedial Law* (Oxford, Oxford University Press, 2019) esp 96–103.

[2] D Winterton and T Pilkington, 'Examining the Structure of Remedial Law' (2021) 84 *MLR* 1137, helpfully capturing the debate to date.

[3] Smith, *Rights, Wrongs, and Injustices* (n 1) 30–47.

see his brilliant elaborations etched out in the years that followed. It was one of many truly memorable days in Steve's company, which began when we first embarked on our research as graduate students together at the same college last century.

I. Suing the Crown: The Problem of Debt

One way to probe the Smithian approach to judicial remedy is to take it into new terrain. Does his model map onto the historical law of debt payments by the sovereign Crown? To answer this question we must scope the application of the old common law petitions of right laid by subjects to claim Crown debts. Such petitions provided the framework for asserting claims against the sovereign person who could not formally be impleaded in his own courts nor subjected to coercive judicial order; the immunity of the king's person applied also to the Crown as a metaphysical office. There were various routes to lay a petition before the king requesting a remedy, whether before Parliament, the Chancery, the Court of King's Bench, the Council, or some other forum closely associated with the king's government.[4] Where the action in question would validly have lain against a normal subject, the claim against the king was known as a 'petition of right'; and a strong expectation grew from 1300 that the Crown should normally permit the claim to be heard and remedied as if it were an ordinary action, as a voluntary submission to jurisdiction. Where there was no possible analogy to a mandatory duty, as when the Crown was called upon to confirm a promised gift or franchise relied upon or hoped for by the subject, then a so-called 'petition of grace' was laid. A vested right to property withheld from the subject was seen as a stronger claim than an action to enforce an executory or precatory obligation, and as such could be claimed by a summary version of the petition of right known as *monstrans de droit*, a demonstration or plea of right. Afforcing these originating actions, a *mandamus* writ might subsequently be moved against a Crown agent, often the Attorney-General, in order to ensure that a Crown duty to pay or convey was performed by a relevant official. Alternatively, *liberate* writs could compel payment by instruction to a Treasury official, issued by the Barons of Exchequer. Equitable suits, as well as legal proceedings, could be brought against the Crown, for example to enforce or release mortgages, or to respect beneficial interests applying to an escheated estate. This jurisprudence developed in the wake of the Crown Debts Act of 1541, balancing Crown priority in debt recovery with defences.[5] The equity courts early made simple decrees recommending that the king act, or release, without probing how the petitionary procedures might be adapted to bind the king's conscience in his own person. Ultimately these equitable procedures merged with the common law petition of right. This complicated petitionary system lasted down to the 1860s, when a series of statutory reforms subjected the

[4] Sources for the history that follows include W Clode, *Law and Practice of Petition of Right* (London, Clowes, 1887) 1–153; F Relf, *The Petition of Right* (Minneapolis, MN, University of Minnesota Press, 1917); L Ehrlich, *Proceedings against the Crown, 1216–1377* (Oxford, Clarendon Press, 1921) 54; W Holdsworth, 'The History of Remedies Against the Crown' (1922) 38 *LQR* 141, 280; MF Spungin, 'A History of the Petition of Right from the Seventeenth Century' (BLitt thesis, University of Oxford, 1959).

[5] 33 Hen 8, c 39, ss 37–58; *Pawlett v Attorney General* (1667/8) Hardres 465, 145 ER 550 (Ex).

Crown directly to obligations as if it were a normal subject. The legislative scheme, developed earlier in Commonwealth jurisdictions, provided mandatory rules in place of the older constitutional method whereby the Crown *usually* accepted liability for debts contracted with private persons – unless it saw good policy grounds to refuse liability.[6]

The history of claims against the Crown for debt at common law, before the reforming statutes, thus reveals an interesting conundrum, whereby the Crown as a judicial public person serves as registrar and adjudicator of an obligational or proprietary claim, and yet as an executive public person stands simultaneously as a counterparty to that claim. Is such dualism consistent with the rule of law – to be both adjudicator and one of the adjudicated?[7] And if political concerns overtly inform judicial enforcement of public debts, does that support (or exceed) the Smithian theory that remedies are often replicative and creative, and do not simply 'rubber-stamp' prior substantive duties?[8]

II. '[A]n Obligational or Proprietary Claim' – Damages versus Debt

The word 'proprietary' was slipped into the last paragraph as a deliberate signifier, for pre-modern common lawyers might be hard pressed to distinguish a claim to collect a sum certain raised upon an obligation, from a claim to the proceeds or transfer of some property. The blurring of obligational and proprietary categories was found most intensely in the form of action for debt, which by the late thirteenth century was used extensively to recover fixed money sums due under loan, sale, rent, pledge or bond.[9] A like union of obligational and proprietary enforcement may be detected in the early feudal actions of account, replevin, distress and waste, and also in the later trespassory actions of detinue, trover, conversion, and assumpsit. Through such personal actions, the law was often concerned to effect the recovery of assets or their value, where title had moved to the obligor subject to some reciprocal obligation. The court's judgment might state that the obligor was liable to pay a liquidated sum equivalent to the value of the asset vested with the obligor, whether on an objective measure set by the court or according to the subjective estimate of the parties set by an accompanying agreement.[10]

[6] Petitions of Right Act 1860 (UK); Crown Proceedings Act 1947 (UK), precursed by Claims Against the Government Act 1866 (Qld), Claims Against the Crown Acts 1861–76 (NSW). See further J McLean, *Searching for the State in British Legal Thought* (Cambridge, Cambridge University Press, 2012) 131–64, 204–40; J Getzler, 'Personality and Capacity: Lessons from Legal History' in T Bonyhady (ed), *Finn's Law: An Australian Justice* (Sydney, Federation Press, 2016) 147; W Bateman, *Public Finance and Parliamentary Constitutionalism* (Cambridge, Cambridge University Press, 2020) 63–80.

[7] cf *Dr Bonham's Case* (1610) 8 Co Rep 10, 777 ER 638, articulating the principle *nemo judex in causa sua*, explored further in R Helmholz, 'Bonham's Case, Judicial Review, and the Law of Nature' (2009) 1 *J Legal Analysis* 325.

[8] cf Smith, *Rights, Wrongs, and Injustices* (n 1) 1–16.

[9] F Pollock and FW Maitland, *The History of English Law before the Time of Edward I* (Cambridge, Cambridge University Press, 1895) ii, 208–14.

[10] See further S Stoljar, *History of Contract at Common Law* (Canberra, ANU Press, 1975) 3–15; AWB Simpson, *A History of the Common Law of Contract: The Rise of the Action of Assumpsit* (Oxford, Clarendon Press, 1975) 9–135.

The various narratives or common counts explained why a debt *sur contract* had arisen by the parties' prior conduct. Such claims could be contrasted with debt *sur obligation*, where a covenant deed or bond had been executed stipulating an agreed debt performance. This mirrored the terrain of classical Roman law, deploying the condiction action to enforce the return of an asset or its value, whether in specie or in some fungible or cash equivalent, in order to satisfy the obligee's settled expectation of return for some original act of transfer to the obligor on terms, contrasting with stipulations enforcing unilateral formal promises independent of exchange.[11] At the head of the common law tradition, Glanvill (around 1187–89) overtly draws analogies between the English debt and covenant actions and the Roman real and stipulatory contracts.[12]

Oliver Wendell Holmes traced an alternative non-Roman genesis of English debt. He saw the earliest common law debt actions as emerging from procedures to repress felonious takings of property, whereby holders were put on proof in the country to show a rightful descent of their title to goods or land.[13] On accusation of a wrongful taking or withholding, the holder of an asset would make a compurgation, 'waging his law' in the sense of invoking friendly self-informing witnesses to vouch for the truth of his oath-taking defence of a decent origin of his possession, sometimes by gift or finding, more commonly by voluntary transaction. This procedure developed into a contractual action, where a plaintiff might bring suit or *secta* swearing that a transfer had been conditioned on a reciprocal obligation requiring the defendant to pay a price, so asserting that a debt was owed. In this context, the suit did not address the defendant's title in order to prove or negate a felonious taking, but rather adduced a liability for unperformed payment under a contract. The defendant would then face the jeopardy of finding compurgators to support his denial of, or defence to, liability.[14] If proved or conceded, the debt claim made for an obligation on the person of the defendant to render a transfer of value in cash form, with the pleading showing the circumstances raising the debt *sur contract*, such as a sale or hire of land or goods, a bestowal of personal service, an executed loan, or a surety for the performance or title of another.

Thus, whether there was direct influence or not, English law debt functionally echoed the Roman condictions, covering many discrete sources of obligation, unified by the core pleading that a reciprocal liquid sum was due to the plaintiff from the patrimony of the defendant. Despite its cumbersome procedures of suit and compurgation, debt provided the key form of contractual action down to the late fourteenth century. The debt action then faded in importance, displaced by actions of covenant, account and assumpsit, which used formal writing, audit and jury trial respectively as superior

[11] Gaius, *Institutes*, 4.1.-9 et seq; Justinian, *Institutes*, 4.6; P Birks, *The Roman Law of Obligations* (Oxford, Oxford University Press, 2014) 27–36, 65–155.

[12] R de Glanvill, *The Treatise on the Laws and Customs of the Realm of England*, ed GDG Hall (London, Nelson, 1965) X, 116–32; D Ibbetson, *A Historical Introduction to the Law of Obligations* (Oxford, Oxford University Press, 2001) 17–21; J Hudson, *The Oxford History of the Laws of England*, vol II: *871–1216* (Oxford, Oxford University Press, 2012) 696–703.

[13] OW Holmes Jr, *The Common Law* (London, Macmillan, 1882) 251–88.

[14] Simpson (n 10) 137–44.

modes of proof of payment obligations.[15] A turning point came with *Slade's Case*,[16] which provided that any contractual agreement hitherto sounding in debt could be brought in the alternative as trespass on the case for assumpsit. The court 'commanded judgment to be entered for the plaintiff', covering payment for damage caused by non-performance as assessed by the jury, plus costs, thus in effect constituting the remedy after weighing the causative facts. The implication was that damage or harm to the claimant's fortune caused by contractual misfeasance now lay at the heart of voluntary liabilities; and this displaced the older mode, seeing debt as the expected return on an executed transfer or performance.

To put all of this in Smithian terms, the creative liability of damages-driven assumpsit was quite different from court discovery of a debt obligation. Under the debt form, parties brought suit to prove (or deny) that, in the opinion of witness-jurors, local people who knew the parties best, a sum certain was owed because that was what the parties had already likely set up. If the obligee was successful, the court would 'adjudge that the plaintiff should recover his whole debt and damages taxed by the court' or 'adjudge the debt proved and amerce for costs'; if not, 'the court adjudges that you take nothing by your writ but be amerced [pay costs], and that [the defendant] go quit'. In either case of judgment, the court purports to discover and maintain the status quo between the parties – who owes what to whom. By contrast, the assumpsit form involved the court in acting to create and impose liability and vary the parties' status after observing what had passed between them post-agreement. A general proof would be offered by plaintiff, showing that on such and such a day a consideration was offered (money or performance) with an expectation of reciprocity defined by agreement, and that no adequate return on the deal had been made, causing damage calling for redress; the defendant could then rebut. If the contract was proved, the court would 'enter judgment for the plaintiff' to 'recover damages and costs' as assessed *ex post*, which might be more or less than any prior agreed contractual exchange.[17] The court set the correct level of payment, not the parties.

III. Restitution of Property from, and Payment of Money by, the Crown

From the later eleventh century, any free subject in England could ask the king's courts to protect seisin in land, or to enforce the due performance of covenants and debts, in a claim brought against another of the king's subjects. The duty holder might be a lord who himself held court with mediate jurisdiction over the plaintiff as a manorial tenant,

[15] RC Palmer, *English Law in the Age of the Black Death, 1348–1381: A Transformation of Governance and Law* (Chapel Hill, NC, UNC Press, 1993) esp 64–78, 140–213, 328–64.

[16] *Slade v Morley* (1598–1602) 4 Co Rep 91, 76 ER 1072; Yelv 21, 80 ER 15; Moo KB 433, 467, 72 ER 677; JH Baker, *Baker and Milsom's Sources of English History: Private Law to 1750*, 2nd ed (Oxford, Oxford University Press, 2019) 460–79; AWB Simpson, 'The Place of Slade's Case in the History of Contract' (1958) 74 *LQR* 381; JH Baker, 'New Light on Slade's Case' (1971) 29 *CLJ* 51, 213; D Ibbetson, 'Sixteenth Century Contract Law: Slade's Case in Context' (1984) 4 *OJLS* 295.

[17] Examples of entries taken from Baker, *Baker and Milsom's Sources of English History* (n 16) 233–34, 475.

in which case the royal court action had qualities of a judicial review, requiring that right be done by lord to tenant within the subordinate feudal forum.[18] But there could also be a non-mediated protection of individual rights in the king's courts, arising from the Crown's core duties to give subjects their dues, to keep courts and officials within the law, and to maintain the peace of the realm. These were the rights common to all Crown subjects, that is, the common law.

It was more difficult to ask the king himself to surrender property or debt wrongly withheld from the subject by resort to law, whether feudal or common. The Court of Exchequer early had a jurisdiction to reckon and enforce the imposition of taxes, such as scutage or military imposts, but this was closer to administrative accounting than legal action.[19] Frederic Maitland adduced plentiful evidence that from around 1300, petitions were addressed to the king seeking redress when the king had failed to pay wages or otherwise honour contracts, or where it was alleged that the king's officers had wrongfully seized lands. Such matters touching the king's own affairs might be dealt with extra-legally in panels of notable barons and clerics advising the king, or be sent to a wider council of influential commoners. Petitionary councils often convened in Westminster Hall alongside the sittings of the established courts of law. Larger gatherings of lords, prelates, and commons might be called by the Crown to handle the most important petitionary business, including Crown requests for aids, a kind of petition from king to subjects. These gatherings were called *parlements* or occasions for speech and discussion; and as parliament came to meet regularly, it became a specially potent court with high political and adjudicative authority.[20]

The adjudication of petitions affecting the king's own interests overlapped with the jurisdiction of the *curia coram rege*, the court in the presence of the king, where a personalised and discretionary justice emanated from the king's person, guided by considerations of policy and favour as much as law or convention. There were curbs on the exercise of such a political or prerogative equity where the cause in the petition closely resembled the kind of private legal claims decided in the regular courts, pre-eminently contracts and conveyances. In the thirteenth century, the royal lawyers began searching for ways to uphold proprietary, promissory, and debt obligations directly touching the Crown, whilst respecting the king's special constitutional position that removed him from the forms of action and the modes of proof available to private litigants.

The starting principle was that one could not sue nor implead a lord in his own court, and this applied *a fortiori* to the Crown. Bracton in around 1230 puts this as follows:

> Among other things we must see who it is that ejects, a prince by virtue of his power or another in his name, or a judge who has decided improperly, or a private person. If it is the

[18] P Brand, 'The Origins of English Land Law: Milsom and After' in P Brand, *The Making of the Common Law* (London, Hambledon, 1992) 203.

[19] R FitzNeal, *Dialogus de Scaccario* [*The Dialogue of the Exchequer*], circa 1180, trs E Amt and S Church (Oxford, Oxford University Press, 2007); SK Mitchell, *Taxation in Medieval England* (New Haven, CT, Yale University Press, 1951); J Sabapathy, *Officers and Accountability in Medieval England 1170–1300* (Oxford, Oxford University Press, 2014).

[20] FW Maitland (ed), *Memoranda de Parliamento 1305* (London, HMSO 1893; Cambridge, Cambridge University Press, 2012).

> prince or king or another who has no superior except God, the remedy by assise will not lie against him; there will only be opportunity for a petition, that he correct and amend his act. If he fails so to do, let it suffice him for punishment that he await God the Avenger ...[21]

This passage both states the royal immunity, and notes the countervailing convention that the king might grant a petition at his discretion, allowing a remedy to correct his own breach of obligation or withholding of property. The discretionary procedure was well established by the 1300s, and by 1400 came to divide between a petition of grace, bestowed at the king's mercy without legal formality, and a petition of right, where there was an expectation that the king should grant a litigant a licence to pursue a claim against the Crown in the king's own courts, in cases where a like claim would have been be viable if brought by one private subject against another.[22] In the latter case, the king would be represented in court by an agent such as the king's attorney, with curial remedy to be addressed to that agent. The king provided redress using the formula '*fiat justitia*', 'let justice [or right] be done', or, to paraphrase, 'I accept the right of the claimant and I accept this to apply to my royal self as a just party as well as the fount of justice'. By this procedure, the king's two bodies both came within the compass of law and acted reciprocally upon each other – the constitutional and juridical Crown applying law to the political person of the king, who *elects* to do no wrong and submits to his own formal justice.[23]

One particular stress point in the medieval system of voluntaristic Crown liability concerned warranty of title. The king might have granted a fee to a tenant by infeudation, but a rival claimant might then challenge the tenant, showing an alternative descent of title. Such conflicts were common enough, as seisins might be lost by escheats, forfeitures, and secretive conveyances in times of civil unrest and divided authority, with possession then restored in new political circumstances. Parties might reach to higher authority to warrant their descent of title in such turbulent conditions. A tenant *in capite* holding directly of the king's grant could not obviously bring the king into a royal court to warrant the tenant's title against the rival. So how was the correct descent of title to be shown? Some lawyers claimed that in the mists of time the king could be compelled to vouch title for tenants in his own court, but this was to idealise practices in the time of Edward the Confessor and the Saxon kings prior to the Norman yoke, and had little to do with the realities of Angevin and Plantagenet monarchy. The better theory was that the king was expected to prevent his own court system from being used to derogate from his own grant; the petition of right served to restrain the king as legal enforcer from undermining rights the king himself should warrant or protect as lord or assignee. William Staunford, a justice of Common Pleas writing in the mid-1500s, put the idea as follows:

> Peticion is al the remedy the subject hath when the king seiseth his land or taketh away his goods from him havinge no title by ordre of his lawes so to do. ... And therefore is his peticion

[21] H de Bracton, *De Legibus et Consuetudinibus Angliae* [*On the Laws and Customs of England*], tr SE Thorne (Cambridge, MA, Belknap Press, 1977) f 171b, iii, 42–43.

[22] Holdsworth (n 4) 147–56.

[23] For further exploration, see E Kantorowicz, *The King's Two Bodies: A Study in Mediaeval Political Theology* (Princeton, NJ, Princeton University Press, 1957).

> called a peticion of right, because of the right the subject hath against the king by the ordre of his lawes to the thing he sueth for.[24]

Petitions of right were regularly heard in a mesne procedure from around 1400 in Chancery or alternatively in Court of King's Bench, as institutions seen to administer the king's prerogative. Those courts could triage cases and send them on for decision in the appropriate fact-finding tribunal, often the Court of Exchequer.[25] A common situation where the subject might petition the king to recover property as of right would involve mistakes in the taking of evidence or some other procedural irregularity in the course of an enquiry known as an 'office', launched by royal officials to justify a recovery of a franchise or presentation in the grant of the king, or to effect an escheat or forfeiture on death, treason, or lunacy. Royal officials, and notably the chief law officers, being the Lord Chancellor, the Attorney-General and Solicitor-General, were highly active pursuing such offices as an important source of royal finance. In the late medieval and Tudor periods, forfeitures by attainders and impeachments channelled through Parliament were joined to executive offices of escheat as methods of raising money for the Crown; and to this day the Crown vigorously pursues escheats to maintain income.[26] Alleviating obvious irregularities in the confiscatory process was an important safety valve protecting the legitimacy of the system.

If the office or inquest into Crown resumption of title was traversed, that is shown to have mistaken the facts or muddied the procedure of notice and witness, then the dispossessed holder or his descendant would petition to recover the estate on the basis that title had never truly departed from the family. The traverse of office to establish an existing property right wrongly held by the Crown came to be known as a 'demonstration of right', or in the law French, a *monstrans de droit*.[27] A variation might occur where the Crown purposed to restore lands to heirs after a felon or traitor was attainted, thus overlooking the theoretical corruption of blood that would normally bar the family inheritance; indeed the wheel of fortune could turn rapidly for landed families as rival dynasts battled to control the Crown, and might offer favour to disgraced families to bind them back into loyalty. A prior forfeiture might then be cut down to a confiscation of a mere life estate, and the remainderman might bring *monstrans de droit* to have the restored estate recognised or perfected. If the pardon had not been formalised then a petition of grace would be the correct remedy, being a request for the king to show favour where the subject had no provable title or right to title. The practice of regular mercy offered by the Crown to the family of a disgraced landholder seems to have been very common up to 1400, using letters patent of pardon, with tens of thousands of

[24] *An exposicion of the kinges prerogatiue* (London, Tottel, 1567) f 72b.

[25] Holdsworth (n 4) 151–53.

[26] For a late example of an office of escheat, see *Burgess v Wheate* (1759) 1 Eden 177, 28 ER 652; W Bl 123, 96 ER 67, where the Attorney-General argued for escheat of a beneficial fee simple, a claim supported in court only by the executive-minded Lord Mansfield, but much later adopted by Parliament: Intestate Estates Act 1884, s 4. Today there are some 7,000 cases of escheat pending before the Crown Estate, which are dealt with at arm's length by the Treasury and private lawyers acting for the Crown, which can register such resumed land as a grant in fee to Himself: Land Registration Act 2002, s 79(1). Controversially, takings of estates by *bona vacantia* continue to enrich the Crown directly within the royal duchies.

[27] *The Sadlers' Case* (1588) 4 Co Rep 54b; 76 ER 1012 (Ch); *Reynel's Case* (1612) 9 Co Rep 95; 77 ER 871.

examples surviving.[28] After that date, personal pardons and restitution of estates generally required a parliamentary bill to reverse or vary a bill of attainder, on the initiative of the Crown or its ministers.[29] Following any such act of mercy, a further petition of right directed to the Crown could be brought to lever the regrant of title following the pardon.

The development of the *monstrans de droit* procedure was entrenched by legislation in 1360–62, helping litigants adduce and review the facts of escheats in order to traverse an office making findings of capacity or title adverse to them.[30] In 1549, Parliament removed delays and simplified procedures to facilitate *monstrans* and traverse-of-office claims, eliminating the need to present a petition to Chancery and have a special inquisitorial commission constituted.[31] Lawyers analogised these remodelled actions to the writ of entry, a speedier method of asserting title that cut away the need for proof of lengthy chain of title, rather focusing parties on recent facts establishing a right to durable possession.

Significantly, this left as a residuum the generic petition of right, now taken to be a process allowing assertion of executory claims, where the king was not wrongfully in possession of an estate in contradiction of a subject's right yet the subject had an inchoate right against the Crown that would have been litigable had that right been held against a common person. The claim to a royal warranty of title against a third party was a core example, as the petitioner could have had a straight claim against a normal or non-royal assignor for a personal guarantee. The king could also resist a *monstrans* or traverse if the controversy over an escheated title concerned a matter of legal record rather than a challenged finding of fact under some royal office.[32]

Other examples of the petition of right emerged on the borderline of contract and property, as where incorporeal hereditaments issuing out of lands led to claims against the Crown. Here the remedy sought might be payment from the profits of land in royal hands, or compensation for harm to easements attached to lands in the tenant's hands. One could not say the payment was a right vested already in the tenant and withheld from him by the king; a petition procedure must first establish the existence and extent of the right to payment. So a claim for rents or corrodies, or for compensation for harm to enjoyment of easements and commons that would normally be effected by *quod permittat* or nuisance writs, would rightly attract a petition of right procedure, and not the more focused *monstrans de droit* for transfer of a right wrongly retained. As Staunford recorded in his treatise,[33] by the mid-sixteenth century the petition of right was being used to pursue a wide range of disseisin and nuisance claims against the Crown, and also for recovery of chattels and protection of incorporeal hereditaments. In the seventeenth century, the petition of right procedure was enlarged on the Latin side

[28] H Lacey, *The Royal Pardon: Access to Mercy in Fourteenth-Century England* (Woodbridge, Boydell & Brewer Press, 2009).

[29] M Steilen, 'Bills of Attainder' (2016) 53 *Houston Law Review* 767, 774–826; Steilen shows how English practice was developed to provide Art III of the US Constitution, s 3: 'no Attainder of Treason shall work Corruption of Blood, or Forfeiture except during the Life of the Person attainted'.

[30] 34 Edw III, c 14 (1360); 36 Edw III, c 13 (1362).

[31] 2 & 3 Edw VI, c 8 (1549).

[32] Holdsworth (n 4) 161–64.

[33] *An exposicion of the kinges prerogatiue* (n 24).

of the Exchequer, and later in Chancery, to allow decrees protecting mortgage and trust beneficiary interests where the Crown came into a title subject to an equitable claim or security.[34] But personal torts were still out of range of the petitionary procedure, defeated by the motto that the king could do no wrong, even if he could be petitioned to do right. We must next explore the contractual implications of the bar on recognition of royal torts.

IV. Debt, *Monstrans de droit*, and Traverses

We have noted that by the early seventeenth century, the Court of King's Bench managed to wrest the lucrative enforcement of normal contractual debt away from the Court of Common Pleas by creative use of the trespassory, damage-based assumpsit action. But what if the promisor were the Crown, who could do no wrong? The king could never be petitioned to pay damages for a tortious breach of a personal duty, including a contractual duty under the trespass procedures recognised in *Slade's Case*. Legal logic pointed back to older debt actions as more congruent with a petition of right procedure, but the core action for debt with wager of law was hardly suitable for royal litigation; and covenant and account were also poor fits, for the Crown would not seal deeds or be subject to auditors to bind over payment of a sum certain.

The road that ended up being taken to sue the Crown *sur contract* was the claim to debt as withheld property. In the 1450s, the notion that a pardoned forfeiture of estate could result in a petition to assert the title of the restored family was engrafted into the field of contractual debt. For example, the king might assert a judgment debt and take payment, but then rescind the underlying contract or otherwise compromise the debt in an *ex post* settlement. The courts held that petition of right, if not *monstrans*, would lie in such cases to return the value of the judgment debt. From the late 1500s to the mid-1800s, dozens of litigations were brought exploring such distinctions, as litigants navigated between petitions of grace, of right, *monstrans* and traverses. All of these methods were used to extract debt payments from the Crown, with *monstrans* for specifically withheld property taking the leading role.[35]

At the same time, the Crown as debtor was special because it could not be forced to pay after judgment or decree by the threat of debtor's prison or bankruptcy, nor could the bailiff or sheriff be sent in to execute against Crown assets. Other levers for enforcement had to be found, taking place at the stage after recognition of primary right and assessment of secondary liquidated remedy. By the later sixteenth century, claims against the Crown to effect payment came to be enforced by the issuing of *liberate* writs within the Exchequer, whereby the Lord Treasurer or the Barons would order officials to 'deliver' a sum of money to satisfy a finding under a petition or *monstrans*. It was unclear

[34] *Hicks v Attorney General* (1661) Hardres 176; 145 ER 439 (Ex); *Pawlett v Attorney General* (1667/8) Hardres 465; 145 ER 550 (Ex). Later authorities are collected in J Mitford, *A Treatise on the Pleadings in Suits in the Court of Chancery, by English Bill*, 2nd edn (Dublin, Lunch, 1789); *Brown v Harris* (1807) 13 Ves Jr 552, 33 ER 401 (Ch) per Lord Eldon LC.

[35] I count some 80 cases in the *English Reports* dealing with *monstrans de droit* alone from 1550–1860; the numbers spiral if one searches for traverse of office, petitions of right and petitions of grace.

if this was an administrative instruction within the Treasury to facilitate payment, or a mandatory order to satisfy a royal debt. The Crown had a hazy prerogative power to block payments by overruling the *liberate*, and the Lord Treasurer also retained a discretion akin to a delegated prerogative power to delay, suspend or remould payment orders independently of the Crown, if he saw fit to do so as a question of policy. The intricacies of such mandatory, permissive, and suspended payment orders were a large part of an intricate and mysterious body of law and custom known as the Course of the Exchequer, and by the late sixteenth and early seventeenth centuries, this had become a highly specialised area of professional legal practice.[36]

V. War, Revolution and Crown Banking (1660–1701)

The breakdown of the constitution in the 1640s, followed by republic in the 1650s, then a restoration of the Stuarts in 1660 and a revolution against them in 1688, led to great changes in the organisation and enforcement of Crown finance and debt. Charles II had agreed to stay within the bounds of parliamentary control of taxation as a condition of his return, but in the 1670s he used extra-parliamentary debt financing, as devised by his courtier George Downing, to maintain his lavish court and launch imperial wars against the Dutch. Downing copied Dutch and French models to promote a prerogative assignment of the excise, being a sizeable revenue that was accorded to the Crown in the 1660 settlement. Bonds staked against anticipated Crown income streams were issued to the London goldsmiths in return for loans brokered from syndicates of secondary creditors. The bond claims in the hands of primary and secondary creditors were then traded to fresh assignees, allowing the income stream to be capitalised by sale onwards to new entrants. The new bond markets depended on the Crown maintaining the flow of interest on the original issues to fix expectations of future value, with pricing varying according to shifts in anticipated default risk and opportunity cost. However, in 1672 the Crown found itself in military and fiscal crisis following defeats inflicted by the Dutch; and on the advice of the Cabal of Tory ministers, the Crown imposed the infamous Stop on the Exchequer, suspending payments on bonds for an entire year, with a promise of heightened compensatory interest to follow. The Stop was then extended indefinitely, and only a trickle of interest was ever paid, with the Crown picking out a few favoured financiers to support and letting others go to the wall, taking the secondary creditors and assignees down with them. Severe disruption to credit and concomitant weakening of faith in government stability contributed to the Monmouth rebellion of 1685, launched by Whig lords opposing Charles' brother James' accession to power.[37]

James II's unpopular regime lasted only three years before imploding. His favouring of Catholic interests at home and abroad, his suspension of legislation, and his attempts to control elections piled political and religious conflict onto financial chaos.

[36] A Graham, 'The "ancient course" and the feudal law: history, ideology and the English Exchequer, 1660–1715' (MS 2022, on file with author).

[37] JK Horsefield, 'The "Stop of the Exchequer" Revisited' (1982) 35 *Economic History Review* 511.

In late 1688, James fled to France, and his daughter Mary and her spouse (and James' cousin) William were installed as dual monarchs. A perpetual Protestant succession and the autonomy and supremacy of Parliament were entrenched by legislation of the revolutionary Convention Parliament. The Glorious Revolution may have successfully rebalanced the constitution, but it did not solve the fiscal crisis of the Crown. The new regime launched fresh and expensive wars against the French, funded by massive new bond issues. The Treasury neglected to pay the old bondholders who had financed the earlier Stuart wars, and in Parliament it was implied that the bonds issued by the prior regime were a kind of odious debt, an illegitimate impost on the present generation who had rightly expelled the rogue kings who had launched a ruinous war against a Protestant neighbour.

The bankers responded to this default by commencing in 1690 a multiparty litigation known as the *Bankers' Case*. The intricacies of the litigation, one of the greatest (and lengthiest) in English legal history, can only be summarised here.[38] Almost all the judges agreed in 1691 that the issue of assignable bonds by letters patent with interest charged against identified taxes was a valid use of the prerogative power. In 1696, the judges also largely agreed that once the Crown had given charters dedicating expected taxes to support specific bond issues and even directing issue of talleys to instigate payment, then the law notionally segregated the funds on accrual in the Treasury, ready to be paid over to the bondholders. Litigants could demand the assigned debt owed to them as a property right now inhering in funds in the hands of the Crown, suing under the non-discretionary *monstrans de droit* procedure. This was a more direct claim even than a real lien affecting freehold lands, as where a creditor brought *elegit* to enforce a registered judgment debt.[39] This is because in the Crown bond case, the property in the excise funds was supposed to have been charged by a prerogative act, requiring no further court action to constitute the claim beyond a payment order internal to Exchequer. In contrast, the judgment creditor had to be constituted a tenant of a moiety of the debtor's lands by the local sheriff charged with executing the *elegit* writ; only then were possessory rights vested.

However, in the *Bankers' Case* the judges ended up dividing over whether the prerogative bond issues backed by letters patent gave the holders a right to extract payment without further authorisation from a judicial or executive official. The majority, led by Holt LJKB, held that sixteenth-century precedents showed that the Barons of Exchequer could enforce the *monstrans de droit* by ordering the Lord Treasurer and his officials via *liberate* writs to appropriate funds and pay out the bonds in order to satisfy the Crown's promises. Opposing Holt, Treby LJCP held that the precedents only showed how *liberate* writs might go to lower officials to activate a Treasury payment mechanism, and further, that without a higher order from the Lord Treasurer using a delegated political

[38] See *Petition of Hornbee* (1691) 1 Freeman 331, 89 ER 246 (Ex); *R & R v Hornby* (1694) Comberbach 270, 90 ER 472 (Ex Ch); (1695) 1 Salkeld 58, 91 ER 56; *R v Hornely & Williams* (1696) (1701) Carthew 388; 90 ER 825; *R v Hornby* (1700) 5 Modern 29, 87 ER 500; *The Bankers Case in Cam Scacc* (1700) Skinner 601, 90 ER 270; *The Argument of the Lord Keeper Sommers … in the Bankers Case* [1696] (Savoy, London, Billingsley, 1733); a fuller analysis of the judges' arguments is offered in my pending study, 'The Bankers' Case Revisited' (MS, 2024, on file with author).

[39] See 4 Will & Mar c 20 (1692) for the contemporary registration requirement.

prerogative from the king, no payments could legally be coerced out of Treasury, not even by the Barons of the Exchequer addressing their fiscal brethren from within the institution. Treby added that to do otherwise would interfere in the most sensitive political discretions of the Government in allocating scarce finance to deal with war and peace emergencies in real time.

Treby's line was then amplified in a further Exchequer Chamber decision by Lord Keeper Somers, who gave a vast judgment taking up more than 130 pages of tightly researched material on the Course of the Exchequer, delivered around half a year after the other judges in late 1696. Somers argued that the assignable debt issued by the Crown against the excise might well constitute a property right suitable for claim under a petition of right or *monstrans*, and the issuing charters were 'sufficient warrant' for payment; but the Lord Treasurer was always left with a choice whether to make the appropriations and payments by *liberate* order, and could not be compelled by any curial process; authority to act was not compulsion. Somers noted that the Lord Treasurer was a high official coequal with the Lord Chancellor, wielding a political discretion as keeper of the king's fiscal conscience to withhold or restrain payments inimical to statecraft or the public interest. On review by the House of Lords in 1699, Holt's analysis binding the Crown and its officers all the way through to the execution stage was preferred; but this still left a further public-law requirement for appropriations to supply the Exchequer, and the Commons delayed voting the necessary funds. Finally a finance bill was passed in 1701 including a clause compromising and reducing the bankers' claims.[40] The remaining creditors were to receive just half the promised interest rate, reduced from 6 per cent to 3 per cent, with no return of capital. Desultory payments were made up to the time of the 1720 South Sea Bubble, and by that late stage most of the bankers were out of business, and political attention had moved elsewhere.

VI. Debt Enforcement, Risk and the Rule of Law

After 1720, new generations of bankers made fresh profits from Crown finance, underpinned by the Bank of England as an independent guarantor of bond payments, as well as swelling incomes from imperial trade. But past credit crises still cast a shadow, and the *Bankers' Case* was studied carefully by lenders for the next two centuries, anxious to understand if there were continuing legal risks in lending to the Crown.[41] The answer seemed to lie in the shrewd risk management of the Bank of England, interacting with deepened bond markets that discounted and priced government debt through constant trading, so determining the costs and supply of fresh finance. The certainties of law and the discretions of politics as determinants of finance were replaced with the probabilities of economics.[42]

[40] 12 & 13 Will 3, c 12, s 15.

[41] See the upholding of the Somers line in *Macbeath v Haldimand* (1786) 1 Term Reports 172, 176–77; 99 ER 1036, 1038 per Lord Mansfield LJKB.

[42] PGM Dickson, *The Financial Revolution in England: A Study in the Development of Public Credit, 1688–1756* (London, Macmillan, 1967); D Kynaston, *Till Time's Last Sand: A History of the Bank of England, 1694–2013* (London, Bloomsbury, 2017).

The history of *monstrans* and petitions, of the delicate balancing of rules and discretions in the recognition and enforcement of Crown debts and assignments, underlines the creative power of judges to create or deny liability – the very factor exposed so brilliantly in Stephen Smith's work. It turns out that his private-law model of curial powers and liabilities, of discretions and remedial orders, also raises basic questions concerning constitutionalism and the rule of law – how power may best be constrained where the public authority is itself adjudged in its private relations. The *Bankers' Case* ultimately showed that no matter how clearly the law specified a primary debt claim against the Crown, or provided secondary remedies to back the claim, the creditor was always prone to defeat at the execution stage. The case is disturbing because it demonstrates how policy pragmatism in the higher courts could provide a path for the ruling authority to evade its promises, with the judges excusing and justifying weakened enforcement in order to protect the fiscal prerogatives of the state. We can see a like move in modern cases where remedies are denied from a concern that strong curial defence of rights might trigger a cascade of unsustainable losses and financial chaos.[43] But as we have seen in our historical account, such selective enforcement is really a story of picking winners, with the more powerful actors proving too important, too 'systemic', too valued to be disciplined by the normal rules. Whether the law should participate in such statecraft has puzzled good legal minds for centuries, and it troubles us still.

[43] Examples may include *Tito v Waddell (No 2)* [1974] Ch 106; *Abbey Life plc v Office of Fair Trading* [2009] UKSC 6; *Pearson v Lehman* [2010] EWHC 2914 (Ch), [2011] EWCA 1544.

10

Trusts as Remedies

ROBERT CHAMBERS*

Trusts are seldom mentioned in Professor Stephen Smith's excellent book, *Rights, Wrongs, and Injustices: The Structure of Remedial Law*.[1] Yet his arguments may have a profound effect on our understanding of constructive and resulting trusts. Most significant is Smith's claim that unjust enrichment does not give rise to a duty to make restitution but merely a liability that a court will order the defendant to make restitution. If true, then we must face the question whether unjust enrichment can give rise to a trust or merely a liability to become a trustee.

Smith defines remedy as a judicial ruling.[2] A judicial declaration of trust is one such remedy, but traditionally the declaration did not create a trust but merely confirmed its existence. To the extent that this is still true, the declaration is a remedy but the trust is not. The Supreme Court of Canada has changed the Canadian law of trusts to add remedial constructive trusts, which are created by court orders as judicial remedies.[3] They now sit alongside institutional constructive trusts and resulting trusts, which are regarded as trusts that come into being without a court order. However, Smith's reasons why restitution of unjust enrichment at common law is a judicial remedy can also be applied to all restitutionary trusts, whether recognised as remedial or not.

I. Restitution of Unjust Enrichment

For Smith, remedies are judicial responses to three different kinds of events: rights-threats, wrongs and injustices. A rights-threat occurs 'when one of the claimant's substantive rights is under threat from the defendant'.[4] The remedy for a rights-threat is an order that the defendant must perform their pre-existing duty or pay a sum equal to the value of that performance. An injustice is 'an unfair loss or gain that has arisen from

* I thank Lionel Smith for his helpful comments on a draft of this chapter.

[1] SA Smith, *Rights, Wrongs, and Injustices: The Structure of Remedial Law* (Oxford, Oxford University Press, 2019) 14 (fn 23), 15 (fn 26), 115 (fn 14), 171, 270 (fn 137).

[2] ibid 19.

[3] *Peter v Beblow* [1993] 1 SCR 980, 101 DLR (4th) 621.

[4] Smith (n 1) 133.

a transaction between the claimant and defendant'.[5] Remedies for injustices include restitution of unjust enrichment and compensation for losses caused by wrongs.[6]

Unjust enrichment can occur without the commission of a wrong when (for example) a claimant pays money by mistake to an innocent defendant. The receipt of such 'a payment is neither a wrong nor a threat to commit a wrong'.[7] If unjust enrichment did give rise to a duty to make restitution, then the corresponding right to restitution would still be a response to an injustice but it would not be a remedy. A court order to make restitution of an unjust enrichment would be enforcing a pre-existing duty and belong in Smith's category as a response to a rights-threat.

II. Restitution as a Remedy

Smith gives three main reasons why unjust enrichment gives rise only to a liability and not to a duty to make restitution. The first is the language used by judges and other writers, who routinely describe the response to restitution as a liability to make restitution.[8] Second, damages are never awarded for a failure to make restitution.[9] If a duty to make restitution did arise when the defendant was unjustly enriched, then a failure to perform that duty should be a wrong for which damages are available.

The third reason is what Smith calls the 'unknowability objection'.[10] A person can be unaware of their unjust enrichment because they do not know either that they have been enriched or that their enrichment was unjust. For example, money can be paid into an account without notice to the account holder or to someone who has no reason to suspect that the payment was made by mistake. For Smith, the imposition of an unknowable duty is inconsistent with 'the most basic requirement of the rule of law'.[11]

Frederick Wilmot-Smith deals with the unknowability objection in chapter 20 of this book. He notes Smith's belief that 'the unknowability objection is conceptual' and applies even though many defendants do know that they are unjustly enriched.[12] For Smith, there can be never be a duty to make restitution of unjust enrichment if some defendants might be ignorant of that duty. Wilmot-Smith considers the possibility of duties that are conditional on the defendant's knowledge of the facts that give rise to the duty.

If Smith is correct and the unknowability objection precludes a duty to make restitution, that does not mean that the defendant's knowledge is irrelevant. The defence of change of position can reduce or eliminate a liability to make restitution, but it is not available to defendants who were aware that they were unjustly enriched when they

[5] ibid 223.
[6] ibid 224–28.
[7] ibid 246.
[8] ibid 239–40.
[9] ibid 240–41.
[10] ibid 243–45 (also see 197–99).
[11] ibid 243 (also see 199).
[12] ibid 244.

changed their position.[13] In other words, the extent and existence of the defendant's liability may depend on their knowledge.

III. Restitutionary Trusts

If there is no duty at common law to make restitution of unjust enrichment, can trusts arise directly in response to unjust enrichment? A trust is normally regarded as a relationship in which the trustee owes duties to the beneficiary. At a bare minimum, this includes the duty to preserve the trust assets and transfer them when required to those who are entitled to receive them. Is the imposition of an equitable duty to make restitution inconsistent with a common law liability to do so? Do Smith's arguments against the common law duty apply with equal force to equitable duties under a trust?

The first of Smith's three main reasons does not help us determine whether trusts can or should arise directly in response to unjust enrichment or only pursuant to a court order. The phrase 'liable as a trustee' is fairly common, but it assumes that a person is liable because they are a trustee. It does not mean that they are 'liable to become a trustee'.

Second, the unavailability of damages is not meaningful because damages are never awarded for breach of trust. If trustees are in breach of trust, the accounting mechanism can be used to make them personally liable for any losses caused by their breach.[14] However, since trustees also have a primary duty to account to their beneficiaries, their liability to account is not a clear indication of wrongdoing. The real question is whether the recipient of an unjust enrichment can be held to account for those assets and thus personally liable for improperly dealing with them. This depends on the nature of the liability for knowing receipt and is discussed below because it is tied directly to the knowledge of the recipient.

The unknowability objection is significant for trusts, because assets can be transferred to honest recipients who do not know that they were transferred in breach of trust. If an unknowable duty to pay a debt is contrary to the rule of law, then so is an unknowable obligation to perform a trust. This finds support in Lord Browne-Wilkinson's obiter dictum in *Westdeutsche Landesbank Girozentrale v Islington LBC*:

> Since the equitable jurisdiction to enforce trusts depends upon the conscience of the holder of the legal interest being affected, he cannot be a trustee of the property if and so long as he is ignorant of the facts alleged to affect his conscience, ie until he is aware that he is intended to hold the property for the benefit of others in the case of an express or implied trust, or, in the case of a constructive trust, of the factors which are alleged to affect his conscience.[15]

[13] See ibid 241–42.

[14] See R Chambers, 'Liability' in P Birks and A Pretto (eds), *Breach of Trust* (Oxford, Hart Publishing, 2002) 1.

[15] *Westdeutsche Landesbank Girozentrale v Islington LBC* [1996] UKHL 12, [1996] AC 669, 705.

Lord Browne-Wilkinson regarded this proposition as 'fundamental to the law of trusts and … uncontroversial'.[16] There are a number of cases in which resulting trusts have arisen without the knowledge of the trustees, but Lord Browne-Wilkinson believed that the trust arose only after the trustees or their 'successors in title have become aware of the facts which gave rise to a resulting trust'.[17]

IV. Trusts and Knowledge

One difficulty with making the creation of a trust conditional on the knowledge of the trustee is that knowledge is not required for the continuation of a trust if the trust assets are transferred in breach of trust to honest recipients. This is set out by Lord Browne-Wilkinson as another fundamental and uncontroversial proposition in *Westdeutsche*:

> Once a trust is established, as from the date of its establishment the beneficiary has, in equity, a proprietary interest in the trust property, which proprietary interest will be enforceable in equity against any subsequent holder of the property (whether the original property or substituted property into which it can be traced) other than a purchaser for value of the legal interest without notice.[18]

Purchasers with notice are bound by the trust, but so too are honest donees who are unaware of it. The honest donee owes none of the usual trust obligations to take care of the trust assets, avoid conflicts of interest, etc, but the beneficiary's proprietary interests can continue without them. There is an important distinction between the beneficiary's rights *in personam*, which are enforceable only against trustees who have undertaken that office, and their right *in rem* to recover the trust assets from people who should not have received them.

Trust beneficiaries can recover assets transferred in breach of trust or their traceable proceeds (subject to any defences the recipients may have), but the recipients will not be personally liable for breach of trust or any loss of trust assets while they are unaware of the trust. Personal liability for knowing receipt or dealing with assets transferred in breach of trust depends on knowledge of the trust or the facts giving rise to it.[19] Once the recipient becomes aware of the trust, they come under a duty to preserve the trust assets and restore them to the persons who are entitled to them. While ignorant of the trust, they owe no duties to the trust beneficiaries but are merely under a liability that they will become accountable as a constructive trustee if they acquire sufficient knowledge while still retaining any portion of the trust assets.

[16] ibid.

[17] ibid.

[18] ibid.

[19] *El Ajou v Dollar Land Holdings plc* [1993] EWCA Civ 4, [1994] 2 All ER 685; S Gardner, 'Moment of Truth for Knowing Receipt?' (2009) 125 *LQR* 20; C Mitchell and S Watterson, 'Remedies for Knowing Receipt' in C Mitchell (ed), *Constructive and Resulting Trusts* (Oxford, Hart Publishing, 2010) 115; R Chambers, 'The End of Knowing Receipt' (2016) 2 *Canadian Journal of Comparative Contemporary Law* 1.

V. Trusts and Liabilities

While unaware of the relevant facts, an honest recipient of assets transferred in breach of trust is only under a liability and has no duty to perform. We might argue about whether the recipient should be called a trustee and whether the beneficiary's continuing proprietary interest in those assets should be called a trust. Equitable proprietary interests can exist in other situations in which someone is liable to become a trustee, but those interests are not trusts. It is useful to consider two of them here: an option to purchase and an option to rescind.

An option to purchase an estate in land is an equitable interest in that estate if the exercise of that option would create a specifically enforceable contract of sale. The option is an offer to sell that is irrevocable for a specified period of time. Its exercise will produce a constructive trust in which the vendor is holding the estate in trust for both vendor and purchaser pending completion of the sale (if the contract is specifically enforceable).[20]

While the option remains open for acceptance, the grantor is under a liability but owes no duty to the grantee. The grantee has an equitable proprietary interest in the estate because they have the power to obtain title to it. As Martland J said in *Canadian Long Island Petroleums Ltd v Irving Industries Ltd*, 'forthwith upon the granting of the option, the optionee upon the occurrence of certain events solely within his control can compel a conveyance of the property to him'.[21] As Jessel MR said in *London and South Western Railway Co v Gomm*:

> The right to call for a conveyance of the land is an equitable interest or equitable estate. In the ordinary case of a contract for purchase there is no doubt about this, and an option for repurchase is not different in its nature. A person exercising the option has to do two things, he has to give notice of his intention to purchase, and to pay the purchase money; but as far as the man who is liable to convey is concerned, his estate or interest is taken away from him without his consent, and the right to take it away being vested in another, the covenant giving the option must give that other an interest in the land.[22]

The equitable proprietary interest created by an option to purchase is not a proprietary right or right *in rem* because there is no corresponding duty placed on anyone. The option is only a power with a corresponding liability, but like a right *in rem*, it can be enforced generally against others. It is a power *in rem*.[23] It can be enforced against successors in title (subject to defences) and can take priority over competing interests (including rights) in the same asset.

If the contract of sale produced by the exercise of the option is not specifically enforceable, then the option is not a proprietary interest because there is no power to obtain title.[24] This is the same reason why a right of pre-emption or right of first refusal

[20] *Jerome v Kelly* [2004] UKHL 25, [2004] 1 WLR 1409 [32]; R Chambers, 'The Importance of Specific Performance' in S Degeling and J Edelman (eds), *Equity in Commercial Law* (Sydney, Lawbook Co, 2005) 431.

[21] *Canadian Long Island Petroleums Ltd v Irving Industries Ltd* [1975] 2 SCR 715, 50 DLR (3d) 265, 277.

[22] *London and South Western Railway Co v Gomm* (1882) 20 Ch D 562 at 581 (CA).

[23] B Häcker, 'Proprietary Restitution After Impaired Consent Transfers: A Generalised Power Model' (2009) 68 *CLJ* 324, 330–31.

[24] *1244034 Alberta Ltd v Walton Int Group Inc*, 2007 ABCA 372, 288 DLR (4th) 360.

does not create an interest in land: the grantee has no power to compel conveyance of the land.[25]

An option to rescind operates in a way similar to an option to purchase. Lord Millett referred to the recovery of assets through rescission as a form of 'specific unperformance'.[26] If a claimant can rescind a contract or other transaction and thereby recover assets that were transferred to the defendant pursuant to that transaction, the claimant has a proprietary interest in the recoverable assets.[27] This happens at common law when there is a voidable contract for the sale of goods.[28] The seller has a proprietary interest in the goods while the contract remains voidable, but is not the owner of the goods until the contract is avoided and title reverts to the seller. Pending rescission, the seller has a power *in rem* that is enforceable generally against others until defeated by a subsequent sale to a buyer in good faith and without notice.[29]

In other situations, an option to rescind is an equitable interest in recoverable assets because the right to rescind is only equitable or because the election to rescind will not cause legal title to revert to the claimant. For example, rescission for undue influence is available only in equity and an election to rescind a transfer of registered land will not affect the legal title until there is a change to the register. The defendant will hold the recoverable assets in trust once the claimant elects to rescind, but there is no trust pending rescission. A defendant who receives assets through a voidable transaction is the beneficial owner of those assets, but subject to a liability that corresponds to the claimant's power to elect to rescind the transaction and recover the assets.[30]

Options to purchase or rescind are not trusts because the person with legal title to the assets is the beneficial owner of those assets, subject to another person's power to obtain them. The honest recipient of assets transferred in breach of trust is in a different position. They are also subject to a liability and not a duty, but they are not the beneficial owner of those assets. There is no transaction that must be created or rescinded in order to shift beneficial ownership from one party to the other.

The liability created by an option to purchase or rescind corresponds to a power held by the person who can exercise that option. The liability of an honest recipient of assets transferred in breach of trust is different because it does not correspond to a power held by the trust beneficiary. The recipient's duty to the beneficiary arises if and when they acquire knowledge of the relevant facts, and as Birke Häcker pointed out, that knowledge can come from sources other than the beneficiary.[31]

Lord Browne-Wilkinson was unwilling to call a continuing equitable interest a trust if the legal owner of the relevant assets was unaware of that interest and thus only

[25] *Canadian Long Island Petroleums Ltd v Irving Industries Ltd* [1975] 2 SCR 715; *Pritchard v Briggs* [1980] Ch 338 (CA). In Alberta and British Columbia, a right of first refusal was declared by statute to be an equitable interest in land: *Law of Property Act, RSA* 2000, c L-7, s 63; Property Law Act, RSBC 1996, c 377, s 9.

[26] PJ Millett, 'Restitution and Constructive Trusts' (1998) 114 *LQR* 399, 416.

[27] R Chambers, 'Tracing and Unjust Enrichment' in J Neyers, M McInnes and S Pitel (eds), *Understanding Unjust Enrichment* (Oxford, Hart Publishing, 2004) 263, 300.

[28] *Car & Universal Finance Co Ltd v Caldwell* [1963] EWCA Civ 4, [1965] 1 QB 525.

[29] Sale of Goods Act 1979, s 23.

[30] Millett (n 26) 416.

[31] Häcker (n 23) 352–53.

under a liability and owing no duties to the trust beneficiary. Lord Millett was happy to say 'that a trust exists whenever the legal title is in one party and the equitable title in another'.[32] He went on to say:

> It has been the common parlance of equity lawyers for centuries is [sic] to describe the legal owner in such circumstances as a trustee and the interest of the equitable owner as arising under a trust. Lord Lindley was content to accept the usage as correct: 'All that is necessary to establish the relation of trustee and cestui que trust is to prove that the legal title was in the plaintiff and the equitable title in the defendant.' But as Lord Browne-Wilkinson himself recognised, this is essentially a question of semantics. He clearly recognises, indeed insists, that the separation of legal and equitable ownership is insufficient to give rise to fiduciary obligations. Unwilling to recognise the existence of a trust shorn of such obligations, he is forced to conclude that such separation of interests does not create a trust. It probably does not matter if we say that the relationship is not a trust relationship, so long as we call it something else. The trouble is that we have no other name for it.[33]

VI. Continuation versus Creation

If the continued existence of the beneficiary's proprietary interest does not depend on the knowledge of the legal owner of the trust assets, then why should the creation of that interest depend on that knowledge? The office of express trustee is undertaken, but constructive and resulting trusts can be imposed on people without their consent. Their intentions should be irrelevant unless they form an essential part of the facts that give rise to those trusts, such as making a specifically enforceable contract, having a common intention to share ownership of the family home or making a secret profit in breach of fiduciary duty.

Unjust enrichment can occur without the recipient's involvement or knowledge. As Smith said, the receipt of the enrichment can give rise to a liability to make restitution but no duty to do so. Is there any reason why it cannot also give rise to a bare trust for the claimant, in which the claimant is the beneficial owner of the assets received by the defendant who is under a liability but no duty with respect to those assets until they become aware of the relevant facts?

A trust can arise when assets are stolen or misappropriated in breach of fiduciary duty. There is no trust prior to the theft or misappropriation, and none is needed so long as the victim retains legal title to the purloined assets.[34] If those assets are used to acquire other assets, a trust will then arise over the traceable proceeds. Typically, this occurs when the wrongdoer deposits the victim's money in their own bank account, or uses it to buy other assets for themselves or their associates. If the wrongdoer uses the proceeds to buy a gift for an honest spouse or friend, the victim's beneficial interest

[32] Millett (n 26) 403.
[33] ibid 404, quoting Lord Lindley in *Hardoon v Belilios* [1901] AC 118, 123.
[34] S Barkehall Thomas, 'Thieves as Trustees: The Enduring Legacy of *Black v S Freedman & Co Ltd*' (2009) 3 *Journal of Equity* 52; R Chambers, 'Trust and Theft' in E Bant and M Harding (eds), *Exploring Private Law* (Cambridge, Cambridge University Press, 2010) 223.

under the pre-existing trust will continue and the gift will be held in trust, even though the donee is unaware of the source of the funds.[35]

In *Black v S Freedman & Co*,[36] a husband stole cash from his employer in a series of thefts over three years. He deposited some of the stolen cash in his own bank account and later withdrew cash from that account and deposited it into his wife's bank account. He deposited much of the cash that he stole directly into his wife's account. The High Court of Australia held that she was a trustee of the funds in her account. It was not established that she was aware of the thefts when the deposits were made. Griffith CJ said:

> The money is identified; it came into her hands as a volunteer, and she is liable to repay it. It was pointed out by Sir George Jessel, in a well known case, that a man may at a certain stage be innocent, but that, if he knows that he has got the advantage of a fraud to which he was no party and says he will keep it, then he becomes himself a party to the fraud and is liable to the jurisdiction of the Court of Equity. In the present case the wife says she holds this money for her separate use and claims it for herself, knowing now, at any rate, the circumstances under which it came to be given to her.[37]

The employer's legal ownership of the cash continued until it was deposited in a bank account. The husband would become a trustee of the funds in his account when the deposits were made. The employer's equitable beneficial interest in those funds would continue and attach to their traceable proceeds: first cash and then the wife's bank account, even if she was unaware of the thefts when those deposits were made. The direct deposits of stolen cash in her account are different, because the trust would be created when those deposits were made or perhaps later. The outcome of the case is consistent with the view that the trust did not arise until the wife became aware of the thefts, but it is also consistent with the view that the trust arose when the deposits were made but her liability became a duty only when she learned of the thefts.

Is there any reason to draw a distinction between the cash that came from the husband's account and the cash stolen from his employer? In either case, the funds in the wife's account are the traceable proceeds of cash stolen from the employer, who was the equitable owner of the cash withdrawn from the husband's account and the legal owner of the stolen cash. If the employer's equitable proprietary interest in the husband's cash can continue to exist as an interest in the wife's bank account when she was unaware of the thefts, then why should it not arise for the first time when the stolen cash was deposited?

VII. Mistaken Payments

There is an ongoing debate over whether mistaken payments should give rise to trusts. Perhaps surprisingly, it continues to revolve around the 1979 first-instance decision of

[35] *BC Teachers' Credit Union v Betterly* (1975) 61 DLR (3d) 755 (BCSC).
[36] *Black v S Freedman & Co* [1910] HCA 58, 12 CLR 105.
[37] ibid 109.

Goulding J in *Chase Manhattan Bank NA v Israel-British Bank (London) Ltd*,[38] in which a New York bank mistakenly paid $2 million to a London bank that became insolvent shortly thereafter. The New York bank wanted to recover the traceable proceeds of the mistaken payment. Goulding J held 'that the equitable remedy of tracing is in principle available, on the ground of continuing proprietary interest, to a party who has paid money under a mistake of fact'.[39]

There is much to criticise about the reasons given for that conclusion, but the question is whether it is correct. I have defended it on numerous occasions.[40] Lord Millett believed that there should be no trust because the payer intended to benefit the recipient (albeit mistakenly).[41] There are reasonable voices on both sides of the debate, which is beyond the scope of this chapter. What concerns us now is Lord Browne-Wilkinson's view that the outcome could be defended on the basis that the London bank learned of the mistake before it became insolvent:

> However, although I do not accept the reasoning of Goulding J, Chase Manhattan may well have been rightly decided. The defendant bank knew of the mistake made by the paying bank within two days of the receipt of the moneys. The judge treated this fact as irrelevant but in my judgment it may well provide a proper foundation for the decision. Although the mere receipt of the moneys, in ignorance of the mistake, gives rise to no trust, the retention of the moneys after the recipient bank learned of the mistake may well have given rise to a constructive trust.[42]

While knowledge of the mistake should be required before any trust duties can be imposed on the recipient, there is no reason why an equitable proprietary interest coupled with a liability cannot arise at the moment of receipt.

VIII. Unknowability

So far, we have considered only one aspect of Smith's unknowability objection: the defendant's awareness of the facts giving rise to a duty. Smith also objected to the imposition of a duty if the content of that duty is unknowable. This is a major reason why he believes that there is no duty to pay compensatory damages for torts or breach of contract, but only a liability that a court will award the payment of such damages. The defendant may know they are liable to pay damages, but they cannot be sure of the amount required before the court order.[43] It is less of concern in cases of unjust enrichment, where it may be relatively easy to calculate the market value of the enrichment received, but that can be complicated by the defence of change of position.[44]

[38] *Chase Manhattan Bank NA v Israel-British Bank (London) Ltd* [1981] Ch 105.

[39] ibid 120.

[40] For example, see R Chambers, 'Distrust: Our Fear of Trusts in the Commercial World' (2010) 63 *Current Legal Problems* 631, 643–45.

[41] Millett (n 26) 412–13.

[42] *Westdeutsche* (n 15) 715.

[43] Smith (n 1) 197–99.

[44] ibid 243–45.

Trusts do arise in circumstances where the essential facts are known but their legal significance is not. The constructive trust of the family home is a good example. The home owner is fully aware of the details of their relationship with their domestic partner and may be aware that their partner is entitled to a share of the home when that relationship ends, but the size of that share may be uncertain in the absence of a court order. This may be a reason why the Supreme Court of Canada shifted fairly quickly from a constructive trust that arises when the facts occur to a trust created by the court as a discretionary remedy.[45]

In England and Wales, the constructive trust of the family home is based on the common intention of the parties, which should in theory be something they know. However, courts are willing to infer a common intention to share beneficial ownership of the home and to determine the size of those shares when the parties have not discussed those issues. As Chadwick LJ said in *Oxley v Hiscock*:

> [I]n a case where there is no evidence of any discussion between them as to the amount of the share which each was to have – and even in a case where the evidence is that there was no discussion on that point – the question still requires an answer. It must now be accepted that … the answer is that each is entitled to that share which the court considers fair having regard to the whole course of dealing between them in relation to the property.[46]

While the trust declared by the court may purport to be a trust that arose during the parties' relationship, the 'share which the court considers fair' is unknowable in advance.

Another example is the constructive trust or other equitable interest created in response to proprietary estoppel. It appears that an equitable proprietary interest can arise when someone acts to their detriment in reliance on a reasonable expectation of acquiring that interest, but the extent of that interest may be impossible to determine without a court order.[47]

The constructive trust created by a contract of sale is problematic. It has long been accepted that the trust arises when the contract is made, but only if the contract is specifically enforceable.[48] In 1964, Donovan Waters heavily criticised this trust as unproductive and a source of problems.[49] Smith was also critical of the trust: '[I]t appears to be a clear example of the law doing exactly what I have argued it should not do, namely, making the existence of a substantive right turn on the availability of a remedy.'[50] Although specific performance is a discretionary remedy, it was routinely available for contracts for the sale of estates in land. The existence and content of the constructive trust were readily knowable without going to court.

[45] Compare Cory J's reasons for judgment in *Rawluk v Rawluk* [1990] 1 SCR 70, 91–92 and *Peter v Beblow* [1993] 1 SCR 980, 101 DLR (4th) 621, 640.

[46] *Oxley v Hiscock* [2004] EWCA Civ 546 [69]; [2004] 3 WLR 715, 750, quoted with approval in *Jones v Kernott* [2011] UKSC 53 [32], [51], [61], [70] and [83]; [2012] 1 AC 776, 788, 794, 796, 798 and 801.

[47] See *Cowper-Smith v Morgan* [2017] 2 SCR 754 [46]–[48]; *Guest v Guest* [2022] UKSC 27, [2022] 3 WLR 911.

[48] *Lysaght v Edwards* (1876) 2 Ch D 499, 506 (CA).

[49] DWM Waters, *The Constructive Trust: The Case for a New Approach in English Law* (London, Athlone Press, 1964) 74–143.

[50] Smith (n 1) 171.

There is a debate over whether the trust created by a specifically enforceable contract of sale is really a trust. There is no doubt that the purchaser acquires an equitable interest that can be enforced generally against others. It is more than a power because the purchaser has a right to conveyance that corresponds to the vendor's duty to convey, but what is it?

A specifically enforceable contract to grant a lease, mortgage, easement or profit à prendre does not create a trust but produces an equitable version of the promised right.[51] The relationship between the parties is not trustee–beneficiary but landlord–tenant or mortgagor–mortgagee, etc. A contract of sale is different because the promised outcome is not an ongoing relationship but a transfer of the beneficial ownership of an estate.

Once the purchase price has been paid in full and the date for completion has arrived, the vendor will be a bare trustee for the purchaser. Until that occurs, the vendor continues to have their own beneficial interest in the estate. As Lord Walker said in *Jerome v Kelly*:

> It would therefore be wrong to treat an uncompleted contract for the sale of land as equivalent to an immediate, irrevocable declaration of trust (or assignment of beneficial interest) in the land. Neither the seller nor the buyer has unqualified beneficial ownership. Beneficial ownership of the land is in a sense split between the seller and buyer on the provisional assumptions that specific performance is available and that the contract will in due course be completed, if necessary by the Court ordering specific performance. In the meantime, the seller is entitled to enjoyment of the land or its rental income. The provisional assumptions may be falsified by events, such as rescission of the contract (either under a contractual term or on breach). If the contract proceeds to completion the equitable interest can be viewed as passing to the buyer in stages, as title is made and accepted and as the purchase price is paid in full.[52]

The existence of the vendor's own beneficial interest is perhaps the main reason for doubting that there really is a trust. However, there is nothing unusual about a trustee's also being a beneficiary. The vendor and purchaser are not co-owners in equity, since they do not share the same rights. Instead, they are similar to income and capital beneficiaries. The vendor has the right to possession and income and to retain title as security for payment of the purchase price, while the purchaser has the right to the capital.[53] Changes to the market value of the estate affect the purchaser and not the vendor. The purchaser holds the hope of gain and bears the risk of loss. This is a hallmark of beneficial ownership and distinguishes it from a mere security interest. While some are reluctant to call it a trust, it is difficult to think of a better name for beneficial ownership of a capital interest in equity.[54]

[51] See, eg, *R v Tower Hamlets LBC, ex parte Von Goetz* [1998] EWCA Civ 1507, [1999] QB 1019; *Theodore v Mistford Pty Ltd* [2005] HCA 45, 221 CLR 612; *Hill v Nova Scotia (Attorney General)*, 1994 CanLII 4392 (NS SC), aff'd [1997] 1 SCR 69; *Mason v Clarke* [1955] AC 778.

[52] *Jerome v Kelly* [2004] UKHL 25 [32]; [2004] 1 WLR 1409, 1419–20.

[53] R Chambers, 'The Importance of Specific Performance' in Degeling and Edelman (eds) (n 20) 431, 452–54.

[54] Millett (n 26) 404.

This area of law was unsettled in Canada by an obiter dictum in a case concerning the quantum of damages for breach of a contract for the sale of land. Sopinka J said 'in future cases, under similar circumstances, a trial judge will not be constrained to find that specific performance is an appropriate remedy'.[55] Although only an obiter dictum, it was from the Supreme Court of Canada and was taken to heart by lower courts across the country. It is now difficult to predict whether land contracts are specifically enforceable or not. As Caldwell JA said in *Raymond v Anderson*:

> In practical terms, this means the prospective purchaser bears the burden of adducing evidence that the subject property is specially suited to the purchaser and that a comparable substitute property is not readily available. These evidentiary points are necessarily intertwined because, on the basis of the evidence, the prospective purchaser must discharge the overall burden of persuading the judge that the subject property is so different from others that damages is an inadequate remedy and that justice dictates the purchaser should have the subject property. The judge, in turn, must conduct a critical inquiry on the evidence as to the nature and function of the subject property in relation to the prospective purchaser.[56]

While the vendor will know that they owe a duty to transfer the land to the purchaser, it may be impossible to know without a court order whether they must specifically perform that duty or can change their mind and pay damages. This makes for an unknowable trust. If the contract is specifically enforceable, then the trust arose when it was made. If not, there never was a trust. Somewhat like Schrödinger's cat, the trust is both existent and non-existent until someone asks a judge for their opinion.[57] The trust depends on an unknowable liability. While the vendor does not know whether a trust exists, they do know that it may exist and this may be a sufficient reason to behave as if it does.

IX. Remedial Constructive Trusts

In *Westdeutsche*, Lord Browne-Wilkinson considered the possibility that the problems in this area might be alleviated by adopting the remedial constructive trust as a judicial remedy:

> Although the resulting trust is an unsuitable basis for developing proprietary restitutionary remedies, the remedial constructive trust, if introduced into English law, may provide a more satisfactory road forward. The court by way of remedy might impose a constructive trust on a defendant who knowingly retains property of which the plaintiff has been unjustly deprived. Since the remedy can be tailored to the circumstances of the particular case, innocent third parties would not be prejudiced and restitutionary defences, such as change of position, are capable of being given effect. However, whether English law should follow the United States and Canada by adopting the remedial constructive trust will have to be decided in some future case when the point is directly in issue.[58]

[55] *Semelhago v Paramadevan* [1996] 2 SCR 415, 136 DLR (4th) 1, 11. See R Chambers, 'The Importance of Specific Performance' in Degeling and Edelman (eds) (n 20) 431.
[56] *Raymond v Anderson* 2011 SKCA 58, [2011] 9 WWR 247 [15].
[57] See Waters (n 49) 98–99.
[58] *Westdeutsche* (n 15) 716.

The remedial constructive trust has not been adopted in England and Wales.[59] If that did happen, then the common law and equitable responses to unjust enrichment would be aligned as concurrent liabilities to be subject to a court order that creates a debt, a trust or both. However, there may be a high price to pay for that alignment. When proprietary interests depend on the exercise of judicial discretion, this tends to generate a large volume of litigation, as demonstrated by the cases concerning family homes or proprietary estoppel. Judicial discretion may be essential in those areas, but it is doubtful whether it is needed elsewhere to that extent.

The remedial constructive trust was adopted in Canada to help with the distribution of family assets at the end of a marriage or similar relationship. While those trusts purport to be responses to unjust enrichment, that is a flag of convenience. The trust is imposed to give effect to the reasonable expectations of the parties and does not provide restitution of unjust enrichment.[60] It is a remedy for an injustice that occurs when a relationship ends and one party has an unfairly large share of the assets acquired during their relationship. The proper size of those shares cannot be determined by using the law of unjust enrichment and their redistribution is not a form of restitution.[61]

X. Conclusion

Some trusts are judicial remedies. Constructive trusts created by equitable estoppel are wholly dependent on a court order for their existence and content, and in Canada, the same is true of constructive trusts of the family home. In England and Wales, the constructive trust of the family home often appears to be a remedy even if it purports not to be. In Smith's framework, these trusts are remedies of injustices.

The constructive trust generated by a specifically enforceable contract of sale is not a remedy because it arises when the contract is made. In Canada, however, the existence of the trust is often unknowable until declared by a court, and in this respect is no different from a remedy.

The trusts that effect restitution of unjust enrichment are also responses to injustices, but they are not remedies. They are not created by court orders but arise when the unjust enrichment occurs. They are somewhat compatible with Smith's view that unjust enrichment does not create a common law duty to make restitution but merely a liability that a court will order the defendant to make restitution. This is because a trust can exist even though the legal owner of the trust assets is merely under a liability and not subject to any duties to the beneficiary while they are unaware of the existence of the trust. While we might be unhappy using the terms 'trust' and 'trustee' in this context, we do not currently have better terms to describe a situation in which one person has bare legal title to an asset while someone else is the beneficial owner of that asset in equity.

[59] *FHR European Ventures LLP v Cedar Capital Partners LLC* [2014] UKSC 45, [2015] AC 250, 274.

[60] R Chambers, 'Constructive Trusts in Canada' (1999) 37 *Alberta Law Review* 173, 197–207.

[61] L Smith, 'The State of the Law of Unjust Enrichment in Common Law Canada' (2015) 56 *Canadian Business Law Journal* 39, 48–50.

When an honest recipient of an unjust enrichment becomes aware of the relevant facts, they can then be subject to a duty to preserve the assets and transfer them as required to the person entitled to receive them. This knowledge does not create the trust but merely gives rise to the duties that are normally associated with the bare trust that arose when the enrichment was received. At that stage, the recipient is subject to an equitable duty in addition to their common law liability. Even if we accept Lord Browne-Wilkinson's view that knowledge is required for the creation of a trust, it would still not be a remedy.

11

Remedial Restitutionary Rights?

WILLIAM SWADLING*

I. Introduction

When Steve Smith left Oxford for McGill, he gave me his bike and gown. I already had a gown, given to me by Peter Birks some years previously. But it was too short, and Steve's hand-me-down fitted just perfectly. As will be seen, so did his views on 'remedial restitutionary rights'.

For Peter, events in the world, such as breaches of contract, the commission of torts and the receipt of unjust enrichments, generated immediate rights in the victim of the wrong or the person conferring the enrichment that the defendant do something to fix the problem, without the need for the claimant to go to court to obtain an order that they do so. Victims of breaches of contract and torts, he said, had *rights* to damages and claimants in unjust enrichment had *rights* to restitution. Any subsequent court order made in response to such an event was, to use Steve's terminology, merely 'duty-confirming'.[1] In this respect, Peter followed the thinking of Lord Diplock, advanced in a series of cases in the 1960s and 1970s,[2] that, at least in the case of contracts, contracting parties had primary rights to performance and secondary rights to damages for non-performance, these secondary rights arising immediately on breach of the primary right, and before any order of a court was made. This approach was adopted more generally by Peter, in fact forming the backbone of much of his work on private law.[3] For him, not only did breaches of contract generate immediate rights

* Alexander Georgiou, Lionel Smith and Frederick Wilmot-Smith made invaluable comments on a draft of this chapter, which is much improved as a result.

[1] SA Smith, *Rights, Wrongs, and Injustices: The Structure of Remedial Law* (Oxford, Oxford University Press, 2019) 238.

[2] *Hardwick Game Farm v Suffolk Agricultural and Poultry Producers Association Ltd* [1966] 1 WLR 287, 341-E–G; *C Czarnikow Ltd v Koufos, The Heron II* [1966] 2 QB 695, 731; *Moschi v LEP Air Services Ltd* [1973] AC 331, 350; *Photo Production Ltd v Securicor Transport Ltd* [1980] AC 827, 848ff. For detail, see D Foxton QC, 'How Useful is Lord Diplock's Distinction between Primary and Secondary Obligations in Contract?' (2019) 135 *LQR* 249.

[3] For instance, Birks' whole taxonomical scheme, that rights arose from 'consent, wrongs, unjust enrichments, and other miscellaneous events', was predicated on this basis.

to the payment of money or some other action, so did the commission of torts and the receipt of unjust enrichments.[4] He traced the idea back to Austin,[5] though as a Romanist, Peter was also no doubt influenced by Gaius, who famously said that 'every obligation arises either from a contract or from a delict'.[6] Though later adopting a four-fold taxonomy, Justinian was no different in this regard, saying 'obligations arise from contract, or as though from a contract, or from a wrong, or as though from a wrong'.[7] On this schema, therefore, there is an obligation to pay damages for the breach of a contract in exactly the same way as there is an obligation to perform it.[8]

Peter's thinking culminated in his Blackstone lecture, where the word 'remedy' was comprehensively banished in favour of 'right'.[9] We have, he said, a *right* to damages for breach of contract, a *right* to damages for the commission of a tort and a *right* to restitution of an unjust enrichment. Moreover, such rights arise as the facts happen. Indeed, for Peter, the rights generated by these events were no different in quality from those generated by the execution of a conveyance, the making of a contract, the taking of possession of land or goods, or the making of a gift. The only difference was that they were 'secondary' rather than 'primary'. Of course, courts make orders against defendants in litigation, so what were these? Does their existence not give the lie to Peter's thesis? Seemingly not. Where a claimant went to court and won his claim, the court's role, according to Peter, was merely 'replicative': 'The judge's order novates the rights that the claimant brings into court … [I]t replicates the right with which the defendant would not willingly comply.'[10] Thus, if a claimant had a right to damages before judgment, though the court order did indeed create a new right, it did so only by way of 'novation' or 'replication' of the pre-judgment right.

If this view were correct, recipients of mistaken payments, of rights transferred because of duress or undue influence, of taxes paid which were not due, indeed of virtually all transfers for which there is an 'unjust factor',[11] would become immediately

[4] P Birks, 'Obligations: One Tier or Two?' in P Stein and A Lewis (eds), *Studies in Justinian's Institutes in Memory of JAC Thomas* (London, Sweet and Maxwell, 1983); P Birks, 'Restitution and Wrongs' (1982) 35 *Current Legal Problems* 53, 76, fn 58; and P Birks, 'Restitution and the Freedom of Contract' (1983) 36 *Current Legal Problems* 141, 161, fn 34.

[5] J Austin, *The Province of Jurisprudence Determined*, vol II (London, John Murray, 1863) ch 45, 450–51. As Rudden noted in B Rudden, 'Correspondence' (1990) 10 *OJLS* 288, the idea can in fact be traced back to RJ Pothier (1699–1772), who, in *A Treatise on the Law of Obligations*, tr WD Evans (London, A Strahan, 1826) §183, wrote 'Obligations are distinguished into primary and secondary; and this division is derived from the order in which they are supposed to be contracted. The primary obligation is that which is contracted principally in the first place and on its own account. The secondary obligation is that which is contracted in case of the non-performance of a primary obligation. For instance, in the contract of sale, the obligation which the seller contracts to deliver and warrant the thing sold is the primary obligation; that of paying the buyer damages, in case of inability to deliver or warrant the thing, is a secondary obligation.'

[6] Gaius, *Institutes*, 3.88.

[7] Justinian, *Institutes*, 3.13.

[8] See generally P Birks, 'Definition and Division: A Meditation on *Institutes* 3.13' in P Birks (ed), *The Classification of Obligations* (Oxford, Oxford University Press, 1997) ch 1.

[9] Birks, 'Rights, Wrongs, and Remedies' (2000) 20 *OJLS* 1.

[10] P Birks, *Unjust Enrichment*, 2nd edn (Oxford, Oxford University Press, 2004) 166.

[11] Although Peter famously moved from 'unjust factors' to 'absence of basis' just before his death, his thinking in terms of primary and secondary rights did not change.

subject to duties to make restitution before any court order were made against them.[12] Moreover, his was not an idiosyncratic view. As Steve observed, although almost every other element of the law of restitution is controverted, the idea of an obligation to make restitution immediately the cause of action arises is unquestioned in the unjust enrichment literature.[13]

For Steve, however, there was no such thing as a 'remedial restitutionary right'. Although recipients of unjust enrichments were liable to be ordered by a court to pay money to the claimant or provide some other form of relief, for example to convey a specific right, they were not duty-bound so to do unless and until so ordered by a court. Court orders making restitutionary awards were therefore duty-*creating*, not, as Birks would have it, duty-*confirming*.[14] The same was true of the commission of breaches of contract and torts. There is no obligation to pay damages for either until a court order is made; court orders here are also duty-creating.[15]

This essay is essentially an appendix to Steve's thinking, focusing specifically on orders to make restitution of unjust enrichments. However, the arguments can apply equally in the context of claims in both contract and tort. This chapter argues that the Birksian view is flawed, in that it fails to take account of the realities of the litigation process; in fact, it sidelines that process completely. It fails to notice that there is, beyond the substantive law, an adjectival law, a law of procedure. In Birks' world, this is entirely superfluous. Steve's model, by contrast, is immune from such criticism and thus a better fit with our law.

II. Steve's Arguments

Focusing on the paradigm case of the receipt of a spontaneous (as opposed to an induced) mistaken payment, Steve put forward several arguments why this could not give rise to an immediate duty on the part of the recipient to make restitution. There were, he said, certain 'justificatory puzzles' and certain 'doctrinal objections'.

[12] This will not be the case where the claimant contracts because of an induced mistake, duress or undue influence; the contract is valid until set aside. There is then a difficult question whether a court order is necessary for such setting aside, or whether it can be effected by the claimant alone.

[13] S Smith, 'A Duty to Make Restitution' (2013) 26 *Canadian Journal of Law and Jurisprudence* 157, 157.

[14] ibid; Smith (n 1) 237–49. See also SA Smith, 'The Restatement of Liabilities in Restitution' in C Mitchell and W Swadling (eds), *The Restatement Third, Restitution and Unjust Enrichment: Comparative and Critical Essays* (Oxford, Hart Publishing, 2013) 227.

[15] SA Smith, 'Duties, Liabilities, and Damages' (2012) 125 *Harvard Law Review* 1727; SA Smith, 'Remedies for Breach of Contract: One Principle or Two?' in G Klass, G Letsas and P Saprai (eds), *Philosophical Foundations of Contract Law* (Oxford, Oxford University Press, 2014) 341. This view was shared with others: J Goldberg and B Zipursky, 'Rights and Responsibility in the Law of Torts' in D Nolan and A Robertson (eds), *Rights and Private Law* (Oxford, Hart Publishing, 2011) 251; J Goldberg, 'The Constitutional Status of Tort Law: Due Process and the Right to a Law for the Redress of Wrongs' (2005) 115 *Yale Law Journal* 524; B Zipursky, 'Civil Recourse, Not Corrective Justice' (2003) 91 *Georgetown Law Journal* 695; N Oman 'Why There Is No Duty to Pay Damages: Powers, Duties, and Private Law' (2011) 39 *Florida State University Law Review* 137.

A. Justificatory Puzzles

One justificatory puzzle was the fact that the mistaken payee was often a mere passive recipient of the money:

> According to the obligation model, if you accidentally wire money into my bank account, the law imposes a legal obligation on me to pay you an equivalent sum of money. Why? What is the justification for imposing that obligation – a positive obligation to benefit you – in a situation where I have not undertaken to do something, or committed a wrong, or indeed done anything at all? To be clear, the puzzle is not the final result: few people would think I should be allowed to keep the money. The puzzle lies in explaining how that result is meant to be achieved. Why am I obliged to fix a problem that I had no hand in creating?[16]

While this is certainly a puzzle for the duty model, as Wilmot-Smith has persuasively argued,[17] it is not clear that Steve's liability model fares any better in this regard. A court order that the defendant pay the claimant a sum of money likewise imposes an obligation to benefit on someone who has done nothing to cause the claimant's problem. Steve saw no issue with this, as he considered that the payment away of money by mistake amounted to an 'injustice', and that the making of a court order, rather than the imposition of a duty, to correct that injustice was legitimate.[18] However, he nowhere addressed the point made by Wilmot-Smith why it is the recipient of the payment who is in the end forced to pay. This problem does not disappear simply by speaking in terms of duty-creating rather than duty-confirming rules.

A second justificatory puzzle was that the duty may be unknowable.[19] If the duty model is sound, said Steve, an obligation to make restitution will arise the moment the cause of action is complete, which in the case of a mistaken payment is the point when the payment is received. Yet at that point, the defendant might not even know of the claimant's performance; in a typical Steve example, the defendant might be out 'hiking in the wilderness', making it physically impossible for them to perform.[20] Let us call this the 'epistemic objection'. It has been argued that such an objection is invalid because of the existence of the strict liability torts.[21] This seems a sound rebuttal. Suppose I take your identical umbrella by mistake from a restaurant, genuinely thinking it is my own; I undoubtedly commit the tort of conversion. As Cleasby B famously said, 'persons deal with the property in chattels or exercise acts of ownership over them at their peril'.[22] But though the epistemic objection itself may be invalid, this does not invalidate Steve's thesis that court orders create, rather than confirm, duties to make restitution.

Third, said Steve, even if the payee sees the money coming into his account and the payor immediately claims it was paid by mistake, how is the payee to know that the

[16] Smith, 'The Restatement of Liabilities in Restitution' (n 14) 228–29.

[17] See the excellent discussion by F Wilmot-Smith, 'Should the Payee Pay?' (2017) 37 *OJLS* 844.

[18] Smith (n 1) 232ff.

[19] The 'unknowability' objection is specifically addressed in a number of other chapters in this volume: see Klimchuk (ch 19); Kramer (ch 16); Wilmot-Smith (ch 20).

[20] Smith (n 1) 243.

[21] S Steel and R Stevens, 'The secondary legal duty to pay damages' (2020) 136 *LQR* 283, 284–85.

[22] *Fowler v Hollins* (1872) LR 7 QB 616, 639.

payor's claim to be both payor and mistaken is genuine?[23] Must he simply accept the payor's word for it? If the payor were to ask a court for relief, it would require the payor to present evidence. Why, asked Steve, should the payee have to accept anything less?[24] Such an objection, he said, applied 'regardless of whether the alleged substantive duty arises when the transfer is made, when the claimant requests restitution, when litigation commences, or at any other time'.[25] This, however, seems to be another manifestation of the epistemic objection. Once again, even if that objection is invalid, it does not necessarily follow that Steve's thesis, that court orders create duties to make restitution, is incorrect.

The justificatory arguments, it would seem, are equivocal. Though they do not rule out the duty-creating model, they do not rule it in either.

B. Doctrinal Objections

Steve was on firmer ground in saying that, beyond the justificatory puzzles, the notion of an immediate obligation to repay a mistaken payment was open to certain doctrinal objections.

First, he said, it is well established that there is no duty to pay damages for not making restitution.[26] If there really was an obligation to pay, he asked, why does the law provide no remedy for its breach? To the argument that such duties cannot be breached because they are not time-limited, Steve's response was that the absence of a date for performance was a reason for questioning the alleged duty's existence, and that if the law wished to impose such a duty, it could just stipulate that it must be performed within a reasonable time.[27] Further, the fact that interest is payable on such awards is no evidence of an obligation to pay, for interest does not equate to loss.[28]

It might also be added that if there were a duty on the defendant to pay money to the claimant before the making of a court order, there would arguably be a further claim for breach of that duty to pay damages for breach of duty, so producing an infinite regression. As was pointed out by Walter Wheeler Cook more than a century ago, it is

> difficult to maintain for a moment that there is any 'right' to damages in the strict sense of right, ie, with a corresponding duty to pay the damages. If there were, it would be violated by non-payment of damages and a new remedial right would arise to be again violated by non-payment, and so on, ad infinitum. The 'right to damages' on analysis, appears to consist of (1) a privilege, and (2) a power with the corresponding liability. There is a liability on the

[23] *Smith* (n 1) 244.

[24] ibid.

[25] ibid. Once again, it might be objected that there is no necessity for an epistemic condition for the presence of duties, that our legal system does recognise duties of which defendants will be unaware. This does not make Steve wrong, however. The issue again is one of fit. What is the best explanation of the current law? Is the law imposing duties to pay immediately the unjust enrichment occurs or only later, when the court makes an order?.

[26] Smith (n 1) 240–41.

[27] ibid 240.

[28] Despite the fact that judges do sometimes see statutory interest as reflecting the fact that the claimant has been kept out of 'their' money.

> part of the defendant to have a judgment entered against him, but no duty to pay until the judgment is entered. The plaintiff through the court has a power to subject the defendant to the imposition of a new obligation known as a debt of record, which is of course a new primary right with its corresponding duty.[29]

Second, the fact that interest awards are assessed at the date of the defendant's enrichment does not show that 'the law presumes that defendants should have made restitution immediately after they were enriched'.[30] The better explanation, said Steve, is that 'interest represents part of the defendant's enrichment'.[31] It might also be added that interest awards are purely the creature of statute. It is trite law that there is no power in courts to make damages awards at common law for the failure to pay damages;[32] by the same token, there can be no liability to pay damages for not immediately repaying a mistaken payment, a fact seemingly forgotten by those who point to the availability of interest as evidence of a common law duty to make restitution on receipt.

The third doctrinal objection concerned the operation of the defence of change of position. 'If there is a substantive duty to make restitution,' asked Steve, 'why should it matter what the defendant does (short of satisfying the duty) after the duty has arisen?'[33] It might be said in reply that the defendant's change of position cuts back the court's willingness to order performance of the duty to make restitution. However, we would no longer be in the realm of the novation of rights, as Birks asserts, for there would now be a disjuncture between the right the claimant has outside the courtroom and the one they have inside.

The upshot was that an unjustly enriched defendant could in Steve's view, only be said to come under a liability to be ordered by the court to make restitution, and that any subsequent court order created a duty to make restitution and did not 'confirm' it. Thus, there were no 'rights' to restitution, merely 'liabilities' to be ordered by a court to make restitution.

III. The Duty-Confirming View is Inconsistent with the Litigation Process

As we have seen, the only function of the court in Birks' world is the passive one of confirming a pre-existing duty on the defendant to pay (or provide some other form of relief).[34] The court, for Birks, simply 'replicates' or 'novates' the existing remedial duty. The argument, however, ignores completely the way our legal system works.

[29] W Wheeler Cook, 'The Powers of Courts of Equity, Part I' (1915) 15 *Columbia Law Review* 37, 45 (footnotes omitted).

[30] Smith (n 1) 241. For an argument in support of Steve's proposition, see A Georgiou and E Rawkins, 'Interest and Enrichment, Again' (2022) 138 *LQR* 186.

[31] Smith (n 1) 241. See also Kramer, ch 16 in this volume.

[32] 'There is no such thing as a cause of action in damages for late payment of damages': *President of India v Lip Maritime Corpn* [1988] AC 395, 425 (Lord Brandon).

[33] Smith (n 1) 242.

[34] Whether the 'right' is one to the payment of money or specific relief is nowhere explained by the duty-confirming theorists.

A. Pleading

First, the argument is inconsistent with the way claims are pleaded. If the claimant pays £1,000 to the defendant by mistake and later brings a claim for restitution, the pleadings will not allege a duty on the defendant to repay at the point of receipt, a failure to comply with such duty and a prayer for a remedy for such breach.[35] The claimant will instead recite the fact that the money was paid by mistake, that it has not been repaid, and will ask for an order that the defendant pay the claimant an equivalent sum.[36] Breach of duty is a wrong, yet mistaken payors do not routinely allege wrongdoing. Indeed, if mistaken payees were always wrongdoers, there would be no room for the operation of the defence of change of position, which is denied to defendants who are wrongdoers.[37] By contrast, Steve's duty-creating view is perfectly consistent with how claims are pleaded.

B. Resolution of Disputed Issues of Fact

As Dixon CJ pointed out in *Bank of New South Wales v The Commonwealth*, 'courts have an advantage over other seekers after truth. For by their judgment they can reduce to legal certainty questions to which no other conclusive answer can be given.'[38] The duty-confirming view denies the fact-finding role of the court altogether.

For Birks, the central case in our subject was *Kelly v Solari*.[39] Yet the case itself is completely at odds with the remedial rights model of restitution. It will be recalled that a widow made a claim on her husband's life insurance policy with the Argus Life Assurance Company. Unbeknownst to her, her husband had failed to pay the quarterly premium due a month before his death, the company noting in pencil on the policy document 'Lapsed'. It nevertheless paid out on her claim. The plaintiff company director brought an action to recover the overpaid sum, alleging it to have been paid by mistake. At trial at *nisi prius*, the plaintiff admitted that the company had known some time before paying out that the policy had lapsed, but alleged that this had been forgotten by the time of payment, two of the company's directors giving evidence to this effect. However, Lord Abinger CB withdrew the case from the jury, holding that the admission of prior knowledge was fatal to the plaintiff's claim.[40] He accordingly directed a non-suit, reserving leave to the plaintiff to move to enter a verdict for the amount claimed, as a way of calling into question that holding on the law.[41]

[35] The same objection applies to claims for breaches of contract and tort, where claimants never seek damages for a breach of the 'duty' to pay damages.

[36] See, eg, W Blair et al, *Bullen & Leake & Jacob's Precedents of Pleadings* (19th ed, London, Sweet and Maxwell, 2022), [108-ZA1], para 3.

[37] *Lipkin Gorman v Karpnale Ltd* [1991] 2 AC 548, 580.

[38] *Bank of New South Wales v The Commonwealth* (1949) 76 CLR 1, 340.

[39] *Kelly v Solari* (1841) 9 M & W 54 formed the subject matter of the first chapter of Birks' last book, *Unjust Enrichment* (n 10), entitled 'A Core Case'. The reason it was the core case was that '[t]he law of unjust enrichment is the law of all events materially identical to the mistaken payment of a non-existent debt': ibid 3.

[40] *Kelly v Solari* (n 39) 54–55.

[41] The procedure, odd to modern eyes, but essentially providing for an appeal, is explained in R Sutton, *Personal Actions at Common Law* (London, Butterworths, 1929) 128–29.

When the plaintiff claimed that verdict, the defendant argued in support of Lord Abinger's ruling at trial. She also made a further argument that restitution could only be ordered where retention of the money was 'unconscientious'. Both arguments failed, however. Lord Abinger held that he had been wrong to withdraw the case from the jury on the ground of prior knowledge: 'the knowledge which disentitles the party from recovering, must mean a knowledge existing in the mind at the time of payment'.[42] As to a need for 'unconscientiousness', Rolfe B said that whenever money 'is paid under a mistake of fact, and the party would not have paid it if the fact had been known to him, it could not be otherwise than unconscientious to retain it'.[43] Unconscientiousness, in other words, added nothing.

The failure of the defendant's arguments meant that the plaintiff should not have been non-suited at trial. The question then was whether simply to grant the relief sought by the plaintiff, or to order a new trial. The court decided on the latter course of action. Although Lord Abinger, having heard the evidence at trial, had 'little doubt … that the directors had forgotten the fact', he held that the defendant 'ought to have had the opportunity of taking the opinion of the jury on the question whether in reality the directors had a knowledge of the facts'.[44] Parke, Gurney and Rolfe BB agreed, Rolfe B saying:

> I agree that Mr Platt [counsel for the defendant] has a right to go to the jury again, upon two grounds: first, that the jury may possibly find that the directors had not in truth forgotten the fact; and secondly, they may also come to the conclusion, that they had determined that they would not expose the office to unpopularity, and would therefore pay the money at all events; in which case I quite agree that they could not recover it back.[45]

Kelly v Solari thus demonstrates that we cannot definitively say there was a mistake before a determination to that effect has been made by the relevant tribunal of fact.[46] The insurance company may well have been telling the truth when it said it was mistaken, and Lord Abinger CB certainly thought it was, but the veracity of that claim was something to be determined by the jury.[47] That is their function in our legal system. How can there be an immediate right to restitution if the event generating that right is dependent on the adjudication of the court?

[42] *Kelly v Solari* (n 39) 58.

[43] ibid 59.

[44] ibid 57.

[45] ibid 59.

[46] Even then, the judge or jury might get the issue wrong. But the 'facts' on which judges make orders are those determined by the relevant tribunal of fact, not those happening in the real world.

[47] Robert Stevens reads the judgments of Lord Abinger CB and Rolfe B as showing that the defendant was entitled to raise a defence that the plaintiff was not mistaken, that all that was needed for the plaintiff to win was a demonstration that there was no legal basis for the payment: R Stevens, *The Laws of Restitution* (Oxford, Oxford University Press, 2023) 71. This is a strained reading of the judgments, which were clearly only concerned to ensure that the defendant was able to put the plaintiffs to proof, to determine the veracity of their claim through cross-examination. Moreover, on Stevens' view, the burden of proof of what would be a non-mistake would be on the defendant, which is odd given that this is something wholly within the plaintiff's knowledge. Finally, mistake on the part of the insurance company was alleged by the insurance company, and it was precisely that which the plaintiff was attempting to prove before his non-suit. The courts certainly treat the burden of proof of any alleged mistake as lying on the claimant: *Holt v Markham* [1923] 1 KB 504, 511 (Warrington LJ); *Avon County Council v Howlett* [1983] 1 WLR 605, 617 (Slade LJ).

Exactly the same approach is seen in the decision in *Kleinwort Benson Ltd v Lincoln City Council*,[48] where the House of Lords laid down the rule that payments made under a mistake of law could be recovered. As to the facts themselves, the trial judge, Langley J, did not decide whether the claimant had made the mistake alleged, taking the view that mistake of law was not a ground of recovery. After a leap-frog appeal to the House of Lords held to the contrary, the case was remitted to trial to determine whether the alleged mistake had in fact been made. Can we really say there was a mistake, and therefore a right to restitution, simply because the claimant alleged it, before the tribunal of fact had investigated the matter?

For the same reason, the remedial rights model is inconsistent with the law of estoppel. In *Avon County Council v Howlett*,[49] the plaintiffs alleged that they had mistakenly paid the defendant, one of their employees, too much in sickness benefits. However, prior to the litigation, the defendant had checked with the plaintiffs whether the payments they had made were due; he was assured that all was in order. As a result, he spent roughly half the money in ways he would not otherwise have done. On this basis, the Court of Appeal dismissed the plaintiffs' claim. Because of the plaintiffs' representation and the defendant's detrimental reliance thereon, the employers were estopped from leading evidence to show they were in fact mistaken. 'Estoppel by representation,' said Eveleigh LJ, 'is a rule of evidence, the consequence of which is simply to preclude the representor from averring facts contrary to his own representation.'[50] As far as the court was concerned, therefore, the plaintiffs never made a mistake, though in the parallel universe we might call 'the real world' they might well have done. If they really were mistaken in the 'real world', it can hardly be said that the refusal of the court to order the defendant to make restitution 'replicated' the plaintiffs' 'right' to the same.

Once again, only Steve's thesis is consistent with the function of the court in the case of disputed facts. Only where the court finds proved the claimant's allegation that the payment was made by mistake, duress, undue influence and so on, can any duty to make restitution possibly arise.

C. Resolution of Disputed Issues of Law

The function of the court is not confined to resolving disputed issues of fact; it must also resolve contested issues of law. As Lords Reed and Hodge said in *Test Claimants in the FII Group Litigation v Revenue and Customs Commissioners (No 2)*:

> It is in the nature of litigation that facts and law are commonly disputed. It is the function of courts to resolve those disputes. Until the court has done so, the parties can, at best, have only a reasonable belief that their assertions are correct.[51]

[48] *Kleinwort Benson Ltd v Lincoln City Council* [1999] 2 AC 349.

[49] *Avon County Council v Howlett* (n 46).

[50] ibid 622.

[51] *Test Claimants in the FII Group Litigation v Revenue and Customs Commissioners (No 2)* [2020] UKSC 47, [2022] AC 1 [196].

This, indeed, is how the common law is made. For the duty-confirming view to work, the law would have to exist separately from the pronouncements of the court. Yet we know this is untrue.

Take as an example *Receiver for Metropolitan Police v Croydon Corporation*.[52] In two separate cases, the defendants' negligence caused police officers to be unfit for work. The claimants were contractually obliged to continue paying the officers' salaries and sought to recover the cost from the defendants. In the first case, Slade J allowed recovery from the defendant tortfeasor.[53] In the second, Lynskey J refused the claim.[54] Both cases were joined for the purposes of appeal, with the Court of Appeal holding that Lynskey J had the better of the argument. Before that decision, the law was in conflict. Only with the decision of the Court of Appeal was that conflict resolved. Yet Birks would have us believe that the law was clear all along.

Another example is *Jazztel plc v Revenue and Customs Commissioners*,[55] a claim for repayment of overpaid tax. The defendant taxing authority claimed the right to charge a particular tax; only later, in *HSBC Holdings v Revenue and Customs Commissioners*,[56] was it established that it did not have that right. Once again, the decision of a court was needed to resolve the dispute.

Again, only Steve's duty-creating view is consistent with the function of the court in resolving disputed issues of law: rights must be contingent on court orders.

D. The Appellate Process

The duty-confirming view is also inconsistent with the existence of the appellate process. Take as an example the swaps litigation. Until the House of Lords handed down its decision (after 14 days of argument) in *Hazell v Hammersmith and Fulham LBC*,[57] we did not know for certain that local authorities had no power to enter into interest rate swaps contracts. Indeed, the Court of Appeal in the same litigation had previously held that they did.[58] Can we really say there was a duty on the local authority in *Westdeutsche Landesbank Girozentrale v Islington LBC*[59] to repay the money the moment the payment was received, when the Court of Appeal in *Hazell* was of the view that such contracts were valid? Moreover, what would have happened had the litigation in *Hazell* stopped after the judgment of the Court of Appeal? Could we really say there was a right to restitution even though an appellate court had held the contracts under which monies were paid were valid?

Similarly, in *Banque Financiere de la Cité v Parc (Battersea) Ltd*,[60] a claim to be subrogated to a lender's right of repayment succeeded at trial, was overturned on appeal

[52] *Receiver for Metropolitan Police v Croydon Corporation* [1957] 2 QB 154.

[53] *Receiver for Metropolitan Police v Croydon Corporation* [1956] 1 WLR 1113.

[54] *Monmouthshire County Council v Smith* [1956] 1 WLR 1132.

[55] *Jazztel plc v Revenue and Customs Commissioners* [2022] EWCA Civ 232, [2022] Ch 403.

[56] *HSBC Holdings v Revenue and Customs Commissioners* [2010] STC 58.

[57] *Hazell v Hammersmith and Fulham LBC* [1992] 2 AC 1.

[58] Overturning the decision of the Divisional Court that such contracts were void: *Hazell v Hammersmith and Fulham LBC* [1990] 2 QB 697.

[59] *Westdeutsche Landesbank Girozentrale v Islington LBC* [1996] AC 669.

[60] *Banque Financière de la Cité v Parc (Battersea) Ltd* [1999] 1 AC 221.

but reinstated by the House of Lords. Can we really say there was a right to subrogation at the point when the money was paid when the Court of Appeal later said there was not? Moreover, what 'duty' is involved when courts allow subrogation claims to discharged debts?

We see a similar phenomenon in *Niru Battery Manufacturing Co v Milestone Trading Ltd*,[61] a claim for contribution between tortfeasors. As the Court of Appeal there explained:

> At the trial both CAI and SGS accepted that if they were both liable they could claim contribution from each other under section 1 of the Civil Liability (Contribution) Act 1978. However, after the judge had handed down his draft judgment on liability in this case, his attention was drawn to the decision of the House of Lords in *Royal Brompton Hospital NHS Trust v Hammond* [2002] 1 WLR 1397, in which Lord Steyn, with whom the other members of the House agreed, disapproved the approach of this court in *Friends' Provident Life Office v Hiller Parker May & Rowden* [1997] QB 85, which had underpinned the parties' approach to contribution. As a result the debate before the judge in the contribution proceedings, in which judgment was given on 8 May 2003, took a somewhat different course from that which it might otherwise have done.[62]

If court orders replicate rights, then we would have to say that there was all along a duty to contribute, which duty was confirmed by the Court of Appeal in the *Friends' Provident* case, but then that there never was a duty to contribute once that case was overruled. Or do we instead say (presumably using some sort of crystal ball) that there never was a duty to contribute because *Friends' Provident* was wrongly decided? Indeed, one unanswered question is how the duty-confirming view copes with judicial error, if that is the right word to describe it.

Another example is *Benedetti v Sawiris*,[63] where the claimant provided services to the defendant in respect of the latter's takeover of a telecoms company. The trial judge ordered the defendant to pay €75.1m, but the Court of Appeal reduced the award to €14.52m, with the Supreme Court reducing it in turn to zero because of payments already received by the claimant. The case involved hugely complicated issues of law,[64] yet the rights-thesis advocates would have us believe that the defendant was obliged to pay nothing from the start. What they would make of both the High Court's order and the Court of Appeal's reduced order is difficult to say. When the trial judge ordered the defendant to pay €75.1m, he could hardly be seen as 'replicating' the claimant's right to be paid nothing; the same is also true of the reduced order of the Court of Appeal.

Finally, there is the already discussed case of *Jazztel*,[65] where the law of limitation changed during the course of the litigation. With regard to payments made under a mistake of law, the House of Lords in *Deutsche Morgan Grenfell Group Plc v Inland Revenue Commissioners* had held that such mistakes were not 'discoverable' for the

[61] *Niru Battery Manufacturing Co v Milestone Trading Ltd* [2003] EWCA Civ 1446, [2004] QB 985.
[62] ibid [27].
[63] *Benedetti v Sawiris* [2014] AC 938.
[64] The Supreme Court judgments spanned 229 paragraphs, with differing views expressed on the concept of subjective devaluation.
[65] Above, text to nn 55–56.

purposes of the postponement of the running of the six-year limitation period until the handing down of the judgment of an ultimate appellate tribunal.[66] Until that point, said Lord Hoffmann, the payee 'could not have discovered the truth because the truth did not yet exist'.[67] The trial judge in *Jazztel*, Marcus Smith J, as he was bound to do by the doctrine of precedent, applied that ruling to the claim, holding that it was not barred by limitation. However, between his decision and the Court of Appeal hearing, the United Kingdom Supreme Court, in *Test Claimants in the FII Group Litigation v Revenue and Customs Commissioners (No 2)*,[68] overruled *Deutsche Morgan Grenfell* on this point. This had the consequence that the claim in *Jazztel* itself was held to have been brought out of time. What, then, of the order made by Marcus Smith J? How can we say that it 'replicated' the pre-existing right of the claimants to restitution when the Court of Appeal later held that it was wrongly made? Nowhere does Birks explain how his thesis fits with the constantly evolving nature of judge-made law.

It might be objected that though this is a problem for the view that a duty arises as the facts occur, it is equally problematic for Steve's liability view. The problems arising from the reality of retroactive judicial law-making are not arguably confined to the view of Birks. Steve also needs an answer to the question just posed about the order of Marcus Smith J; even though he would not say it was replicative, he would have to say it had some juridical effect, and then would have to deal with the retroactive effects of the rulings of higher courts as much as Birks or anyone. Such an objection is, however, unfounded. There is no doubt that a ruling made by a judge has legal effect unless and until it is overturned by a superior court. Steve would not have to say that the original order was a nullity. To take an example from the criminal law, if a defendant is convicted and imprisoned, but then released on appeal, it is trite law that those who imprisoned him are not liable for wrongful imprisonment. That is perfectly consistent with what Steve is saying. Yet on Birks' view, they would seem to be tortfeasors from the start.

E. Issues of Judgement

Litigation sometimes involves an exercise of judgement by the court, yet another thing the duty-confirming view cannot accommodate. There are many examples, one being the computation by the court of a 'just sum' under section 1(3) of the Law Reform (Frustrated Contracts) Act 1943. Another is that involved in contribution proceedings, where courts are required to determine the amount that is 'just and equitable having regard to the extent of that person's responsibility for the damage in question'.[69] In both cases, it is impossible to say that the claimant brings to court pre-existing rights, for they are both dependent on an exercise of judgement by the court. Once again, Steve's thesis does not encounter this problem, for rights are being created by the court order, not simply confirmed.

[66] *Deutsche Morgan Grenfell Group Plc v Inland Revenue Commissioners* [2006] UKHL 49, [2007] 1 AC 558.

[67] ibid [31].

[68] *Test Claimants in the FII Group Litigation v Revenue and Customs Commissioners (No 2)* [2020] UKSC 47, [2022] AC 1.

[69] Civil Liability (Contribution) Act 1978, s 2(1).

IV. Conclusion

The problem with the remedial rights thesis put forward by Birks is that it fails to distinguish between substantive and adjectival law. For him, there was only substantive law. It is, however, wrong to see there as being both rights to the performance of a contract and rights to damages for its breach; wrong to think there are rights not to be defamed, assaulted and so on and rights to damages for breach of such obligations; and wrong to say there is an obligation to make restitution of an unjust enrichment by the mere fact of receipt. Such 'remedial' or 'secondary' rights are the creature of the court, of the adjectival not the substantive law. They do not exist until a court order is made in the claimant's favour. Court orders to pay damages or make restitution are therefore duty-creating, not duty-confirming.

I have sought to bolster Steve's arguments by showing how his duty-creating model fares better as an explanation of court orders than Birks' duty-confirming alternative, by demonstrating the incompatibility of the duty-confirming view with the way our legal system operates, with our adjectival or procedural law. Birks simply ignores it, turning judges into mere slot-machines. The adjectival law must not, however, be left out of account. It was shown that the duty-confirming view is inconsistent with the process of litigation in five ways. First, unjust enrichment claims are not pleaded in terms of a duty to repay and a breach thereof, but simply pray for an order to repay. Second, the duty-confirming view bypasses the role of the courts in resolving disputed questions of fact, whereas defendants are entitled to put claimants to proof, as demonstrated by the leading case of *Kelly v Solari*.[70] Third, the duty-confirming view bypasses the role of the courts in resolving disputed issues of law, ignoring the way the common law is made. Fourth, it is incompatible with the appellate process: if an order of a trust judge is overturned, how could the trial judge's order have 'replicated' the claimant's rights? Fifth, and finally, the duty-confirming view fails to accommodate the fact that many cases involve courts in exercising judgement.

These inconsistencies with the operation of the legal system mean that it is impossible to say there is a duty to make restitution on receipt of a mistaken payment. At best, recipients come under liabilities to be ordered by a judge to make restitution: there are no 'remedial restitutionary rights'. Just as Steve's gown was a better fit for me, so too is his explanation of the content of court orders in the law of restitution a better fit for the common law.

[70] *Kelly v Solari* (n 39).

PART III

Contract

12

The Scope of Restraint of Trade

ROBERT STEVENS

I. From the End to the Beginning

Today, at least in England, anyone seeking an academic post in a serious law faculty would be expected to have a doctorate in law. In the 1990s this was not so, and I obtained my first academic job at Oxford on the time-honoured basis of appearing to be a Good Thing.

Steve Smith by contrast, did his doctorate in Oxford: 'The common law of restraint of trade: a theoretical analysis',[1] under the supervision of Joseph Raz and Hugh Collins. It combines, as its title indicates, a keen interest in the substantive legal doctrine and what might in principle justify it, that was to characterise all of his work. He not only appeared to be a Good Thing: he was.

The doctorate led to his articles 'Of Remedies and Restrictive Covenants'[2] and 'Reconstructing Restraint of Trade',[3] and the ideas foreshadowed there are also found in his later work on duress,[4] penalties[5] and interpretive accounts of law.[6]

When, some months before he died, I said to Steve that I intended to write about his doctorate, he tried to put me off. He had the embarrassment many of us feel for our juvenilia. However, the younger man was much more able than the older had recalled, and the mature scholar had something to say to his younger self of 30 years before.

In his last, and major, work, he succeeded in showing that the law of court orders in private law is distinctive.[7] It gives rise to different concerns from the substantive rights we have one against another. This chapter makes two claims that follow on from the late and early work. First, that the restraint of trade doctrine does not concern the validity of the agreement between the parties but its enforceability. It too is best understood as part of the law of court orders. Second, that Lord Reid's formulation of the restricted scope

[1] S Smith, 'The common law of restraint of trade: a theoretical analysis' (DPhil, Oxford University, 1993).

[2] S Smith, 'Of Remedies and Restrictive Covenants' (1994) 7 *Journal of Contract Law* 164.

[3] S Smith, 'Reconstructing Restraint of Trade' (1995) 15 *OJLS* 565.

[4] S Smith, 'Contracting under Pressure: A Theory of Duress' (1997) 56 *CLJ* 343.

[5] S Smith, 'Performance, Punishment and the Nature of Contractual Obligations' (1997) 60 *MLR* 360.

[6] S Smith, *Contract Theory* (Oxford, Oxford University Press, 2004) ch 1.

[7] S Smith, *Rights, Wrongs and Injustices: The Structure of Remedial Law* (Oxford, Oxford University Press, 2019).

of restraint of trade in *Esso Petroleum Co Ltd v Harper's Garage (Stourport) Ltd*[8] was correct, follows from the justification for the doctrine, and that the abandonment of this restriction by the United Kingdom (UK) Supreme Court for one of what is accepted in 'trading society' in *Peninsula Securities Ltd v Dunnes Stores (Bangor) Ltd*[9] was mistaken.

II. What is Objectionable to Clauses in Restraint of Trade?

The most common examples of agreements in restraint of trade are post-employment covenants (employees promising not to use what they have learned in the course of their employment in competition with the employer), sale of business no-compete covenants (such as a restraint on a seller of a retail business to stop them from setting up shop in competition with the buyer) or, more unusually, attempts to create cartels to the prejudice of third parties.

The doctrine of restraint of trade is unfortunately commonly lumped together in textbook accounts with the quite separate rules on the effect of illegality in enforcing a contract.[10] That latter doctrine has nothing to do with what is just as between the two contracting parties, indeed the effect of its operation will only ever be to refuse to do what would otherwise be just as between them. It ensures that our private law rules cohere with the reasons for criminal prohibitions. There is nothing necessarily illegal about agreements in restraint of trade. It is tempting, but wrong, to think of the restraint of trade rule as similarly based upon a 'public policy' wholly external to the parties to the contract: promoting economic efficiency by ensuring competition and eliminating cartels. However, it has been convincingly shown that the law as it is cannot be understood in such crude economic terms.[11] The courts do not engage in a wide-ranging consideration of when, if ever, a particular covenant will be economically optimal.[12] This is unsurprising, as the courts lack both the technical competence and political legitimacy to engage in this enquiry. The doctrine of restraint of trade is primarily, but not solely, concerned with the protection of the promisor.

Steve's view was that the restraint of trade doctrine 'can be defended on the ground that autonomy is a crucial ingredient in individual well-being and that the law should not help individuals to give up future autonomy unnecessarily'.[13] Subject to a qualification

[8] *Esso Petroleum Co Ltd v Harper's Garage (Stourport) Ltd* [1968] AC 269.

[9] *Peninsula Securities Ltd v Dunnes Stores (Bangor) Ltd* [2020] UKSC 36, [2021] AC 1014.

[10] eg H Beale (ed), *Chitty on Contracts*, 34th edn (London, Sweet & Maxwell, 2021) (hereinafter '*Chitty*') ch 18; E Peel, *Treitel on the Law of Contract*, 15th edn (London, Sweet & Maxwell, 2020) (hereinafter '*Treitel*') ch 11; J Beatson, A Burrows and J Cartwright, *Anson's Law of Contract*, 31st edn (Oxford Oxford University Press, 2016) (hereinafter '*Anson*') ch 11.

[11] M Trebilcock, *The Common Law of Restraint of Trade: A Legal and Economic Analysis* (Toronto, Carswell, 1987) 407–14; Smith (n 1).

[12] *Texaco Ltd v Mulberry Filling Station Ltd* [1972] 1 WLR 814, 827, per Ungoed-Thomas J: '[R]estraint of trade … is based on and directed to securing the liberty of the subject and not the utmost economic advantage. It is part of a doctrine of common law and not of economics.'

[13] Smith (n 3) 570. See also P Benson, *Justice in Transactions* (Cambridge, MA, Harvard University Press, 2019) 197. cf *Petrofina (Great Britain) Ltd v Martin* [1966] Ch 146, 169, per Lord Denning MR.

concerning third parties discussed in section III, this seems to be both the best reason available to account for the law as it generally is and one that also (happily) accords with considerations of justice as to what it ought to be.

A close cousin to the restraint of trade doctrine is the rule that the law will not specifically enforce contracts for the provision of personal services, such as employment contracts.[14] We do not use state resources through its powers of enforcement to promote a system of slavery, even one voluntarily entered into. This too is nothing to do with 'public policy', if by that we mean considerations of justice unrelated to the parties before the court. The restraint of trade doctrine goes further in ruling out not only specific relief, but also any claim for damages for breach.

Enforcing restrictive covenants is, in one sense, much less objectionable than enforcing promises to provide personal services. After all, compliance with a restrictive covenant only stops the promisor from doing one thing, the full range of other options on how to live remains open; being forced to work, on the other hand, excludes all other options during that time. But in practice, if promisors are to be prevented by a covenant from doing the only trade for which they are suited (eg, a professional footballer unable to play; a dentist prevented from drilling teeth), their productive lives are sterilised by the restriction.

However, looked at from the other side of the relation, such clauses are more suspect than a positive covenant to provide a service. If work is performed, the promisee gets the benefit of that work. If a restrictive covenant is respected, the promisee merely obtains the 'not doing' by the counterparty that almost everyone else in the world is simultaneously not doing. Directly, the promisee obtains essentially nothing. The direct cost to the promisor may be high, the direct benefit to the promisee non-existent.

There may of course be significant consequential or ancillary benefits for the promisee from giving effect to a restrictive covenant. Traditionally, if a master blacksmith took on an apprentice and agreed to train him, he would not want to train up a competitor, and so it would be agreed that the apprentice would not work in the vicinity once his employment came to an end. If such a clause is not to be given effect, the master will not pass on his skills to others. In the modern era, if a business is to be sold at a price that reflects its goodwill, this will only be possible if the seller's promise not to compete, and thereby take the goodwill away, is enforceable. The reason for the inclusion of such clauses is the consequential economic benefit that flows from them, which explains why damages for breach should be, and in England are, confined to special damages for consequential economic loss.[15] Unlike the performance of a promise to deliver goods or services, the performance of a purely negative covenant is not valuable for itself.

Not all restrictive covenants are therefore objectionable. If the promisee shows both that he has a legitimate interest to protect through the clause and that it is reasonable as between the parties to it, and the promisor does not show that it is unreasonable in relation to the public interest, it is enforceable.[16]

[14] See also *Harwood v Millar's Timber and Trading Co Ltd* [1917] 1 KB 305, CA for another near relative.
[15] *Morris-Garner v One Step (Support) Ltd* [2018] UKSC 20, [2019] AC 649.
[16] *Nordenfelt v Maxim Nordenfelt Guns and Ammunition Co Ltd* [1894] AC 535, 565, per Lord Macnaghten.

III. Third Parties: The Public Interest

Attempts by contracting parties to prevent third parties from working or trading are more objectionable than the situation where a party has agreed to give up their own freedom and been provided with consideration in exchange for their promise. The best modern example of how the interests of third parties to the agreement may engage the restraint of trade doctrine, other than through the general interest we all have that the promisor not be restrained from working or trading, is the decision in *Eastham v Newcastle United Football Club*.[17] The decision arose from the 'retain and transfer' system then in operation in the English football league. That system was a creation of the agreement between the clubs who made up the League. At that time, a club could put a player previously under contract with it on a 'retained' list, thereby preventing him from playing for another club. If, by contrast, the player was placed on the 'transfer' list, the player could apply to the League's management committee to have the fee reduced or eliminated, and could transfer to a club outside of the League without any transfer fee. The 'retained' list was effectively a transfer list that removed these options from the player. Wilberforce J concluded that this 'retain' system was unenforceable as in restraint of trade: it unreasonably interfered with the liberty of players to work.[18] A declaration to that effect was made against Newcastle United, the League and the Football Association. The transfer list system, under which a player after the termination of his contract could move to another club only if a fee were paid for his registration, was not formally ruled upon, although Wilberforce J indicated that it was unobjectionable.[19] It survived until the *Bosman*[20] ruling, when the European Court of Justice struck it down as incompatible with freedom of movement for workers under the Treaty of Rome.

Similar, although more difficult, is the subsequent decision of the Court of Appeal in *Nagle v Fielden*.[21] Florence Nagle was a trainer and breeder of racehorses. The Jockey Club was in charge of flat race meetings in Great Britain. By its rules, no horse was entitled to run unless trained by a licensed trainer, and it had a monopoly on the granting of licences. Nagle applied for a licence, which was refused without reasons being given but was in fact because she was a woman (she had previously bypassed this effective ban on women trainers by having her 'head lad' apply for and obtain a licence). She applied for a declaration that the practice in refusing a licence to women was void as against public policy, and an injunction ordering the stewards to grant her a licence. The court concluded that, although she had no contract with the Jockey Club, it was arguable that the practice was contrary to public policy, violating her 'right to work', and refused to strike out the action.

The unenforceability of the express contractual rules of the associations prejudicing third parties in *Eastham v Newcastle United*, and of the implicitly agreed rules in

[17] *Eastham v Newcastle United Football Club* [1964] Ch 413.
[18] ibid 427.
[19] ibid 427–38.
[20] Case C-415/93 *Bosman* [1995] ECR I-4921.
[21] *Nagle v Fielden* [1966] 2 QB 633.

Nagle v Fielden, follows *a fortiori* from the more usual case of the unenforceability of restraints that limit the freedom of the promisor to work and trade. However, although an injunction was thought arguably available in *Nagle v Fielden*, the doctrinal basis upon which this would be so is obscure. It is one thing to conclude that an agreement to the prejudice of a third party is unenforceable, quite another to decide that the third party has a right to prevent its performance.

This limited approach to how and why the interests of third parties to have the liberty to work or trade ('the public') may render a contract unenforceable reflects the conception of the doctrine in England but not in the United States. In the United States, an agreement not to bid at an auction or similar bidding competition is caught by the doctrine.[22] In England, this has never been so.[23] The agreement may remove a potential bidder, but it does not set back in any significant degree the freedom of a seller to trade. The seller can protect themselves by setting a reserve price and would, without more, be left with no remedy if the conspirators adhered to their bargain, even if it is unenforceable. It should not be enough for the doctrine to apply that the agreement, if adhered to, would leave a third party worse off. It is not, properly, a freebooting power of the courts to regulate competition, and it is unknowable whether enforcing such agreements is, overall, a good or bad thing in economic terms.

IV. Unenforceable

Contract textbooks refer to clauses that fall foul of the restraint of trade rule as 'void' and 'unenforceable' almost interchangeably.[24] In almost all litigated cases, the distinction does not arise. The usual issue is whether the promised restraint can either be enforced by an injunction, or a claim for damages be awarded for breach of it. In such a case, it does not matter whether the promise is void or merely unenforceable.

However, in some cases it would matter. What if the agreement is fully executed, neither party realising that it is objectionable on the grounds of being in restraint of trade? Could payments made in exchange for the restraint be recovered? Alternatively, if, unusually, the restrained party is to be paid after they have forborne for a period from working or trading, can they recover the sum promised them, or is their performance and the promise to pay in exchange a nullity?

The correct position, it is suggested, is that restraint of trade should only potentially render promises in an agreement unenforceable, not void. Once fully executed, the agreement should not be susceptible to being unwound on the basis of being in restraint of trade. The agreement between the parties provides a good justification for the performance rendered by each party. The reasons for the restraint of trade doctrine (usually,

[22] *Fletcher v Johnson*, 102 NW 278 (Mich 1905); The American Restatement (Second) of Contracts § 187 illustrations 3 and 4.

[23] *Rawlings v General Trading Co* [1921] KB 635 (Bankes and Atkin LJJ, Scrutton LJ dissenting).

[24] *Treitel* (n 10) [11-063] consistently describes them as 'void'. *Chitty* (n 10) [18-123] states 'unenforceable' but then muddies the waters by saying 'void in the sense of unenforceable.' *Anson* (n 10) 429 cannot make up its mind ('unenforceable or void'). The American Restatement (Second) of Contracts § 186 uses 'unenforceable'.

the protection of one party to the relation) go to the enforceability of the contractual rights, not their validity as between the parties *inter se*.

Further, whether sums of money promised in relation to restrictions that have been adhered to should be actionable as an agreed sum due should depend upon whether the restraint is objectionable because of the interests of the promisor or those of third parties.[25] Where the restraint is unenforceable for purposes of protection of the promisor, there is no objection to requiring the counterparty to adhere to his side of the bargain and pay. This too follows from the justification for the doctrine. The courts will not lend the aid of enforcement to covenants that restrict another's freedom without adequate justification, but the promise to pay in exchange is not caught by the same reasoning. In the early decision of *Bishop v Kitchin*[26] this was the result, but this has subsequently been doubted.[27]

Where however, as in *Eastham*, the doctrine applies in order to protect third parties, neither parties' covenant should be enforceable. We do not wish in such a case to encourage adherence to the restriction by awarding payment for it. By contrast, in *Wyatt v Kreglinger & Fernau*,[28] a wool broker was promised a pension if he would not re-enter the wool trade. Nine years later, the Court of Appeal rejected his claim for arrears of pension. Assuming that the employer's promise to forfeit the pension if he worked again was capable of constituting consideration, which divided the Court, it was held that such a promise was 'void' as in restraint of trade and so incapable of supporting the counter-promise of the pension. As *Treitel* says, however, 'the view that a restraint on an elderly wool broker at the time of his retirement was likely to injure the public may be regarded with some scepticism'.[29] *If* the broker had proved that he had refrained from working as a result of the promise of the pension, this should then have been recoverable, notwithstanding the unenforceability of his promise to do so.

V. Pre-existing Freedom

For many years, the leading decision on the scope of the doctrine of restraint of trade was the decision of the House of Lords in *Esso Petroleum Co Ltd v Harper's Garage (Stourport) Ltd*.[30] The defendants were the owners of two petrol garages. They entered into separate agreements with respect to the premises with Esso, under which they undertook to sell only fuel supplied to them by that supplier. One agreement had a term of restriction of four years and five months, the other a term of 21 years, contained in

[25] *Peninsula Securities* (n 9) [1], per Lord Wilson, 'unenforceable against the covenantor unless it is reasonable'.

[26] *Bishop v Kitchin* (1868) 38 LJ (QB) 20; cf *Joseph Evans Ltd v Heathcote* [1918] 1 KB 418, 431, per Bankes LJ: '[S]ome day it may have to be decided whether, in a case like the present, where the consideration has been wholly executed by the party setting up the account stated, the other party will be allowed to dispute the original debt on the ground merely that the contract under which the debt was incurred was in unreasonable restraint of the trade of the party suing on the account stated.'

[27] *Wyatt v Kreglinger & Fernau* [1933] 1 KB 793.

[28] ibid.

[29] *Treitel* (n 10) [11-081].

[30] *Esso* (n 8).

a mortgage irredeemable for that period. The plaintiff sought an injunction restraining the selling of petrol other than as supplied by them. Mocatta J held that the restraint of trade doctrine only applied to restraints on persons and not those relating to particular pieces of land, a distinction rejected by both the Court of Appeal and the House of Lords. The House of Lords held that the covenants were within the scope of the rule, that the 21-year tie could not be enforced as it was in restraint of trade, but that an injunction could be granted in relation to the shorter tie as being reasonable.

Mocatta J's approach was derived from cases where a brewer had conveyed[31] or leased[32] land to a publican who had covenanted to sell no beer other than the brewer's on the premises, where the doctrine had not been applied. This was so despite the fact that bare agreements tying a publican to sell only one brewer's beer had been subject to review.[33] How was the non-application of the doctrine to be explained in those cases if Mocatta J's approach was rejected?

Lord Reid stated:

> Restraint of trade appears to me to imply that a man contracts to give up some freedom which otherwise he would have had. A person buying or leasing land had no previous right to be there at all, let alone to trade there, and when he takes possession of that land subject to a negative restrictive covenant he gives up no right or freedom which he previously had. I think that the 'tied house' cases might be explained in this way.[34]

Lord Morris expressed the point as follows:

> There is a clear difference between the case where someone fetters his future by parting with a freedom which he possesses and the case where someone seeks to claim a greater freedom than that which he possesses or has arranged to acquire. So, also, if someone seeks to buy a part of the land of a vendor and can only buy on the terms that he will covenant with the vendor not to put the land to some particular use, there would seem in principle to be no reason why the contract should not be honoured.[35]

Lord Hodson made the same point, albeit in a less generalised way:

> All dealings with land are not in the same category; the purchaser of land who promises not to deal with the land he buys in a particular way is not derogating from any right he has, but is acquiring a new right by virtue of his purchase. The same consideration may apply to a lessee who accepts restraints upon his use of land; on the other hand, if you subject yourself to restrictions as to the use to be made of your own land so that you can no longer do what you were doing before, you are restraining trade and there is no reason why the doctrine should not apply.[36]

Since in *Esso* the petrol garage owners were giving up a freedom they otherwise possessed, the restrictions fell within the scope of the rule, and so it fell to the court to consider their reasonableness.

[31] *Catt v Tourle* (1869) LR 4 Ch 654 (CA).

[32] *Luker v Dennis* (1877) 7 ChD 227; *Clegg v Hands* (1890) 44 ChD 503 (CA); *Courage v Carpenter* [1910] 1 Ch 262. cf *Foley v Classique Coaches Ltd* [1934] 2 KB 1 (sale of land for use as petrol garage with tie).

[33] eg *Thornton v Sherratt* (1818) 8 Taunt 529.

[34] *Esso* (n 8) 298.

[35] ibid 309.

[36] ibid 316–17.

Lord Pearce agreed with the majority that restrictions contained in a sale or lease fell entirely outside the doctrine,[37] but *in addition* proposed:

> The doctrine does not apply to ordinary commercial contracts for the regulation and promotion of trade during the existence of the contract, provided that any prevention of work outside the contract, viewed as a whole, is directed towards the absorption of the parties' services and not their sterilisation.[38]

This quite separate limitation, which the other members of the court did not endorse, would rule out from review exclusivity agreements during the currency of employment, the idea being that they are justified in ensuring that the employee's work is not diluted by also being engaged elsewhere (something anyone who has employed a builder will have sympathy with).

What is the justification for the majority's 'existing freedom' test of scope? Straightforwardly, clauses that do not cut back the promisor's liberty or freedom fall entirely outside of the mischief that the restraint of trade doctrine exists to tackle.[39] A condition attached to a freedom or power acquired because of a contract is not the same as agreeing not to exercise a pre-existing freedom or power. The former does not set back or restrict the overall future freedom or autonomy of the promisor at all. The condition comes as part of a package that, overall, increases the freedom the promisor has.

The reasoning of the majority of the House of Lords was prefigured by earlier case law on resale price maintenance agreements. Such clauses were not subject to the rules on restraint of trade.[40] As the seller has the power not to sell at all, they are entitled to impose any conditions they so choose on the buyer in relation to the thing bought, unless the scheme operates as a cartel to the prejudice of third parties. The restrictive condition to which the buyer is subject cannot be operating as a restraint of any interest in trading they have as they would not have the ability to resell the goods *at all* unless the seller were prepared to sell to them. As Lord Hanworth MR explained in *Palmolive Company (of England) v Freedman*:

> The case we are considering here is one in which a merchant is unable to become a trader in certain goods except upon the terms imposed by the vendor of them. The vendor may fix a price so high as to be ridiculous and then fail to sell his goods. That is his loss. But if a man accepts the terms offered, I cannot see that the Court must declare the terms imposed and accepted unreasonable, in order to give the acceptor terms more agreeable to his judgment, when his general trade, and trading power otherwise, is not affected by the contract entered into. There is no restriction as to the defendant selling other soap, or the preparations of other manufacturers or proprietors. He is as free to deal with them as he was before the contract was signed.

[37] ibid 325.

[38] ibid 328.

[39] But see Smith (n 2), accepting Heydon's criticisms of Lord Reid's formulation, discussed below; and Smith (n 3) 571, accepting the need for a scope test but not adopting Lord Reid's restriction: '[C]ourts should scrutinize only contracts that satisfy one or (preferably) more of three criteria: (1) the restraint is relatively onerous; (2) the parties' self-interest is a weak check; (3) there is a high risk of cognitive error in the framing of the contract.'

[40] *Elliman Sons & Co v Carrington & Sons Ltd* [1901] 2 Ch 275.

> Different considerations might possibly apply if the contract provided that the defendant should in any event purchase a periodic and definite amount of the plaintiffs' preparations, or if his power to sell other goods was restricted by it.[41]

Such further restrictions would indeed be potentially a restraint of trade because they would deprive the buyer of a liberty that they had independently of the purchase; it would not simply be a condition attached to the power to sell acquired by purchasing the goods.

Unfortunately, one other member of the *Esso* court gave a different formulation for the scope of the doctrine, which subsequently gained support. Lord Wilberforce stated:

> [J]udges have been able to dispense from the necessity of justification under a public policy test of reasonableness such contracts or provisions of contracts as, under contemporary conditions, may be found to have passed into the accepted and normal currency of commercial or contractual or conveyancing relations.[42]

VI. Trading Society

The Supreme Court's unanimous decision in *Peninsula Securities*[43] disapproved of the approach of the majority in *Esso*, instead endorsing that of Lord Wilberforce, under the strong influence of the commentary of the former High Court of Australia judge, Dyson Heydon.

A developer of a shopping centre in Northern Ireland leased part of it to a retailer. He covenanted that he would not allow any substantial shop to be built on the rest of the centre in competition with the retailer. The landlord then assigned his interest to the claimant, who decided that the centre was declining without further redevelopment and sought a declaration that the covenant was unenforceable as in restraint of trade. The issue before the Supreme Court was whether the doctrine was engaged, not whether the restraint was reasonable. It concluded that it was not, and in doing so rejected the 'pre-existing freedom test'.

Their lordships' primary reason for doing so was that '[t]he passage of half a century since [*Esso*] established the pre-existing freedom test has not generated a reasoned defence of it'.[44] It was perceived as an ad hoc limitation introduced to explain away an otherwise problematic line of authority.

Reliance was placed upon the following passage from *Treitel*:

> [T]he reasoning is hard to reconcile with the emphasis placed in the Esso case itself on the element of public interest; for restrictions on the use of land may cause harm to the public where they are imposed at the time when the land is acquired, no less than where they are imposed later.[45]

[41] *Palmolive Company (of England) v Freedman* [1928] Ch D 265, 273–74.

[42] *Esso* (n 8) 332–33.

[43] *Peninsula Securities* (n 9). The leading judgment is given by Lord Wilson in his last case, with whom Lord Lloyd-Jones, Lady Arden and Lord Kitchin concurred. Lord Carnwath gave a short concurring judgment.

[44] ibid [43].

[45] *Treitel* (n 10) [11-151].

However, as we have seen, the doctrine is usually engaged, and was in *Esso* itself, because of the interests of the promisor, not those of the public more generally. The promisor is not prejudiced in any way by a restriction on a liberty or power acquired by virtue of a contract: they did not have that freedom or power before the contract and still do not. The ability of the promisor to choose how to live their life in the future is not set back by the agreement.

The effect on third parties of a lease (or a sale) of land with a covenant not to use for a particular purpose is that instead of one party's having a veto over how the area of space is to be used, two now do so. Prior to the sale (or lease), third parties have no entitlement that the land be used in any particular way. Such an agreement between two parties cannot be objectionable on the basis that it rises to the status of a cartel, prejudicing the freedom of third parties, unless there is no other land reasonably available for this particular use. Unless there is a shortage of retail outlets, or land for their development, in that area of Northern Ireland, it is hard to see how the interest of third parties (ie the public) was engaged at all. Indeed, presumably, the reason the landlord thought that the site was declining was because of competition from others.

In criticising the *Esso* restriction, Heydon gave the following example, which the Supreme Court cited with approval in *Peninsula Securities*:

> If all the landowners in Yorkshire agree not to trade on their Yorkshire land, the restraint of trade doctrine would apply because the landowners are fettering a pre-existing freedom, and the agreement would certainly be held unenforceable. But if X buys all the land in Yorkshire, covenanting with each seller not to trade on the land, the Esso test prevents the doctrine applying, so that the covenants are all enforceable. In each case the public and the parties restricted are equally damaged[46]

The first example is indeed a case where a cartel has been created by agreement, which potentially impacts on third parties because of its wide-ranging scope (all the land in Yorkshire) so as to be unenforceable. Third parties would no longer have the ability to trade in Yorkshire because of the covenants. The doctrine should therefore apply because of the potential prejudice to third parties created by the restrictive covenants, which should not be enforceable.

The second example is entirely different. The potential prejudice to third parties is not primarily created by the restrictive covenants, but rather by the fact that X now owns all the land in Yorkshire. If X bought up all the land and chose not to use it, the prejudice to others would be precisely the same even if there were no restrictive covenants at all. That the various portions of land are subject to the choice of two people, rather than one, by virtue of the restrictive covenants is not the gist of the problem. In the first case it is the restrictive covenants that create the monopoly, and so they should not be enforceable; in the latter it is the owning of all the land, not the covenants, that creates the monopoly. It is not true that the interests of the parties and public are equally damaged by the covenants in each case.

[46] *Peninsula Securities* (n 9) [31], citing D Heydon, *The Restraint of Trade Doctrine*, 4th edn (Sydney, Butterworths, 2018) 281–82.

The Supreme Court states that the doctrine is based upon 'public policy' but does not set out what that policy might be.[47] If the rule were based upon general consideration of economic efficiency and competition, it might be concluded that Lord Reid's restriction should be discarded. However, the courts have not hitherto sought to explain the doctrine in such terms, and if taken seriously it would require the law to be redrawn.

It is sometimes claimed that Lord Reid's formulation is artificial or formal. Again, Heydon gives the following example, cited with approval by the Supreme Court:

> X, who owns two shops, sells one to A and A and X mutually covenant that neither shop shall be used as a butcher shop, the restraint of trade doctrine will apply to X's obligations but not to A's; X's may be held unenforceable but not A's.[48]

When looked at *ex post*, it may appear that the two restrictions are the same and so should be treated in the same way. Looked at *ex ante*, at the time of contracting, which is the correct perspective, they are quite different. Again, the reason why the doctrine should not apply to A's covenant is that they have not restricted their future self by the agreement at all. They have acquired a liberty subject to a condition. The apparently formal rule flows from the substantive justification for the doctrine.

It could be that the parties would in such a case attempt to evade the doctrine. X could lease the shop they intend to retain to A, take back a sub-lease of the same premises and covenant in that sub-lease not to use the premises as a butcher's shop. Would the covenant in the sub-lease be enforceable? Courts had shown no hesitation in looking through such structures, which are analogous to disguised penalties.[49]

However, instead of abandoning any restriction on the class of covenants susceptible to review, the Supreme Court in *Peninsula Securities* adopted instead the formulation of Lord Wilberforce in *Esso* that the courts

> dispense from the necessity of justification under a public policy test of reasonableness such contracts or provisions of contracts as, under contemporary conditions, may be found to have passed into the accepted and normal currency of commercial or contractual or conveyancing relations.[50]

The Supreme Court concluded that as the restriction in the case before it satisfied the 'trading society' test, it should not be subject to review.

This test is both wider and narrower in some respects than that of Lord Reid. Commercially accepted restrictions on existing freedoms are no longer subject to review, but novel attempts to impose conditions upon a liberty acquired as a result of an agreement now are.

The problems with this test are obvious. First is one of uncertainty. How are litigants to know or prove whether a particular practice has passed into normal currency? Second, and more fundamentally, what, as a matter of 'public policy', makes a restriction

[47] *Peninsula Securities* (n 9) [44]; cf *Egon v Zehnder Ltd v Tillman* [2019] UKSC 32, [2020] AC 154 [22] per Lord Wilson (Baroness Hale, Lord Kerr, Lord Brigs and Lady Arden agreeing).

[48] *Peninsula Securities* (n 9) [31], citing Heydon (n 46) 281–82.

[49] *Amoco Australian Pty Ltd v Rocca Bros Motor Engineering Co Pty Ltd* (1973) 133 CLR 299; *Alec Lobb (Garages) Ltd v Total Oil GB Ltd* [1985] 1 WLR 173.

[50] *Esso* (n 8) 331–33.

legally acceptable by virtue of its being longstanding and commercially widespread? The retain and transfer system in the English football league was in existence from 1893 to 1963, until the *Eastham*[51] decision challenged it. Seventy years of operation had rendered it part of normal currency in football, but the court, with a judgment given by Wilberforce J, still found it in restraint of trade. This was so despite the operation of a near identical system in the UK in rugby league[52] and similar systems in other professional leagues elsewhere,[53] such as the 'reserve clause' in American baseball, still operating at that time. Many injustices are longstanding or ordinary; that does not make them acceptable. Indeed, on the new 'test', the more widespread and deep-rooted the problem, the more it becomes unassailable.

The Supreme Court's preference for the 'trading society' test is expressed in terms of the common law as a 'living system' that is 'inevitably a patchwork' which adopts a 'pragmatic test'.[54] No doubt there were, and are, good commercial reasons why anchor tenants desire and pay a premium for such a restrictive covenant in a lease. However, circumstances can be contemplated where such a clause would be so wide-ranging as to be unreasonable. The 'trading society' restriction would only be of substantive significance in such a case if it now rules out its being challenged. If, therefore, the 21-year restriction in *Esso* had been 'accepted and normal', it would presumably no longer be reviewable on the approach of the Supreme Court. Fundamentally, the reason for the Court's adopting this 'pragmatic' test is that it is unable to articulate *why* the restraint of trade doctrine exists at all.

Lord Carnwath, in a concurring judgment, stated:

> Less important than history is whether, in the light of established practice, there is in the relevant context any public policy reason for interfering in the free process of negotiation between the parties, or seeking to redress the balance of interests between them.[55]

Although expressed as a concurrence, this is a quite different test. Instead of looking to the *fact* of how widespread the adoption of such clauses are, and how long-established their usage is, it appeals to the *reasons* why such a restriction is appropriate. Unfortunately, vague appeals to 'public policy' provide no firm foundation for defining such limits.

VII. Conclusion

It is a great shame that Lord Reid never explained the basis for the restriction on the restraint of trade doctrine. That he did not is probably explicable on the basis that he

[51] Text at n 17.

[52] The High Court of Australia applied *Eastham* in *Buckley v Tutty* (1971) 225 CLR 353, in holding that the retain and transfer system in rugby league was an unreasonable restraint of trade. This system remained in place in rugby league in Britain until 1987: T Collins, *Rugby League in Twentieth Century Britain: A Social and Cultural History* (London, Routledge, 2006) 179–80.

[53] *Eastham* (n 17) 438.

[54] *Peninsula Securities* (n 9) [45]; cf *Egon v Zehnder Ltd v Tillman* [2019] UKSC 32, [2020] AC 154 [26], per Lord Wilson.

[55] *Peninsula Securities* (n 9) [61].

and the other members of the *Esso* majority thought it axiomatic, following from the justification for the rule. Which indeed it is. There is nothing further that needs to be, or can be, said by way of justification. It is only in the unusual case, such as *Eastham*, where the gist of the problem is the harm to the future autonomy of third parties where it does not follow naturally. Even in that context, it is impossible to think of any example where the prejudice to third parties does not take the form of the parties' agreement not to exercise a pre-existing freedom to deal with them.

It is to be hoped that *Peninsula Securities* will cause no more damage than the incurring of needless costs. If a court is presented with a case where the promisor has not given up any pre-existing freedom, it will only potentially be unenforceable if it is unreasonable. Sensible judges should, as a matter of course, say that all clauses that do not involve the giving up of any pre-existing freedom are reasonable.

Perhaps surprisingly, the Court of Appeal in *Quantum Actuarial LLP v Quantum Advisory Ltd*[56] subsequently rejected the proposition that the 'trading society' test was the single scope of application test to be universally applied, as this would entail that any entirely novel form of agreement would necessarily be within it.[57] Instead, it preferred a somewhat more free-form assessment of whether 'public policy' was engaged, following Lord Carnwath's approach. The Court's enquiry looked very similar to determining whether the clause was commercially unreasonable, collapsing the different stages of the doctrine. Were a case such as *Peninsula Securities* to occur again, but where the restriction was unreasonable, the 'trading society' test is probably sufficiently opaque to allow the court to conclude that it does not satisfy it.

It is, however, disappointing that the conceptual basis for an earlier decision of the House of Lords was not understood by the Supreme Court.

This chapter has sought to show how Steve Smith's work provides us with a way of understanding part of the law of contract. It has argued that the distinction in his final work between reasons for invalidity and unenforceability helps us to understand restraint of trade, and that his justification for that doctrine enables us to explain its proper scope. I have argued that he was even more right than he knew.[58] However, he would have been very disappointed if I had no words of criticism for him. His doctorate commences:

> Why does the law enforce contracts? This fundamental question of contract law can be approached in either of two ways. The first is by examining the kinds of agreement which the law enforces. The other, less common, approach is that of examining agreements which the law refuses to enforce. Asking why the law does not do some things may be the best, or at least a good, way of discovering why it does things.

In this context, this seems untrue. There are many *countervailing* reasons why an obligation that on its face meets all the necessary conditions for validity may still be unenforceable. It would not be thought, for example, that understanding the justification

[56] *Quantum Actuarial LLP v Quantum Advisory Ltd* [2021] EWCA Civ 227, [2022] 1 All ER (Comm) 473. Discussed in W Day, 'In Restraint of Trade' [2022] *Lloyd's Maritime and Commercial Law Quarterly* 135, 141–43.

[57] *Quantum* (n 56) [72]–[73].

[58] See n 39.

for statutory limitation periods provides us with a secure basis for determining why tortious or contractual obligations arise. That the restraint of trade doctrine exists in order to protect, in some sense, the 'autonomy' of the promisor or third parties does not tell us why promises that are agreed should create enforceable legal duties. It is that general rule, not the restraint of trade doctrine that is an exception to it, that is the greater mystery.

13

What Might Contract Theory Be?

GREGORY KLASS

The first question any legal theorist should ask is: What the hell am I doing here? What is the point of legal theory? What counts as success in the project?

Among the many virtues of Stephen Smith's 2004 *Contract Theory* is its first chapter, which explains what Smith seeks to do with his theory of contract. Smith informs the reader that he will provide an interpretive theory:

> Interpretive theories aim to enhance understanding of the law by highlighting its significance or meaning. … [T]his is achieved by explaining why certain features of the law are important or unimportant and by identifying connections between those features – in other words, by revealing an intelligible order in the law, so far as such an order exists.[1]

More specifically, *Contract Theory* will provide an interpretation of contract law that aims to satisfy four criteria: fit with the existing law; internal coherence; moral attractiveness; and transparency to legal actors. Chapter One discusses these four criteria, distinguishes several versions of each, identifies which Smith will employ and explains why. Few works on contract theory begin with so comprehensive a discussion of method.

This chapter examines Smith's approach to contract theory through a close reading of his explanation of these four criteria. Section I argues that Smith's account is shaped in part by a picture of the theorist as spectator. For Smith, the legal theorist observes the drama of the law without playing a role in it. Though the picture of theorist as spectator influences Smith's account, I suggest it also fails to fully support it. In fact, the picture generates some tensions amongst Smith's four criteria and leaves some gaps in the argument.

Section II suggests an alternative picture, one that emphasises a possible continuity between legal practice and legal theory. Such an approach can, like Smith's, be interpretive. And its guiding principles can include the criteria Smith identifies. But the reasons for and implementations of those criteria differ from what one finds in Smith.

[1] SA Smith, *Contract Theory* (Oxford, Oxford University Press, 2004) 5.

I. The Legal Theorist as Spectator and the Goals of Interpretive Theory

The English word 'theory' comes from the Greek 'θεᾶσθαι', to behold, contemplate or examine. Theory, one might say, takes a step back from its object to observe it from a distance. 'Θεᾶσθαι' is also the root of 'theatre'. If all the world is a stage, the theorist is a spectator working to make sense of the drama.

This picture of theorist as spectator is a familiar one. Consider Copernicus' explanation of the paths of the planets through the night sky. People had been watching the planets for millennia, but without a theory it was difficult to make sense of their trajectories. ('Planet' derives from 'πλάνης', meaning 'wanderer'.) Copernicus' suggestion that the Earth and other planets followed elliptical paths around the Sun made new sense of those observed facts – better sense, it turned out, than Ptolemy's system of deferents, epicycles and equant points.[2] In constructing his theory, Copernicus did not interact with the planets. Nor did his theory change their courses. He observed them from a distance, saw patterns in their movements and proposed an explanation that rendered those movements intelligible.

There are important differences between explanations of the planets and explanations of a social institution like the law. A mechanistic explanation can render planetary movement fully intelligible. Further explanation, such as a purpose to their trajectories, is not only superfluous but suspect. Like the planets, people and social institutions are natural phenomena subject to the laws of physics. But mechanistic explanations of them are incomplete. Humans also act for reasons, with purpose, in accordance with rules. Their behaviour and the institutions they create can be rendered intelligible in a way the planets cannot be.

Anglo-American legal theorists often make a related point by saying that reductive causal and incentive-based theories of law are unable to account for the *internal point of view* of those participating in legal practice. The phrase is from HLA Hart's 1961 *The Concept of Law*. It refers, roughly speaking, to the perspective of participants in the law who accept and use legal rules to guide their behaviour.[3] Smith emphasises the importance of the internal point of view in his interpretive theory of contract law: 'To understand a human practice – to make it intelligible – it is necessary to understand what the participants in the practice think they are doing. In other words, it is necessary to understand how the practice is regarded internally.'[4]

What is the internal point of view on a social practice or institution? One finds subtle shifts and some ambiguities in Hart's use of the term, and scholars have since assigned various meanings to it depending, for example, on whose point of view counts

[2] See TS Kuhn, *The Structure of Scientific Revolutions*, 2nd edn (Chicago, IL, University of Chicago Press, 1970) 68–69.

[3] '[F]or it is possible to be concerned with the rules, either merely as an observer who does not himself accept them, or as a member of the group which accepts and uses them as guides to conduct. We may call these respectively the "external" and the "internal points of view."' HLA Hart, *The Concept of Law*, 2nd edn (Oxford, Oxford University Press, 1994) 89.

[4] Smith (n 1) 13–14.

as internal and what practical commitments the point of view entails.[5] Smith does not fully explain what he means by the internal point of view. I will say more about his conception below. For the moment I limit myself to two observations.

First, the internal point of view for Smith, like for Hart, is the perspective not of all legal subjects but of legal officials acting and importantly speaking in their official capacity. For example:

> Because it is the public institution of the law, and not the inner minds of legal actors, that a legal theory seeks to interpret, the theorist is interested in how legal actors explain what they are doing when they are acting as legal actors. The relevant evidence of this understanding is found in judicial reports, parliamentary debates, and lawyers' arguments in courts.[6]

Second, a theory that seeks to explain the internal point of view need not itself adopt the internal perspective. A theorist can describe the point of view of participants in a practice without becoming a participant. Although Hart maintains that a complete explanation of the law must account for the internal point of view, Hart's theory is not guided by those rules and does not assume their legitimacy. Hart the theorist stands outside the practice and looks in.

Smith and Hart focus on different types of questions. Whereas Hart seeks to construct a general theory of law, Smith aims to provide a theory of an existing area of law: the common law of contract. Nonetheless, Smith adopts a spectator's perspective akin to Hart's. That perspective can be seen in Smith's explanation of his four criteria for assessing interpretive theories. It also, I will argue, generates some gaps and tensions in his account of them.

A. Morality

Smith's picture of theorist as spectator appears most clearly in his account of the morality criterion. Smith argues that an interpretive legal theory is to be preferred if it shows the law to be morally justified. Why seek out interpretations of the law as morally justified? Because, Smith argues, moral justification accounts for a key aspect of the internal point of view: that 'the law is understood internally as a *legitimate* authority'.

> One of the fundamental features of law's self-understanding is that it presumes a close link between law and morality. More specifically, laws are understood, from the inside, as providing morally good or justified reasons to do what the law requires. From the internal perspective, it is considered wrong, and not merely foolish, irrational, or contrary to self-interest to disobey the law.[7]

To make sense of the law's self-understanding as a legitimate authority, a theory of law must be able to explain how legal actors could believe laws to be morally justified.

[5] See, eg, SJ Shapiro, 'What is the Internal Point of View?] (2006) 75 *Fordham Law Review* 1157; CL Barzun, 'Inside-Out: Beyond the Internal/External Distinction in Legal Scholarship' (2015) 101 *Virginia Law Review* 1203.

[6] Smith (n 1) 14.

[7] ibid 15.

Given this reason for the morality criterion, an interpretive theory need not show that the law *in fact is* morally justified. Legal actors might be wrong in their belief. This leads Smith to reject a strong version of the morality criterion, which 'holds that a theory of law is better if it portrays the law in a morally appealing light, that is, if it portrays the law as morally justified'.[8] Smith's argument suggests that participants who accept the law's claim to authority adhere to something like the strong morality criterion. Because they treat the law as legitimate authority, they must believe it to be at least for the most part morally justified. But the theorist is not a participant: '[A] good legal theory should explain the law in a way that shows how the law *might be thought to be* justified even if it is not justified.'[9] Smith's moderate morality criterion is of a piece with his picture of the theorist as standing outside legal practice.

Despite this understanding of the theorist as spectator, Smith rejects a weaker morality criterion according to which 'it is enough that a theory explain why legal actors might claim, *sincerely or not*, that the law is morally justified'.[10] He explains 'It is just not plausible to suppose that legal actors are involved in a mass conspiracy.'[11] I will call this the 'sincerity postulate'. The sincerity postulate does not follow from other elements of Smith's theory. It is an empirical claim used to rule out a hypothesis otherwise consistent with the picture of theorist as spectator.

Smith's reliance on the sincerity postulate reveals something about his conception of the internal point of view. The postulate is a claim about the attitudes of actual judges, legislators and other legal officials in Anglo-American legal systems. This empirical conception of the internal point of view is of a piece with Smith's aim: to provide a theory not of contract law generally but of the contract law we theorists in common law jurisdictions find in our legal systems. It also marks a difference between Smith's and Hart's projects. Whereas Hart is interested in the range of theoretically possible attitudes that might be associated with law's claim to authority, which might include systematic insincerity, Smith's concern is the plausible attitudes of the actual legal officials who have created and apply the common law of contract.

One final point about Smith's morality criterion: even granting Smith the sincerity postulate, his argument for the morality criterion relies on a non sequitur. Sincerity requires that legal officials attribute moral authority to the law. They must believe that a valid law imposing a legal duty to *A* gives persons subject to it a new moral reason to *A*. But a belief that the law has moral authority need not be accompanied by a belief that the substance of any given law, or even of an entire domain of law, is morally justified. Consider absolutist theories of the divine right of kings.[12] If one believes the law's moral authority derives from the sovereign's divine authority, the fact that the sovereign has issued a law suffices to render it morally authoritative. No further substantive justification, moral or otherwise, is required. Smith needs a theory of the law's claim to moral authority to get from the premises that the law claims moral authority and that legal actors sincerely believe it to be authoritative to the conclusion that those actors

[8] ibid 13.
[9] ibid 28.
[10] ibid 13 (emphasis added).
[11] ibid 16.
[12] See G Burgess, 'The Divine Right of Kings Reconsidered' (1992) 107 *English Historical Review* 837.

must believe that the rules of contract law are in substance morally justified. Smith does not provide such a theory. This is a gap in his argument for the morality criterion.

B. Transparency

Like his argument for the morality criterion, Smith's argument for transparency is premised on a claim belonging to the internal point of view. Despite that similarity, however, the two arguments are in tension.

The law is transparent, in Smith's usage, 'to the extent that the reasons legal actors give for doing what they do are their real reasons'.[13] Just as the law claims moral authority, Smith argues, the law claims transparency:

> That law is understood, *from the inside*, as transparent is clear: law-makers, and in particular judges, give reasons for acting as they do and those reasons are presented as their real reasons. The report of a legal decision is not presented as mere window dressing; it is meant to explain why the plaintiff did or not win.[14]

The law's claim to transparency imposes an additional constraint on legal theory: '[T]o *account for* law's claim to be transparent a legal theory of the common law must, *inter alia*, take account (in a way yet to be specified) of the reasons that judges give for their decisions.'[15]

Smith identifies three ways in which a theory might take account of those reasons. A theory satisfies a strong transparency criterion if its explanation 'of the law will support the explanation that legal officials give'.[16] A theory satisfies a moderate transparency criterion if it 'explain[s] the law in a way that shows how legal officials could sincerely, even if erroneously, believe the law is transparent'.[17] A theory satisfies a weak transparency criterion if it 'explain[s] why legal actors might claim, sincerely or not, that the law is transparent'.[18] As with his morality criterion, Smith deploys a Goldilocks argument for moderate transparency. The strong transparency criterion is too demanding. The 'linking of intelligibility and truth seems unwarranted. A false statement or belief may be perfectly intelligible so long as a plausible explanation is given for holding that statement or belief.'[19] The weak criterion is not demanding enough. It allows for the theories that legal officials systematically to hide the real reasons for their decisions, violating the sincerity postulate. Having eliminated the alternatives, we are left with a moderate transparency criterion.[20]

There is, however, a difference between Smith's arguments for his morality criterion and for his transparency criterion. The strong morality criterion is rejected because legal actors might be mistaken about the requirements of morality. They might believe the law to

[13] Smith (n 1) 24.
[14] ibid 25.
[15] ibid.
[16] ibid.
[17] ibid.
[18] ibid.
[19] ibid 27.
[20] For a critical account of this form of argument, see RH Gaskins, *Burdens of Proof in Modern Discourse* (New Haven, CT, Yale University Press, 1992) 205–39.

be morally justified, though in fact it is not. Smith rejects the strong transparency requirement because 'the linking of intelligibility and truth seems unwarranted'. But in the case of transparency, the possible mistake is to believe that the law is transparent when in fact it is not. It is for legal officials to believe that the reasons they give for a rule are the real reasons for it, when in fact they are not. The moderate transparency criterion rests on the idea that legal officials might be mistaken about the actual reasons for the rules they employ.

The twentieth century is replete with theories claiming that humans regularly misunderstand the true reasons for their actions. Paul Ricoeur, in his book on Freud, Marx and Nietzsche, uses the phrase the 'hermeneutics of suspicion' to describe this outlook.[21] (Smith, somewhat confusingly, calls these 'functionalist explanations'.[22]) The hermeneutics of suspicion does not take the meaning of the object of interpretation at face value but looks behind it for hidden causes or meanings. If the object of interpretation is a literary text, the interpreter finds a meaning other than the one its author or contemporary audience intended or understood. If it is a social practice, the interpreter looks for causes, functions or other explanations that participants in that practice might not recognise, accept or even comprehend – the collective unconscious, the material conditions of society, the will to power. The hermeneutics of suspicion seeks to unmask or demystify. The goal is to 'clear the horizon for a more authentic word, for a new reign of Truth, not only by means of a "destructive" critique, but by the invention of an art of *interpreting*'.[23]

Although his moderate transparency criterion makes room for a legal hermeneutics of suspicion, Smith wants nothing to do with such explanations. He deploys two arguments against them. First, 'it seems implausible, in light of their training and sophistication, that all or even many judges are in the grips of a collective false consciousness'.[24] Like the sincerity postulate, this argument makes an empirical claim. Call it the 'self-awareness postulate': legal officials know the real reasons for which they act. Smith's second argument is a version of a classic riposte to philosophical scepticism: if false consciousness is pervasive, it also infects the theorist who attributes it to legal actors, rendering the theorist's own claims suspect.[25]

Both arguments strike me as ad hoc, and neither as especially convincing. (Query how the self-awareness hypothesis squares with Smith's rejection of strong transparency.) Smith also suggests that the hermeneutics of suspicion fails to render the law intelligible:

> Insofar as a theorist's explanation of the law reveals the law to be based on concepts that are external to legal reasoning – on concepts, in other words, that are not just different from those

[21] P Ricoeur, *Freud and Philosophy. An Essay on Interpretation* (New Have, CT, Yale University Press, 1970) 32–36.

[22] Smith (n 1) 29: '[A] "functionalist" explanation … supposes that legal actors are controlled by external forces that are typically unacknowledged and unknown.'

[23] Ricoeur (n 21) 33.

[24] Smith (n 1) 28. See also ibid 20: 'Given the number, variety, and sophistication of the actors involved in making law's claims to authority, the suggestion that these actors have all wildly misunderstood the reasons with which they explain the law is prima facie implausible.'

[25] ibid 20: 'If the hidden forces that drive the development of the law work as successfully and covertly as the explanation suggests, the obvious question is why are those defending the explanation – and everyone else for that matter – not subject to the same or similar types of unconscious forces. Functionalism, at least in its stronger versions, is self-defeating.'; ibid 28: '[I]f it were plausible, then it seems likely that legal theorists would be in the grip of similar forces.'

> that the judge did use but from those that the judge might have used – then the law's belief that its reasons were real reasons is not just mistaken, but conceptually confused (and hence not intelligible).[26]

This, I believe, is the root of Smith's objection. It relies, however, on a narrow understanding of rendering a practice intelligible. If a toddler has a meltdown in a supermarket and the parent says to a passerby 'She missed her nap this afternoon', the parent has rendered the toddler's behaviour intelligible – whether the toddler would accept the explanation or not.[27] Legal officials are not toddlers. Among other things, they have a greater capacity to reflect on the reasons for their actions. It does not follow, however, that they always know the full explanation of their decisions. Historical examples like coverture, colonialism, slavery and apartheid suggest it would be Panglossian to rule out the possibility of shared false consciousness amongst sincere legal officials. The hermeneutics of suspicion might not be the whole story in legal theory. But it is unduly optimistic for a theorist standing outside the practice to exclude it tout court.

Regardless of whether Smith's argument against the hermeneutics of suspicion is convincing, his decision to rule it out transforms his moderate transparency criterion into something stronger. Whereas originally the criterion required 'explain[ing] law in a way that shows how legal officials could sincerely, even if erroneously, believe the law is transparent',[28] the goal is now to 'explain the law using concepts that are recognizably "legal" … even if those concepts are not the same legal concepts that were employed by judges'.[29] I will call this the 'moderately strong transparency criterion'. Smith calls explanations that satisfy the moderately strong transparency criterion 'internal' or 'legal' explanations. Although the theorist remains a spectator who stands outside and looks in on legal practice, the theorist's explanations must be in the vernacular of the practice. The best theory of contract law will provide an explanation that legal actors could accept, even if it is not the explanation they would give.

To construct such a theory, Smith needs a way of identifying what does and does not count as a legally acceptable explanation, what distinguishes 'internal' legal arguments, which are on the table, from 'external' legal arguments, which are off it. Here Smith recurs to the judgments of actual legal officials: '[A]n explanation is legal if it is recognized as such by the consensus of those familiar with the law.'[30] This rests on another empirical claim, which I will call the 'vernacular postulate': there exists a consensus among those familiar with the law regarding what counts as a legal argument and what does not, a consensus within the legal community regarding the legal vernacular. Like the other postulates I have identified, the vernacular postulate is an empirical claim that might be true or false depending on the legal system.

One last comment on Smith's moderately strong transparency criterion. Smith's moderate morality criterion holds that an interpretive theory should look for the actual reasons of actual legal officials, even if they are based on a moral mistake. Smith's

[26] ibid 29.
[27] See 'Big brother tells sister she needs nap' (7 January 2015) at https://youtu.be/A-Vn_fmkCuc (accessed 18 July 2023).
[28] Smith (n 1) 25.
[29] ibid 29.
[30] ibid 30.

argument for his moderately strong transparency criterion, in distinction, holds that an interpretive theory should not limit itself to the actual reasons of actual legal officials – the reasons sincere legal officials give for their decision. Moderately strong transparency permits the theorist to seek reasons that are better than those given by officials. Unlike Smith's moderate morality criterion, Smith's moderately strong transparency criterion allows for a gap between the explanations sincere legal officials give for the law and the explanations the best interpretive legal theory gives for it.

C. Coherence

Smith's argument that a theory should render the law coherent does not rest on the law's claims and a wish to explain the internal point of view. A minimal coherence requirement follows directly from the goal of interpretive theory: to render the law intelligible. 'Consistency in the sense of non-contradictoriness is a basic requirement of intelligibility.'[31]

Smith considers whether legal theory should seek a stronger form of coherence. Maximally, a theory might seek to show that 'all [contract law's] constituent parts flow from a *single* master idea or principle'.[32] He rejects maximal coherence as being unnecessary to render contract law intelligible. 'Unless one assumes (as few people do) that all reasons for acting can, in the end, be reduced to a single master principle, it is accepted as perfectly intelligible, indeed appropriate, that people act for different reasons in different situations.'[33]

Smith does not, however, recur to minimal of coherence, or non-contradiction. He again aims for a middle way. If perfect unity is too much to expect, 'a good theory must show that *most* of the core elements of contract law can be traced to, or are closely related to, a single principle'.[34] This coherence is not maximal. Other principles might work around the edges. But it is relatively strong: an interpretive theory should seek out a single principle that explains and justifies as much of contract law as possible. Chapters Three and Four of the book find such a principle in the promissory obligations contractual agreements generate and the promisee's corresponding right to performance.

Chapter One does not explain why this relatively strong form of coherence is preferable to the minimal requirement of non-contradiction. Smith does not suggest, for instance, that contract law claims to flow from a single principle. Nor does he identify reasons to expect such unity in a body of law built by many hands through the resolution of individual disputes over the course of many centuries. And given Smith's outsider perspective, it is not obvious why he would want to rule out *ab initio* the possibility that the common law of contract law has more than one aim or is justified by multiple, non-contradictory principles. This is another gap in Smith's account: Smith does not explain the reasons for his relatively strong coherence criterion.

[31] ibid 11.
[32] ibid 11–12.
[33] ibid 12.
[34] ibid 13.

D. Fit

The fit requirement follows directly from Smith's picture of the theorist as spectator. According to that picture, the job of a theorist is to explain the observed data. Copernicus' theory of the movement of the planets ultimately beat out Ptolemy's not because it was more elegant but because 60 years later Galileo pointed his telescope at the sky and provided additional data that fit Copernicus' theory and not Ptolemy's.[35] 'A theory "fits" if it is consistent with, and supported by, the relevant facts.'[36] To qualify as an interpretation of the law, a theory must to some degree fit the legal data. The better the fit, the better the theory.

This fit requirement generates a new question for Smith: 'Fit with what?' Which legal facts should a theory of contract law aim to interpret and explain? The spectator theorist needs to know what play to attend:

> A theory of contract fails the fit criterion if it rejects as an exception or as misclassified so much of contract law that those familiar with the law would not recognize what remains as 'contract' law (though such an account might qualify as a good theory of something else …).[37]

Smith's answer is that an interpretive theory of contract law should fit with what legal sophisticates understand the core elements of contract law to be:

> Contract law – pre-interpretation – is rightly regarded as that which people familiar with the law (lawyers, judges, legal scholars) take to be contract law. The parameters of contract law, and also the identification of what is central and what is peripheral to contract law, are determined by the consensus of those familiar with the law.[38]

Again Smith's approach relies on an empirical claim: that there exists a consensus amongst legal sophisticates regarding the core of contract law. Call this the 'doctrinal core postulate'.

The doctrinal core postulate is of a piece with Smith's attachment to a strong coherence criterion. A commitment to seeking a single principle to explain contract law's core assumes that 'contract law' is not just a convenient label for a loosely related family of rules but a unified whole. The assumption of unity suggests that a good theory of contract should not be expected to fit the rules of tort, property, unjust enrichment or other areas of law. Fit must be fit with that which counts as contract law.

II. The Legal Theorist as Participant

I have taken a deep dive into Chapter One of *Contract Theory* because Smith's answer to the question 'What is contract theory?' is so thoughtful, thorough and forthright. Whether one agrees with him or not, one cannot help but learn from Smith's careful

[35] TS Kuhn, *The Copernican Revolution: Planetary Astronomy in the Development of Western Thought* (Cambridge, MA, Harvard University Press, 1957) 219–28.
[36] Smith (n 1) 7.
[37] ibid 10.
[38] ibid 9.

explanations of what he means by 'interpretive theory', his criteria for assessing interpretations of contract law and his reasons for choosing them.

Although I have doubts about several moves in Chapter One, I am sympathetic to Smith's idea of interpretive legal theory. This section suggests modifications based on a different understanding of the theorist's role. Whereas Smith views the legal theorist as spectator, a contract theorist might instead understand themselves as in conversation with legal officials and, in this way, to be a participant in legal practice. The point is not that one must participate in a legal practice to understand it – a thesis Smith associates with Ronald Dworkin and Ernest Weinrib and, I believe, rightly rejects.[39] The point is that the theorist might want to do more than render the law intelligible. They might also want to make it better.

Contemporary contract law poses any number of difficult doctrinal questions. When if ever should the parties' intent to contract be a condition of contractual liability? Is the proper test for good faith a subjective or an object one? What precontractual duties do parties owe one another and what consequences should the law attach to their violation? When if ever should parties' contractual obligations turn on a writing's plain meaning? How should courts take account of unread terms in standard consumer contracts? When should a court grant injunctive relief? Do some breaches call for exemplary damages? What is up with promissory estoppel?

Different common law jurisdictions, including different US States, provide different answers to these and other doctrinal questions. The existence of difficult doctrinal questions suggests two things. First, the fact of doctrinal divergence amongst common law courts is part of the data for an interpretive theory of the common law of contact. It too requires explanation. I return to this point below. Second, answering such questions often requires recurring to the level of theory. To decide whether or when liability should turn on parties' intent to contract, we would want to know whether contract law aims to confer on parties the power to undertake new legal obligations, to impose on them legal duties they might not have chosen or both. Decisions regarding the enforcement of standard terms in consumer contracts turn in part on the scope and meaning of freedom of contract, on parties' responsibility for own their decisions and on their responsibilities to one another. To decide whether specific performance should be more readily available, we might want to know whether contract law is guided by the principle *pacta sunt servanda*, by considerations of efficiency or party preference, or by something else. Because theoretical questions are intrinsic to legal practice, the contract theorist can occupy an on-stage role in it.

Viewing contract theory as continuous with the practice of courts and other legal officials provides theorists with a new reason to take an interpretive approach, especially in domains shaped in significant part by judicial decisions. The law's commitment to *stare decisis* entails that every judicial decision is answerable in part to the best

[39] SA Smith, 'Taking Law Seriously' (2000) 50 *University of Toronto Law Journal* 241, 252–53. Smith cites R Dworkin, *Law's Empire* (Cambridge, MA, Harvard University Press, 1986) 14 ('[t]his book takes up the internal, participants' point of view; it tries to grasp the argumentative character of our legal practice by joining that practice and struggling with the issues of soundness and truth participants face') and E Weinrib, *The Idea of Private Law* (Cambridge, MA, Harvard University Press, 1995) 11 ('not only does an internal account orient itself to the features salient in legal experience, but it also understands those (and other) features as they are understood from within the law'): ibid 252, fn 5.

interpretation of decisions that went before. To use a well-worn metaphor, common law judges are like the sailors on Neurath's ship: responsible for replacing individual planks as conditions require, but always in a way that fits with the current design of the whole and that keeps the ship afloat.[40] Interpretive theories of the common law can look for basic design principles that judges and even legislatures should use to maintain, repair and extend the common law.

This picture of the contract theorist as participant in the shared project of using available materials to achieve the best possible law of contract suggests rethinking Smith's four criteria for assessing interpretive theories of contract.

The morality criterion receives a new argument and new content. If contract theory is continuous with the practice of legal officials, we have a new reason to prefer morally attractive explanations: to realise a morally defensible contract law. When courts consider doctrinal change – whether because the question is open, because existing authorities are in conflict or because a rule seems ripe for change – they look to moral considerations, broadly understood – to contract law's *raisons d'être*, to considerations of justice, to whether a rule will benefit or harm future parties, to what the rule might signal and so forth. The more morally compelling a theory's explanation of contract law, the better its answers to such doctrinal questions. The practical theorist need not take a (possibly misguided) detour through law's claim to authority to explain the morality criterion.

This practical argument entails replacing Smith's moderate version of the morality criterion with a stronger one. From the perspective of practice, the goal of contract theory is not merely to 'explain the law in a way that shows how legal actors could sincerely, even if erroneously, believe the law is morally justified',[41] but also to show how the law is or might be morally justified. The goal is to provide a morally attractive account of contract law and to achieve a morally attractive law of contract.

The strong morality criterion means that the theorist is no longer exclusively interested in the reasons legal officials give for their decisions. This shift aligns the morality criterion with Smith's moderately strong transparency criterion, which seeks explanations that 'use concepts that are recognizably "legal" … even if those concepts are not the same legal concepts that were employed by judges'.[42] The theorist who is a participant in the legal practice aims, *inter alia*, to address to legal officials arguments of the form 'You think the best grounds for your decision is *R*, but I want to convince you it is *S*.' Like morality, the argument for transparency does not require a detour through the law's claims. The transparency criterion follows directly from the theorist's interest in providing reasons legal officials will respond to when deciding hard doctrinal questions, which means speaking in a legal vernacular.

[40] 'We are like sailors who on the open sea must reconstruct their ship but are never able to start afresh from the bottom. Where a beam is taken away a new one must at once be put there, and for this the rest of the ship is used as support. In this way, by using the old beams and driftwood the ship can be shaped entirely anew, but only by gradual reconstruction.' O Neurath, 'Protocol Statements' in O Neurath, *Philosophical Papers 1913–1946*, eds RS Cohen and M Neurath (Dordrecht, Reidel, 1983) 91, 96.

[41] Smith (n 1) 13.

[42] ibid 29.

A practical contract theory might, however, employ a more open-ended conception of legal vernacular than Smith's. A theorist outside the practice looking in must rely on practitioners' understanding of what counts as a legal reason and what does not. Hence Smith's vernacular postulate, which assumes a consensus amongst legal sophisticates regarding what does and does not count as a legal argument. I have doubts about whether any such consensus exists, and if it does, whether the legal vernacular is as narrow as Smith believes. Be that as it may, a practical theory of contract does not require prior guidance regarding which explanations are internal to the law and which are not. It is open to anyone participating in a conversation on a difficult doctrinal question to say 'Yes, but until now you have not considered *S*', where *S* is a type of explanation, reason or justification previously not part of the conversation.

From this practical perspective, even the hermeneutics of suspicion is on the table. Consider Mary Keyes and Kylie Burns' argument that the intent-to-contract requirement has served in English law to create 'a highly effective default principle which impedes enforcement of family agreements, and performs a powerful symbolic function delineating the realm of law from the realm of the family and the feminine, privileging the former over the latter'.[43] Or the overwhelming evidence that during the Jim Crow era in the United States, Southern courts used facially neutral contract doctrines to effectively bind formerly enslaved Blacks to their former owners.[44] Smith is correct to note that these interpretive explanations of contract law differ from other types of legal argument. But I find it easy to imagine a contemporary judicial discussion about what contract law should be taking account of them.[45] It would be a mistake for the theorist who wants to participate in those conversations to exclude this form of argument altogether.

My advocacy of a more capacious conception of the legal vernacular is of a piece with my doubts about Smith's claim that 'a good theory must show that *most* of the core elements of contract law can be traced to, or are closely related to, a single principle'.[46] There is a familiar practical argument for Smith's moderately strong coherence criterion. Theories that ascribe independent, non-ordered justifications to contract law cannot provide determinate answers to difficult doctrinal questions when those justifications conflict. If one believes the job of legal theory, practically speaking, is to provide such answers, this argues for a unitary theory. Smith does not make such an argument. But if he were to take a practical turn, it would be available to him.

My own view is that the unitary theories of contract tend to paper over real conflicts between competing principles, as evidenced by jurisdictional splits on difficult doctrinal questions. From this perspective, the job of contract theory is not merely to answer difficult doctrinal questions; it is to identify conflicts, explain why they exist and elucidate the values different doctrinal choices implicate. I hope Smith would grant that such a theory can render contract law intelligible, even if he might consider it second-best.

[43] M Keyes and K Burns, 'Contract and the Family: Whither Intention?' (2002) 26 *Melbourne University Law Review* 577, 585–87.

[44] See, eg, J Roback, 'Southern Labor Law in the Jim Crow Era: Exploitative or Competitive?' (1984) 51 *University of Chicago Law Review* 1161.

[45] For an example and analysis of a critical historical argument entering judicial reasoning, see Charles Barzun's discussion of the opinions in *Seminole Tribe v Florida*, 517 US 44 (1996). Barzun (n 5) 1266–70.

[46] Smith (n 1) 13.

This practical approach I am sketching can also do without Smith's assumption that contract law has a doctrinal core. Smith's doctrinal core postulate serves to ensure that the spectator theorist is not observing or explaining the wrong social practice. That is not a risk for a contract theory that starts from the hard doctrinal questions practice presents and which is not committed to a unified interpretation.

This is not to say that fit is irrelevant to such a theory. For Smith, the fit criterion follows from the very nature of interpretive theory. For an interpretation to be about the interpretandum, it must in some sense fit it. Practical contract theories have other reasons to aim for fit. One has already been mentioned: *stare decisis*. Fit with the existing case law belongs to the vernacular of common law courts. As or more importantly, I would argue, theorists can learn from case law. This point was central to Arthur Linton Corbin's empiricism:

> A study of the appellate court decisions can never decrease in value or interest, for the reason that they constitute the living evidence of the continuing evolutionary process of our judicial system, both in the statement of its 'working rules,' and as to its success or failure in the administration of 'justice.'[47]

Corbin's attitude here is of a piece with his scepticism toward 'the quest for absolutes', his embrace of contingency in the law, as well as his basic optimism.[48] Contract theory should take case law seriously – should seek to fit with it – because, despite many errors along the way, there is wisdom to be found there.

III. Conclusion

In his Lectures on Pragmatism, William James emphasises the role of temperament in the production of theory:

> Of whatever temperament a professional philosopher is, he tries when philosophizing to sink the fact of his temperament. Temperament is no conventionally recognized reason, so he urges impersonal reasons only for his conclusions. Yet his temperament really gives him a stronger bias than any of his more strictly objective premises. It loads the evidence for him one way or the other, making for a more sentimental or a more hard-hearted view of the universe, just as this fact or that principle would. He trusts his temperament.[49]

James's observation is not intended as an indictment. It is a description of how actual philosophers, James included, work. Theory is not handed down from on high: it is crafted. Any serious theory reflects the concerns, values, habits of mind, cultural background and, broadly speaking, temperament of the living person who created it.

[47] AL Corbin, 'Sixty-Eight Years at Law' (1964) 13 *University of Kansas Law Review* 183, 188.

[48] AL Corbin, 'Farewell of Arthur Corbin to the Yale Law School Faculty' in G Calabresi, *The Future of Law and Economics: Essays in Reform and Recollection* (New Have, CT, Yale University Press, 2016) 173, 174–75. For more on Corbin's approach to contract theory, see G Klass, 'Arthur Linton Corbin (1874–1967)' in J Goudkamp and D Nolan (eds), *Scholars of Contract Law* (Oxford, Hart Pubishing, 2022) 201.

[49] W James, *Pragmatism, A New Word for Some Old Ways of Thinking* (London, Longmans, Green & Co 1907) 7.

My disagreements with Smith on what contract theory might be stem in part, no doubt, from my own acculturation in US law schools, where we regularly teach doctrinal splits between States and where, for historical reasons, scholars tend to embrace methodological diversity. My sense is that the postulates and occasional gaps I identified in section I reflect Steve Smith's personal philosophical temperament, which stems in part from the culture of Oxford legal positivism. Smith is inclined to believe that legal officials are basically trustworthy; that the common law is the product of judicial attempts to do justice between parties; that the law is not only coherent but principled. At the same time, Smith's analysis in Chapter One, as well as the theory he develops in the rest of the book, suggests an openness to complexity. Fit, coherence, morality and transparency are multiple, potentially competing goals that Smith nowhere attempts to reduce to a single principle. Smith's account of interpretive theory is complex. Although I disagree with him on the substance of what contract theory can and should be, I admire and will miss Steve's way of theorising.

14

Rights, Wrongs, Injustices and the Three Strata of Contract Law

MARK P GERGEN

This chapter draws on Stephen Smith's later book, *Rights, Wrongs, and Injustices*,[1] to revisit the subject of his earlier volume, *Contract Theory*.[2] The earlier book argues that an analytic theory of contract should aspire to give a single, unifying answer to the questions 'what sorts of events give rise to a contractual obligation and what the content of the obligation thus created is'.[3] Smith achieves this goal by defining contract law as the law of bilateral agreements, which he argues is best explained by promissory theories of contract. He acknowledges promissory theories of contract do not explain other parts of contract law. This chapter focuses on two of these other parts of contract law. I will refer to them as the law of debt (which is the oldest stratum of contract law) and the law of invited reliance (which is much newer). I will argue *Rights, Wrongs, and Injustices* illuminates the differences between these parts of contract law and the law of bilateral agreements.

Section I uses the distinction Smith draws between remedial and substantive law in *Rights, Wrongs, and Injustices* to argue the law governing contract enforcement contains a mix of remedial and substantive rules, and that rules governing debt enforcement are almost entirely substantive (putting bankruptcy law to the side) and do not require a creditor to act reasonably in enforcing a debt (unlike rules on contract termination). Section II argues Smith's taxonomy of remedies law supports and refines the claims in Fuller and Purdue, 'The Reliance Interest in Contract Law',[4] that there is an ascending scale of enforceability in contract law and debt is at the top of this scale. Section II also argues the causative event of the obligation to pay a contractual debt is a half-completed exchange. Together sections I and II argue the law of debt is analytically distinct from the law of bilateral agreements, with respect both to the event that gives rise to an obligation

[1] SA Smith, *Rights, Wrongs, and Injustices: The Structure of Remedial Law* (Oxford, Oxford University Press, 2019).

[2] SA Smith, *Contract Theory* (Oxford, Oxford University Press, 2004).

[3] ibid 43.

[4] LL Fuller and WR Purdue, 'The Reliance Interest in Contract Law' (1936) 36 *Yale Law Journal* 52 (Part I), 373 (Part II).

and to the content of the obligation. Section III takes up contract claims near the bottom of Fuller and Purdue's ascending scale of enforceability. It uses the example of indefinite agreements to show contract law has a third, invited-reliance stratum of rules.

I. Remedial and Substantive Rules in Contract Enforcement

In *Contract Theory*, Smith argues that a contract theory should aspire to show 'contract law to be coherent in the sense of being unified', so that 'all of its constituents parts flow from a *single* master idea or principle'.[5] In the Preface to *Rights, Wrongs, and Injustices*, Smith remarks that when he taught remedies law, he was unable to 'find a common thread – an overarching principle, concept, or question – to tie the materials together'.[6] The unifying thread Smith eventually found in remedies law is a difference he saw between remedies law and substantive law. According to Smith, substantive law instructs people how to treat each other, while remedies law instructs courts on what they may command a defendant to do when a claimant seeks a court's assistance.[7]

Smith argues this is normatively important. Even if you believe private law is about interpersonal justice (eg, how people should treat each other as individuals), remedies law inevitably involves consideration of the public interest because the claimant is asking for the state's assistance,[8] and because a violation of a court order is a wrong against the state and not against the claimant.[9] (One way to think about Smith's project is that by separating remedies law from substantive law, he makes it more plausible to argue substantive law is about interpersonal justice.)

Much of contract law is substantive law. Contract law is composed of rules that are power-conferring, duty-imposing or both (ie, composite rules).[10] These rules instruct people how to treat other people in the making and performance of contracts. My interest is the rules governing contract enforcement, specifically debt enforcement.

Contract enforcement is governed by a mix of substantive and remedial rules. Rules governing contract termination (eg, the substantial performance and material breach rules and rules on conditions)[11] are substantive because they instruct the injured party how to respond to non-performance by the defaulter. On the other hand, the rule governing the choice between remedial cost and loss of market value as the measure of damages for incomplete or defective construction is part of remedies law.[12]

[5] Smith (n 2) 11.
[6] Smith (n 1) vii.
[7] ibid viii–ix.
[8] Smith (n 1) 88, 102–03, 276.
[9] ibid 58, 83.
[10] G Klass, 'Three Pictures of Contract: Duty, Power, and Compound Rules' (2008) 83 *New York University Law Review* 1726.
[11] See generally, MP Gergen, 'Contract Termination' in M Chen-Wishart and P Saprai (eds), *Research Handbook in the Philosophy of Contract Law* (Cheltenham, Edward Elgar, forthcoming).
[12] Restatement, Second, Contracts § 348(2).

So, too, are the doctrine of undue burden in the rules governing specific performance[13] and the rule invalidating a penal liquidated damages term.[14] These rules instruct courts on what they may command the defaulter to do. The duty to mitigate is both substantive and remedial. The rule instructs both the injured party how to respond to breach and the court on what damages the defaulter may be ordered to pay.

To be clear, these substantive and remedial rules serve broadly similar purposes.[15] The default rules governing contract termination require the injured party to act reasonably in response to breach, balancing her interest in obtaining the benefit of her bargain (which is paramount), the defaulter's interest in minimising his loss on breach and the defaulter's bad faith.[16] Courts weigh these same factors in choosing between remedial cost and loss of market value as the measure of damages and whether an order of specific performance would impose an undue burden on the defaulter. And a court will invalidate a liquidated damages term as a penalty only if enforcing the term would give the injured party a windfall and impose forfeiture on a defaulter. The similarity of purpose of these rules is unsurprising for rules that guide people and courts in choosing the appropriate response to a breach of contract should serve similar purposes.

But there are also differences between these rules that justify distinguishing the two types of rules. Obtaining a damages award as compensation for a harm generally requires more in the way of justification by the injured party than terminating a contract to avoid a harm. And when an injured party seeks an injunction, she will also have to persuade the court that the order will be easy for the court to enforce. This is just as Smith says. In addition, some of the remedial rules apply to non-contract claims. The rule governing the choice between remedial cost and loss of market value as a measure of damages applies to tort claims involving harm to property, as well as breach of contract claims for defective or incomplete work. And the undue burden doctrine applies to claims for injunctive relief generally.

Putting bankruptcy law to the side, most rules governing debt enforcement are substantive and not remedial, because the rules instruct creditors how they may treat debtors when collecting debts. This includes rules governing 'self-help' repossession of property and rules governing a creditor's harassment of a defaulter to induce him to pay. These rules give creditors a great deal of power to recover property from a defaulter or to harass a defaulter, even if the creditor's action harms the defaulter (again, putting bankruptcy law to the side). Unlike the rules governing contract termination, there is no requirement of reasonableness in debt enforcement. Thus, the rule governing self-help in recovering property forbids a creditor from breaching the peace but does not require a creditor to forbear because a debtor has a desperate need for the property. And creditors generally are permitted to take punitive measures against defaulters

[13] Restatement, Second, Contracts § 364(1)(b).

[14] Restatement, Second, Contracts § 356.

[15] cf *Aetna Casualty and Surety Co v Murphy* (1988) 538 A.2d 319 (Conn Sup Ct) (Peters, J) (noting the 'family resemblance' of rules that permit 'a fair allocation of profit and loss' between the injured party and defaulter on breach of contract).

[16] Gergen (n 11).

without inquiring into whether punishment is warranted. A modern example is using an electronic kill switch to turn off a machine owned by the defaulter.[17] Finally, as Smith explains, when a creditor turns to a court for assistance to enforce a debt, a court generally has no discretion in the matter. I turn to this point now.

II. Debt's Place in Contract Law's Ascending Scale of Enforceability

In *Rights, Wrongs, and Injustices*, Smith divides remedies law into three main private law causes of action (what a claimant had to prove to obtain a remedy) and associated remedies (what a court could order a defendant to do). The three types relate to substantive duties in different ways. *Rights-threats-responding remedies* are orders to a defendant to perform a substantive duty he owes to a claimant. Examples include an order to pay a debt, an order to return property (ejectment or replevin) and most injunctions (including specific performance). These remedies required 'proof that the defendant is unwilling to comply with the claimant's substantive rights'.[18] *Wrongs-responding remedies* are orders to a defendant to pay a sum of money for committing a wrong when the sum is not appropriately understood as based on a claimant's loss. Clear examples include nominal damages, punitive damages and damages based on property's use-value (eg, a reasonable royalty for use of intellectual property and mesne profits for use of land).[19] Compensatory damages are in Smith's third category, which he labels *injustice-responding remedies*.[20]

Smith emphasizes the challenge his account of remedies law poses to the continuity thesis.[21] This is the thesis that remedies are duties of repair that follow in some normatively straightforward way from the substantive duties that are breached.[22] Thus one version of the continuity thesis states that a violation of a substantive duty gives rise to a duty of repair to make it 'as if' a wrong never happened.[23] Only in Smith's first

[17] MP Gergen, Contract Law's Morality and Punitive Debt Enforcement, SSRN Abstract 4976632, https://ssrn.com/abstract=4976632.

[18] Smith (n 1) 9.

[19] ibid 208–13. Smith also includes gains-based damages and damages for pain and suffering in this category: ibid 214, 218. This is debatable.

[20] ibid 93. Smith also includes loss-based restitutionary remedies in the third category. This also is debatable.

[21] US readers may find it difficult to get their minds around Smith's challenges to the continuity thesis because they tend to think of both substantive and remedial private law in more functionalist terms. Smith does not challenge functionalist justifications of remedies law: ibid, 202, 204 and 248. His interest in *Rights, Wrongs, and Injustices* is analytic clarity and not justification: ibid 25 (stating 'this book's primary aim is not to reform the law or even to evaluate it, but simply to understand it'). Nevertheless, the book has an important message for US readers because it challenges a central pillar of remedies law in the US. This pillar is the make-whole principle and the idea that the dominant purposes of remedies are compensation for past harm and deterrence of future harm. Protecting people from harm is so central to how lawyers in the US think about rights and remedies that some argue a claimant must allege harm to have a right to a court's assistance. The US Supreme Court said something like this in *TransUnion LLC v Ramirez*, 594 US 413 (2021), holding that standing to bring a claim in federal court requires a plaintiff to plead an 'injury', 'injury-in-fact', 'harm' and 'concrete harm', as if they mean the same thing.

[22] Smith (n 1) 181–84. See also S Steel, 'Compensation and Continuity' (2020) 26 *Legal Theory* 250 (comparing duty continuity, reasons continuity and rights continuity).

[23] A Ripstein, 'As If It Had Never Happened' (2007) 48 *William & Mary Law Review* 1957, 1958.

category (right-threats-responding remedies) does a judicial order directly correspond to a substantive duty. In this category, the order is to perform the duty and not to repair the violation.[24] The continuity thesis takes compensatory damages as the benchmark remedy, because in principle the goal of compensatory damages is to make it 'as if' the wrong never happened. Among other grounds,[25] Smith challenges the claim that compensatory damages make, or are meant to make, the claimant whole, 'as if' the wrong never happened.[26] This is certainly true of compensatory damages in contract law. These often make the claimant less than whole because of the requirements of foreseeability, mitigation and certainty, and a general rule precluding recovery for non-financial losses.

This account of remedies law supports and refines claims in Fuller and Purdue, 'The Reliance Interest in Contract Law'.[27] The article is renowned for challenging the moral basis of contractual obligation and expectation damages as the remedy for breach.[28] Fuller and Purdue had a more parochial target. This was the Williston project to create a general body of contract law that took as the paradigmatic contract a bilateral business agreement, and specifically Williston's position that when a promise is enforceable as a contract the claimant should recover expectation damages.[29] Fuller thought the article's major contribution to contract theory was presenting 'an analysis which breaks down the Contract-No-Contract dichotomy and substitutes an ascending scale of enforceability'.[30] According to Fuller and Purdue, at the very top of the scale, presenting 'strong claims for the most complete relief', is 'a half-completed exchange'.[31] In other words, at the very top of the scale is debt, either a promise to pay a sum of money embodied in a written instrument or the duty to pay the market price for performance received in an exchange transaction.[32]

Fuller and Purdue attribute the historic primacy of the expectation measure in contract law to the role of debt 'in a society in which credit has become a significant and pervasive institution'[33] and a process by which 'an enforceable promise [came to] be regarded as a kind of property'.[34] They describe 'the (bargain) promise to pay money'

[24] The definition of remedies in the second category (wrong-responding remedies) requires damages not be based on the harm caused by the defendant's wrong. The harm caused by the defendant's wrong is only one of several factors that bear on the assessment of the sum of money due. Other factors include 'the importance of the relevant right' (Smith (n 1) 221) and the character of 'the defendant's conduct', including 'the defendant's awareness of, and motivations for, the relevant actions' (ibid 207).

[25] Smith also argues the continuity thesis does not account for liability-imposing rules that do not require the defendant to have committed a wrong. His examples include much liability in restitution and non-fault-based liability in tort (e.g, strict liability): ibid 224–25.

[26] ibid 253–56.

[27] Fuller and Purdue (n 4).

[28] See, eg, P Benson, *Justice in Transactions* (Cambridge, MA, Harvard University Press, 2019) 5.

[29] Fuller and Purdue (n 4) 64, 69, 89.

[30] RS Summers, *Lon L. Fuller* (Redwood City, CA, Stanford University Press, 1984) 133 (quoting a 1938 letter by Fuller to Karl Llewellyn).

[31] ibid.

[32] Fuller and Purdue (n 4) 67. Fuller and Purdue refer to these as 'real contracts'. Their main goal in this part of the paper is to use real contracts to illustrate the divergence of the measure of damages and the reasons for enforcing a promise. The measure of damages for debt is the expectation interest, while the reasons for enforcing a debt are the benefit received by the debtor and reliance by the creditor.

[33] ibid 59.

[34] ibid.

(ie, a debt) as the 'ideal contract from the perspective of the credit system', because it is liquid and relatively easy to value (particularly if it is in a form that either minimises or makes it possible to price credit risk).[35] They add 'The farther removed a contract is from the credit system, the less is the judicial incentive to grant the expectancy, the less pressing are the basic policies which justify the granting of the expectancy in the ordinary business agreement.'[36] They place 'bilateral business agreements' just beneath debt on the scale as the other major category of contract that ought to be enforced without proof of reliance.[37]

Rights, Wrongs, and Injustices supports and refines Fuller and Purdue's claims that there is a scale of enforceability of contracts and debt is at the top the scale. Smith zooms in on expectation-based remedies at the upper end of the scale and shows there are large differences in remedies in this part. One reason debt is at the very top of the scale of enforceability is that a debt is enforced by an order to the debtor to pay the debt, with an immediate threat of bad things to follow if the debtor does not pay.[38] Just below debt on the scale of enforceability is the remedy for breach of a bilateral contract, when the claimant is able to complete the exchange in a substitute transaction.[39] Significantly below these remedies on the scale of enforceability is the remedy of compensatory consequential damages. Smith explains that the rules governing compensatory consequential damages basically instruct the court to fairly apportion the claimant's loss from the breach between the claimant and the defendant.[40] Rules on mitigation, foreseeability and certainty are tools to achieve a fair apportionment.

Debt claims are also substantively simple. Much of contract law is composed of rules that were created when courts began to enforce promises in informal executory agreements. Most of these rules are irrelevant to a debt claim.[41] The irrelevant rules include the statute of frauds, the requirement of definiteness, the rules on offer and acceptance, the doctrine of frustration and damages rules (eg, mitigation, foreseeability and certainty). The requirements of consideration and (in English law) intent to create a legal relationship are relevant but rarely come up. Consideration arises only when a debt is incurred gratuitously (and, in England, when a debt is not embodied in a sealed instrument or a deed).[42] Intent to create legal relations only comes up when a debt is incurred in a social or domestic arrangement.[43]

[35] ibid 65.

[36] ibid 66.

[37] ibid 70.

[38] Smith (n 1) 89, 138. The similarities between the remedy on a debt claim and the remedies to recover property (replevin and ejectment) are obvious to English lawyers, because under English law the creditor brings the action for an agreed sum to enforce a debt, and not a breach of contract claim. The action of debt has largely disappeared in the US, so a creditor is likely to bring a claim for compensatory damages. This makes no practical difference other than with respect to the duty to mitigate, and this is an issue only in the unusual case in which the creditor chooses to perform after repudiation. MP Gergen, 'Debt as a Contractual Type' in Chen-Wisehart and Saprai (eds) (n 11).

[39] Smith (n 1) 172 (discussing substitutionary damages), 213 (discussing market price damages).

[40] ibid 253–56. Fuller and Purdue make a similar point with respect to the foreseeability requirement: Fuller and Purdue (n 4) 84–86.

[41] Gergen (n 38).

[42] See, eg, *Dougherty v Salt*, 125 NE 94 (NY) (1919).

[43] See, eg, *Balfour v Balfour* [1919] 2 KB 571 (CA).

Debt claims are simple substantively because of the character of the causative event of a duty to pay a debt. The causative event of a duty to perform a promise in a bilateral agreement is an exchange of promises, as in by offer and acceptance. Traditionally, debt had two possible causative events: the delivery of a prescribed formal instrument (eg, a sealed bond) or performance by the creditor in an exchange transaction. Even in legal systems that enforce a sealed bond (or other prescribed formal instrument), almost all debt is incurred in an exchange transaction for a performance rendered.[44] So it is fair to say that performance generally is the causative event of a duty to pay a debt.

In *Contract Theory*, Smith equates contract law with the rules in the bilateral agreement stratum of contract law. He treats an exchange of promises as the paradigmatic contractual type, and the rules on offer and acceptance as the 'core' of contract law.[45] This choice strengthens Smith's case that promissory theories best explain contract. But this choice also means Smith must look outside of contract law to the law of unjust enrichment or to estoppel to explain why there 'is a duty to pay for requested services'.[46] Smith deserves credit for his candour on this point. Explaining the duty to pay for requested services with the offer-acceptance framework requires describing the debtor's request as an offer and the creditor's performance as an acceptance of the offer. This stretches the terms 'offer' and 'acceptance' beyond their usual meaning. The debtor wants performance, not a promissory acceptance; and the creditor may not undertake any further duty when she performs (eg, when the debt is for a loan of money). When the creditor performs at the debtor's request, she is engaging in half of an exchange, she is not agreeing to engage in an exchange in the future.

It is even harder to explain with the offer-acceptance framework why there is a duty to pay for unrequested services when a recipient knows a service provider expects to be compensated and a recipient has an opportunity to reject the services. The Restatement, Second, Contracts jams this into the offer-acceptance framework by saying the recipient's 'silence and inaction operate as an acceptance'.[47] It is simpler and more accurate to say there is a duty to pay for performance received in an exchange transaction. Broadening the analytic account of contract to include a contract based on performance also makes it possible to describe a barter exchange as a contractual transaction.[48] It is a small step from saying a half-completed exchange is a contract to saying an apparently completed exchange is a contract. This makes it easier to explain the existence of implied warranties in a barter exchange.[49]

[44] AWB Simpson, *A History of the Common Law of Contract* (Oxford, Oxford University Press, 1975) 73; D Ibbetson, *A Historical Introduction to the Law of Obligations* (Oxford, Oxford University Press, 1999) 32.

[45] Smith (n 2) 167.

[46] ibid 194.

[47] Restatement, Second, Contracts § 69.

[48] Smith (n 2) 176–77, argues this is not governed by contract law.

[49] *Pennsy Supply, Inc v American Ash Recycling Corp*, 895 A.2d 595 (Pa Superior Ct 2006) illustrates and adds a wrinkle. The defendant offered treated ash aggregate on a 'first come, first served' basis to contractors, on the understanding it would be used in paving work. This was to save itself the expense of disposing of the material, which was classified as hazardous waste. The claimant used the material in paving that experienced cracking for reasons the claimant attributed to defects in the materials (which had nothing to do with its classification as hazardous waste). The claimant sued for breach of the implied warranty of merchantability. The defendant argued the transaction was a gift. The court held the complaint stated sufficient facts to find a bargain.

Debt and bilateral agreement should be thought of as ideal types. Shades of difference between these two types of contracts eventually become differences in kind. Parties can try to create a contract by an exchange of promises but fail because the promises exchanged do not match. When this occurs, parties may end up being bound because they perform or accept performance. Classical contract law explains the existence of a contract in this case by treating performance or acceptance of performance by the original offeror as 'acceptance' of the terms of a counteroffer. A more sensible rule is UCC § 2-207(3). This is to explain the existence of a contract by conduct of both parties recognising the existence of a contract. This explanation makes it possible to treat neither party as assenting to the terms of the other party's writing.

There are other payoffs to recognising debt and bilateral agreement as analytically distinct contractual types.[50] This highlights a feature both share: they involve exchange transactions. Contract law mostly is the law of 'this for that'.[51] Contract theory should pay more attention to the element of exchange. The most basic and fundamental object of consent in contract law (defining an object of consent as something people typically actually have in mind when they consent) is to engage in an exchange transaction.[52] And whether people consider a transaction to be a gift or an exchange is the only way to distinguish a conditional gift from conditional bargain.[53]

Recognising debt as an analytically distinct contractual type also helps to clarify the relationship between contract law and property law. As Smith observes, contract law is like property law in that each body of law 'specifies the acts that are required to create a particular sort of right, and the content of the right thus created'.[54] Contract law enables people to create new rights as well as to transfer existing rights. A difference between contract law and property law is that contract law enables people to tailor rights. But many contractual transactions involve well-established right types. Debt illustrates that some contract right types have property-like attributes, such as assignability and the right of a purchaser to hold an asset free of upstream claims (aka negotiability).

[50] In 'Debt and the Morality of Contract Law' (n 17) I argue that some prominent theories of contract, including Fried and Shiffrin's account, misfire because they equate contract with bilateral agreement.

[51] J Gardner, 'The Contractualisation of Labour Law' in H Collins et al (eds), *Philosophical Foundations of Labour Law* (Oxford, Oxford University Press, 2018) 33, 44–46. For a critique of Gardner's conclusion that therefore contract inevitably involves a debased type of human interaction (eg, alienation and subordination), see H Dagan, 'The Liberal Promise of Contract' in H Psarras and S Steel (eds), *Private Law and Practical Reason: Essays on John Gardner's Private Law Theory* (Oxford, Oxford University Press, 2023) 311.

[52] See MP Gergen, 'Consent Across Private Law' in S Bray et al (eds), *Interstitial Private Law* (Oxford, Oxford University Press, 2024) 89, 96–98. The second most basic object of consent in contract law is to a writing as an expression of the terms of an agreement. The specific terms of a contract, which includes many promises, is a distant third. People often make contracts without having specific terms in mind.

[53] To make this point, Williston uses the famous hypothetical in which 'a benevolent man says to tramp "If you go around the corner to the clothing shop there, you may purchase an overcoat on my credit."' S Williston, *Williston on Contracts*, 1st edn (New York, Baker, Voorhis & Co, 1921) § 112.

[54] Smith (n 2) 103.

III. A Third Strand of Contract Law and the Knowability Value

Debt and bilateral agreement share another characteristic: ideally, people undertake a contractual duty intentionally. Debt usually is intentionally incurred because people generally know when they obtain performance in an exchange transaction. The objective approach makes it possible for people to be bound to a bilateral agreement they did not intend to make. The law of bilateral agreements is made complicated by rules that shield people from unintended contractual obligations. These obligation-shielding rules include the consideration requirement, the statute of frauds, the definiteness requirement, the mirror-image rule and the power to revoke an offer prior to acceptance. These obligation-shielding rules are qualified in turn by shield-piercing rules, further complicating matters.

My interest in this section is cases in which an obligation-shielding-rule is pierced to protect the claimant's reliance. Fuller and Purdue lumped together performance-based and reliance-based claims on 'contracts imperfect in expression or legal effect'[55] because it supported their claim about the importance of the reliance interest in contract law. This was disingenuous. Performance-based claims generally involved courts' use of common counts like quantum meruit and money-had-and-received to allow what would have been, in the writ of debt's heyday, a debt claim based on obtaining performance in an informal exchange. It is unsurprising that courts found ways to allow these claims, even though they ran afoul of rules like the statute of frauds and the certainty requirement that were developed to deal with problems that arose when courts began to enforce informal promises in executory agreements. Reliance-based claims are a different kettle of fish. They are a new stratum of duty and liability rules associated with contract law.

This section uses what is called the 'puzzle of indefiniteness' to show that contract law has a third, invited-reliance stratum of duty and liability rules. It will also argue that contract theory should pay more attention to what Smith calls the knowability requirement of a duty. Indefinite agreements rank low on Fuller and Purdue's ascending scale of enforceability for both substantive and remedial reasons. When an agreement is indefinite, it can be difficult for a claimant to establish breach. It also can be difficult for a claimant to quantify expectation damages with a reasonable degree of certainty. Under classical contract law, when a claimant rendered performance under an indefinite agreement, he would bring what is now called a restitution claim to recover the market value of the performance.[56] Again, Fuller and Purdue argued these cases were authority for awarding reliance damages.[57] While this may have been disingenuous, Fuller and Purdue succeeded. It is now well-established in US law that a claimant can bring a promissory estoppel claim and recover reliance damages when an agreement is too indefinite to be enforced as a contract.[58]

[55] Fuller and Purdue (n 4) 386.
[56] See, eg, *Kearns v Andree*, 107 Conn 181, 139 A.695 (1928).
[57] Fuller and Purdue (n 4) 394–96.
[58] See, eg, *Wheeler v White*, 398 SW.2d 93 (1965).

A promissory estoppel claim requires the claimant to establish that the defendant broke a promise. This creates a puzzle: how can a promise be too indefinite to enforce on a contract claim but for it still be possible to find a breach of promise to sustain a promissory estoppel claim?[59] In a moment I will answer this question. But first I want to set to the side indefiniteness problems that can be solved within the bilateral agreement framework. This requires me to say a word about Smith's position that a duty must be knowable.

Smith develops the knowability requirement as part of his challenge to the continuity thesis. He argues that a rule is appropriately described as imposing a duty only if the person who is subject to the rule's command can 'reasonably be expected to know' what the rule commands him to do.[60] Relatedly, he argues a violation of a rule is appropriately described as wrong only if the action violating the rule is considered 'undesirable' and 'something that we should not do'.[61] My point does not require you to accept Smith's position that these are requirements for a rule to be described as a duty and conduct to be described as wrong. It only requires you to accept it is valuable that people know what the law commands them to do. I assume this is uncontroversial.

An indefiniteness problem arises when people make a contract that fails to resolve an issue that arises in performance. The facts in *Academy Chicago Publishers v Cheever*[62] illustrate the point. A contract between Mary Cheever and Academy required her to collaborate with Denius to produce a book of her late husband John Cheever's uncollected stories. It was Denius's task to find the stories. He found an unexpected treasure trove. Cheever and Denius disagreed on what to do with it.[63] This presented an indefiniteness problem, for the contract did not resolve this issue.

Under modern contract law, this is framed as a balancing problem. The court must balance the desire to protect Denius's reasonable expectations with the desire not to impose an obligation on Cheever that she did not agree to and probably would not have agreed to.[64] The trial court resolved this balancing problem by declaring that Cheever was obligated to consent to a very short book (140 pages) containing stories of her choosing. Academy was unhappy with this resolution and appealed. The Illinois Supreme Court resolved this balancing problem by declaring the contract was

[59] *Garwood Packaging, Inc v Allen & Company, Inc*, 378 F.3d 698 (7th Cir 2004).

[60] Smith (n 1) 197–99, 243–45. For example, Smith argues (ibid, 198) that it is improper to say a wrongdoer has a duty to pay damages for emotional distress he inflicts because 'it is impossible, even in theory, to determine in advance of litigation the amount wrongdoers might owe'. He explains 'the unknowability objection is not merely a version of the familiar idea that it is difficult to apply general rules to particular circumstances. The objection is that the relevant facts are in the hands of the duty's beneficiary' and are not 'available to those' who are subject to the rule's command: ibid 244.

[61] ibid 258. For example, Smith opposes describing the liability to pay compensatory damages in *Vincent v Lake Erie Transportation Co*, 109 Minn 456 (1910) as wrong-based, because the court held the defendant acted appropriately in tying up to the dock to protect his ship from the storm: Smith (n 1) 261. He takes the position that the action in these cases should not be described as a breach of a substantive duty on the view '[f]rom the law's perspective, to state there is a legal duty to do X means that, all things considered, X should be done': ibid 274–75, fn 3. He acknowledges the contrary view, which he attributes to John Gardner: ibid 261.

[62] *Academy Chicago Publishers v Cheever*, 578 NE 2d 981 (Ill 1991).

[63] Academy was a small academic publisher; Cheever wanted a major publishing house to publish the entire collection.

[64] *Rego v Decker*, 482 P.2d 834 (Alaska 1971).

unenforceable on grounds of indefiniteness. The trial court's resolution of the problem is in the spirit of modern contract law (the trial court invoked the duty of good faith); the Illinois Supreme Court's resolution is in the spirit of classical contract law (it invoked the maxim that courts do not make contracts).

The knowability value adds another concern: the party in Cheever's position should be able to know what the law commands her to do. In the case, Academy tried to finesse this concern by suing for a declaratory judgment. But the problem cannot be kept out of the case. A decision in favour of Academy creates the possibility that a claimant could rely on this precedent in a future case to sue for damages for breach of contract. To ensure that people in Cheever's position in the future can know what the law commands them to do, in deciding for Cheever the court must enunciate a rule that would have enabled Cheever to know that the law prohibited her from doing what she did, if the rule had already been established. Basically, modern contract law allows a court to enforce an indefinite agreement by creating a rule that will eliminate a similar indefiniteness problem in a future case.

The trial court's decision would be all right on this score if it were grounded on a rule that applies when a contract allows a range of ways to perform a promise. The rule allows and requires a promisor to choose to perform at any point in the range.[65] If this rule had already been established then Cheever could reasonably be expected to know of the rule and that it commanded her to agree to a very short book with stories of her choosing. A decision giving Academy more and better stories might also be acceptable on this score if the court adopted Benson's position that a general requirement to act reasonably within the framework of the agreed exchange attaches to every contract.[66] I am not interested in the relative merits of these two rules. What I want to call to your attention is that both explanations of a judgment for the claimant in *Academy Chicago Publishers* can be explained within the bilateral agreement framework, because Cheever violated a duty that could be derived from the parties' agreement. Neither explanation requires reference to the promissory estoppel doctrine or to invited reliance.

Some cases in which the claimant prevails on a claim involving an indefinite agreement cannot be explained in this way. These cases are best explained by invited reliance. *Hoffman v Red Owl Stores, Inc*[67] illustrates this. Hoffman relied in definite and substantial ways on representations by a local Red Owl manager (Lukowitz) that $18,000 capital (which was all Hoffman had) would suffice to set him up in a Red Owl grocery store. When Hoffman got down to negotiations with Red Owl's senior managers, they said that a store would require significantly more capital. Hoffman broke off negotiations and sued. He recovered reliance damages on a promissory estoppel claim.

It is hard to see what Red Owl's senior managers did wrong. They honestly believed more capital was needed, and they probably thought that in demanding adequate capital they were acting in Hoffman's interest, as well as in the company's interest. It is even

[65] *Mears v Nationwide Mutual Ins, Co*, 91 F.3d 1118 (8th Cir 1986).

[66] Benson (n 28) 156–64. Smith takes the position that the duty of care in negligence law does not violate the knowability requirement. It follows that the knowability requirement does mean that the person subject to a duty must be able to predict precisely where the line will be drawn when the duty is a standard.

[67] *Hoffman v Red Owl Stores, Inc*, 26 Wis.2d 683, 133 NW2d 267 (1965).

harder to formulate a rule that would instruct people in a similar position what not to do in the future. This has led some to propose the doctrine of negligent misstatement as a sounder basis for the decision.[68] A decision on this ground would be all right on the knowability score, because someone in Lukowitz's position could reasonably be expected to know that the law commanded him not to carelessly mislead Hoffman about the capital needed for the store, once a duty of care in conveying information about prospective dealings is established. Alternatively, Smith's analytic framework would allow a court to order Red Owl to pay damages for Hoffman's reliance loss to avoid an unjust loss. Presumably, this would be justified by a rule that allows a court to impose liability when one person misleads another about the likelihood of prospective dealings.

Whichever ground is chosen, invited reliance is the basis for the duty or the liability in *Hoffman v Red Owl*. The duty or liability is imposed because Lukowitz reasonably appeared to intend to invite Hoffman to rely on his representation of the capital needed for a store. Invited reliance also is the basis for the rule in Restatement Second § 87(2), protecting reliance on an offer.[69] And invited reliance is a possible basis for the claim under Restatement Second § 90 for breach of a gratuitous promise. Looking outside of contract law to tort law, invited reliance is the basis for imposing a duty of care in supplying information to guide another generally (and not just with respect to future dealings), and it is the basis for imposing a duty of care when one person gratuitously undertakes to perform a service to assist another.[70]

Now I can explain the answer to the puzzle: how can a promise be too indefinite to enforce on a contract claim but for it still be possible to find a breach of promise to sustain a promissory estoppel claim? The answer has three parts. Sometimes, as in *Academy Chicago Publishers v Cheever*, an indefiniteness problem can be resolved within the bilateral agreement framework and does not require reference to the promissory estoppel doctrine. This leads to the second part of the answer: the promissory estoppel doctrine allows a claim for breach of promise when a claimant cannot establish the promise broken was part of a bilateral agreement. The rule in Restatement Second § 87(2), protecting reliance on an offer, is an example of this, if one accepts the position that an offer covered by the rule includes an implicit promise of irrevocability. *Hoffman v Red Owl* illustrates the answer's third part: sometimes a duty or liability is based on non-promissory assurances about the prospect of future dealings.

It is tempting to equate the invited-reliance stratum of contract law with what is described as 'pre-contractual liability'[71] (plus, perhaps, a promissory estoppel claim for breach of a gratuitous promise). But once invited reliance is recognized as a distinct basis for duty or liability in contract, it invites reconsideration of some rules of contract formation. This brings me back to *Contract Theory*. Smith argued that while

[68] MP Gergen, Liabilty for Mistake in Contract Formation, (1990) 64 U.S.C.L. Rev. 1. Restatement, Third, Torts: Liability for Economic Harm § 5(5), rejects a tort claim for negligent misrepresentations made in the course of negotiating a contract.

[69] Drennan v. Star Paving, (1958) 333 P.2d 757 (Cal.) is the template.

[70] MP Gergen, 'Negligent Misrepresentation as Contract' (2013) 101 *California Law Review* 953; MP Gergen, 'The Ambit of Negligence Liability for Pure Economic Loss' (2006) 48 *Arizona Law Review* 749.

[71] Smith (n 2) 195–206.

an objective approach is appropriate with respect to the *meaning* of an agreement,[72] a subjective approach is appropriate if the question is 'the very intention to make a contract.'[73] As already noted, often a claimant brings a reliance-based claim to pierce a rule shielding a defendant from unintended contractual obligation. This is consistent with Smith's challenge to the objective approach. And one could go even further, to explain that contract generally requires both parties to subjectively intend to commit to an exchange, in the absence of invited reliance.

IV. Conclusion

I have argued that contract law has at least three distinct strata of duty and liability rules involving debt, bilateral agreement and invited reliance. For each of these strata of rules it is possible to give a single, unifying answer to the questions posed by Smith at the outset of *Contract Theory*: 'what sorts of events give rise to a contractual obligation and what the content of the obligation thus created is'.[74] As a practical matter, the most important stratum is debt. A half-completed exchange gives rise to a debt, and the obligation is to pay a debt or face potentially punitive consequences. Separating debt as a contractual type from bilateral agreement reveals that much of the law of bilateral agreements consists of rules, like the definiteness requirement, that qualify the objective approach by shielding people from contractual obligations they did not agree to undertake, and which they probably would not have agreed to undertake, in the absence of invited reliance.

[72] ibid 272.
[73] ibid 174.
[74] ibid 43.

15

Conceptualising the Law of Contractual Modifications: A Different Framework

PETER BENSON*

I. Introduction

In a characteristically thoughtful and careful article, 'Contracting under Pressure: A Theory of Duress', Stephen Smith drew our attention to two different ways in which parties can be induced by pressure to enter contracts or to modify existing contractual terms.[1] The first way involves a *wrongful threat* by the promisee to bring about unwelcome consequences for the promisor if the latter does not agree to a proposed transaction or modification. The canonical case of this is threatened (unjustified) bodily harm: a contract signed at gunpoint.[2] Here, the wrongfulness of the threat is an essential prerequisite, and Smith assumed that to be wrongful, there must standardly be some threatened violation of the promisor's rights.[3] Moreover, unless such wrongful pressure had no impact on the promisor's decision, the law does – and, Smith thought, should – deem the resulting transaction or modification voidable.[4] This, according to Smith, is not because there is an actual absence of will or intention on the promisor's part but rather because the law cannot uphold a claim by the promisee against the promisor that has arisen through the former's wrongdoing against the latter.

But Smith also emphasised that wrongful pressure of this kind does not exhaust the grounds upon which the law does – or at least might reasonably – relieve the promisor. There is a second reason, he argued, that is based on the promisor's lack of consent and that aims to uphold her autonomy vis-à-vis the promisee, and he was at pains to identify its distinctive conditions and implications for the law relieving parties from agreements contracted under pressure.[5] For this consent or autonomy principle to apply,

* For my friend and valued fellow-traveller in the realms of contract law and contract theory, Steve Smith, who was always kind and courageous in all circumstances.

[1] SA Smith, 'Contracting under Pressure: A Theory of Duress'(1997) 56(2) *CLJ* 343.

[2] ibid 344.

[3] ibid 351–53.

[4] ibid 354–56.

[5] ibid 344–45, 358 ff.

it is not necessary that the promisee exerted *any* wrongful pressure on the promisor. Smith instead referred to the promisor's defence here as 'duress by necessity', suggesting salvage scenarios as a clear instance.[6] Here, a ship is induced to contract with a second ship for the latter's salvage services in circumstances of dire necessity that have in no way been brought about by the second ship but that result in the endangered ship's having no one but the second ship to provide this service. According to Smith, for the first ship to be able to claim lack of consent as a defence to enforcing the agreement, it must show that there was a complete absence of reasonable alternatives and that this absence affected the *terms* of their agreement. The fact that the party entered an agreement would, by itself, normally not suffice to impugn the requisite voluntariness of her consent. In the salvage scenario, the crucial fact is that there was no other ship to provide the service, and what must be shown is that this fact affected the terms agreed upon between the parties. So, for example, if the terms were seriously out of sync with what (hypothetically) would have been charged had there been a range of rescue ships, that is, a competitive market price, the consent defence could apply. Smith contended that agreements contracted under such non-wrongful pressure can in principle be relieved to the extent that the contract terms are unfair or unacceptable to the promisor.[7]

In my view, Smith was right to insist on this distinction between the two grounds for relief from contracting under pressure. He was also right to characterise the contrast between them by emphasising that the 'existence [including terms] of a contract is peripheral to the application of the wrongdoing principle'.[8] Indeed, this is a fundamental insight. Since I will draw on it in developing my own argument, a brief elaboration of it is in order here.

According to Smith, the wrongdoing principle applies as a ground for relief to *whatever legal effect* the wrongdoer seeks to impose on the innocent party. To establish wrongful pressure of this kind, it is not necessary to determine whether there has been a contract or what its terms are. The analysis is not in any sense internal to – it neither draws on nor reflects – these factors. The latter are relevant only in so far as they specify the effect (eg, claim) the wrongdoer is asserting against the victim and whether the threat has been effectual in reality. So, whether consideration has been satisfied, whether the terms are otherwise fair and reasonable, and so on, are matters that are irrelevant per se. All this is abundantly clear in the canonical example of a contract signed at gunpoint: what counts is simply whether there has been a wrongful threat or action that has affected the victim in a way that sufficiently relates to the claim asserted by the wrongdoer against her. The ground for relief is *conceptually external* to the specific nature of the transaction – the effect – that has been induced by the wrongful threat.

In sharp contrast, the consent basis for relief *must* refer to the particular nature and terms of the agreement in order to apply *at all*. According to Smith, these aspects go to the *essential* constitutive conditions and operation of the consent principle: the latter is thus *internal* to – it reflects and draws on – the nature of the transaction that

[6] ibid 363, 373 and 365 ff.
[7] This is Smith's formulation: ibid 366, fn 72 and text.
[8] ibid 351.

it underpins. Indeed, Smith emphasised that the definition of consent that should be applied in the context of contracting under pressure is not some universal definition immediately suited for all (even non-contractual) circumstances of alleged pressure but, to the contrary, should be specified in a way that is appropriate for determining the existence of contractual obligations. This follows from the fact that, according to Smith, the consent defence always has to do with whether and when a person (here a party claiming release from her promise) should be able to disclaim responsibility for her actions, and thus presupposes – and must engage – the prior determination that she could otherwise have been bound by those actions.[9]

I would like to draw on this core contrast to develop a tentative framework for understanding the law of contract modifications, which Smith himself characterised as 'the most complex variant of a pressure case' and which he discussed at various points in his article.[10] Almost three decades after his article was published, the treatment of contract modifications in contract law is still unsettled or not clearly and fully enough worked out, and, beyond this, it certainly continues to be a topic of serious scholarly controversy that goes to the very nature of contractual obligations. On the one hand, there seems to be a prevailing view – particularly among commentators – that the general requirement of consideration, even though doctrinally formulated as applicable to *any* promise not under seal and therefore viewed as necessary for contract formation, need not apply, exceptionally, to the promises constituting contract modifications. This challenge to the traditional so-called 'pre-existing duty' doctrine, which often denied enforceability to a contract modification simply on the basis of an absence of fresh consideration, raises the fundamental question of what should be the criterion for deciding this. And increasingly courts – and especially commentators – have formulated ideas of so-called 'economic duress' for this purpose. Yet, on the other hand, basic issues going to the very meaning, scope and legal consequences of economic duress – including its relation to other doctrines, such as good faith and unconscionability, and more generally to forms of wrongdoing – remain highly controverted and judicially unsettled.

My aim in this chapter will be to outline an analysis of contract modifications that is consistent at all levels with general principles of contract law, including those of contract formation with its central requirement of consideration, but which at the same time properly takes into account the movement of ideas and concerns stated in the case law about the apparent rigidity of past applications of the pre-existing duty rule, the need to recognise legitimate interests of parties in adjusting their on-going transactions reasonably and fairly, and the relevance of good faith or other doctrines that protect against illegitimate advantage-taking in the particular context of contract modifications. The proposed analysis differs fundamentally from most scholarly approaches precisely because it attempts to be wholly internal to, and framed by, the conception of consent that is required by the common law of contract formation, in this way following through on Smith's core insight as discussed above.

[9] ibid 364 and elsewhere.
[10] ibid 371; also ibid 369 and elsewhere.

II. The Pre-existing Duty Rule and its Critics

Since the late sixteenth century, it has been, and still remains, a settled necessary requirement for the *contractual* enforcement of non-formal promises (ie, those promises not under seal or some other legal formality) that they be supported by consideration.[11] This is not a controverted proposition of the common law of contract. More exactly, as doctrinally presented and understood, it is a *general* requirement that applies to *any and every non-formal promise whenever and however it arises.* Following Smith's important insight that both the conception of consent and that of non-wrongful pressure vitiating such consent should be defined in a way that is appropriate to the contractual relations that are under scrutiny, it seems more than plausible to suggest that the nature of contractual consent – viewed non-reductively and in terms of how it is doctrinally specified[12] – should first and foremost be understood by how it is specified via this central requirement of consideration.

This should hold no less for the nature and existence of consent (as well as of consent-based duress) in circumstances of contract modifications. For, given its general character and scope, the consideration requirement must apply to, and be satisfied by, any promises made in the context of a contractual modification. Thus, where there is an already existing contract between two parties and one of them promises the other something more than or different from what was already included in the express or implied terms of their contract, this new promise (as I will refer to it) must prima facie itself be supported by consideration. This *must* be an incontrovertible conclusion, because it merely applies in a consistent way the general requirement of consideration for any non-formal promise. Any other conclusion would directly contradict – hence abolish – the settled core meaning and definition of consideration. Since consideration so understood remains an essential prerequisite for contract formation, even criticism of the pre-existing duty rule must also accept this conclusion, if it is to be doctrinally relevant.

Rightly accepting this conclusion, the traditional pre-existing duty rule, however, *takes the further step* of holding that, in these circumstances of promised modification, what the other party – the promisee – gives or promises in return for the new promise *cannot* count as consideration if it *only* amounts to what the promisee already gave or promised under the express or implied terms of their existing contract.[13] It is with respect to this further step that modern critics of the rule mount their challenge.[14]

There have been many different criticisms of the pre-existing duty rule motivated by widespread and often legitimate dissatisfaction with what is viewed as the rule's mechanical, indeed sometimes arbitrary and distorting, treatment of on-going transactions.

[11] I will define a promise as 'contractually enforceable' if performance as promised is itself directly enforceable via expectation damages or specific performance, independently of any detrimental reliance by the promisee upon the promisor.

[12] Smith emphasises that this is how he thinks these and other contractual issues should be approached. See Smith (n 1) 360–61 and elsewhere.

[13] The clearest and most influential judicial statement of this view is still Lord Ellenborough CJ's judgment in *Stilk v Myrick* (1809) 2 Camp 317 (KB), which should be read in conjunction with the later *Hartley v Ponsonby* (1857) 7 El & Bl 877 (QB) (per Lord Campbell CJ).

[14] In section III, I try to show how the law is correct in taking this step and suggest that, properly understood, it is untouched by the standard criticisms.

Here, I want to focus on the basic premises of the alternative views proposed by its critics. Despite differences in approach, the latter generally turn on the role they ascribe to the consideration requirement in general and also in this context of post-formation modifications and adjustments.

In a nutshell, these critics view consideration's role in purely instrumental terms as evidencing a serious intention by the parties to enter contractual relations – this they take as the fundamental prerequisite for the contractual enforcement of promises – and they presuppose that the principal way in which consideration performs this role is by establishing a bargain relation between the parties. This positive basis for enforcement is then qualified by a negative requirement that the parties' intent, as operating in their bargain relation, must *not* be vitiated by duress or unfair conduct. As long as a promise satisfies these positive and negative requirements, it should be contractually enforceable.

Now, according to these critics, the positive requirement is easily satisfied by modifications made in the context of on-going contractual relations simply in so far as parties reasonably view themselves as already in an existing bargain relation – which will always be the case unless the parties have ended their pre-existing contract. With modifications viewed in this way as *ancillary to a bargain relation*, the contention is that there should normally be no issue as to the existence of serious intent with respect to the modification or, it can be added, as to the potential economic or social importance of the modification. In other words, the role and reason for consideration are in principle always and fully met in these circumstances, and therefore promisors should prima facie be held to their promises, notwithstanding the fact that there may be a new promise that has not itself been made in return for the promise (or doing) of something beyond what was already included in the express or implied terms of the existing contract. Notice that, on this view, the consideration requirement is met, not because the parties' modification can be shown to involve the traditional doctrinally required quid pro quo involving mutually requested legal benefits and legal detriments, but instead if the underlying rationale, which these critiques attribute to consideration, is sufficiently satisfied in the circumstances. It is not by chance that courts and commentators taking this view treat as sufficient any so-called 'practical' or factual benefit accruing to the promisor as a result of the promisee's performance of his original promise; or, going the whole way, they simply dispense altogether with the need for consideration as traditionally defined for modifications. The underlying approach is the same.

Having reached this conclusion about consideration, the central issue for these critics – and the sole focus of virtually all scholarly discussion – becomes whether the new promise should be *voidable* because *vitiated* by some form of unfairness, economic duress or otherwise illegitimate pressure. As to what constitutes the relevant kind, scope and juridical basis of the pressure that is sufficient to deny enforceability at this second step, the contemporary literature and recent case law suggest a variety of answers, including procedural and substantive fairness, the avoidance of opportunistic or unconscionable conduct, community standards of good faith and so forth. Despite these differences, they generally seem to share the following pattern.

On the one hand, consistent with the conclusion about the relevance and role of consideration at the first step – that is, that it is always effectively satisfied and so superfluous in circumstances of pre-existing bargain relations – this second step, with its vitiating factors, is worked out and explained in complete abstraction from an internal analysis of the principles of contract formation and the conception of consent that these embody. Thus, the relevant normative criteria or factors need neither start from nor be framed by what consideration itself might require, constrain or entail. (If consideration is mentioned at all at this second step, it is merely to note that its only plausible function could be to prevent duress or unfairness but that, for these purposes, it is a very blunt and unreliable instrument.) On the other hand, the vitiating factors and sources of economic duress or unfairness in these modification scenarios need not involve the kinds of rights violations characteristic of wrongful pressure cases. Rarely do these situations rise to the level of contracting under a threat of violence, duress of goods or other clear-cut violations of rights that are protected independently of contracting.

In other words, the core analysis proposed by these criticisms of the pre-existing duty rule, being neither fully internal nor external to the contractual relation, cannot fit readily within *either* of the two categories of contracting under pressure that, according to Smith, are the valid bases for relief. This apparent conceptual confusion is also reflected in the fact that while, so far as content goes, the vitiating factors (unconscionability, bad faith and so on) can normally be aspects of a contractual analysis that is consent-based, the way these factors are assessed is standardly taken directly from the very different analysis appropriate for external wrongful pressure cases.[15]

Although the approach just described is dominant, it is important to acknowledge that more recent literature and case law have included proposals for determining the validity of modifications that rely on criteria internal to contracting scenarios in the following way: modifications should not be enforced if made in bad faith or unfairly, and – very importantly – whether this is so is decided in light of what the parties originally agreed under their pre-existing contract and how, against this background, they dealt with circumstances, usually arising post-formation, that impacted the performance of their original contractual rights and duties.[16] I think that these efforts point in the right direction. In sections III and IV, I will try to outline a framework that, I hope, clarifies and develops such an internal, contract-centered orientation in a way that is both fully consistent with the principles of contract formation and also properly responsive to the concerns raised about the application of these principles to on-going contractual transactions, with their changing circumstances and party-initiated adjustments.

III. The Pre-existing Duty Rule and the Requirements of Consideration

In contract law, any question concerning potential relief from a promise made under pressure presupposes that a party might be prima facie *held* to that promise. Otherwise, there is nothing to avoid or relieve. For this conceptually prior step, there must be a

[15] As Smith insightfully noted. See Smith (n 1) 344–45 and elsewhere.

[16] See, eg, B Kain and J Nasseri, 'Economic Duress after *Bhasin v Hyrnew*: Does the Organizing Principle of Good Faith Offer a New Framework?' [2016] *Annual Review of Civil Litigation* 43.

positive juridical basis. That basis must at least be in the party's promise. But at common law, only promises supported by consideration are contractually enforceable or even contractually relevant. So, the ground on which parties can be contractually held to their promises must be specified in terms of consideration. How, then, does the requirement of consideration apply in the context of a promised modification of pre-existing contractual terms? In answering this question, it is crucial to apply the doctrine of consideration in its settled meaning and scope, always keeping in mind that it purports to be a *general* prerequisite for the contractual enforceability of any non-formal promise.

Rather than adopting the terms of standard criticisms by starting from some presupposed purpose(s) that the requirement of consideration is thought to serve, we should begin with what it does.[17] And what it does is to require the establishment of a certain kind of promissory relation between the parties that is qualitatively distinct from and irreducible to a so-called 'gratuitous' promise. The latter is, by definition, a promise that is not supported by consideration and that, as such, is contractually unenforceable as a matter of basic principle, even though it may give rise to a non-coercible moral (ethical) duty to comply and no matter how seriously and unconditionally the promisor intended performance or communicated to the promisee a commitment to perform.

To be contractually enforceable according to its terms, a non-formal promise must be made for a legally valid consideration that can be either a reciprocal promise (hence mutual promises) or a reciprocal act, which is *requested* by the promisor and *moved* by the promisee to the promisor in return for the latter's promise as part of one unified transaction. Moreover, what is promised as consideration must, in legal contemplation, be something of value, in the sense of being something – whether a thing, service, money, right, liberty and so forth – that, in virtue of its *specific concrete features*, can be wanted, used or otherwise enjoyed by a party to the exclusion of the other. And since the consideration that you promise me must be something that I can want or use *qua* requested by me in return for what I promise you, it must be *qualitatively different* in some way from whatever consideration I promise you in return – otherwise it would not make sense for me to want the item as part of a bilateral reciprocal transaction with you. Hence the characterisation of mutual promises as quid pro quo: *some*thing of value for something *else* of value. This is the only thing that counts: whether the two sides are in any way proportional or equivalent in terms of exchange value and any further comparisons between them are irrelevant so far as the consideration requirement goes. Whether a given voluntary interaction between parties can be construed as meeting these criteria is always decided from a legal point of view in accordance with the objective test of contract formation and interpretation. It must be possible for a court to conclude that the parties can reasonably be held to have dealt with each other and treated the items promised in this way.[18] This is an important point to which I return in section IV.

[17] I discuss consideration in more detail in P Benson, *Justice in Transactions: A Theory of Contract Law* (Cambridge, MA, Harvard University Press, 2019) ch 1.

[18] As put by Cardozo J in *McGovern v City of New York*, 138 NE 26 (1923), 31 (citations omitted): '"Nothing is consideration," it has been held, "that is not regarded as such by both parties" … Promisor and promisee must have dealt with it as the inducement to the promise'.

A promised consideration, I have said, must be construable as being *moved from one party to the other*. This entails, first, that it must be possible to view what is promised as *originating* solely on the side of the party who promises it, such that it is, initially, actually or potentially under her exclusive control, or at least not under the other party's. The item can be thought of as something that she might actually or potentially have dealt with for other purposes, independently of her interaction with and excluding the other. But, second, in promising the consideration, the party is taken to have moved it *from out of her control and into that of the second party*, who, in turn, accepts it via his own promise in return. This is exactly what is represented in the element of the parties' mutual and completely reciprocal promises. Thus, *each* party's promise necessarily and simultaneously performs *two* functions: both moving and taking consideration, respectively, to and from the other. There must be this unified two-way movement represented *as taking place* between the parties, and contract formation consists of nothing but this. The doctrine of consideration requires that a promissory interaction be such a relation if it is to be contractually enforceable or even contractually relevant.

Supposing that there has been contract formation, this two-fold movement of promised considerations has therefore *already and completely* taken place, prior to and independently of delivery or actual performance. This essential feature of mutual promises that satisfy consideration bears on the analysis of contract modifications in the following way.

Let us suppose a fully – not just prima facie – enforceable agreement consisting of mutual promises the terms of which are certain and clear, and that, at some point after formation but before the parties have completely performed, one of them promises to give the other something more (or to accept something less) than originally agreed in return for the very thing already promised by the other. This new promise, we also suppose, is not already included in the original express or implied terms of their pre-existing contract and so stands on its own. As such, it must itself be supported by consideration. But if, finally, we assume that the original terms continue to be contractually effective and binding, there seems to be an evident problem if the second party presents (whether in the form of a promise or an act) the very same performance as a consideration for the new promise: as between the parties and via their pre-existing promissory representations, the second party has *already* moved it to the other side and so it can no longer originate with him in the required sense, nor can it be his to provide anew to the other. This simply applies the settled meaning of the general features of consideration other.[19] And in so far as the pre-existing duty rule says *only* this and applies within the parameters supposed above, it would seem, prima facie, to be a correct entailment of the doctrine of consideration.[20]

Common objections to the pre-existing duty rule do not shake this conclusion. As I discussed in section II, these critiques generally rest on the assumption that the aim of the doctrine is to evidence a serious intent to enter legal (contractual) relations, and that this is satisfied if modifications are made as ancillary to an on-going bargaining relation. As part of such a relation, particularly a business relation that is at arm's length,

[19] For further development of this argument, see P Benson, 'The Performance Interest and the Promissory Basis of Contract Law' in P Saprai and M Chen-Wishart (eds), *Research Handbook on the Philosophy of Contract Law* (Cheltenham, Edward Elgar Publishing, forthcoming).

[20] Note the qualification 'in so far as [it] says *only* this'. I shall come back to this point in section IV.

the parties can be presumed in their post-formation interaction to intend legal relations, with their promises being legally enforceable. To describe their modifications as 'gratuitous', it is often said, is fatuous and unrealistic. This criticism rests on the further premise that there is a divergence between the way parties may view their relation and the legal point of view imposed by the doctrine of consideration. Value should be understood as in the parties' eyes, not the law's: a bird in the hand is worth more than one in the bush.

It is certainly true that from the standpoint of the parties as business transactors, individuals may view themselves and want to be understood by each other as bound by their modifications. They may view proposed adjustments and changes to the original terms as essential to their on-going business relation, both in the short and longer terms. And they may see these modifications as part of a give-and-take through which both parties expect to benefit because of presumed business norms of reciprocity and reasonableness. But, even assuming all these points, this does not track the contractual contrast between enforceable and gratuitous, which is distinct from how it might be understood in other domains. The legal contrast demands a *particular kind* of reciprocal relation that, as discussed above, is inherently and thoroughly two-sided, and in which no element – no promise, nothing purporting to be a benefit, detriment or something of value – operates except as part of this two-sidedness. The law deems this necessary if the parties are to be held (objectively) to promises that are *coercively* enforceable (via legal remedies) and not merely morally binding.[21]

Thus, it is perfectly intelligible that promises which parties may view as rational, serious and binding in their business relations are not two-sided in the way required by contract law and so, for this reason and in this way, deemed to be gratuitous. The idea of bargain in the doctrine of consideration is the *juridical* idea of quid pro quo stated above. It is conceptually different from the idea of bargain in the commercial, business sense.[22] And since, in legal contemplation, parties move at formation the full and complete value of the represented promised consideration from and to each other, not only is there no remaining value of the original promise still on a party's side to promise or provide again but also, contractually speaking, this value, complete and intact, has moved to the other, with whom it has vested in accordance with the contract's express and implied terms. From the standpoint of consideration and contract analysis, this second party, from formation on, already (juridically) has the bird in her hands. There can be no contractually relevant bird in the bush that counts for more.

IV. The Contractual Relevance of Parties' Post-formation Interactions

In section III, I argued that, if it is presented and understood within certain parameters, the pre-existing duty rule as originally stated seems to be correct. This is because it simply follows through and applies the general core requirements of consideration in

[21] Whether the law is (morally) justified in taking this view is clearly an important question requiring much more discussion than is possible in this short piece.

[22] For further discussion of this difference, see Benson (n 17) 413–25.

the context of promises that vary pre-existing, still fully binding contractual terms. It is crucial to set out explicitly the limits that define the rule as so justified. First, the new promise must be of something that is more than or different from what was already included in the express and implied original terms (being so included it would not need fresh consideration), whereas the other's promise or act must be of something that *is* so included and so apparently identical. But in addition, this latter promise or doing must be same with respect to an original promise that is construed as *still* subsisting and contractually binding on the parties. There must be, in other words, *nothing in their post-formation interaction* that changes this. Only if this second condition is also satisfied is the pre-existing duty rule correctly applied to invalidate the new promise as a matter of general contract law principles. By recognising this limit, contract law can also reasonably make room for contractually relevant and effectual post-formation party-initiated modifications, as I now explain.

To illustrate with a familiar example, suppose that before both sides completely perform, there is a bona fide disagreement or dispute between the parties as to the meaning, scope or effects of an express term or of some implied aspect of their contract, and on this basis they agree to settle and to continue on different terms, involving one party's promise of more for the same performance by the other. Assume also that, if the dispute had instead been litigated, a court would *not* have taken this view of their pre-existing contract but would have enforced the original terms as they stand. Despite this, it is settled law that the new terms can be contractually enforceable as a compromise or settlement.[23] Even though in some sense a modification of the original terms, a compromise is never explained as an 'exception' to the pre-existing duty rule. The only question is: Did the parties' interaction amount to the kind of transaction that counts as a compromise? Here, as I will now elaborate, is a post-formation interaction that involves something other than the mere repetition of an original promise, still subsisting, for the new.

The accepted analysis of binding compromises entails that it is the *parties themselves* who can fix the interpretation that becomes enforceable as a compromise, even though, as just noted, they might instead have litigated their dispute and – very importantly – a court might have taken a different view of the proper interpretation of their contract and enforced the original terms. In this way, what parties do and how they view what they are doing that can potentially be contractually relevant: this is just as true for post-formation interaction as it is for determining whether there has been the requisite interaction satisfying consideration in the first place. At the same time, the compromise example makes clear that, for the parties' interaction and understanding to have this significance and effect, these must satisfy certain definite legal prerequisites for a valid contractual transaction – here a compromise. In particular, a court must be able to infer that the parties reasonably (objectively) interacted in a way that evidences their intended closing of an honest dispute by way of settlement.

[23] For instructive discussion, see J Beatson, 'Duress, Restitution and Contract Modification' in J Beatson, *The Use and Abuse of Unjust Enrichment* (Oxford, Clarendon Press, 1991).

If, for example, a party knew that the claim or interpretation that formed the basis of his demand was completely false, dishonest or without any semblance of plausibility, the new terms cannot count as a valid compromise. That it must be bona fide or honest in this way is an internal feature or constituent condition of a compromise that is contractually enforceable in accordance with general principles of contract formation.

What this last point means is that, conceptually, there is no need to go further than this transactional analysis establishing the existence of a bona fide compromise and ask whether the new agreement should be avoided for unlawful or even illegitimate (as distinct from unlawful) pressure. The transactional analysis that ascertains whether the constituent elements and conditions of a valid compromise exist does all the work. If a bona fide compromise can be established, whatever pressures existed are part and parcel of their contractual situation. Also, because it does not matter that a threatened non-performance would, if litigated, have been deemed *post facto* a breach and wrongful, the example of compromises suggests that the analysis of contract modifications resulting from threatened non-performance, not involving contractually independent threats to persons or property, is not oriented in the right direction by the model of contracting under pressure *wrongfully* caused.

Historically, courts have upheld compromises even while insisting on the validity of the pre-existing duty rule. I now want to explain why, in doing so, they need not have not been guilty of any inconsistency.

To begin, there is – and can be – nothing in the pre-existing duty rule that precludes parties from making new agreements between themselves that do not come within the purview of and so possibly conflict with that rule. Otherwise, a rule of contract formation would itself prevent parties from forming new agreements that are consistent with general principles – an absurdity.

But what brings a transaction, for example a valid compromise, outside the purview of, and thus not necessarily at odds with, the pre-existing duty rule? It must be possible to construe what, on its face, is the same performance for a promise of more, *not as a variation within the framework of the first, pre-existing contract viewed as an on-going, still binding transaction but instead as arising from and anchored in a new, second transaction that is either distinct from or displaces the first.*[24] And this is something that must be *inferred* on the basis of the parties' post-formation interactions, which standardly involve such things as demands for renegotiations, implied or even express threatened non-performance unless changes are made, new promises or other representations as to adjustments, and so on.

Right away, this criterion clearly precludes as unnecessary and indeed misguided the idea of trying to find in the new interaction a 'practical' benefit that will meet the requirement of consideration within the framework of the pre-existing contract. Nor does it dispense with the requirement of consideration for the modification viewed as within that framework, shifting the focus to the question of economic duress or

[24] For an excellent analysis framed in terms of this distinction between a first and second transaction, see *King v Duluth, M & N Ry Co*, 63 NW 1105 (SC Minn 1895).

some other kind of unfairness. If the compromise analysis did any of these things, it would directly contradict the general requirements of consideration as well as the pre-existing duty rule.

To the contrary, by the proposed criterion, the actual performance (or re-promising it) that appears merely as a repetition for something new is assessed only as to whether it can be objectively construed as part of an interaction that meets the desiderata of a compromise and thus of *a second transaction with its own distinctive framework, irreducible to the first.* All the elements considered for this purpose, including whether the claims or dispute and settlement have been made honestly and in good faith, belong to and are applied as part of this second framework only. A bona fide valid compromise manifests the parties' joint intent, reasonably construed, to displace the original terms by new terms, which alone are enforceable and irrevocable. The parties have dealt with each other and the original terms in a way that juridically can be construed as such a contractually valid and effectual release and replacement – and of course, it is always within the contractual competence of parties to do this, no less than to enter the original contract in the first place. The pre-existing duty rule has no application to this second transaction. But if, on the particular facts, the elements for such a compromise *cannot* be shown, the result must be, all things equal, that the new promise stands on its own, neither as part of a second transaction nor as supported by fresh consideration: a merely gratuitous promise, according to the general requirements of consideration.

I have chosen to discuss the example of a compromise in some detail because it has been long accepted, concurrently with the traditional pre-existing duty rule.[25] My argument is that they are mutually compatible and that, in seeing this, we can not only understand the proper limits and basis of the pre-existing duty rule but also develop an approach to contract modifications that encompasses other instances where the rule does – or need – not preclude courts' according contractual significance to parties' post-formation interactions. I conclude with a very brief discussion of the more important of these other instances.

By far the most important instance, which has been widely recognised in US contract law, concerns the contractual significance of parties' adjusting their terms in response to circumstances and events that are different from what the parties subjectively knew or anticipated at formation and that seriously impact at least one of the party's costs of completing performance according to the original terms.[26] Supposing that the new terms are not supported by fresh consideration, these situations are divided into two different categories, depending on whether the pre-existing contract *clearly* did or did not allocate the risk of that event. If the contract did *not* clearly either expressly or (less often) implicitly allocate the risk, the parties' good faith and

[25] Smith mentions compromises and the policy in favour of settlement but does not consider their possible significance for a consent-based account of contracting under pressure. See Smith (n 1) 356.

[26] The most illuminating judicial analysis of this scenario remains *King v Duluth* (n 24). See also *Restatement (Second) of the Law of Contracts* (1981) § 89, to be read in conjunction with § 73. For helpful scholarly discussion, see R Halson, 'Opportunism, Economic Duress and Contractual Modifications' (1991) 107 *LQR* 649. Smith refers positively to this approach as consistent with his consent (versus wrongdoing) basis for relief, writing 'it can be expected that the English courts would do the same although there does yet appear to be a case in point': Smith (n 1) 371.

reasonable adjustment of terms to reflect the impact of this unanticipated event will be construed as establishing a second or new transaction that supersedes their original bargain: the party promising more for the same will then be held to have intended that the other's uncompleted performance on the original terms be excused, and together they will be held to have created a new bargain displacing the original contract. There must be this objective basis for the law's construction of their interaction to be fair and reasonable. Where, by contrast, the pre-existing contract *clearly* allocated the risk of this very kind of event or circumstance, the modification will not be treated as part of or as establishing a new transaction but simply as a purported variation of the one pre-existing contract; and being without fresh consideration, it will be found contractually unenforceable.

Paralleling the compromise analysis, this approach to unanticipated circumstances recognises the capacity of parties to decide to treat their performances as excused – hence releasing each other from them – even if a court would have concluded that their contract was not frustrated and should not be set aside had the parties litigated it instead. At the same time, the analysis requires that there be a fair and reasonable basis for parties *to be able to hold each other* to have unequivocally made this decision, even though not expressly but only impliedly and under the pressures arising from their uncompleted performances. Factors such as the promisee's dishonesty, bad faith manoeuvring and so on would ordinarily preclude this inference and are thus constituent elements of the test. But, as with compromises, if this second transaction can be established, any pressure arising from the parties' being in a situation of bilateral monopoly is otherwise irrelevant. There is no basis or need for a further separate inquiry into illegitimate pressure. Finally, at no point, it must be emphasised, does this analysis treat the actual or re-promised performance as a practical benefit that functions as a variation within the framework of the initial pre-existing contract. There is no conflict with the pre-existing duty rule or with the basic conception of consent that is required for contract formation.[27]

V. Conclusion

At a time when the near unanimous view among Anglo-Commonwealth courts and scholars was that there was just one model for and rationale underlying the avoidability of contracts entered under pressure – embracing everything from threats of physical duress and undue influence to economic duress[28] – Stephen Smith challenged this orthodoxy by suggesting that there are at least two, qualitatively different bases, and that one – but only one – of these relies on notions of consent and reasonableness

[27] Even if an objective basis for reasonably imputing an implied release and replacement has *not* been met, there are further possibilities of reasonable construction: the new promise, though gratuitous, may be enforceable to the extent of a promisee's reasonable reliance; or it may sometimes establish a distinct unilateral contract; or, finally, where the promisor can just as readily obtain the same performance from a third party or via an adequate remedy, it might be reasonable to imply rescission and replacement of the original terms.

[28] As stated influentially by Lord Diplock in *Universe Tankships Inc of Monrovia v International Transport Workers' Federation* [1983] 1 AC 366, 384 (HL).

internal to contract law. Now, almost three decades later, his fundamental insight is taking hold, and the further development of Anglo-Commonwealth contract law seems increasingly to reflect the second, contractually internal model. In grappling with this still-challenging issue in contract law and contract theory – as with so many other such questions – Smith sought approaches and answers fully anchored in his understanding of the dynamics and normative ideas internal to the practice of contracting. This was fitting and appropriate for the author of that magnificent exploration of the autonomy of contract law, *Contract Theory*.[29]

[29] SA Smith, *Contract Theory* (Oxford, Oxford University Press, 2004).

16

Applying Smith to the Practice of Contract Damages

ADAM KRAMER

At the start of the millennium, I was lucky enough that my legal journey took me to McGill University in Montreal, Canada, and to Steve. He supervised my Master's dissertation[1] and I got paid to assist some of his research towards *Contract Theory*[2] and *Atiyah's Introduction to the Law of Contract*.[3]

Even then, it was clear that we shared a taxonomic bent. It may be that this is an inherent part of analysis, but I tend to think it is also a matter of inclination, temperament or personality. His taxonomy of theory[4] stayed with me like the core insights of the best theorists do (eg, Hart's internal point of view, Dworkin's Hercules). In my small number of years as a full-time academic, following my time in Montreal, I fancied myself a mid-level theorist doing interpretive accounts like Steve did in his early contract law articles. But I have since moved into practice at the English Bar, and our journeys both converged and diverged. They converged, in that we both ended up with a focus on remedies, Steve with his ambitious and alarmingly readable (given its subject matter) *Rights, Wrongs, and Injustices: The Structure of Remedial Law* in 2019[5] and me with my *The Law of Contract Damages* textbook.[6]

But we clearly diverged, as those works show, in that I have moved away from theory. There is no doubt in my mind that my textbook is part of the problem identified by

[1] Which, no doubt in large part due to his steer, became my article on contract remoteness, published a few years later with Ewan McKendrick's encouragement and cited by the House of Lords in *Transfield Shipping Inc v Mercator Shipping Inc (The Achilleas)* [2009] 1 AC 61. The phrase 'agreement-centred' in the title of that article was Steve's. I remember that my prior title was terrible, although thankfully can no longer recall what it was.

[2] SA Smith, *Contract Theory* (Oxford, Oxford University Press, 2004).

[3] SA Smith, *Atiyah's Law of Contract*, 6th edn (Oxford, Oxford University Press, 2006). This taught me one of Steve's important life lessons – try to find work so interesting you would have done it for free. I remember being there when Steve was deciding whether to agree to Patrick Atiyah's suggestion that Steve take his text on. Very exciting for a Master's student!

[4] Smith (n 2) 4ff.

[5] SA Smith, *Rights, Wrongs and Injustices: The Structure of Remedial Law* (Oxford, Oxford University Press, 2019).

[6] A Kramer, *The Law of Contract Damages*, 3rd edn (Oxford, Hart Publishing, 2022).

Steve when, in discussing what he called 'the most important question about the content of a judicial order: what is its relationship to the claimant's substantive rights?', he said '[y]et the literature on remedies almost never asks this question';[7] and when he then said '[e]ven textbooks on remedies rarely discuss the form, creation, or legal effects of orders'.[8]

And this does seem odd now Steve raised it. Unlike Steve, I routinely draft judicial orders (as counsel) in my day job. I argue about them at post-judgment hearings dealing with consequential matters. I do so shortly after arguing about substantive rights at trial. That sometimes comes after previously advising clients on whether they or the other parties are in breach (especially in those sweaty meetings considering whether a party has a right to terminate a contract), and what the implications of that mean. And I talk in detail about what remedies are available for breach of contract in my textbook.

So, for my contribution to this book I wanted to catch up with Steve's work, especially in his 2019 book, and consider what it means for me, and for my legal practice. Does it make sense of what contract remedies, in particular, feel like in action? Does it matter?

I. When Does the Duty to Pay Damages Arise?

One of the first points Steve considered when analysing contract (and other) damages[9] is whether there is duty to pay damages following breach, but prior to the court's making an award. Is an order to pay damages (when the court does eventually make one) an order that the defendant do something it already had a substantive duty to do? Does a substantive contractual duty to perform include a duty to give as close to performance as possible even after breach, including to pay compensatory damages? (As Steve said, the argument that this is what is going on is strongest in delay cases: just because you missed the deadline, you still need to perform, and damages for loss caused by the delay would be the best way to comply as fully as possible now that it is impossible to perform on time.[10])

Of course, we have always been schooled that there is an obligation to pay damages. This is what Lord Diplock told us in *Photo Production Ltd v Securicor Transport Ltd*,[11] when explaining why some contractual obligations (jurisdiction clauses, exclusion clauses, etc) survive breach:

> Every failure to perform a primary obligation is a breach of contract. *The secondary obligation on the part of the contract breaker to which it gives rise by implication of the common law is to pay monetary compensation to the other party for the loss sustained by him in consequence of the breach* … This secondary obligation to pay compensation (damages) for non-performance of primary obligations I will call the 'general secondary obligation.' …
>
> …

[7] Smith (n 5) 6.
[8] ibid 48.
[9] ibid 179.
[10] ibid 182 and 185.
[11] *Photo Production Ltd v Securicor Transport Ltd* [1980] AC 827.

> *Where such an election* [to terminate for repudiatory breach] *is made (a) there is substituted by implication of law for the primary obligations of the party in default which remain unperformed a secondary obligation to pay monetary compensation to the other party for the loss sustained by him in consequence of their non-performance in the future and (b) the unperformed primary obligations of that other party are discharged.* This secondary obligation is additional to the general secondary obligation; I will call it 'the anticipatory secondary obligation.'[12]

Lord Diplock is a clear proponent of what Steve (after John Gardner) called the 'continuity thesis', which provides that breach gives rise to an obligation to pay damages in relation to that breach; termination gives rise to an additional obligation to pay damages that replaces the substantive obligations to perform that cease upon termination; the 'primary obligation is converted into a secondary [obligation]'.[13] This happens not two years later, when the court makes its award, but rather, according to Lord Diplock, at the date of breach. This was Lord Diplock's 'system of primary and secondary obligations'.[14]

Steve's simplest reason for concluding that Lord Diplock is wrong is derived from the fact that damages are unavailable for failure to pay damages.[15] For the practitioner, it is difficult to give much weight to this objection. Under ordinary principles, the law awards pre-judgment interest compensating for loss of use of money from the date when the claimant would have had it (whether lost earnings that would have been made employing the money, or borrowing costs), as part of the ordinary compensatory calculation putting the claimant in the position it would have been in but for the breach.[16] A claimant does not just get lost profits (for example), or a defraying of increased costs, but also lost profits on the lost profits or the money spent on the increased costs.[17] And there could be no room for any loss beyond that rate of interest (contrary to what Steve has said;[18] he is of course live to this point), because the compensation for loss of use of money is limited only by the same rules on compensation that would also apply to a claim for damages for failure to pay damages, that is, it is an at-large calculation of the loss resulting from loss of use of money. There are also statutory awards for simple interest (not compounded) on an abstract basis (ie not specific loss of use of the particular claimant) that are expressly an award of interest 'on damages'.[19] Clearly, this award is a strong signal that the law treats the defendant as obligated to pay the damages from the

[12] ibid 848ff (emphasis added).

[13] *Afovos Shipping Co SA v Pagnan* [1983] 1 WLR 195 (HL), 203 (Lord Diplock).

[14] *Lombard North Central plc v Butterworth* [1987] QB 527 (CA) 538 (Mustill LJ). Lord Diplock was probably referencing Austin's or else Pothier's primary and secondary rights and duties (B Dickson, 'The Contribution of Lord Diplock to the General Law of Contract' (1989) 9 *OJLS* 441; B Rudden, 'Correspondence' (1990) 10 *OJLS* 288; D Foxton, 'How useful is Lord Diplock's distinction between primary and secondary obligations in contract?' (2019) 135 *LQR* 249.

[15] Smith (n 5) 194ff. Although see SA Smith, 'Duties, Liabilities and Damages' (2011–12) 125 *Harvard Law Review* 1727, 1741, fn 40.

[16] See more recently *Sagicor Bank Jamaica Ltd v Seaton* [2022] UKPC 48, reaffirming the re-establishment of such loss of use claims in *Sempra Metals Ltd v Commissioner of Inland Revenue* [2008] 1 AC 562.

[17] And, as Sandy Steel and Robert Stevens point out, in S Steel and R Stevens, 'The secondary duty to pay damages' (2020) 136 *LQR* 283 288–89, this also applies to non-pecuniary loss, implying that the defendant is being held liable for not compensating for the non-pecuniary loss at the date at which it was caused (interest on a non-pecuniary amount being less clearly a loss caused by the original wrong, unless the interest is a proxy for non-pecuniary loss of use of the injured leg, etc).

[18] Smith (n 5) 194, fn 35.

[19] Senior Courts Act 1981, s 35A. And in Scotland the Interest on Damages (Scotland) Act 1958, s 1.

date of harm, and these feel like damages for failure to pay damages. And it is difficult to identify any further irrecoverable losses (other than perhaps the legal costs of suing the defendant[20]) that could be caused by breach of a duty to pay damages immediately and are not compensated in this way.

And, as Steve I think accepted,[21] the English law rule that one cannot recover damages for late payment of an insurance indemnity[22] does not tell us much. That is based on the characterisation/fiction of indemnity insurance as an obligation to hold harmless against the insured fire, etc, meaning that the insurer's payment under the insurance contract is characterised as a payment of damages for the breach in being responsible for the fire damage, rather than as performance of a primary obligation to pay a sum under the insurance contract. For that reason, the case law provides that the insurer is not liable to compensate for loss caused by delay in paying its insurance claim. But that does not tell us much, because consequential losses resulting from the fire/from not having the building burned down by fire (including for loss of use of the building or money) are in principle recoverable, although whether they are recoverable under the particular insurance policy depends upon the policy wording (likely of the business interruption section).

In any event, since 2017, statutory intervention does allow an award for late payment of indemnity insurance claims in England, and it does so by a deemed implied term that the insurer must pay any sums due within a reasonable time.[23] Accordingly, the law deems a contractual obligation to pay damages (the 'sums due', which must be paid in a reasonable time, being damages for failure to hold the insured harmless against (say) the fire), which rather undermines Steve's analysis on this point.

II. Are Damages Unknowable?

Steve also contended that the contract breaker could not be expected to know the amount of damages until the court judgment, and therefore '[i]f a substantive duty to pay damages existed, it would be an unknowable duty'[24] and thus could not guide behaviour.[25]

This objection does not resonate with my practical experience. The uncertainty as to whether there has been a breach and what damages will be ordered is of the same type as the uncertainty as to whether the contract was entered into, whether

[20] Which for various policy reasons are excluded from damages awards. The costs of litigating against the defendant in the present claim are the exclusive preserve of costs rules and cannot be awarded as damages: *Hutchinson v Harris* (1978) 10 BLR 19 (CA), 39–40; *Seavision Investment SA v Evennett (The Tiburon)* [1992] 2 Lloyd's Rep 26 (CA); *ENE Kos v Petroleo Brasilero SA* [2009] EWHC 1843 (Comm) [65] (Andrew Smith J); and L Merrett, 'Costs as Damages' (2009) 125 *LQR* 468.

[21] Smith (n 5) 195, fn 36.

[22] *Ventouris v Trevor Rex Mountain (The Italia Express (No 2))* [1992] 2 Lloyd's Rep 281, 292 (Hirst J); *Sprung v Royal Insurance (UK) Ltd* [1999] Lloyd's Rep IR 111 (CA); *Mandrake Holdings Ltd v Countrywide Assured Group plc* [2005] EWCA Civ 940.

[23] Insurance Act 2015, s 13A.

[24] Smith (n 5) 197.

[25] ibid 199.

it has been terminated or subsists, and what the particular contractual obligation requires on its correct interpretation.[26] These are uncertainties as to the facts (what has actually happened) and how legal principles are applied to them.[27] Damages for breach of contract at least (ie leaving aside other damages awards) are not discretionary.[28]

Moreover, the unknowability characterisation of contract damages (and other damages) is rather belied by Part 36 of the English Civil Procedure Rules. Under those Rules, if a defendant makes an offer to settle and ultimately the claimant is awarded a lower sum than was offered, the claimant receives the court judgment amount but, despite winning, has to pay the costs of the litigation from around the date of the offer. (Similar consequences obtain in reverse where the claimant makes an offer to accept a particular sum in settlement.) In effect, the costs of litigation are treated as legally caused not by the breach of the contract but by the failure to accept an offer that turns out to have been better then the result ultimately obtained. In other words, the damages may be the responsibility of the breaching party, but the legal costs after refusal of an offer that ultimately was not beaten are the responsibility of the innocent party.

This encourages both parties to predict what damages will be awarded, and to make offers relating to that sum far before judgment, forcing the other party to take sides on the offeror's bet as to the outcome. The stakes are the costs of the litigation thenceforth, including of the trial, which are often as much as the damages award itself. But the important point for present purposes is that this works in practice. This is not finger-in-the-air stuff. Sensible predictions of the damages quantum can almost always be made, although of course settlement offers often take account of many factors other than the quantum of the claim, including prospects of success and publicity. It rarely feels like the damages are unknowable and that any offer or response to an offer is just a guess at an unknowable. Quite the opposite.

This Part 36 offer dynamic is also relevant to the question of the pre-payment rule. Steve relies on the fact that a pre-payment of damages would not be a defence to a claim[29] as further evidence that the law does not recognise a duty to pay damages prior to a court order.[30] But although 'an offer to pay equal to or greater than the court's award' is not a 'good defence against such an award',[31] an offer of payment does in fact put a lot of legal rule-created pressure on the parties to stop the litigation early and for the defendant to then pay up.[32] Couple that with the fact that an agreed settlement upon acceptance of the Part 36 offer will be a defence to a claim, and you have what looks like a duty to pay damages that lives from the date of breach.

That said, and returning to the question of unknowability but this time supporting Steve, there is something to be made for his argument from the award of post-judgment

[26] See also Wilmot-Smith, ch 20 in this volume, section V.B.ii.

[27] See also Steel and Stevens (n 17) 284–85.

[28] See further section V, especially the subsection on 'Remoteness'.

[29] Smith (n 5) 196.

[30] See also Smith, 'Duties, Liabilities and Damages' (n 15) 1741ff.

[31] Smith (n 5) 200.

[32] See also J Gardner, 'Damages without duty' (2019) 69 *University of Toronto Law Journal* 412, 415.

interest. In the United Kingdom, interest on any sum found due in a court judgment is payable under the Judgments Act 1838, section 17 at a rate of (simple, not compound) interest prescribed by legislation from the date judgment is given.[33] This rate has since 1993 been 8 per cent.[34] (It was 15 per cent before that.) Normally that rate is much higher than any actual loss of use is likely to be. But this rate is reserved for the period after judgment and does not apply from the date of the breach.

Further, case law confirms a reluctance for the court to award such a potentially penal interest rate,[35] even after judgment, where the defendant could not be expected to pay the sum awarded because that sum was not quantified. Thus, in a case of a split/bifurcated trial, the date on which interest starts to run at the Judgments Act rate has been held not to be the date of the judgment on liability but that of the later judgment on quantum, when the sum payable was known and so it was justifiable to impose such a rate.[36] This is a reflection of the view that the Judgments Act rate is an often punitive rate, applicable where a defendant is at fault for not paying the damages or other sum awarded, and also of the view (consistent with Steve's) that until quantum is fixed the defendant cannot be treated as at fault in this way.[37]

More likely, however, the question of when the Judgments Act rate of interest applies is not determinative of whether or not there is a duty to pay damages from the date of breach, but rather is a question of degree. Defendants can still be under a moral duty to compensate, and damages can still be knowable and predictable, but nevertheless the law recognises that there is *some* uncertainty in the damages award (and perhaps whether there has been a breach at all) that means that things do become different when a quantified court order to pay is made. From that point onwards, the prior liability is subsumed into the court order and the failure to pay that order is a separate and serious matter, punishable by contempt and justifying a potential punitive interest rate under the Judgments Act 1838.

[33] Civil Procedure Rules, r 40.8.

[34] The Judgment Debts (Rate of Interest) Order 1993 (SI 1993/564).

[35] It has been described as 'not prescribed by way of penalty' but having a 'commercial character' that is penal when the commercial rate of interest was only 1.5%: *Excalibur Ventures LLC v Texas Keystone Inc* [2015] EWHC 566 (Comm) [6] (Clarke LJ).

[36] *Persimmon Homes (South Coast) Ltd v Hall Aggregates (South Coast) Ltd* [2012] EWHC 2429 (TCC) [39]–[42]; *Sycamore Bidco Ltd v Breslin* [2013] EWHC 174 (Ch) [39]–[43]. Similarly, courts have established a practice to only award Judgments Act interest on costs that are to be subject to detailed assessment from a date three months from the date of judgment, because the defendant could not until around then, when the assessment process is underway, be expected to make a realistic assessment of the amount of its liability: 'I do not think it just to make an order under which interest begins to run at the rate appropriate for unpaid judgment debts before the paying party could reasonably be expected to pay the debt', *Involnert Management Inc v Aprilgrange Ltd* [2015] EWHC 2834 (Comm) [23]–[24] (Leggat J). This is just the sort of geeky procedural point that Steve would have been excited by.

[37] There may be an argument that the Judgments Act rate be payable from the date of a judgment on liability, but only in relation to the part of the quantum that is predictable and highly likely. In effect this is what happens in relation to costs (rather than the damages themselves) where subject to detailed assessment: a payment on account is ordered of the most likely amount that will later be awarded on detailed assessment, and Judgments Act interest runs on that payment on account until paid, and it is only the rest of the costs for which the Judgments Act rate is deferred for three months to allow for the detailed assessment process to start and the sum to become more knowable.

III. How Does it Feel?

Many contract-breakers that I encounter – and they are typically commercial parties – understand that they will or might breach by their proposed action, or have or may have breached by their past actions, the terms of the contract. Part of my role may be to help them understand how likely that is and to argue that they have not breached. But they also understand that if they have broken the contract, they will have to pay damages to compensate for the other side's loss. I may need to advise them on the likely amount of those damages.

What I am saying is that from the point of view of the contract party, there is little difference between:

(a) being under a duty to the contract counterparty to pay damages immediately after breach, that counterparty therefore having what Steve called an 'ordinary' 'substantive right',[38] with such duty/right ultimately to be adjudicated upon by a court but with interest running in the meantime; and
(b) not being under a duty, but knowing that a court likely will impose a liability to the contract counterparty to pay those damages at a later date, following the law of damages, which are rules directed at the court that create 'remedial rights' in the innocent party, then giving the counterparty a 'court-ordered' 'substantive right'.[39]

Steve rightly observed that

> from a practical perspective this issue may not matter very much to the parties to an actual or potential dispute. With rare exceptions it will not matter to someone who has wrongfully injured another … whether the damages rules are directed at courts or directed at him.[40]

On either alternative, no one can *make* the breaching party pay damages until the court does in a year or two, its being clear that even if there were a right to damages immediately, the law does not permit self-help enforcement by going and seizing the breaching party's things. But also on either alternative, when that trial comes, the court probably will make the breaching party pay then, including awarding interest dating back to now. And on either alternative, the breaching party can compromise any such current or future obligation to pay damages by making offers and settling the claim now.

Or, from the point of view of the innocent party: what is the difference between a right to damages enforceable by going to court, and a right to a court order giving an enforcement right in relation to a then newly created obligation owed by the defendant to the state to pay damages?[41]

[38] S Smith, 'The Law of Damages: Rules for Citizens or Rules for Courts?' in D Saidov and R Cunnington (eds), *Contract Damages: Domestic and International Perspectives* (Oxford, Hart Publishing, 2008) 33.

[39] ibid.

[40] ibid 47–48.

[41] For the latter formulation, see J Penner and K Quek, 'The Law's Remedial Norms' (2016) 28 *Singapore Academy of Law Journal* 768, 783–84.

This is not the place to dive into Austin, Hart, Holmes and others (and I am no longer equipped to do so). I will merely observe that real people are motivated by the anticipation of sanctions: here, the cost of compensatory damages is for commercial defendants a business cost that has to be allowed for and, in some cases, managed so that it arises at a suitable time. A contract claim is for most commercial people not much more than an asset or liability to manage. The prospects of paying damages certainly guide behaviour, but not primarily understood as an obligation, more as a prediction of a cost (or, in Hohfeldian terms, as a recognition of a liability[42]).

But I also detect an acceptance of a moral duty to pay damages. Most commercial parties if in breach not only accept the likelihood of having to pay damages, they also accept that it is appropriate that they do so. Penner and Quek's view that there is a 'moral duty of repair', although not a legal duty to pay damages, may well be right.[43] It is hard to unravel the motivations of hard-headed commercial people, and they would likely ask why it should matter anyway. An asset/cost is an asset/cost; and good business people anticipate and pay their bills.

IV. Conflicts of Laws

Steve made the point that one rare legal area where it matters whether damages rules are rules of private obligation or rules for courts is conflicts of laws.[44] If damages rules are rules for courts, they are typically treated not as part of the foreign applicable law (*lex causae*) but instead as governed by the law local to the forum (*lex fori*). So if a foreign law applies to a dispute in England, to what extent do English damages rules apply and to what extent foreign damages rules? For contract law, at common law questions of remoteness, legal causation and heads of damage are questions of the *lex causae* and questions of measurement or quantification are questions of the *lex fori*.[45]

Although Steve thought this common law position (with questions of quantification being rules for the courts, not part of a substantive obligation that would fall to the *lex causae*) might indicate that there was a duty to pay that has arisen upon breach,[46] under the Rome I Regulation, all legal rules of assessment of damages are a matter for the *lex causae*.[47] But the conflicts position may not ultimately tell us much about that. While classifying these rules as procedural could indicate no duty to pay until court order, in classifying them as substantive the courts are really only asking whether there are principles of law that designate the scope of the damages claim for breach

[42] Although see Wilmot-Smith, ch 20 in this volume, as to Smith's particular conception of a liability.

[43] Penner and Quek (n 41) 794.

[44] Smith (n 38) 50ff.

[45] *J d'Almeida Araujo LDA v Sir Frederick Becker & Co Ltd* [1953] 2 QB 329; *Cox v Ergo Versicherung AG* [2014] UKSC 22, [2014] AC 1379; L Collins et al, *Dicey and Morris: The Conflict of Laws*, 14th edn (London, Sweet & Maxwell, 2006) [4-044]. See *Cox v Ergo Versicherung AG* [2014] UKSC 22, [2014] AC 1379 (tort claim) as to mitigation, legal causation and collateral benefits.

[46] Smith (n 38) 51.

[47] Regulation (EC) No 593/2008 of the European Parliament and of the Council of 17 June 2008 on the law applicable to contractual obligations (Rome I) [2008] OJ L177/6, Art 12(1)(c); Collins et al (n 45) [4-045].

of contract. That does not, I think, tell us whether or not those principles are directed at courts or citizens.

V. Steve's Schema of Contract Damages and the Content of Damages Rules

Steve's main focus was on restitution/unjust enrichment and tort law, but his schema for contract damages appeared to be the following:

(a) *Compensation for financial loss.* Following his conclusion that there is no moral duty to pay damages that a compensatory contract damages award could be enforcing (so no '*rights-threat*' to which the law can be responding[48]), Steve concluded that compensatory contract damages, at least where the harm was financial (consequential loss[49]), are not wrong-responding, because they are measured by loss and not at large or focused on the degree of wrongdoing like punishment. On the contrary, they are corrections to the unjust losses the claimant has suffered.[50] The breach of contract is a condition of the award (that renders it just to require compensation) but not the reason for issuing it.[51] Rules of remoteness, causation and mitigation are part of determining a just award, that is, of measuring what is just.[52]

(b) *Market-price damages.* Damages measured by the market price of goods (such as in sale of goods cases of non-delivery or defective goods), or the market price of services, are wrong-based because they are not measured by loss.[53]

(c) *Substitutionary awards.* Where damages permit the purchase of a substitute performance (ie cost-of-cure damages), they may be based on a rights-threat, that is enforcement of the primary obligation for which the substitution is determined by the court at the moment of judgment, although only if the contract has not been terminated and not if the cost of cure is awarded as compensation for a cost the claimant has incurred or will incur.[54]

(d) *Compensation for non-pecuniary loss.* Damages for loss of amenity and other non-pecuniary loss are not compensation for 'loss' and the quantification is picked out of the air, so they are wrong-based.[55]

(e) *Negotiating damages and gain-based damages and nominal damages.* Rare awards of negotiating damages and gain-based damages, and more common awards of nominal damages, are wrong-based because they are not measured by loss.[56]

[48] Smith (n 5) 251.
[49] ibid 249.
[50] ibid.
[51] ibid 250 and 266–67.
[52] ibid 254–55.
[53] ibid 213–14.
[54] ibid 174–75.
[55] ibid 218–19.
[56] ibid 2089, 212–13 and 214–15.

As set out above in sections II to V, I tend not to agree that there is no duty to pay damages, meaning that at least all compensatory awards could be a response to a rights-threat in Steve's terminology, that is, enforcement of a secondary duty to pay damages that arises on breach of the primary contractual duty (per Lord Diplock). But I do have some further observations on Steve's schema and on his views of contract damages rules.

A. Remoteness

In *Contract Theory*, Steve saw remoteness as largely irrelevant to the nature of contract remedies, and instead saw it as a generalised rule applicable to all obligations for probably the same reasons.[57] In *Rights, Wrongs, and Injustices*, Steve not dissimilarly saw remoteness as an open-textured question of 'true discretion' for which there was 'no formula',[58] which shows for him that contract damages are unknowable. He also saw remoteness as inconsistent with contract damages as a response to a wrong, rather than being a response to an unjust loss.[59] He further recognised the differences between the contract test and the tort test, and relied on them to discredit the continuity thesis that contract damages are just an attempt to do the next best thing to performing the primary contractual obligation, because, he said,[60] that cannot explain why there is any difference between tort and contract cases.

The answer to all of these points – at least my answer – is that contractual remoteness is about construction of the contract.[61] It depends upon the implicit allocation of risk, the answer to the question of what losses the parties would have expected the defendant to be responsible for.[62] Accordingly, this is the part of contract damages that is close to enforcing a contractual obligation (or, at least, a contractual agreement as to the response when the obligation is breached), rather than (merely) responding to a breach of one. Remoteness is the shaping of contract damages by the parties' agreement. Accordingly, contract remoteness is applicable for the same reasons contracts are enforced (whatever reasons they are). It gets in before questions of the remedy are engaged, just as an express exclusion or limitation or liquidated damages clause would. It is no surprise that the parties' agreement can successfully modify what the secondary obligation to pay damages would otherwise require (as Lord Diplock expressly accepted[63]), even if that secondary obligation is imposed by law and is not itself even an implied term of the contract.[64] And it is not discretionary or causative of uncertainty as to the ultimate award.[65] So contractual remoteness has very little to

[57] Smith (n 2) 426–27.

[58] Smith (n 5) 198. And Smith, 'Duties, Liabilities and Damages' (n 15) 1743, where Smith says that contract damages are always to an extent 'discretionary' because of the remoteness rule.

[59] Smith (n 5) 227 and 254–55.

[60] ibid 188, fn 14.

[61] *The Achilleas* (n 1).

[62] A Kramer, 'An Agreement-Centred Approach to Remoteness and Contract Damage' in N Cohen and E McKendrick (eds), *Comparative Remedies for Breach of Contract* (Oxford, Hart Publishing, 2005) 249.

[63] eg *Hardwick Game Farm v SAPPA* [1966] 1 WLR 287, 341.

[64] Lord Diplock said they arose by implication of law, although that does not take us much further.

[65] Nor is it about fair apportionment, contra Gergen, ch 14 in this volume, text to n 40.

tell us about contract remedies, and cannot be used to show that contract damages are not measuring loss or responding to a wrong, since in either case the parties' agreement would trump or shape that measurement or response simply because the parties agreed it.

B. Non-pecuniary Loss

Steve's first point on non-pecuniary damages[66] was that, because money never can measure non-pecuniary loss, such damages do not measure loss and so cannot be a response to unjust loss.

This point is unpersuasive: difficulties of putting a monetary value on non-pecuniary harm do not mean that the award is not compensatory for that (unjust) harm. Steve was right in his earlier writings to refer to 'compensation for non-pecuniary loss'.[67] Judges, when awarding damages for non-pecuniary loss in contract (often loss of amenity or discomfort), do attempt to find a monetary sum that is in proportion to the non-pecuniary loss. One can debate how best to do that: Do you take a negotiating damages approach – what sum would the claimant accept in return for suffering the loss? How subjective should it be? Does that depend upon what idiosyncrasies of the claimant were within the parties' shared contemplation? But that does not mean that the courts do not rightly understand themselves to be attempting to translate the non-pecuniary loss into money. This is no more than a genuine attempt to follow the basic dictum of Baron Parke in *Robinson v Harman*,[68] who foresaw this problem: '[H]e is, *so far as money can do it* to be placed in the same situation, with respect to damages, as if the contract had been performed.'[69] Non-pecuniary awards in contract are not special in this regard, they are just compensation.

Steve's second point concerns the fact that (as he accepts) non-pecuniary losses attempt to measure the degree of harm. He argues that this is still consistent with an aim of measuring the wrongfulness of the wrong, as the seriousness of the wrong may be not merely a function of moral culpability – the more obvious sense in which a wrong is more or less serious – but also about the degree of harm caused.[70] This is probably uncontroversial on its own terms, but undermines Steve's general point that damages for *pecuniary* harm cannot be wrong-based because the 'massively detailed set of rules for determining' the contract damages award would be 'ultimately arbitrary' as they do not reflect culpability.[71] As Steve rightly observes in relation to non-pecuniary loss, a calculation based around the extent of the harm can still be wrong-based and geared to the seriousness of the wrong, and that must be as true for damages for pecuniary loss as for those for non-pecuniary loss. And unless one takes the view that the only appropriate response to a wrong is punishment for culpability, not compensation for the loss

[66] Smith (n 5) 218–19.
[67] Smith (n 2) 430.
[68] *Robinson v Harman* (1848) 1 Ex 850.
[69] ibid 855 (emphasis added).
[70] Smith (n 5) 219.
[71] ibid 227 and 249.

caused (ie reflection of the degree of harm), which is a slightly more extreme version of the thesis Steve proposed, there is nothing in compensation that makes it necessarily a response to unjust loss rather than to a wrong. The unjust loss element here then seems to be an unnecessary extra element that is not necessary to justify the core characteristic element of the awards that they measure loss. Steve might say, with some justification, that although measuring harm is to respond to the seriousness of wrongdoing in one sense, if compensatory damages were driven by the wrong, they would also respond to the degree of culpability, which is a core feature of wrongfulness. Perhaps. However, culpability is singularly inappropriate for contract law, which is a form of strict liability. The seriousness of the wrong of breaching contract is about no more than the degree of harm, being the degree by which the breaching party has forced the innocent party to deviate from the position promised.

C. Non-compensatory Damages

Steve also overstated the heterogeneity of contract damages remedies. Contract damages are about compensating for loss. In contract law, restitutionary and negotiating damages are applicable in vanishingly small ranges of situations, and themselves may be best justified as compensatory.[72] And (dealing with other categories he identifies) contract damages are in general not substitutionary. In particular, the market price award in contract cases (non-delivery or defective goods, for example) is not a substitutionary award but rather based on principles of legal causation, including mitigation.[73] The market measure is only applicable where the claimant's independent choice not to resort to the market breaks the chain of causation. It therefore measures the legally caused loss, and does not provide an award that is greater than that loss. That rule of legal causation is part of everyone's concept of what compensation means, so its justification sits outside this debate, but it follows that market measure damages are measuring loss.

VI. Conclusion

Where does that leave this practitioner's view of the court order for damages? Steve's points about the measure of damages do not convince that contract damages are not about measuring loss or that they are discretionary. Indeed, contract damages awards are rule-based and have a high degree of predictability, and they do not feel like an unpredictable discretionary remedial response divorced from loss.

[72] See, eg, Kramer (n 6) chs 22–23.

[73] Contra Smith (n 5) 213–14. See, eg, *Bunge SA v Nidera* BV [2015] 3 All ER 1082 (SC) [17] (Lord Sumption); A Dyson and A Kramer, 'There is no "Breach Date Rule": Mitigation, the Difference in Value and Date of Assessment' (2014) 130 *LQR* 259. As for services, the simple point is that there are also no substitutive awards in services cases: see Kramer (n 6) [2-35] et seq. It may be that, in contrast, damages in lieu of specific performance are substitutionary. This is only where there is a damages award which is not measured by reference to compensation in the ordinary way, but rather the calculation of which is affected by its function in replacing specific performance. As Smith notes at Smith (n 5) 174, these awards are rare.

It does not follow that there is an obligation to pay damages upon breach, only, perhaps, that there can be. To some extent the further question of whether there is such a duty is above my theory pay grade, as it is of next to no relevance for the practitioner or litigant. However, the predictability and rules-based nature of the contract damages award, and the award of damages for loss of use of money (interest) and Part 36 costs rules that incentivise settlement, support the sense that there is a damages obligation of sorts that arises upon breach. Certainly (like dark matter perhaps), one can detect such an obligation by inference from the behaviour of litigants and the rules around them. So, as a practitioner, I must, always respectfully and tentatively, disagree with Steve on this one. But that is not to diminish the value of his shining a light on this area, and doing so as elegantly as he did.

17

In Defence of 'In Defence of the Third-Party Rule'

JASON W NEYERS

I. Supposed Difficulty

Stephen Smith's 'Contracts for the Benefit of Third Parties: In Defence of The Third-Party Rule'[1] is a legal classic and one of his most important works in the law of contracts.[2] In it he makes two powerful claims. The first is that the doctrine of privity necessarily flows from the legal idea that contractual obligations are voluntary obligations that are 'undertaken to particular persons, extending to and only to those persons'.[3] To bring home this point, Smith offers a simple example (with his usual familial twist):

> A agrees with B that in return for B paying A £100, A will do C's gardening for one year (C is B's sister). A receives the money, does C's gardening for one month, and then goes on holiday for the rest of the year.

As Smith explains, the 'simple but profound' reason why 'C should not be able to enforce A's promise is the fact that A did not make a promise to C. The promisor A has a duty to perform his promise, but the duty is owed to B, the promisee, not to C.'[4]

Smith's second claim is that most of the perceived problems with the doctrine of privity are in reality general problems in the law of obligations that manifest themselves in, but are not limited to, situations involving third parties. As one example of this,[5] Smith asks us to imagine that

> in our gardening contract, A has breached his contractual obligation to B to do C's gardening and thus B can bring an action for breach of contract against A. The difficulty for B is that

[1] SA Smith, 'Contracts for the Benefit of Third Parties: In Defence of The Third-Party Rule' (1997) 17 *OJLS* 643 reprinted in P Kincaid (ed), *Privity: Private Justice or Public Regulation* (Farnham, Ashgate, 2001) 147.

[2] In fact, Steve himself agreed with this assessment. When I asked him, as I was preparing to write this essay, why there was not a chapter on privity in SA Smith, *Contract Theory* (Oxford, Oxford University Press, 2012), but rather only a short paragraph (ibid 60), he answered by saying that he had been content to point the reader to 'In Defence of The Third-Party Rule' since he had said all he wanted to say in that article. As would be expected, many of the arguments from that article also find their way into SA Smith, *Atiyah's Introduction to the Law of Contract*, 6th edn (Oxford, Oxford University Press, 2005) esp 338–41.

[3] Smith (n 1) 645.

[4] ibid.

[5] For arguments related to reliance, see ibid 654–57; and restitution, see ibid 657–58.

> under the traditional approach to damages he is unlikely to obtain more than a nominal sum. The explanation given for this result is that since it was C's garden that was untended, B has not suffered a loss. If B sues for specific performance a similar response will be given: nominal damages are an adequate remedy because B has not suffered any loss. It should be evident that the traditional rule is unsatisfactory.[6]

But, as Smith points out,

> insofar as the promisee's interest in performance is insufficiently protected in privity cases the reason is not the third-party rule, but artificial limitations on recovery of difficult to quantify losses (or on the availability of specific performance). The problems that these limitations cause can and do arise in standard two-party contract cases. If we are willing to live with the limitations in two-party cases, then we should be willing to live with them in privity cases, and vice versa.[7]

In addition, he argues that these problems are magnified in situations where the promisee has died since, even were the law to develop so as to recognise that B routinely had a claim to substantial damages or specific performance,[8] executors are entitled to enforce a deceased's contracts

> only where enforcement would benefit the deceased's estate financially and only in order to benefit the estate. Thus an executor will normally not demand specific performance of a contract to benefit a third party … nor hand over any damages awarded in compensation to the third party.[9]

Thus, as he explains, the problem in cases like *White v Jones*[10] lies with estate law and the general lack of recognition for after-death interests in the law of obligations rather than with the doctrine of privity, since if the law developed to allow the full panoply of remedies to B, then B (if alive) could sue, as promisee, to make sure that his intentions vis-à-vis C were satisfied.[11]

Given the clarity and profundity of his arguments, it is not surprising that 'In Defence of The Third-Party Rule' is routinely cited in textbooks and articles[12] as an example of a work supporting the traditional concept of privity. Unfortunately, and perhaps due to the force and logical precision with which Smith makes his arguments, most of the textbook discussions (which for the most part are at least mildly critical of, if not downright hostile to, privity) do not extensively engage with or attempt to rebut his arguments. Instead, they generally note his theoretical defence of the rule before: (i) explaining how the rule causes inconvenience in practice (often using the arguments marshalled in the 1996 UK Law Commission Report);[13] and (ii) proceeding (depending on jurisdiction) to examine the contemporary statutory

[6] ibid 650, citation of *The Albazero* [1977] AC 774, 846 omitted.

[7] Smith (n 1) 651.

[8] See *Beswick v Beswick* [1968] AC 58.

[9] Smith (n 1) 651.

[10] *White v Jones* [1995] 2 AC 207.

[11] See R Stevens, 'The Contracts (Rights of Third Parties) Act 1999' (2004) 120 *LQR* 292.

[12] My searches have revealed that it has been cited in more than 60 articles and essays and almost 20 textbooks, treatises and monographs.

[13] Law Commission, *Privity of Contract: Contracts for the Benefit of Third Parties* (Law Com 242, 1996).

exceptions[14] or the Canadian principled exception[15] that have attenuated privity's perceived baleful effects.

A notable exception to this pattern, however, is provided by the work of Angela Swan, in the fourth edition of her textbook, *Canadian Contract Law* (now co-written with Jakub Adamski and Annie Na).[16] As might be expected, given the book's overall focus on reasonable expectations and commercial reality, Swan, Adamski and Na are critical of Smith's approach. They argue that the examples given by Smith, which focus on the personal nature on the relationships between the parties and the rights and duties that flow from those relationships, are overly 'simple' and 'not realistic'. As they comment:

> The modern example of the problems of the third party beneficiary rule do not involve facts like those in *Beswick v Beswick* or *White v Jones* or even of the kind of relation at issue in *Tweddle v Atkinson* … The problems that create difficulties now raise instead (and to take only a few prominent examples): (1) the need to preserve the allocation of risk (and the consequent identification of the insurer who is to bear the loss) in an enterprise, the completion of which requires the co-operation of many separate parties; [and] (2) the vulnerability of employees to personal actions for negligence in circumstances where their employer cannot be sued (because of a contract between it and the plaintiff) … In these situations, the idea that, for example, the contract between a shipper and a carrier is personal so that the exemption from liability of the carrier does not or should not extend to the stevedores who unload cargo – the facts of Midland Silicones – is belied by the facts that (1) the shipper as consignor can transfer title in the cargo to the consignee (who will often be the (nominal) party suing the third party) and (2) the only question in issue is which of two insurers will bear the risk of loss caused by the stevedores' negligence. … The other situations that have been mentioned do not support an argument that the personal element is important.[17]

Thus, instead of focusing on simple examples (or simple personal relationships) and from them designing abstract rules beholden to internal conceptions of contract law, they suggest that commentators and courts should design privity rules justified in terms of achieving desired results in light of the more complex factual circumstances with which contemporary courts typically are faced. In this regard, the authors contend that the key idea to understanding developments relaxing privity (at least in the Canadian

[14] See, eg, Contracts (Rights of Third Parties) Act (UK) 1999; Law Reform Act RSNB 2011, c 184, s 4; Contracts (Rights of Third Parties) Act of 2001 (2002 rev edn) (Singapore); Property Law Act 1969 (WA) 1969, s 11; Property Law Act 1974 (Qld) 1974, s 55; Law of Property Act 2000 (NT) 2000, s 56.

[15] The doctrine finds its origins in *London Drugs Ltd v Kuehne & Nagel International Ltd* [1992] 3 SCR 299, where the majority decided that employees could rely on exclusion clauses in contract between their employers and third-party customers when (i) the limitation of liability clause explicitly or impliedly extended its benefit to the employees who sought to rely on it; and (ii) the employees were acting in the course of their employment and thereby performing the very services provided for in the contract between their employer and the customer when the loss occurred. In *Fraser River Pile & Dredge Ltd v Can-Dive Services Ltd* [1999] 3 SCR 108, the court unanimously recognised that what it termed the 'principled exception' to privity of contract was not limited to the employer–employee relationship.

[16] A Swan, J Adamski and AY Na, *Canadian Contract Law*, 4th edn (LexisNexis Canada, 2018) §3.21–§3.31. See also D Nolan, 'Reforming the Privity of Contract Doctrine' in M Andenas and N Jareborg (eds), *Anglo-Swedish Studies in Law* (Uppsala, Iustus Förlag, 1999) 288, criticising Steve's article for assuming that a promise-based, as opposed to a facilitation-based, theory of contract law is the appropriate starting point for theorising about contract law.

[17] Swan, Adamski and Na (n 16) §3.21.

law) is not the idea of personal interaction but rather the concept of 'enterprise'.[18] Their view is succinctly summarised in *Halsbury's Law of Canada* (itself written by Adamski and Swan):

> The [policy] concern underpinning almost all instances of the recognition of the principled exception is that commercial activities that involve multiple parties should not be able to avoid the consequences of the risk they freely bore in some contracts structuring the activity by pursuing other participants who were not parties to the contract. In this sense, the principled exception functions to conflate the parties to a contract structuring part or whole of some activity (privity of contract) with parties engaged in that activity (ie, a kind of 'privity of activity' or enterprise).[19]

Interestingly, in coming to this conclusion, Swan and Adamski cite an 'idea' that has a 'long pedigree', namely, the concept of 'vicarious immunity'.[20]

The history of vicarious immunity has been detailed elsewhere, so only the briefest of summaries is necessary.[21] In a nutshell, the concept was developed by Scrutton LJ in his judgment in the Court of Appeal in *Paterson, Zochonis & Co Ltd v Elder, Dempster & Co Ltd*,[22] and found (varying degrees of) favour in a number of subsequent trial and appellate court judgments,[23] most notably in the judgments of Lord Cave,[24] Viscount Finlay[25] and Lord Carson[26] when *Elder, Dempster* was appealed to the House of Lords.[27] In the later case of *Mersey Shipping and Transport Co Ltd v Rea Ltd*, Scrutton LJ explained the principle as follows:

> I think that the reasoning of the House of Lords in the Elder Dempster case shows that, where there is a contract which contains an exemption clause, the servants or agents who act under

[18] ibid §3.107–§3.124.

[19] *Halsbury's Laws of Canada (online), Contracts*, 'Third Party Beneficiary Rule' (IV) (2021 Reissue) HCO-80.

[20] ibid HCO-80, fn 2.

[21] See B Coote, *Exception Clauses* (London, Sweet & Maxwell, 1964) ch 9; M O'Meara, 'From Elder Dempster to London Drugs: The Saga of Vicarious Immunity' (2005) 21 *Journal of Contract Law* 131; FMB Reynolds and FD Rose, *Carver on Bills of Lading*, 5th edn (London, Sweet & Maxwell, 2022) §7-015 et seq.

[22] *Paterson, Zochonis & Co Ltd v Elder, Dempster & Co Ltd* [1922] 1 KB 420 (CA), 441: 'The real answer to the claim is in my view that the shipowner is not in possession as a bailee, but as the agent of a person, the charterer, with whom the owner of the goods has made a contract defining his liability, and that the owner as servant or agent of the charterer can claim the same protection as the charterer. Were it otherwise there would be an easy way round the bill of lading … the owner of the goods would simply sue the owner of the ship and ignore the bill of lading exceptions'.

[23] See, eg, *The Kite*, [1933] P 154; *Gilbert Stokes & Kerr, Prop, Ltd v Dalgety & Co, Ltd* (1948) 81 LlL Rep 337 (NSWSC); *Waters Trading Co Ltd v Dalgety & Co Ltd* [1951] 2 LlL Rep 385 (NSWSC Full Court); *AM Collins & Co v Panama R Co*, 197 F.2d 893 (5th Cir 1952); *Pyrene Co Ltd v Scindia Navigation Co Ltd* [1954] 2 QB 402.

[24] *Elder, Dempster & Co Ltd v Paterson, Zochonis & Co Ltd* [1924] AC 522, 534: 'It was stipulated in the bills of lading that "the shipowners" should not be liable for any damage arising from other goods by stowage or contact with the goods shipped under the bills of lading … It may be that the owners were not directly parties to the contract; but they took possession of the goods (as Scrutton LJ says) on behalf of and as the agents of the charterers, and so can claim the same protection as their principals.'

[25] ibid 548: '[W]hen the act is done in the course of rendering the very services provided for in the bill of lading, the limitation on liability therein contained must attach, whatever the form of the action and whether owner or charterer be sued. It would be absurd that the owner of the goods could get rid of the protective clauses of the bill of lading, in respect of all stowage, by suing the owner of the ship in tort. The Court of Appeal were, in my opinion, right in rejecting this contention, which would lead to results so extraordinary as those referred to by Scrutton LJ, in his judgment.'

[26] He agreed with the judgments of both Lord Cave and Lord Sumner, see ibid 565.

[27] *Elder, Dempster* (n 24).

> that contract have the benefit of the exemption clause. They cannot be sued in tort as independent people, but they can claim the protection of the contract made with their employers on whose behalf they are acting.[28]

Unfortunately, after its early successes, judicial doubts in relation to the doctrine started setting in.[29] These doubts ultimately culminated in the purported excising of the doctrine from the common law, as being inconsistent with privity, by Fullagar J (with whom Dixon CJ concurred) in *Wilson v Darling Island Stevedoring & Lighterage Co Ltd*.[30] This result was enthusiastically and subsequently accepted by the House of Lords, over Lord Denning's sole dissent, in the case of *Midland Silicones Ltd v Scruttons Ltd*.[31] Interestingly, the United States Supreme Court, in *Krawill Machinery Corporation v Robert C Herd & Co Inc*,[32] also relying on the analysis of *Elder, Demspter* provided by Fullagar J in *Wilson*, rejected the doctrine (despite the more relaxed views on privity taken in the United States) on the basis that American law had consistently held that agents were liable for their own torts, 'unless exonerated therefrom, in whole or in part, by a statute or valid contract binding on the person damaged'.[33]

The tenor of the argument of Swan, Adamski and Na is therefore clear: we can either have a doctrinally pure law of contract with a robust idea of privity that does not accommodate contemporary patterns of contracting and business organisation, or we can have a law of contract shorn of traditional ideas of privity that does so accommodate. In other words, you can have the principle-based law defended by Smith or a state-of-the-art policy-infused law according to Swan, Adamski and Na, but not both.

In defence of Smith's views as to the centrality of privity, I would like to suggest that this is a false dichotomy. A judge or jurist who eschews policy could accept *both* a doctrine of privity as elucidated by Smith and a doctrine of vicarious immunity similar to that presented by Scrutton LJ (and therefore go a long way to answering Swan, Adamski and Na's concerns), because both are principled doctrines that operate at different levels and answer different questions. Thought of in this way, the doctrine of privity tells us who has rights in relation to contractual performance and other entitlements (ie, only a person to whom a promise was made), whereas the doctrine of vicarious immunity is part of the larger law of agency (in the loose sense), which tells us both when one person can be said to be acting as a representative of another (and so assimilated to them for certain purposes) and also what the legal consequences of so acting are.

The fact that such a reconciliation is possible is even suggested by Swan, Adamski and Na when they argue that 'the "enterprise" basis for the recognition of third party

[28] *Mersey Shipping and Transport Co Ltd v Rea Ltd* (1925) 21 LlL Rep 375 (DC), 378.

[29] See, eg, *Adler v Dickson (The Himalaya)* [1955] 1 QB 158 (CA).

[30] *Wilson v Darling Island Stevedoring & Lighterage Co Ltd* (1956) 95 CLR 43 (HCA). Kitto J agreed that the doctrine of vicarious immunity was not good law but did not think that privity resolved the issue. Instead he concurred in the result on the basis that the exclusion clause in the contract between the plaintiff shipper and the carrier, as properly interpreted, did not cover the defendant stevedores, and that therefore they could not raise consent or voluntary assumption of risk as a defence to their negligence. Williams and Taylor JJ dissented on the basis that *Elder, Dempster* had supported a concept of vicarious immunity.

[31] *Midland Silicones Ltd v Scruttons Ltd* [1962] AC 446, mentioned by Swan, Adamski and Na (text at n 16). See Viscount Simonds, *Midland Silicones* at 472: 'In [*Wilson*], … the late Fullagar J delivered a judgment with which Dixon CJ said that he entirely agreed. So do I – with every line and every word of it'.

[32] *Krawill Machinery Corporation v Robert C Herd & Co Inc*, 359 US 297 (1959).

[33] ibid 303.

claims deals easily with the two principal objections to the enforcement of third party beneficiary rights, ie, that the third party has given no consideration and is not party to the contract'.[34] If one substitutes the concept of 'representative' or 'agency' for that of 'enterprise', the basis of such a reconciliation becomes clear. And beyond its functionality in analytically allowing such a reconciliation, the concept of vicarious immunity also has an intuitive normative appeal. As O'Meara notes, it makes '"obvious common sense" that an employee, agent or independent contractor … performing his or her employer's or principal's ("employer") contractual obligations to another person ("the customer") should enjoy the employer's immunities from common law tortious liability to the customer'.[35] The difficulty then becomes a doctrinal one: given that apex courts across multiple jurisdictions have firmly stated that vicarious immunity is not part of the common law, could a contemporary court now revive the concept consistently with its judicial requirement to develop the private law incrementally and by analogy to established doctrines?[36]

In section II, I will suggest that the answer to this question is 'yes', on the basis that the arguments presented by the courts against the idea of vicarious immunity are not as cogent as was assumed by the judges making them, meaning that the path is open for contemporary courts to reinvigorate the idea, even in jurisdictions that have not accepted the principled exception to privity.

II. Arguments against Vicarious Immunity Examined

Judges, especially those who participated in the leading Commonwealth cases of *Wilson* and *Midland Silicones*, have made at least three arguments against vicarious immunity; namely, that the concept is inconsistent with: (i) the doctrine of privity; (ii) general principles of agency; and (iii) judicial authority relating to the personal liability of servants and agents of the Crown. In what follows, I would like to suggest reasons why these arguments are not as compelling as they first appear, and to also suggest why, in some cases, they might have found favour despite their lack of cogency.

A. The Conflict with Privity

As Treitel stated in 'The Battle over Privity', the rejection of vicarious immunity in *Midland Silicones* was 'entirely abstract' and was 'presented simply as a deduction from Lord Haldane's statement of the privity doctrine in *Dunlop v Selfridge*'.[37] The same might be said about the judgment of Fullagar J (with which Dixon CJ agreed) in *Wilson*.

[34] Swan, Adamski and Na (n 16) §3.124.

[35] O'Meara (n 21) 131, quoting UK Law Commission, *Privity of Contract: Contracts for the Benefit of Third Parties* (Law Com 121, 1991) §3.31.

[36] See *Fraser River* (n 15) [43]–[44].

[37] G Treitel, 'The Battle over Privity' in G Treitel, *Some Landmarks of Twentieth Century Contract Law* (Oxford, Oxford University Press, 2002) 60, referencing *Dunlop Pneumatic Tyre Co v Selfridge & Co* [1915] AC 847.

Yet if agency and privity operate at different levels and in relation to different questions, the existence of a robust doctrine of privity does not logically undercut vicarious immunity. Beyond this point, there are two additional reasons for thinking this. The first is that none of the judges in *Elder, Dempster* gave any indication that what they were proposing conflicted with privity. As Lord Reid commented, '[t]hey cannot have thought that any important question of law or novel principle was involved'.[38] One would have especially expected Lords Dunedin and Sumner, who had themselves participated in *Dunlop v Selfridge*, to have said something or attempted some sort of reconciliation if they thought that their judgments in *Elder, Dempster* were inconsistent with a fundamental principle they had previously accepted.[39] Second, as Trietel noted, another difficulty with treating privity as 'a decisive ground' for rejecting vicarious immunity is that in the United States the principle was also 'rejected even though there is no doctrine of privity'.[40]

If it is true, then, that there is no necessary incompatibility between the two doctrines, why did the majority of the judges in *Wilson* and *Midland Silcones* think there was? A plausible three-fold answer might be advanced. The first and most simple explanation is that that was how the case was put by counsel for the defendant appellants in *Midland Silicones*. In his submissions, Eustace Roskill QC (later Lord Roskill) argued that *Elder, Dempster* had recognised an exception to privity in relation to the carriage of goods by sea, and that this qualified what was decided in *Dunlop v Selfridge*.[41]

The second and more pervasive factor was Lord Denning. In a series of cases,[42] he used *Elder, Dempster* as a weapon in his 'assault' on the doctrine of privity.[43] Rather than presenting vicarious immunity as justified by the relationship between the employer and their servant or agent, and therefore as consistent with privity, he used it as evidence for the proposition that contracts for the benefit of third parties should generally be enforceable despite privity. As O'Meara notes, this represented 'a significant re-casting of vicarious immunity for it presents it as "a new general principle of the law of contract" in direct opposition to the doctrine of privity … [and] it does not appear that this is the way Scrutton LJ or Viscounts Cave and Finlay in *Elder, Dempster* saw the matter'.[44] Even in his dissenting speech in *Midland Silicones*, Lord Denning takes this line of argument. After explaining vicarious immunity and why it is unlikely that either Scrutton LJ ('this great master of commercial law') or 'the members of this House' in *Elder, Dempster* forgot about privity,[45] in the very next paragraph Lord Denning's argument pivots to disparaging privity as 'a discovery of the nineteenth century' of which 'Lord Mansfield and Buller J knew nothing'.[46]

A final reason, which I will address in section II.B, is that the courts were not presented with any real affirmative case for vicarious immunity as a matter of principle; instead, they were offered consequential arguments that vicarious immunity was

[38] *Midland Silicones* (n 31) 477.
[39] ibid 455 (Counsel's arguments).
[40] Treitel (n 37) 61.
[41] *Midland Silicones* (n 31) 457 (Counsel's arguments).
[42] See, eg, *White v John Warick* [1953] 1 WLR 1285 (CA).
[43] O'Meara (n 21) 140, citing NE Palmer, *Bailment* (Sydney, Law Book Company, 1989) 1627.
[44] O'Meara (n 21) 140 citing *Wilson* (n 30) 74 (Fullagar J).
[45] *Midland Silicones* (n 31) 483.
[46] ibid.

justifiable merely on the basis of its ability to produce the 'good outcomes' of protecting the agreed allocation of risk between the parties.[47] This was an argument doomed to fail before the principled and legally conservative Anglo-Australian judges hearing the cases.

B. The Conflict with Agency Law

As Lord Reid perplexingly noted in *Midland Silicones*, although the judges who decided *Elder, Dempster* 'must all have thought that they were merely applying an established principle to the facts of the particular case … when I look for such a principle I cannot find it'.[48] Similarly, Lord Keith stated that the 'proposition favoured by Scrutton LJ 'does not appear to me to proceed on any known principle in English law.'[49] Comparable language was used by Fullagar J in *Wilson*: 'When no precise legal ground for supporting an immunity can be found, there must be strong reason for suspecting that the immunity cannot be supported at all.'[50] Beyond its perceived inability to fit with privity, the judges made two additional arguments as to its lack of fit with common law principles. The first was that vicarious immunity is inconsistent with the basic principle that a servant or agent is liable for their own tortious conduct, even when they are acting on behalf of their employer.[51] Unfortunately, Scrutton LJ's use of the terminology of not being 'sued in tort as independent people',[52] in his summary of vicarious immunity in *Mersey Shipping*, amplified concerns that what he was proposing was a total abrogation of this principle, and this confused some of the judges. For example, in *Midland Silicones*, Viscount Simonds stated:

> [I]f the cargo owner sues a stevedore for negligence, he sues him not as a dependent or independent tortfeasor but just as a tortfeasor. It may be that, if he is a 'dependent' tortfeasor in the sense that he is the servant or agent of a master or principal, the latter may be made vicariously liable, but that does not touch his personal liability.[53]

The second related argument was that the principle of vicarious immunity depended on a loose and inexact use of the term 'agent', which should be reserved for situations where a person has the power to enter into contracts or other legal relations for another. As Lord Reid commented in *Midland Silicones*:

> The use of the term 'agent' is one difficulty: [Scrutton LJ] cannot have been using that word accurately in its legal sense. The charterer or anyone else under obligation to do certain things employs servants or independent contractors and instructs them to do those things. But they do not act as agents …[54]

[47] An outcome of course not accepted as intrinsically 'good' by either Fullagar J (and Dixon CJ) in *Wilson* (n 30) 71, or Viscount Simonds in *Midland Silicones* (n 31) 472.

[48] *Midland Silicones* (n 31) 477.

[49] ibid 480–81.

[50] *Wilson* (n 30) 73.

[51] PG Watts, *Bowstead and Reynolds on Agency* (London, Sweet & Maxwell, 2022) paras 9-115–9-116. See also *Restatement (Third) of the Law of Agency* (2006) § 7.01.

[52] *Mersey Shipping* (n 28) 378.

[53] *Midland Silicones* (n 31) 470–71.

[54] ibid 478.

Similar definitional concerns were expressed by Fullagar J in *Wilson*:

> [T]he word 'agent' appears to me to be often misused in this connection, and one cannot help feeling that this misuse is largely responsible for at least one of the views which have been entertained of the Elder Dempster Case. It seems to me quite wrong to say that a stevedoring company engaged by a shipowner to load or unload a ship is an 'agent' of the shipowner, just as it would be wrong to say that a builder is an 'agent' of a building owner. ... Agency in the legal sense simply does not come into the matter.[55]

In response to the first argument, it is clear that the principle of vicarious immunity as presented by Scrutton LJ is not an abrogation of the general rules for tortious liability of servants and agents. The argument is *not* that because you are a servant or agent acting for an employer you are immune from suit but that you are – subject to an important limitation that will be discussed in section II.C – immune from suit where you are acting as a servant or agent for an employer; and had your employer acted personally, they would have been immune from such a suit.

In response to the proper use of the term 'agent', there is nothing to this objection since it is merely semantic. As Lord Denning pointed out in his dissent in *Midland Silicones*, 'the books are full of the use of the word "agent" in the sense used by Scrutton LJ"'.[56] If, however, one wanted to be technical and to save the term 'agent' only for a subset of those representatives with authority to enter into legal relations for their principal,[57] and to use another term (such as perhaps 'representative') for the wider category of persons performing actions as another (and including servants, those akin to servants and agents properly so called), then this would not affect the cogency (or not) of vicarious immunity.

Beyond showing that the arguments against the doctrine are not as strong as they first appear, is there a positive case to be made for vicarious immunity? The first and more subtle argument is that the law clearly recognises a doctrine of vicarious liability that renders an employer liable for torts committed by representatives (ie servants, employees, those who are akin to employees, agents, etc) when those torts are sufficiently or closely connected to the conduct authorised by the employer.[58] If, as has been suggested, the best understanding of this legal phenomenon is that such liability is justified by the fact that the legal positions of the servant or agent and the employer are assimilated by attributing the acts or wrongs of the representative back to the employer,[59] it is just that such a servant or agent should prima facie be entitled to the privileges and immunities of the person they are representing when they are performing acts on account of that person and on their behalf. In other words, that the assimilation of legal positions should go both ways.[60]

[55] *Wilson* (n 30) 70.

[56] *Midland Silicones* (n 31) 483.

[57] For a discussion, see R Leow, 'Two Kinds of Agency' (2019) 93 *Supreme Court Law Review* 2.

[58] See *John Doe v Bennett*, 2004 SCC 17; *Various Claimants v Catholic Welfare Society* [2012] UKSC 56.

[59] See R Stevens, *Torts and Rights* (Oxford, Oxford University Press, 2007) ch 11; JW Neyers and J Kiss, 'Vicarious Liability: The Revolution in Canada' in P Giliker (ed), *Vicarious Liability in the Common Law World* (Oxford, Hart Publishing, 2022) 19.

[60] See Stevens (n 59) 267: 'These rules for identifying an agent or employee with his principal or employer are a species of the same set of rules of which vicarious liability forms a part.'

The second more obvious argument in favour of vicarious immunity is that the law has consistently, and seemingly uncontroversially, recognised an almost identical doctrine protecting servants and agents – namely, that of vicarious privilege.[61] As Atiyah explains:

> Notwithstanding the general principle that a servant or agent cannot rely on superior orders as a defence to an action in tort there are some circumstances in which the whole character of the servant's act is altered if it is done by his master's authority so that it is, in the result, not a tort at all. This is because the master may be entitled to do some act which is prima facie tortious, and may also be entitled to do that act through a servant or agent instead of doing it himself. If a privilege of this kind is thus delegable the servant will not be liable any more than the master and may be said to enjoy vicarious [privilege]. Obvious examples of this occur when a master authorizes his servant to eject a trespasser from his premises, or to seize his property from someone with no right to it … Vicarious [privilege] is not confined to servants but extends to any agent acting by the authority of another, so, for instance, it has been said that someone assisting a sheriff's officer to levy execution 'may justify as the officer may do' and that a person levying distress by authority of a landlord shares the landlord's immunity.[62]

As Stevens notes in *Torts and Rights*, the doctrine also protects a servant or agent who publishes a defamatory statement on behalf of an employer where the employer possesses a privilege to do so but where the representative does not possess any independent privilege of their own.[63] As both Atiyah and Stevens point out, the doctrine of vicarious privilege can even apply where there is no prior authority for the servant's or agent's acts, so long as the those acts are subsequently ratified by the employer.[64] Thus, as Stevens argues, as a result of the *Midland Silcones* decision, English law apparently has 'a doctrine of "vicarious privilege" but no doctrine of vicarious immunity'.[65]

Why did the judges in *Midland Silcones* and *Wilson* not make any analogies with vicarious liability or grapple with the issues of vicarious privilege in attempting to make sense of what *Elder, Dempster* had decided? Beyond the obvious answers related to what counsel argued and their Denning-provoked preoccupation with privity, a reason, which has some initial plausibility, relates to the way in which English lawyers were taught about agency in the relevant time period. As Falconbridge noted in 1939, in England, agency was 'usually treated as a mere appendix to the Law of Contract and Tort'.[66] This meant that English knowledge of agency ideas was compartmentalised, commercially focused and non-integrated. In contrast, in Canadian and American law schools of the time, agency was 'the subject of a major course'[67] (sometimes mandatory) that analysed the rules of agency and the ideas of representation in relation to contract and tort together, thereby inviting comparisons and analogies across the whole field of

[61] See Watts (n 51) para 9-115, citing *Hull v Pickersgill* (1819) 1 B & B 282; Stevens (n 59) 266–67; Coote (n 21) 129–33. See also *Restatement of the Law of Agency* (1933) § 343; *Restatement (Third)* (n 51) § 7.01.

[62] PS Atiyah, *Vicarious Liability in the Law of Torts* (London, Butterworths, 1967) 401–02, citing *Piggott v Kemp* (1832) 1 C & M 197 (ejecting trespassers); *Blades v Higgs* (1861) 30 LJCP 347 (seizing property); *Britton v Cole* (1697) 1 Salk 408 (agent levying execution and distress).

[63] Stevens (n 59) 267, relying on *Egger v Chelmsford* [1965] 1 QB 248 (CA). See also, Atiyah (n 62) 402.

[64] Atiyah (n 62) 402; Stevens (n 59) 266–67, citing *Buron v Denman* (1848) 2 Exch 167.

[65] Stevens (n 59) 267.

[66] JD Falconbridge, 'The Law of Agency' (1939) 17 *Canadian Bar Review* 248, 249.

[67] ibid.

this body of law.[68] Thus, the argument goes, it might never have occurred to the Anglo-Australian lawyers or judges involved in *Midland Silcones* and *Wilson* that vicarious liability or the privileges of servants and agents in relation to trespass or distraint were particularly relevant to the issues they had to decide.[69] On the other hand, the fact that the court in *Krawill* also dispensed with the doctrine (albeit under the influence of the decision in *Wilson*) suggests that this difference in educational technique could not have been decisive.

C. The Conflict with Crown Servant or Agent Liability

A final prominent criticism that is made of vicarious immunity is that it is inconsistent with cases that have held servants or agents of the Crown personally liable for their torts. As Southin JA explained in *London Drugs Ltd v Kuehne & Nagel International Ltd*,[70] citing cases such as *Entick v Carrington*[71] and *Rogers v Ragjendro Dutt*:[72]

> In my opinion, there is no such doctrine [of vicarious immunity]. A servant could be sued for trespass to goods even though his master, because he was immune from suit, could not be. Thus, the servants of the Crown could be so sued even though their master, the Sovereign, since he could do no wrong, could not be.[73]

Similar concerns were raised by Fullagar J in *Wilson*,[74] relying on *Williams v Commissioner for Main Roads*, where Jordan CJ held that although the Crown at common law enjoyed complete immunity, 'it has never been suggested that a servant of the Crown who commits a tort when acting within the scope of his authority can shelter behind the immunity of his principal'.[75] In light of this line of cases, is it possible to suggest, as I seek to do, that vicarious immunity provides a means to integrate Smith's views of privity with the complex nature of contemporary contracting invoked by Swan, Adamski and Na as a criticism of those views?

Although, as we have seen above, commentators (such as Stevens) have indicated that there is a doctrine of vicarious privilege in the common law but no doctrine of vicarious immunity, Atiyah instead argued that there is no stark distinction between the two ideas. This is because the apparent difference could be explained by the concept of delegability. As Atiyah explained, 'A servant or agent will only be entitled to vicarious

[68] For a comparison between the rules on scope of employment in vicarious liability and the concept of usual authority in contract prompted by the first *Restatement of the Law of Agency* (1933) (n 61)), see C Wright, 'Restatement of Contract and Agency' (1935) 1 *University of Toronto Law Journal* 17.

[69] See also Coote (n 21) 130.

[70] *London Drugs Ltd v Kuehne & Nagel International Ltd* (1990) 70 DLR (4th) 51 (BCCA).

[71] *Entick v Carrington* (1765) 19 St Tr 1030.

[72] *Rogers v Ragjendro Dutt* (1860) 13 Moore PC 209.

[73] *London Drugs* (BCCA) (n 70) 129–30. The Supreme Court of Canada choose not to examine vicarious immunity, preferring to deal 'head on' with whether to create the principled exception, see *London Drugs* (n 15) [194].

[74] *Wilson* (n 30) 69.

[75] *Williams v Commissioner for Main Roads* (1940) 40 SR (NSW) 472 (SC), 478, citing *Raleigh v Goschen* [1898] 1 Ch 73; *Mackenzie-Kennedy v Air Council* [1927] 2 KB 517; *Skinner v Commissioner for Railways* (1937) 37 SR 261 (NSWSC).

immunity when the privilege or immunity of his employer is a delegable one, and although most privileges are delegable, most immunities are not.'[76] He also reasoned that the answer to the question of whether the privilege or immunity will be delegable depended on an interpretation of the relevant statute, contract or legal rule that created the privilege or immunity at issue. Thus he argued that, even in relation to privileges, not all will be delegable, since it would be absurd to maintain that a member of a club could send their servant or agent into the club premises when this was contrary to the rules of the association.[77] When this is understood, the idea of delegability can be used to explain the traditional lack of vicarious immunity for Crown servants and agents, since the immunity of the Sovereign does not intuitively seem to be the type that should be shared by its subjects. Moreover, under modern law, if the immunity of the Crown were delegable, an important purpose of Crown proceedings statutes – to make the Crown vicariously liable for the torts of its servants and agents in a manner similar to that of a private employer[78] – would be thwarted.[79] This is because a substantive immunity for Crown servants and agents would make such vicarious liability impossible – there would be no tort committed by its representatives for which the Crown could be held vicariously responsible, which is one of the orthodox prerequisites of the modern doctrine.[80]

When this idea of delegability is kept in mind, one can see a way forward to rehabilitating the concept of vicarious immunity consistently with the incremental development of the common law. On this basis, *Elder, Dempster* is easy to explain: the immunity clause explicitly provided for protection for the 'shipowner', which was reasonably interpreted as being for the benefit of all persons involved with the storage of the cargo on the ship.[81] Thus it is clear that the immunity was eminently delegable and was available to be enjoyed by the servants or agents of the carrier/contracting party (such as the shipowner) when they were acting as that party according to the general principles of representation. And it is for this reason that none of the judges involved saw any concern with the doctrine of privity: not because they forgot about an important principle, but rather because they did not think it was imperilled by this sort of agency reasoning.

In contrast, in *Midland Silicones* the court was tasked with interpretating whether the term 'carrier' in the United States Carriage of Goods by Sea Act, 1936 (which the bill of lading incorporated) included a stevedore, and thus whether the immunity provided for the carrier under the relevant rules was one that was delegable or not. Given that the United States Supreme Court in *Krawill* had already decided that the term did not include stevedores, and given that it was important that statutes incorporating

[76] Atiyah (n 62) 404.

[77] ibid.

[78] See B Feldthusen, 'Unique Public duties of Care: Judicial Activism in the Supreme Court of Canada' (2016) 53 *Alberta Law Review* 955, 959–61, discussing the various Canadian Crown liability and proceedings Acts. As an example, see the Crown Liability and Proceedings Act, 2019, SO 2019, c 7, sch 17, ss 8(1)(a), 8(3), where this vicarious liability technique for Crown liability is employed.

[79] See *Williams* (n 75) 478; Atiyah (n 62) 403.

[80] See JW Neyers, 'Vicarious Liability' in E Chamberlain and SGA Pitel (eds), *Fridman's The Law of Torts in Canada*, 4th edn (Toronto, Thomson Reuters, 2020) 317, discussing the vicarious liability of the Crown.

[81] See *Edler, Dempster* (n 24) 534 (Lord Cave); *Gilbert Stokes* (n 23) 340.

international agreements were given common meaning by different national courts,[82] the House of Lords can be understood as deciding that the immunity given under the Act was one that was personal to the carrier and not one that could be relied upon its servants, agents or representatives even when acting as and for their employer. A similar analysis might be provided for the High Court of Australia's decision in *Wilson*, based on the interpretation of the bill of lading given by the majority of the court.

Finally, bringing the focus back to Swan, Adamski and Na's invocation of the principled exception, the Supreme Court of Canada's decision in *London Drugs*[83] could, from the perspective of vicarious immunity, be seen as a contemporary example of a finding by the court that an immunity contemplated in the contract was not personal to the corporate employer, and therefore could be enjoyed by its servants and agents when they acted in its stead.[84] As the majority stated:

> When all the circumstances of this case are taken into account, including the nature of the relationship between employees and their employer, the identity of interest with respect to contractual obligations, the fact that the appellant knew that employees would be involved in performing the contractual obligations, and the absence of a clear indication in the contract to the contrary, the term 'warehouseman' … must be interpreted as meaning 'warehousemen'. As such, the [employees] are not complete strangers to the limitation of liability clause.[85]

III. Conclusion

In this chapter, I have attempted to suggest three things. First, that it is possible to accept, on a principled basis, *both* (i) the austere and simple concept of privity that Smith defended in 'In Defence of The Third-Party Rule' and (ii) that (in certain situations) servants or agents of one of the contracting parties might be protected by exclusion clauses in contracts to which only their employer and the employer's customer are parties. Second, that a reason for this protection could be provided by the venerable concept of vicarious immunity that is part of the larger law of agency or representation that assimilates the legal positions of servants or agents and their employers when one is representing the other; and in so doing, overcomes concerns about lack of privity or consideration. Third, that, despite what was said in *Wilson* and *Midland Silicones*, it would be possible for contemporary courts to reinvigorate vicarious immunity, provided that they were sensitive to the issue of whether the immunity granted by the relevant statute, contract or legal rule was purely personal and hence non-delegable to a servant or agent. In light of these suggestions, it is submitted that the criticisms made by Swan,

[82] See *Midland Silicones* (n 31) 494: 'It would be deplorable if the nations should, after protracted negotiations, reach agreement, as in the matter of the Hague Rules, and that their several courts should then disagree as to the meaning of what they appeared to agree upon'.

[83] *London Drugs* (n 15).

[84] See O'Meara (n 21) 148–49; Reynolds and Rose (n 21) §7-019; and G Huscroft, 'Bad Doctrine and Incremental Reform' (1994) 7 *Journal of Contract Law* 181, 185, where it is noted that the reasoning in *London Drugs* seems very similar to the doctrine of vicarious immunity.

[85] *London Drugs* (n 15) [267].

Adamski and Na lose much of their force. The law can, justly and on a principled basis, achieve commercially sensible results in relation to many of the complex and impersonal factual circumstances with which contemporary courts are faced, by combining privity and vicarious immunity.

I very much hope that Steve would have enjoyed these suggestions. Like all the contributors to this volume, I am deeply saddened that he will not get to read them and offer the insightful criticisms and refinements for which he was justifiably famous.

PART IV

Law's Normativity

18

Trying and Succeeding

JOHN CP GOLDBERG AND BENJAMIN C ZIPURSKY

We are grateful and honoured to have this occasion to engage our friend Steve Smith's remarkably broad and deep scholarly corpus. For it, we have chosen to focus on one of his writings, titled 'Duties to Try and Duties to Succeed'.[1] As our own title conveys, we have chosen this piece because, even though we approach it with a critical eye (as we imagine he would want us to), we regard it as very much a success. In a manner characteristic of all of his work, it combines analytical rigour, a broad and powerful theoretical vision, and a deep command of doctrine and history. And it identifies and illuminates fundamental and difficult issues of private law theory.

I. Smith's Argument

The chapter we are analysing begins with the perennial question of the role of fault in private law. As a way into this question, Smith starts with a distinction drawn by John Gardner between two types of duty,[2] then builds out from it two models private law and asks what role fault plays in each. These models are offered as analytical constructs, not descriptions of the rules of a given legal system.

The first is the *outcome model*. According to it, private law's duties are what Gardner dubbed *duties to succeed*. The tort of trespass to land recognised in Anglo-American law, or something like it, illustrates this type of duty. Conforming to the duty it specifies requires something more than reasonable efforts to avoid entering another's land; one must succeed in not entering. The second model is the *conduct model*. On this account, private law duties are (again, in Gardner's terms) *duties to try*. Illustrative of this sort of duty would be a negligence-like tort that imposes a duty to take reasonable efforts to try not to injure others.

Smith's chapter next suggests that, while both models can accommodate a notion of fault, they do so on quite different terms. In the outcome model, the absence of fault is

[1] SA Smith, 'Duties to Try and Duties to Succeed' in A Dyson, J Goudkamp and F Wilmot-Smith (eds), *Defences in Tort* (Oxford, Hart Publishing, 2015) 65.

[2] ibid 68 and fn 10, 73 (invoking Gardner's work for this distinction).

relevant only as a potential *excuse* that might spare a legal wrongdoer from liability for their wrong. To return to the trespass example: if an actor has entered another's land, the actor's fault is neither here nor there on the question of whether the duty has been breached. It has. Instead, lack of fault (for example, reasonable care taken in an unsuccessful effort to avoid trespassing) at most provides grounds for a more lenient response to the breach. Meanwhile, on the conduct model, fault 'always' figures in determinations of wrongfulness.[3] The duty to try to avoid harming another just is a duty to make reasonable efforts, such that its breach consists of fault.

According to Smith, the different roles played by fault in the two models indicates that the two instantiate different conceptions of wrongdoing. The gist of the breach of a duty to try is a *failure to treat others with proper concern*. The lack of even so much as an effort to avoid injuring another shows disrespectful indifference to the interests of others. A breach of a duty to succeed, by contrast, is wrongful in that that it generates a setback to another's right or interest, irrespective of whether it shows disrespect. A trespass to land is still a wrong, on this model, even if the trespasser was scrupulous in attending to the interests of the possessor.

According to Smith, the two models also generate distinct conceptions of *liability*. When an actor is made to pay damages for the breach of a duty to succeed, the payment, in principle, undoes the bad outcome for the victim. Damages for the breach of this sort of duty thus lend themselves to descriptions such as those provided by the 'continuity thesis' – according to which the duty-bearer who breaches is still obligated to perform the duty, but, being unable to perform it fully, must do the next best thing, which is to compensate for harm done by the breach, thereby (in principle) making it as if the breach never happened. By contrast, according to Smith, compensatory damages for breaches of duties to try have as their primary aim the restoration of the parties' formal equality. Damages in this context operate expressively, in the manner of a criminal punishment – they aim to restore the moral balance between wrongful injurer and victim. As such, they cannot plausibly be characterised as a way of complying with the original duty to try.[4]

Having isolated the two models, the chapter considers whether a body of private law could in principle adopt a hybrid model that recognises both duties to try and duties to succeed. After canvassing three possibilities, it concludes that only the third is 'even prima facie stable'.[5]

1. *Combination regimes*. The law might combine the two types of duties *conjunctively* (for example, by recognising both a duty to try not to trespass and to succeed in not trespassing, the breach of either of which, or both, would generate liability) or *disjunctively* (by recognising a duty not to trespass by means of failure to try to avoid trespassing). In Smith's view, both of these constitute 'ad hoc mixtures of qualitatively different and independently complete concepts'.[6] As we have seen, on his view, it is coherent to combine a duty to succeed while recognising *excuses* for

[3] ibid 66.
[4] ibid 77.
[5] ibid 78.
[6] ibid.

the breach of such a duty. What cannot be done is to identify wrongs that impose on actors, at once, an obligation to try to avoid an outcome and an obligation to succeed in avoiding that outcome. Any genuine duty – that is, obligation of conduct – must be one or the other.

2. *Overlapping regimes*. The law might recognise two independent yet 'overlapping' wrongs, one involving a duty to succeed, the other a duty to try. For example, trespassing and failing to try to avoid trespassing might be separate torts. Smith suggests that such a regime would be 'impossibly complicated',[7] in part because in cases in which each duty is breached by a single action (eg, an actual trespass), it will be difficult to know how to assess damages without conflating the two very different conceptions of liability that correspond to the different types of duty or providing the victim with double recovery.
3. *Non-overlapping regimes*. Under this approach, different rights are protected by the different kinds of duties. For example, possession of property is protected by a duty to succeed, whereas bodily integrity is protected by a duty to try. While this would be a coherent system, according to Smith there is no obvious account that tells us when the legal system should use one type of duty or the other to protect different rights.

The final portions of the chapter consider how the two models map onto actual English and Commonwealth tort law. Its first suggestion is that existing legal rules for determining when an actor is subject to liability could *in theory* be made to fit either model. Thus, the outcome model nicely captures the rules for liability contained in direct-interference torts such as trespass to land and battery.[8] And it can be made to fit consequential wrongs such as negligence (understood as imposing a duty to succeed in avoiding injuring another subject to an excusatory defence of reasonable care). The conduct model, meanwhile, seems readily to capture the core of negligence, understood to be a duty to make reasonable efforts to avoid injuring. (However, it then needs an explanation – presumably grounded in practical considerations – as to why liability for the actual tort of negligence is limited to cases in which the lack of such efforts actually causes harm). As for direct-interference torts, the conduct model has to 'bite the bullet' and treat these as instances of liability without wrongdoing.

Having allowed for an in-principle reconciliation of each model with extant doctrine, the chapter goes on to suggest that neither in fact accounts for the terms on which courts *actually characterise* liability for torts such as trespass to land or negligence. Instead of consistently following the language and logic of one model or the other, courts seemingly invoke features of each model in a willy-nilly fashion, which makes actual tort law something of a hodgepodge when it comes to articulating the legal duties to which we are subject. The tort of negligence, for example, is typically described by courts on terms that seem, incoherently, to hinge liability on a failure to try *and* a failure to succeed.[9] Thus, while either model could in principle explain the law, neither actually does.

[7] ibid 80.
[8] ibid 81.
[9] ibid 83.

The chapter closes with an historical explanation for this rather sorry state of affairs. Anglo-American private law, Smith reminds us, grew out of the writ system, working backwards from remedies to rules. For centuries, the rules of private law were rules for judges that guided *them* on how to resolve disputes, not primary rules for guiding everyday conduct. It is only with Blackstone that an effort began to draw from the pattern of remedies under the writ system to a set of rules specifying primary rights and duties of individuals. Almost inevitably, this has created confusion, because liabilities can be related to duties in different ways (as discussed above). In the end, Smith concluded that more work needs to be done in figuring out whether private law should be structured around duties to succeed or duties to try.[10]

II. Duties of Noninjuriousness and Duties of Noninjury

In what follows, we will – by turning from abstract models to tort doctrine – take up the challenge Smith rightly laid down: whether there is a way to make sense of the pattern of fault-requiring and non-fault-requiring private law wrongs, and the cluster of legal attributes attached to each.

In this section, we will suggest that tort law, at least, is not as much of a mishmash as Smith suggested is the case across private law. To see this, however, requires that the distinction between duties to try and duties to succeed be recast as a contrast between 'duties of noninjuriousness' and 'duties of noninjury'.[11] With this alternative distinction in place, we make two further claims: that it is perfectly coherent to combine *these* two types of duties within a single legal wrong, and that this is precisely what courts have done for torts traceable to the writ of trespass *on the case*, particularly negligence. In the next section, we will suggest that torts that harken back to the writ of trespass *vi et armis* do not work quite the same way, yet are similar in that they, too, involve what we call *qualified duties of noninjury*. Thus, on the overall picture we sketch: (i) all torts involve breaches of duties of noninjury; (ii) all of these duties of noninjury are qualified; but (iii) only for some is the qualifier a breach of a duty of noninjuriousness.

Smith and Gardner were both right to point out that torts and tort duties are defined partly in terms of 'success' conditions. This is what we mean to capture when we say that tort law specifies 'duties of noninjury' that correlate to rights against being wrongfully injured. To learn the law of torts is to learn that there are legal rules specifying (among other things) that one must not defraud others, batter others, defame others or interfere with others' possession of their lands. In each case, there is no breach of legal duty unless the right sort of interference with another actually occurs.

However, our concept of a duty of noninjury differs in important ways from the concept of a duty to succeed. In particular, Smith characterised duties to succeed by contrasting them with conduct norms, apparently on the assumption that, in private law,

[10] ibid 83–84.

[11] This distinction was first invoked and elaborated in A Ripstein and BC Zipursky, 'Corrective Justice in the Age of Mass Torts' in G Postema (ed), *Philosophy and the Law of Torts* (Cambridge, Cambridge University Press, 2001) 214.

the relevant notion of 'conduct' refers to acts divorced from consequences (for example, the act of driving without due care, as opposed to the consequence of another being injured by such driving). We reject this assumption and instead maintain the norms containing duties of noninjury *are* norms of conduct. Consider the injunctions listed above. Each, we would say, enjoins a species of conduct. Defrauding, battering, defaming and trespassing are things that an actor does. Second, Smith offered the descriptive or interpretive claim that only *some* torts involve duties to succeed, whereas our view is that *all* torts involve duties of noninjury. To say this is not to say that torts are either all fault-based or never fault-based: some are, and some are not. It is instead to say that every tort specifies injury as an element, such that there cannot be a tort in the absence of an injury.[12]

We also depart from Smith in maintaining that, in certain contexts (especially in the domain of negligence), the appropriate contrast to a duty of noninjury is not a *duty to try* but rather a duty of noninjuriousness – that is, a duty to refrain from acting in a manner that has a tendency to cause a certain kind of injury to a certain set of persons. The difference between a duty of noninjuriousness and a duty to try – as well as the difference between a duty of noninjuriousness and a duty of noninjury – may be illustrated by considering a simple negligence hypothetical.

Suppose Green hires Lancaster to spruce-up Green's yard. Lancaster sprays the yard with what he believes to be a vinegar-based herbicide that poses no danger to humans. Unfortunately, Lancaster confused the name of that herbicide with a different herbicide that is suitable for industrial use only, and that contains ingredients that can burn human skin. Because Lancaster told Green that she was using a pesticide that posed no risk of harm, Green – as he does each day – entered his yard, barefoot, to retrieve his morning newspaper shortly after Lancaster sprayed the yard. As a result, Green suffered serious burns on his feet.

Green v Lancaster would make for a straightforward negligence case. And yet the analytic structure of Green's claim is not simple. Indeed, if one were to ask the question 'Under negligence law, what was Lancaster's duty?', there are two plausible answers: (i) 'Lancaster's duty was to take reasonable care while working on Green's yard to prevent persons, including Green, from being physically harmed'; and (ii) 'Lancaster's duty was to avoid causing physical harm to persons, including Green, by failing to exercise reasonable care while working on Green's yard.'

The first of these formulations describes what is often referred to in textbooks and judicial opinions as 'the duty of care' or the 'duty element of negligence'. The idea is

[12] By 'injury' we refer not to material harm but to an interference with some right or interest of the plaintiff. The victim of a trespass to land that causes no property or other tangible harm has still been 'injured' in this sense – the victim's legal right against others intentionally entering their land has been violated. According to Smith, for all torts defined in terms of a breach of a duty to try, no such setback is required to render an actor's conduct wrongful. Thus, the wrong of negligence, understood as specifying a legal duty to try, occurs just as soon as an actor fails to make the appropriate effort to avoid injuring another. To be sure, he acknowledges that such failure, without causation of injury, is not sufficient to generate liability. But, on Smith's view, this merely shows that negligence liability requires something more than wrongdoing. Smith (n 1) 74. As noted above, he also claimed that the remedy for what he classified as duty-to-succeed torts is essentially continuous with the primary duty breached, as opposed to being oriented towards empowering the plaintiff to redress the wrong done to them. We reject this view as well.

that negligence requires us to exercise due care against injuring persons of a certain (abstract) description. So understood, the duty is one that can be breached or fulfilled before anyone gets injured. Lancaster's mistaken application of the dangerous herbicide, of itself, was a breach of this duty.

But, of course, the careless mistaking of the herbicide itself is not sufficient to subject to Lancaster to liability for negligence. Thus, Green's neighbour, who, from the safety of her own home, happened to observe Lancaster's mistake but was not injured by it, could not prevail in a negligence suit against Lancaster. The most immediate explanation for this result is the neighbour's lack of injury. But the requirement of injury also sheds light on the content of the legal duty that comes with the tort of negligence. In Hohfeldian terms, the claim-right conferred by negligence law is the right against being *injured* by the carelessness of others. It is not a right against others acting carelessly, full stop. And the duty correlative to this right is a duty owed by others to avoid carelessly injuring persons such as Green and the neighbour. In this sense, the second formulation of the duty issue in negligence – the duty to avoid injuring through carelessness – is no less apt than the first formulation, in which injury does not figure.

As readers will perhaps have surmised, we think the two dimensions of duty in negligence law are captured nicely by the distinction between a duty of noninjuriousness and a duty of noninjury. The first duty described above (the 'duty of care') is a duty of noninjuriousness – that is, a duty to refrain from acting in a way that generates an unacceptable risk of a certain kind of injury to certain others (roughly, those who one can foresee might be injured if one were to act carelessly). Lancaster's mistaken spreading of an unduly dangerous herbicide in a residential area is a breach of this duty. But breaching this duty is not the same thing as committing the tort of negligence. The tort, after all, requires not just a breach of the duty of noninjuriousness but also a breach of the duty of noninjury.

Replacing Smith's (and Gardner's) 'succeed'/'try' distinction with the 'noninjury'/'noninjuriousness' distinction offers several advantages.[13] First and foremost, while we agree that compliance with a duty of care defeats negligence liability even if an injury occurs – even if there is no success in the effort to avoid injuring someone – we think it is misleading to use terms such as 'try' to capture what it means to comply.[14] To heed the duty of care (the duty of noninjuriousness within the tort of negligence) requires something more than an attempt or a try. Whether one has complied with the duty turns on what one has *done* or *not done*: whether one has actually taken adequate precautions or failed to do so, whether one has acted competently or failed to do so, etc. While it is true that such performances are often in aid of achieving some end – and in that sense, are attempts to achieve those ends – 'trying' tends to denote a

[13] We will not pursue it further here, but we also question Smith's suggestions that wrongs built around duties to try, unlike wrongs built around duties to succeed, involve disrespect, and that wrongs built around duties to succeed are particularly suited for damages that restore the victim to the status quo ante. Smith himself suggested that negligence (or something quite like it) is emblematic of a wrong involving the breach of a duty to try and thus as a prototypical wrong of disrespect, yet it seems somewhat odd to select negligence *over* intentional torts like battery or defamation as quintessentially about disrespect. Conversely, accident cases involving physical injury strike us as the most apt for compensation limited to an amount that makes the plaintiff whole.

[14] See JCP Goldberg and BC Zipursky, 'Tort Law and Moral Luck' (2007) 92 *Cornell Law Review* 1123, 1157, fn 115.

subjective or volitional state of mind that is not a part of the inquiry into whether, so far as negligence law is concerned, a person has acted in a careless manner. To return to our imagined case, whether, at the time of acting, Lancaster was actually making an effort to avoid injuring Green has no bearing on the question of whether Lancaster exercised the care required of her. (In this sense, the duty of care is no less a 'success' idea than the duty not to injure through carelessness: to heed the duty of care requires that one succeed in exercising the appropriate level of care.)

Second, even if Smith was correct to assert that it is incoherent to define a wrong to include both a duty to try and a duty to succeed, this claim does not carry over to duties of noninjuriousness and duties of noninjury. On his view, no single tort, including negligence, can coherently require an actor to try not to injure and to succeed in not injuring. For example, if negligence law is to be coherent, it must be that the second 'duty' (the 'duty' not to injure) is not a genuine duty at all but instead a rule of liability.[15] In purporting to establish that there is something fundamentally ad hoc about identifying wrongs that purport to combine duties to try and duties to succeed, Smith offered the following thought:

> As we have seen, the wrong of failing to achieve a particular outcome is not affected by whether the wrongdoer also did, or did not, try to achieve that outcome. Similarly, the wrong of failing to try to achieve an outcome remains the same whether or not the wrongdoer actually achieved the outcome. To be sure, a legal system that consisted exclusively of duties to succeed might decide that liability for breaching such duties should be subject to an excusatory defence of reasonable behaviour; similarly, a legal system that consisted exclusively of duties to try might decide that liability for breaching such duties should be conditional on the breach causing harm. … But at the stage of articulating duties, there appears to be no reason to combine duties to try and duties to succeed. Two wrongs are worse than one, but a single wrong remains a wrong. Duties to try and duties to succeed are complete in themselves.[16]

On our view, there is a very strong prima facie reason for tort scholars to accept that the two types of duty we have set forth (unlike Smith's duties to try and duties to succeed) *can* be combined. For, as we have seen, this is exactly what the common law of negligence purports to do (as Smith acknowledged). A negligence defendant will avoid liability unless the plaintiff shows a breach of both duties we noted above in discussing *Green v Lancaster* – there must be both *injury* and *conduct breaching the duty of care.* This is not to deny Smith's initial concern that 'combination duties' seem like they might be unstable mixtures. We agree that duties to succeed and duties to try are qualitatively different, and we tend to think the same is true of duties of noninjury and duties of noninjuriousness. The challenge is to say why the combination is not ad hoc.[17]

[15] As noted, while, on Smith's view, law can impose a genuine duty not to injure another, such a duty has to be a simple or unqualified duty – for example, a duty to avoid physically injuring another, full stop. To be sure, for a wrong consisting of the breach of a duty not to injure, the law might recognise excuses, including the excuse of having taken reasonable care. But even if it did, the wrong in question would be the injuring, not a failure to take care against injuring. The injurer who behaves reasonably would thus still be a wrongdoer but might avoid liability by virtue of having an excuse, as might a person who injures another while acting under duress.

[16] Smith (n 1) 78–79.

[17] As an aside, it does not follow from the (putative) fact that both forms of duty are independent and complete concepts that there is anything problematic about combining them. 'Cheese' and 'burger' arguably

In fact, we favour the somewhat clunky phrases 'duty of noninjuriousness' and 'duty of noninjury' in part because they are supportive of such an explanation. In a tort such as negligence, the relationship between the duty of noninjuriousness and the duty of noninjury is a *qualifying* relationship. Indeed, it would be false to say, without qualification, that negligence law imposes a duty not to injure others. What it actually imposes is a qualified duty not to injure: a duty not to injure others *through conduct of a certain sort* (namely, careless conduct). Moreover, in negligence, the relation of the duty of noninjuriousness and the duty of noninjury is organic (and indeed almost teleological). The plaintiff not only must demonstrate that the injury was caused by the breach of the duty of noninjuriousness (the breach of the duty of care), but also that the causal connection amounts to a realisation of one of the risks that rendered the defendant's conduct a breach of the duty of noninjuriousness. Hence negligence law's proximate cause requirement.[18]

Perhaps our most basic point is that duties of noninjuriousness and duties of noninjury are co-dependent rather than independent or complete in the relevant respects. A tort is an act that the common law understands to warrant the recognition of a right of action by a person against the actor who committed it. Tort law does not count an act as a legal wrong warranting a right of action for a plaintiff unless it consists in part of an injuring of the plaintiff. This is for fundamental reasons of political morality. A person's having actually been injured is the basis for them to be entitled to claim a power to use the courts to hold the wrongful injurer to account. The plaintiff must herself have been the actual victim of a 'realised wrong' committed by the defendant in order to claim the power to make a legally enforceable demand for redress.[19]

What about breaches of duties of noninjury? Are these not complete and independent? We maintain they are not. An injury of itself is not enough to count as having been *wronged* by the defendant. It must have resulted from the defendant's having violated the right sort of legal norm – a norm of conduct or a guidance rule. As Smith and Gardner both rightly emphasised, norms of this sort can be extremely unforgiving, and thus can be violated even by actors who are earnestly trying to do right, who are diligent and who cannot be faulted in some strong sense of 'fault'. It is in this sense apt to describe such duties as duties to succeed. It does not follow, however, that these are wholly unqualified duties to avoid bringing about certain states of affairs.[20] Generally speaking, tort law hinges liability on the defendant's at least having had *the capacity* to

denote independent and complete concepts in a way that 'mortar' and 'pestle' do not, but this does not render the concept of a cheeseburger objectionable.

[18] If Lancaster's use of the wrong herbicide did not burn anyone, but instead unexpectedly caused Green's weeds to turn an unnatural neon shade of pink, and if their new hue captured the attention of a startled passerby, such that the passerby walked into a nearby telephone pole and was injured, Lancaster would not face liability. He would not because the causal connection between the breach of the duty of noninjuriousness and the injury was not a realisation of one of the risks that rendered Lancaster's conduct a breach of the duty of noninjuriousness.

[19] JCP Goldberg and BC Zipursky, *Recognizing Wrongs* (Cambridge, MA, Harvard University Press, 2020) 207–08. In certain special contexts, some courts have deemed a person's being exposed to a risk of physical harm an injury of itself. When and on what grounds they are entitled to do so is a complex question beyond the scope of this chapter. See JCP Goldberg and BC Zipursky, 'Unrealized Torts' (2002) 88 *Virginia Law Review* 1626, 1650–60.

[20] Goldberg and Zipursky, *Recognizing Wrongs* (n 19) 189–98.

avoid bringing about the injury, or *a meaningful opportunity* not to breach the duty of noninjury to the plaintiff. The wrongs of tort are rights invasions, and rights invasions are actions by others that we are entitled to expect them not to do. Pure unqualified duties of noninjury may be coherent, but it is not clear that one can – in anything but a stipulative manner – regard the breach of such duties as *wrongs* to the plaintiff. If this is so then, in tort law, duties of noninjury are not complete but require some kind of qualification.

To sum up, all torts involve breaches of duties of noninjury. Moreover, because there is nothing ad hoc or incoherent about qualifying a duty of noninjury with a duty of noninjuriousness, there is room in tort law for such combinations. And indeed the tort of negligence involves precisely such a combination. This is not to say, however, that all torts combine duties of noninjuriousness and duties of noninjury. Trespass to land illustrates this point: it does not qualify the duty to refrain from entering another's land by incorporating a duty to refrain from engaging in conduct that has a tendency to cause one to enter another's land. But this does not mean that trespass and other torts consist of *un*qualified duties of noninjury. Instead, they consist of qualified duties of noninjury where the qualification consists of something other than a duty of noninjuriousness. This, we will now argue, is the main lesson of one of the 'chestnuts' of American tort law.

III. From *Green v Lancaster* to *Brown v Kendall*

As explained in section I, while Steve's models are constructs, he suggested that they resemble the pair of medieval writs out of which modern private law grew. We thus turn attention to them to defend our view that, even for torts that do not combine duties of noninjuriousness with duties of noninjury, the duties of noninjury in question are still qualified duties.

In the beginning was the writ of trespass *vi et armis*, which by its terms enabled victims of directly inflicted, forcible harms to obtain redress from the wrongdoer in the royal courts. Later, the courts developed the writ of trespass *sur la case*, through which claimants could obtain redress for indirect harms wrongfully committed without force.

The trespass/case distinction has been understood on somewhat different terms by different jurists and in different eras. Still, the two writs had consistently distinctive features.[21] The terms on which wrongs were pleaded under the writ of trespass were quite sparse. The plaintiff would allege simply that the defendant, with force and arms, had directly injured him. Moreover, injury was defined in 'boundary-crossing' terms – touching a person, confining a person, entering a person's land – without setting a threshold of harmfulness that had to be met before there could be a viable claim.[22] By contrast, a plaintiff invoking the writ of trespass on the case was required to elaborate

[21] JH Baker, *An Introduction to English Legal History*, 5th edn (Oxford, Oxford University Press, 2019) 428–34.

[22] The idea of trespass *quare clausum fregit* (breaking the close), as well as 'least touching' formulations of battery (trespass to the person), capture this aspect of claims under the writ of trespass. See W Blackstone, *Commentaries on the Laws of England*, vol 3 (Chicago, IL, University of Chicago Press, 1979) (originally published 1768) 120, 209.

on the qualities of the defendant's action that rendered it wrongful, and to plead and ultimately prove temporal or tangible harm. Thus, a suit brought in 'case' against a veterinarian for what would today be called malpractice would allege not merely that the defendant touched or treated the plaintiff's horse, but that he had done so *negligently* and to the detriment of its health. Likewise, an action on the case for interference with a possessor's use and enjoyment of his land (ie, private nuisance) would generate liability only if the interference was substantial and unreasonable.

This no doubt over-simplified description might seem to support the supposition that Anglo-American 'tort' law has long included wrongs involving the breach of *un*qualified duties of noninjury (once actionable via the writ of trespass *vi et armis*) and wrongs involving the breach of qualified duties of noninjury (once actionable via the writ of trespass *sur la case*). But it does not. Indeed, the claim that it does not is arguably at the core of Chief Justice Shaw's opinion for the Massachusetts Supreme Judicial Court in *Brown v Kendall.*[23] *Brown*, we will suggest, is a landmark precisely because it insisted that all torts, whether they once fit the rubric of 'trespass' or 'case', incorporate qualified duties of noninjury.

At least since Holmes made it a centerpiece of his discussion of negligence in *The Common Law*,[24] *Brown v Kendall* has been considered a foundational decision of American tort law. This is understandable. The decision was rendered at a pivotal moment in which modern tort law was emerging out of the collapse of the writ system and Shaw's Court was perhaps the nation's leading State court. And Shaw himself, though in some respects a controversial figure, was generally held in very high regard as a jurist.

In other respects, however, *Brown* seems like a poor candidate for landmark status. Its facts did not raise the big-ticket issue of the era – namely, whether and when railroads and other modern industries would be held liable for the carnage they caused. Also, the literal terms on which the suit proceeded were obsolete at the time the case was decided.[25] Brown sued Kendall for 'assault and battery'. Yet the suit was not for what lawyers today would call an intentional tort. Rather, these terms were being used – as they had been for centuries – to refer to a forcibly and directly inflicted personal injury actionable via the writ of trespass *vi et armis.*[26]

So what did *Brown* hold, and why was it significant? We start with the first question. The plaintiff's and defendant's dogs were fighting. To break up the fight, Kendall raised a long stick with which to hit them, accidentally striking and injuring Brown, who was standing behind him. At trial, which ultimately resulted in a plaintiff's verdict, the defendant requested that the judge instruct the jury that it must find for Kendall if it were to conclude that he was using 'ordinary care' when he struck Brown. The trial court instead instructed the jury that, if Kendall had *chosen* to try to separate the dogs

[23] *Brown v Kendall*, 60 Mass 292 (1850).

[24] OW Holmes, Jr , *The Common Law* (Boston, MA, Belknap Press, 1881) 105–06.

[25] Indeed, the Massachusetts legislature abolished the old English writs within a year of *Brown*'s having been decided. GE White, 'The Intellectual Origins of Torts in America' (1977) 86 *Yale Law Journal* 671, 679–80 (noting that Massachusetts abolished writ pleading in 1851).

[26] *Brown* (n 23) 294 ('This is an action of trespass, *vi et armis*, brought by George Brown against George K Kendall, for an assault and battery …').

(rather than doing so in the fulfilment of an obligation), he should be deemed liable to Brown unless Kendall had exercised 'extraordinary care' such that the injury to Brown was 'inevitable'.[27]

Shaw's opinion deemed the trial court's instruction erroneous, and on that basis (among others) ordered a new trial. The trial court's reasoning, it maintained, displayed a misunderstanding of the distinction between the writs of trespass and case. The trespass writ, Shaw maintained, was properly invoked when 'the damage complained of is the immediate effect of the act of the defendant', whereas 'case' was the proper writ if the damage is 'consequential only, and not immediate'.[28] From this difference, the trial judge had mistakenly inferred that, for a wrong actionable under the writ of trespass, there need *only* be a showing of a harm directly inflicted by the defendant, irrespective of whether the act that caused the harm was in some sense deficient or 'unlawful'. Not so, insisted Shaw. Such a claim, he insisted, requires for liability that the defendant's action failed to meet a *standard of conduct* set by the law, where the notion of a standard of conduct stands apart from the mere fact of injuring. Specifically, according to Shaw – citing Harvard Law Professor Simon Greenleaf's evidence treatise – there must be evidence that the defendant acted either with 'an intention that was unlawful' or 'fault'.[29] As there was no evidence of any intent on the part of Kendall to interact in an unlawful way with Brown, there could be no liability in this case based on a showing of unlawful intent.[30] Instead, it would have to be based on fault. Hence the trial court should have given to the jury the defendant's requested jury instruction.

To repair to our terminology, the apparent mystery of *Brown*'s importance can be explained precisely in Shaw's contention that the wrongs actionable via the writ of trespass, no less than the wrongs actionable through the writ of trespass on the case, were wrongs involving the breach of a *qualified* duty of noninjury. To say roughly the same thing in Smith and Gardner's terminology, it was a mistake for the trial judge in *Brown* to map onto the distinction between trespass and case a distinction between duties to try and duties to succeed. For the wrongs actionable under each writ, the relevant duties were duties to succeed, and for both writs the duties to succeed contained important qualifiers.

While the categories of trespass and case are long gone, Shaw's point still stands. Each tort specifies a qualified duty of noninjury. As we have explained, for negligence, the qualification comes in the form of a duty of noninjuriousness – the duty to take due care that must be breached before causation of injury will be actionable. For battery (as defined in modern tort law) there is also a qualification, but not one that consists of a

[27] ibid 292–94.

[28] ibid 295.

[29] ibid 296. Whether Shaw was correct in his assertions about the basis for liability under trespass and case as those operated in medieval English law is a matter of debate. According to Sir John Baker, wrongs actionable via the trespass writ were qualified in our sense of that term, because juries were understood to have the authority to decline to impose liability if they concluded the defendant had acted reasonably and otherwise acceptably. Baker (n 21) 429–32.

[30] Shaw did not have occasion to spell out what, precisely, was meant by 'unlawful intent'. Forty years later, the Wisconsin Supreme Court, citing the same language from the Greenleaf treatise, concluded that, for personal injury claims, 'unlawful intent' does not require an intent to injure or offend, but only an intent to perform a touching of a sort that tends to cause bodily harm or is otherwise regarded as unacceptable. *Vosburg v Putney*, 50 NW 403 (Wisc 1891).

duty of noninjuriousness. Instead, it is the requirement that the defendant acted with the intent to perform a certain kind of touching of another. Only a touching so intended is actionable. For trespass to land, the qualification likewise comes in the form of an intent requirement – the intent to occupy space that is in fact lawfully possessed by the other with which the actor must have acted before the occupation will be actionable.[31]

IV. Conclusion

It is painful to acknowledge that Steve Smith, like John Gardner, was deprived of the opportunity to develop his remarkable insights over the course of the sort of lifespan one hopes to have. We would like to think, however, that we are taking up their cause and developing it in ways that they would find interesting, even if not in all respects agreeable. This is certainly the spirit in which we have offered the sometimes critical reflections contained in this essay.

Whatever the nature of our disagreements with Steve, we share entirely his sense of the need to work out how, in tort law and private law more generally, legal duties are 'combination' duties that link conduct with outcomes. In particular, one crucial question flagged by the way in which 'Duties to Try and Duties to Succeed' divides up tort law is how to capture accurately the *different qualifiers* that courts have built into different torts, and what (if anything) might explain these differences. For there is indeed an important distinction between torts for which the exercise of due care shields defendants from the conclusion that a wrong has been committed and those in which it does not. And in the latter camp, there are further divisions between torts that rely on qualifiers so thin as to barely mark off wrongs (trespass to land being the prototype) and torts that rely on thicker qualifiers (such as assault, or false imprisonment).

Why does tort law have these different kinds of wrongs? Is one more basic than the other? Which, if any, should be preferred? Why is the paradigm of a thinly or minimally wrongful tort one that *protects property rights*, while more robust requirements of wrongdoing prototypically, although not uniformly,[32] apply to *invasions of bodily integrity*? To these important questions, we, like Steve, see no easy answers. But we can thank him for forcing us to engage in the search.

[31] A driver who veers to avoid a road obstruction that falls from the sky without warning, directly in front of his car, and who intends by veering only to avoid the obstruction while staying on the road, cannot be held liable for trespass to land if the car, against the driver's intentions, leaves the road and ends up on private property. There is no trespass because the driver never intended for the car to be in that location.

[32] Thus, the law of strict products liability in the US imposes a duty of noninjury qualified only by a requirement that the defendant sold a product that happens to have been dangerously defective at the time of sale.

19

The Unknowability Objection

DENNIS KLIMCHUK*

At more than one point in his defence of his account of the law of damages, Stephen Smith relied on what he came to call 'the unknowability objection'. Though I believe he thought it was plainly sound, I don't quite feel the force of it. I will explain it and my misgivings, and try to diagnose what the heart of my disagreement with him on this point was. If my analysis is right, we might get some insight into the work done by some general themes in legal theory in Smith's deeply illuminating work on private law doctrine.

I. The Unknowability Objection

Smith articulated the unknowability objection three times. The first was in an article, 'Duties, Liabilities, and Damages'.[1] There it was cast in support of a general thesis about damages for civil wrongs. The second and third were in his final book, *Rights, Wrongs, and Injustices*.[2] There Smith raised the unknowability objection first in support of a claim concerning compensatory damages in tort and contract, and then again in a later chapter in defence of a claim about restitution for unjust enrichment. The main thesis in these passages is the same, and there are shared considerations. The key supporting arguments in 'Duties, Liabilities, and Damages' and *Rights, Wrongs, and Injustices*, however, are different. I do not know whether Smith regarded *Rights, Wrongs, and Injustices*, on this point, to reflect his more considered view. In either case, the arguments are consistent and, I will suggest, expressive of the same general jurisprudential orientation. So I will treat them as collectively comprising one body of argument.

* I ran some of the ideas of this chapter by my colleagues in the Department of Philosophy at Western University in an informal series we run called 'Philosophical Briefings'. I would like to thank them, and David Benatar who was visiting Western at the time, for their many helpful questions and suggestions. Thanks very much, as well, to John Goldberg and Fred Wilmot-Smith for their many insightful comments on an earlier written draft.

[1] SA Smith, 'Duties, Liabilities, and Damages' (2012) 125 *Harvard Law Review* 1727.

[2] SA Smith, *Rights, Wrongs, and Injustices* (Oxford, Oxford University Press, 2019).

The collective core claim is this: there is neither a substantive duty to pay compensation for civil wrongs nor a substantive duty to pay restitution for unjust enrichment, because in each case the defendant cannot know in advance of a court order exactly what they owe. (If there were a duty, it would arise at the moment of the commission of the civil wrong or receipt of the enrichment.) A 'duty' whose content is unknowable in this way is not properly speaking a duty at all. In each case the defendant, rather than being under a duty to pay damages, is better understood as being subject to a liability to do so.

A 'duty' whose content is unknowable in this way is not properly speaking a duty at all because – and this is the heart of the argument – such a duty, Smith argues, would be incapable of guiding behaviour. Bearing this capacity is in the very nature of duties and rules. But the point is not *quite* merely analytic: 'The existence of an impossible-to-perform legal duty is not a logical impossibility. It is, however, highly unlikely … [and] should be accepted on only the clearest evidence.'[3] (And Smith does not find such evidence.) The claim instead is substantive: an impossible-to-perform legal duty, Smith argues, would be at odds with (i) the maxim that 'ought' implies 'can' (the argument in 'Duties, Liabilities, and Damages') and (ii) the rule of law (the argument in *Rights, Wrongs, and Injustices*). I will treat each argument in turn. But first, a few thoughts on a general proposition implicit in Smith's argument.

II. An Implicit Proposition

Implicit in Smith's argument is something like the proposition that you can be under a duty to *x* only if you know what it requires of you, that is, what you must do to discharge it. I will call this *the implicit proposition*. Reflecting on the implicit proposition for a moment or two will help set up our consideration of Smith's explicit arguments.

First: if knowing what a duty requires of you means knowing in advance what physical actions one must perform or refrain from performing, or what event or state of affairs in the external world one must undertake to bring about or realise, then the implicit proposition is arguably false. It is arguably false because it is arguably overbroad. What I have in mind, as a counterexample, are what Kant calls imperfect duties.[4] A good example is the duty of beneficence. It is, I think, reasonably well accepted that part of ordinary (and not just Kantian) morality is that we have a duty to undertake to help others in need, and that one's motive in discharging this duty matters from the moral point of view. It would be good if I gave to charity, whatever my motive. But it would be better, and I would more fully discharge the duty of beneficence, if I gave to charity because morality requires it, than if I did so, say, to impress someone. On Kant's view, as an imperfect duty, what the duty of beneficence requires is that one adopt an end, namely, the promotion of the well-being of others. This is, in part, a kind of mental

[3] Smith (n 1) 1744.

[4] Here I draw on the account Kant develops in the *Doctrine of Virtue*, the second half of the *Metaphysics of Morals*. See M Gregor (ed and tr), *Kant: Practical Philosophy* (Cambridge, Cambridge University Press, 1996) 512–40, 571–73.

act, but importantly it is not just that. It is not enough that I hope that others do well. In Kant's language, that is wishing, not willing. I will have made others' well-being an end only if I in fact undertake to promote it and do so because morality requires it. But, and here is the crucial point, necessarily I have discretion in how to discharge the duty. It is up to me, for example, whether I give my time or my money and, within limits,[5] how much I give. What I must do, if by doing we mean acting in the physical world, cannot be specified in advance.[6]

There is an obvious response to the claim that imperfect duties are a counterexample to the implicit proposition: they are moral and not legal duties (duties of virtue rather than right, in Kant's terms). Indeed, this is necessarily so. If a sanction were attached to discharging the duty of beneficence, and I acted on it, I would fail to properly discharge the duty because my motive would be the amoral one of avoiding the sanction. Though, as we shall see in section III, Smith draws a particular link between moral and legal duties, his concern in the end is with the law, so perhaps we should set aside imperfect duties of virtue.

Arguably, however, there are plainly legal duties that share some of the properties of the duty of beneficence that makes it a counterexample to the implicit proposition. Consider, for example, the duties imposed on a lifeguard.[7] We cannot specify in advance whom, if anyone, she will have to help at a given moment or on a given day, nor exactly what she will need to do. She will have been trained to take particular steps in particular circumstances – unconscious victims need to be treated differently from conscious ones, for example – but presumably in many emergencies, what is required of her is that she use her skills as her best judgement directs her.

Now these duties, too, are exceptional in certain ways. They are positive and tied to a role or office requiring qualification and licensing. Perhaps this explains their being an exception to the implicit proposition. Consider, however, the duty of care in negligence. It is not exceptional in these ways, but is no less indeterminate and discretionary. And it is as entrenched a private law duty as any. Is it a counterexample to the implicit proposition?

No, says Smith, and seeing why this is so is key to understanding his argument. Drawing the contrast with the (putative) duty to pay restitution for unjust enrichment, Smith argues:

> Even if it can be difficult to determine what is required to take 'reasonable care not to injure another', the relevant facts are available to those bound by this duty. A substantive duty to make restitution, if it existed, would be different.[8]

[5] A pittance will not do. On the other hand, I ought not to give so much that I make myself dependent on the beneficence of others.

[6] John Goldberg pointed out to me that some conventions fix some duties of beneficence to a degree that makes them relatively precisely action-guiding. Consider, for example, tithing. Fair enough, though it seems to me that the more precise the specification, the more perfect the duty becomes; the more, to take this example, the tithe is akin to a tax.

[7] I owe this example to David Benatar.

[8] Smith (n 2) 244.

It would be different because significant facts are unknowable (or very likely unknown) as they are, as Smith puts it, in the plaintiff's hands. Consider, for example, the receipt of a mistaken payment.

> Suppose that you transfer money into my bank account by mistake. And suppose further I happen to be viewing my account online at that moment, so that I am instantly aware of the transfer … Even in these circumstances, I cannot be certain that I am under a duty to return the money to you until I know two additional things: first, I need to know that it was you who made the payment; and, second, I need to know that you made the payment because of a mistake.[9]

Likewise, in the case of a wrong,

> [t]he extent of a victim's losses depends on the victim's income, business prospects, leisure activities, medical expenses, pain and suffering, insurance, pre-existing medical conditions, living arrangements, life expectancy, and so forth. Even a simple claim for the value of goods that were destroyed, damaged, or lost, depends on the goods' characteristics and condition.[10]

Why does the fact that in each case there are facts in the plaintiff's hands bear such significant weight? Though he does not draw this line explicitly, I think we can fairly sort the reasons Smith gives into two groups. The first are epistemic. Because these facts are in the plaintiff's hands, they are especially inaccessible to the defendant. That is not just because, at first, only the plaintiff knows them; it is also because the plaintiff will likely not be quick to share them with the defendant, at least in some cases. '[M]any victims,' Smith notes, 'understandably want nothing further to do with those who have injured them.'[11]

The other group of reasons are normative or, perhaps we could say, juridical. First, not only might you be unwilling to share relevant facts with me; I usually also have no right that you do so. Second, even if you offered them up, what if we disagreed? Suppose I thought you inflated your income and so losses, or misrepresented your motive for transferring payment to me (say, you intended it as a gift you now regret giving). Neither of us would be bound to defer to the other.

Let us pause for a moment to review before going on. As well as concluding that we should stick here with legal duties, there are two main conceptual lessons to take from this consideration of what I have called the 'implicit proposition', two things to bear in mind as we turn to consider Smith's main arguments in defence of the unknowability objection. First, knowability is a matter of degree. To make a philosophers' argument, even the duty to pay someone a specific sum of money on a particular date by a particular method does not spell out each physical action one must take. Even 'you must pay $25 via electronic transfer by midnight on the first of April' is not the finest-grained level of description available. The question is what level of generality is tolerable. As we have seen, on Smith's account – and to make the point in a more serious way – though the duty of care is to a degree indeterminate, and how one discharges it is to a degree a matter of discretion, it is tolerably so. Second, an essential feature of what makes the unknowability of what a least some duties require intolerable is their being in the hands of another, with the epistemic and juridical barriers that imposes.

[9] ibid 243–44.
[10] ibid 197.
[11] ibid 198.

III. 'Ought' Implies 'Can'

Smith justifies enlisting the maxim that 'ought' implies 'can' – I will call this simply 'the maxim' – in support of the unknowability objection in a complex argument. We do not need to engage with all of it here, but I will start by reproducing it in full, because it is a bit tricky to disentangle the claims that, I will argue, are illuminative of the case Smith makes for the unknowability objection. I will number the steps of the argument, to help keep track:

> [1] The existence of an impossible-to-perform legal duty is not a logical impossibility. [2] It is, however, highly unlikely. [3] Legal duties are meant to express moral duties – [4] that is why they are called 'duties' – and [5] in morality 'ought' generally implies 'can.' [6] The suggestion that the law recognizes a legal duty to do something that individuals cannot reasonably be expected to do should be accepted on only the clearest evidence. [7] The prepayment rule shows that in the case of an alleged duty to pay damages, the evidence points in the opposite direction.[12]

The prepayment rule is the rule that, in Smith's formulation, 'payment of damages prior to litigation is no defence to a claim for damages',[13] except in cases in which payment is accepted as part of a settlement. Smith's reasoning is that if there were a substantive duty to pay damages for a wrong, it would arise at the moment of the commission of the wrong, and so surely if I wronged you and set it right with a payment, I would discharge the duty. But then why would I still be liable to pay damages? The question contains the answer: what the wrong gives rise to is a liability to be subject to an order to pay damages, not a duty to do so. Tying this all together, then, the argument goes something like this: the law inherits from morality a commitment to the maxim; this commitment takes the form of a presumption in its favour, rebuttable only with clear evidence that the positive law defeats it; so far as the law of damages goes, the evidence points otherwise; therefore the positive law of damages is committed to the maxim. This commitment expresses itself interpretively: it supports the claim that, on the best reconstruction, civil wrongs and unjust enrichments give rise to liabilities rather than duties.

Now, a bit of pruning. To start, I propose setting aside, for the rest of this chapter, Smith's claim that the law inherits its commitment to the maxim from morality and morality's commitment to the maxim, that is, steps [3]–[5]. I am not sure what is meant by the claim that legal duties are meant to express moral duties, and I see no reason to hold that the fact that legal duties are called 'duties' indicates any particular link between morality and law. More importantly, my main question here is whether Smith is right that accepting the maxim entails accepting the unknowability objection. So I think we can in this chapter avoid engaging the difficult questions to which the claims in [3] and [4] are answers, and grant that the law is committed to the maxim, without relying on any particular justification for the claim that it is so committed.

To help isolate the question on which I want to focus in this section, I will also set aside, though just for now, two further parts of the argument. I will suggest another way

[12] Smith (n 1) 1744.
[13] ibid 1741.

to interpret the message sent by the prepayment rule in section IV, but for now let us grant that Smith has reckoned the weight of the evidence supplied by the prepayment rule correctly, and so allow [7]. And I will set aside for now, but return to in section VI, the idea contained in [1], [2] and [6], that the law's commitment to the maxim has the particular status of an interpretive presumption rebuttable by sufficiently clear counter-evidence supplied by positive law. I will enlist this in support of a hypothesis that Smith's defence of the unknowability objection relies on a certain orientation to some questions of general jurisprudence.

So: does the maxim support the unknowability objection? There is a reasonable sense in which I cannot discharge a duty *x* if I do not know what it would take to do so. Does it follow that the unknowabilities that Smith argues burden the (purported) duties to pay compensation for civil wrongs and restitution for unjust enrichment show that they are not, in fact, duties?

I don't think so. The starting point to seeing why is to note that often incapacities do not defeat duties. Sometimes they serve to determine what a duty requires of particular persons or groups of persons in particular circumstances. The acuity of my eyesight and, in a different way, my expertise, for example, can shape what the duty of care asks of me in particular circumstances, as can the limitations of both.[14] Second, sometimes incapacities ground excuses. That I could not conform my actions to the requirements of the law – because, say, I was having a seizure or because I had been threatened – does not show that I was not subject to a duty to do so. Instead, it excuses my failure to do so. Of course, at some point, incapacities do go so far as to defeat duties. I am probably not in breach of any duty if I do not attempt to rescue a drowning person because I do not know how to swim. But we cannot get from the mere fact of someone's being unable to do what a duty asks that they are not subject to it, or that it is not a duty properly speaking.

My suggestion is this: just as incapacities have this qualifying rather than defeating role in these settings, we can likewise see the unknowability to which Smith has drawn attention as serving to shape rather than defeat the duties to compensate for civil wrongs and make restitution for unjust enrichment. Recall that the telling unknowables on his account are those that arise because some facts are in the hands of the plaintiff. And recall, as well, that there are two relevant properties of these unknowables, one epistemic and the other juridical. My idea is that each has its own implication. It follows from the fact that there will be things that the defendant almost certainly cannot know before they are determined by a court that she is excused from paying pending their judicial determination. And it follows from the fact that the plaintiff is entitled to have these issues settled through judicial proceedings – not electing, that is, to settle out of court – that the defendant's duty to pay damages expresses itself in a duty to accept the outcome of those proceedings.

Or so I want to suggest. I will develop the second ideas more in section IV, where we have a look at Smith's second defence of the unknowability objection.

[14] The incapacities in these examples are both different from one another and each from the kind at issue in the unknowability objection. I start with them because they are, I think, familiar and help introduce the general point about incapacity and duty I want to introduce.

IV. The Rule of Law

'A rule that imposed substantive duties to pay damages,' Smith argues, 'could not fulfil the most basic role of legal rules – and the most basic requirement of the rule of law – namely, to guide behaviour.'[15] There are undeniable truths in this claim. It is true, for reasons that Smith has outlined, that I cannot know exactly what a duty to pay damages would require of me prior to settlement or the outcome of litigation. And it is true that a law that, for whatever reason (its obscurity, its retroactivity, its secrecy) could not guide those subject to it, would, for that reason, fail to realise an ideal of the rule of law. But I do not think the rule of law supports the unknowability objection, or that respect for the rule of law requires us to reject the view that remedial duties, properly speaking, issue from civil wrongs and unjust enrichments. That is because I think duties do not have to issue self-executing directives to play a role in the realsation of the rule of law. And while it is among the desiderata of the ideal of the rule of law that legal rules be action-guiding, I am not sure that is its most basic requirement. Or, in any case, to consider Smith's claim we need to start by seeing where in the bigger rule-of-law picture this requirement fits.[16]

It will be helpful, I think, to begin by asking what the basis of our commitment to the rule of law is. I say 'our' commitment to refer to the place the ideal of the rule of law occupies in at least broadly liberal democratic legal orders. This is not to say that illiberal undemocratic orders might not respect at least some of what are generally understood to be requirements of the rule of law, but the interpretation of those requirements is, I think, guided by what justifies their adoption and, more basically, what justifies a polity's commitment to the ideal of the rule of law. I want to suggest that in a liberal democratic order, it is an idea at the heart of liberal democracy itself: our commitment to recognising our standing among one another as equals.

Though, so cast, the rule of law is an early modern ideal, we can find the idea that it issues from a commitment to equality at least as far back as Aristotle. In a discussion of democracy in *Politics*, Aristotle considers the democrats' idea that, among equals,

> everyone should be ruled as well as rule, and therefore … all should have their turn. We thus arrive at law; for an order of succession implies law. And the rule of law, it is argued, is preferable to that of any individual.[17]

It is not clear that Aristotle himself, in the end, accepts that the rule of law is always preferable to that of any individual. And he thinks that in holding that each should take a turn ruling, democrats make a mistake, namely, wrongly thinking that persons equal in one respect (entitlement to citizenship) are therefore equal in all (including fitness to govern). But I believe that he thinks it is correct that, among persons who regard

[15] Smith (n 2) 199.

[16] The account I offer of the rule of law here is quite sketchy. I develop some of the ideas in a bit more detail elsewhere. See D Klimchuk, 'Equity and the Rule of Law' in L Austin and D Klimchuk (eds), *Private Law and the Rule of Law* (Oxford, Oxford University Press, 2014) 247; and D Klimchuk, 'State Estoppel' (2020) 39 *Law and Philosophy* 297.

[17] Aristotle, *Politics*, tr B Jowett, in *The Complete Works of Aristotle*, vol II, ed J Barnes (Princeton, NJ, Princeton University Press, 1984) 2042 (3.16, 1287a15–20).

themselves as equals, authority to govern issues from the rule according to which those in authority have taken their place (or simply their turn, as the radical democrats would have it).

We can think of the rule of law, so understood, as answering a puzzle posed by equality to political authority: if each of us is one another's equal, why should anyone have the right to make laws, settle disputes, execute verdicts or, generally, subject another to coercion? The answer cannot be because of the person they happen to be, the child of the parents they happen to have. It can only because they occupy offices constituted by a legal order to which all are subject. This casts the rule of law in the context of the vertical, state–citizen relationship of public law. But the same basic consideration expresses itself likewise in private law. Among equals, one can compel another (to pay damages, to move a fence, to reinstate one's employment, etc) only through public institutions of law to which are all subject.

Now, how do we get from this to the idea – which, again, I agree is central to the rule of law, if not its most basic requirement – that the ideal of the rule of law requires that the rules to which persons are subject be able to guide them? The link is this: I will be able to understand myself as indeed subject to the law upheld by those who occupy the offices it constitutes rather than to those persons (or to their wills, as it is sometimes said) only if their actions can be justified in terms of laws that are in some sense available to all *and* that can explain, at least roughly, why things turned out as they did – why I am now subject to this punishment, or injunction, or order to pay damages. At the limit of the ideal, in this respect, the rule of law suggests that persons are subject to a government of laws and not of persons (as it is sometimes cast) if they are capable of governing themselves by the law. Let us call this the ideal of self-governance. From it follows the familiar list of rule-of-law desiderata: laws must be publicly accessible, intelligible, apply prospectively, not be rife with contradictions and (crucial here) not demand the impossible.

This last step might just seem to make Smith's point. To see why it does not, we need to get the bigger picture I have drawn back into focus. We just saw that in a legal order that respects the rule of law, one can compel another (to, say, pay damages) only through public institutions of law to which are all subject. There is arguably a tension between this and the ideal of self-governance. The tension can be understood to reveal a genuine contradiction only if you think the ideal of self-governance is realised only by laws understood to issue precise self-executing directives. But not only is there no reason to think that: taking the rule of law seriously, I want to suggest, rules it out.

While the rule of law is not a buffet of ideas from which one can help oneself as one pleases, it is a set of ideas that suggest institutional arrangements that can be worked out in more than one way. What guides the working out is the anchor of the ideal in our commitment to take seriously our standing as equals. That means interpreting the consequences of that commitment in a way that tries to respect them all, even when they seem, in some settings, to pull in different directions.

With this in mind, I would like to suggest that Smith's rule-of-law argument for the unknowability objection miscasts what the ideal of self-governance requires by implying that it would be realised by a duty to pay damages for civil wrongs or unjust enrichment only if that duty could be discharged in full, in a way that would satisfy the plaintiff's claim, moments after it arose. One might think this only if one treated the ideal in isolation from the rest of the rule-of-law picture. Bringing that bigger picture into focus reminds us that respect for the rule of law also requires parties to a private dispute to accept that the authoritative calculation of damages owed awaits judicial determination.[18] This means that the duty to pay damages for civil wrongs and unjust enrichments *does* guide action.[19] As I suggested at the conclusion of section III, the defendant's duty to pay damages expresses itself in a duty to acknowledge the legitimacy of the proceedings[20] that, for general rule-of-law reasons and for the particular reasons to which Smith has drawn attention, are the only means through which the quantum of damages owed can be settled. This justifies the prepayment rule. And it tells the defendant they must now submit to these proceedings and honour their outcome.[21]

The duty to pay damages respects the rule of law, I suggest, in playing this formal or procedural role. But that is not its only place in the larger rule-of-law picture. It plays a correlative substantive role as well. Recall that I argued that we will be able to understand ourselves as governed by law only if the outcomes of legal proceedings can be justified in terms of laws that are in some sense available to all *and* that can explain, at least roughly, why things turned out as they did. This directs us to a second rule-of-law-realising role played by the duty to pay damages for civil wrongs and unjust enrichment: it justifies the court's order that the defendant pay the plaintiff the amount it has determined is owed. In short, it explains to the defendant *why* it was owed.

V. Smith's Likely Reply

Smith's answer to my argument, I think, would be that I have in the end just described liabilities, in each of the two roles I have suggested the duty to pay damages can be understood to play. Let me consider each in turn.

Smith considered as a possible reply to the unknowability objection the idea that the duty to pay damages is an inchoate duty. On this view, 'the duty to pay damages exists "in principle" from the moment of injury, but the duty is not crystallized – and so not in force – until a court has specified its content'.[22] According to this approach, the prepayment rule is just a response to a practical difficulty. Would that it were possible to determine the precise amount owed before trial; the defendant would be subject to a duty to pay it then. But it is not possible, so they have to await the outcome of the legal proceedings.

The problem with this response, Smith argues, is that

> it is not clear that an inchoate substantive duty is a duty at all. Duties should be able to guide those subject to them. By definition, inchoate duties cannot provide guidance. A substantive

[18] Unless, of course, they both agree to settle privately. Please think of this qualification applying throughout my argument.

[19] As Wilmot-Smith also argues in ch 20 of this volume.

[20] That is, the particular proceedings. It explains to this defendant why they are answerable in court to that plaintiff. The particular breached duty does not ground the more general duty to acknowledge and submit to the legal order; what explains that is the core question of political philosophy. Thanks to John Goldberg for showing me I needed to sharpen this point.

[21] And perhaps also to not in the meantime act in a way that would render those proceedings practically pointless by, say, divesting themselves of their assets or otherwise making them inaccessible to the plaintiff.

[22] Smith (n 2) 199.

> duty that is inchoate until confirmed by a court seems indistinguishable from a duty that is simply created by a court.[23]

And so, really, the claim that the duty to pay damages is an inchoate duty just amounts to the claim that it is a liability.

Now, the view I defended above is not that the duty to pay damages is inchoate, at least not as Smith characterises that idea. On my view, the duty *is* in force throughout. It just expresses itself, at first, as a duty to submit to the proceedings through which the quantum owed is determined. Rather than accommodate a practical problem, the prepayment rule respects a normative feature of the circumstances in which the defendant finds themselves. My hunch is that Smith might reply that this is a distinction without a difference: that a duty to submit to the proceedings through which the quantum owed is determined is *just* a liability to pay the quantum owed once determined.

I am not sure that is right. To see why, let us consider Smith's reply to the idea that the duty to pay damages serves to justify the order to pay damages. In this case, we do not have to speculate as to what Smith would say. Immediately after the claim I quoted at the beginning of section IV:

> A rule that imposed substantive duties to pay damages could not fulfil the most basic role of legal rules – and the most basic requirement of the rule of law –namely, to guide behaviour.

Smith continues (and I will number the claims):

> [1] The only practical role that such a rule could fulfil would be to provide a basis for awarding damages once a court had determined what the duty required. [2] But if that is all that a duty-imposing rule is doing, it is actually a liability-imposing rule.[24]

I must admit that I do not see the move from [1] to [2]. Here is how Smith explains the contrast between duties and liabilities:

> Duties describe things that we must do; liabilities describe things that may be done to us. To say that we have legal duties to do X means that, from the law's perspective, we must do X. In contrast, to say that we have liabilities to X, means that X may be done or imposed on us by another person or institution.[25]

However, as justifying the order to the defendant to pay the determined sum of damages to the plaintiff, the duty to pay damages does not simply put the defendant on notice that they will be subject to that order, nor even merely make them normatively vulnerable to being so subject. It also answers the defendant's question 'Why must I pay?' In short, it justifies the remedy; it does not merely prepare the defendant for being ordered to pay it. Similarly, in directing the defendant to submit to the legal proceedings through which the precise quantum of their debt to the plaintiff will be determined, the duty to pay damages does not *just* put the defendant on notice that they will have to pay some as-yet-undetermined sum to the plaintiff. It also, in requiring the defendant to submit to a procedure that respects the equality of the parties to the dispute, legitimates the order to pay the sum once thereby determined.

[23] ibid.
[24] ibid.
[25] ibid 192.

VI. The Even Bigger Picture

At the heart of much of the imagined exchange between Smith and me that I have just charted is a disagreement about how to think about the rule of law. Stepping further back, there may even be something more basic at issue here. There is, I think, a kind of positivism implicit in Smith's arguments. This reveals itself in at least three places. The first is his claim that the law could in fact impose an impossible-to-perform legal duty, notwithstanding that he argues that such a 'duty' would not be a duty at all. This nearly says that the positive law can, by fiat, make the impossible actual, an idea that seems to be staked in accepting a rather stark version of the separation thesis. The second is in Smith's quite *a*moral characterisation not only of liabilities, but even of duties, again: '[t]o say that we have legal duties to do X means that, from the law's perspective, we must do X'. And finally, most deeply though implicitly, there is I think something positivist about Smith's claim that not just legal rules that uphold or impose duties have a point, but also that duties themselves do. That makes sense if duties are created by someone: we can then ask what they hoped to achieve. But that is to say that duties, in some sense, are posited.

Putting my claim this way suggests that I am accusing Smith of holding a set of views that I believe he would have been happy to endorse. It is well beyond the scope of this chapter for me to explain my misgivings about them. I am pretty sure Steve would not have been persuaded by my arguments, or by my objections to the unknowability objection. I am not sure what his replies would have been. I do know they would have been surprising, challenging and deep, as is the body of work we are so fortunate he left us with.

20

Must We Know What We Owe?

FREDERICK WILMOT-SMITH*

I. Hostage Rescue

The path to a doctorate at the University of Oxford has a hurdle, just before the final submission, known as 'confirmation of status'. My confirmation was conducted by John Gardner and Robert Stevens. It was as bracing as you might imagine. When I came to write up, I clung to chance remarks my examiners had thrown in during their merry evisceration. And I kept in mind, in particular, John's statement that I had a few too many 'hostages to fortune'.

John examined my doctorate with Steve Smith. It was a calmer affair. Later, and after a few drinks, I spoke to Steve about the process. He said that my thesis was a little frustrating (sc. boring) since I had refused to 'stick [my] neck out' on points of controversy. I told him of John's comment. 'Ah, well,' he said, 'you'd shot all the hostages.'

This was more than a quick-witted quip. Academic work can be inspirational when there are hostages to fortune – unguarded claims to which the author is deeply committed – left for future scholars to protect or to liberate. In this chapter I consider one of Smith's, included as part of his objections to remedial duties. His worry, I claim, was misplaced; the hostage should be freed.

II. Duties and Liabilities

A. On Duties

A duty to ϕ is, on Smith's account, composed of two features. It provides a reason for the duty-bearer to ϕ and a second-order or 'exclusionary' reason for the duty-bearer not to act on any of the reasons they have not to ϕ.[1] The 'most basic role' of legal duties is,

* I am grateful to John Goldberg and Robert Stevens for their comments on a draft.

[1] SA Smith, 'Duties to Try and Duties to Succeed' in A Dyson, J Goudkamp and F Wilmot-Smith (eds), *Defences in Tort* (Oxford, Hart Publishing, 2015) 65, 69–70.

Smith tells us, 'to guide behaviour'.[2] This means that 'Duties should be able to guide those subject to them.'[3] It is worth dwelling on this last formulation to highlight three points. Notice first that Smith does not say that legal norms must guide behaviour (or guide it well) for the norms to count as legal duties. A retrospective legal duty – which, by definition, cannot provide guidance at the moment it primarily applies – remains a legal duty. Smith's claim is only that legal duties *should* do this. The requirement that duties be able to guide provides a standard to evaluate duties (whose existence is ascertained in some other way).

Second, the guidance ideal is complex and worthy of further study. Not all guidance that norms may offer is, from the standpoint of the rule of law, apt. Suppose that a legal system contains two laws governing speed limits: one enjoins drivers to drive above 40 miles per hour and another says they must not exceed 40 miles per hour.[4] Each law, taken alone, gives clear guidance. The conjunction of laws also offers guidance: do not drive on the motorways. But it seems odd to say that the system of laws is justified by the lights of the rule of law on that basis. We should say, then, that some norm guides, in the relevant sense, if its positing can (in some to-be-specified sense) contribute towards better conformation with its content by duty-bearers.

The third and final point is that Smith's formulation does not say that a duty is justified only if it can always provide precise guidance to all subjects in all respects. He says only that a duty should be able to guide. That statement can be interpreted in different ways – and there is some textual evidence that Smith himself *would* hold duties to higher standards.[5] But we need not interpret the injunction in that manner, and (I will argue) a very strict standard leaves no room for ordinary features of legal practice, such as the need for legal rulings to provide more precise guidance than the legal rules themselves offer.

B. On Liabilities

A legal liability is the correlative of a legal power, which is, in turn, an ability to change the existing legal position.[6] Thus, if *A* offers to sell his land to *B*, once the offer has been received, *B* 'has the power to impose [by "dropping a letter of acceptance in the box"] [an] … obligation *ex contractu* on *A* and himself', and the correlative 'liability of *A* will continue for a reasonable time unless, in the exercise of his power to do so, *A* previously extinguishes it'.[7]

[2] SA Smith, *Rights, Wrongs, and Injustices: The Structure of Remedial Law* (Oxford, Oxford University Press, 2019) 199.

[3] ibid. See, too, ibid 245.

[4] I adapt this example from A Ross, *Directives and Norms* (Abingdon, Routledge & Kegan Paul, 1968) 172, §36. Thanks to Giovanni Ratti for bringing the passage to my attention.

[5] See his claim, discussed in section V.B.ii, that 'it is sufficient, for [the unknowability objection], that there *could be circumstances* in which it is not possible for individuals bound by the alleged duty to know they are bound': Smith (n 2) 244 (emphasis added).

[6] WN Hohfeld, *Fundamental Legal Conceptions as Applied in Judicial Reasoning and Other Legal Essays*, ed Walter Wheeler Cook (New Haven, CT, Yale University Press, 1923) 60.

[7] ibid 55.

Legal liabilities therefore enjoin nothing – *B* is under no duty to accept the offer; they can let it lapse. This does not mean that a liability cannot provide guidance: someone subject to a legal liability might be led to flee the jurisdiction for that very reason. Yet this guidance connects to the liability only indirectly (just as the guidance not to drive on the motorway bears only an indirect relation to the contradictory duties): there is, in other words, nothing the law itself requires by placing an individual under a liability.

Many scholars think that a wrongdoer has a duty, following a wrong, to compensate for the losses owed.[8] The wrong also, it is often supposed, generates a power in the wronged party to institute a claim, asking the court's assistance in enforcing the underlying duty.[9] In a series of influential papers – with the canonical account in his last book – Smith argued that all this is muddled.[10] There is, he claimed, no legal duty to pay damages or make restitution of a mistaken payment; defendants are, instead, under a liability to be ordered by a court to pay damages or make restitution (and *only* that).

The Hohfeldian model of liabilities does not fit Smith's account easily.[11] Hohfeldian liabilities are canonically relations between two parties, where one has the power to change the legal position of the second simply by acting.[12] Yet Smith's 'liability' account of remedial claims is not like that. Individuals are, in his formulation, under liabilities to be ordered by courts to pay damages.[13] Since courts do not act of their own motion, Smith's *explanandum* has three parts – *A*, *B* and the court (which makes the ultimate order).

This is not a trivial issue: the important question is what (if anything) there is to say about the relationship between *A* and *B* unmediated by the court's role. *B* is under a liability to become subject to the court's process (contingent on *A*'s issuing a claim form) and the court has a contingent power, on issue of a claim, to make an order against *B*.[14] *A* holds a power to issue a claim and the court is under a liability to issue the claim form. But what relation holds between *A* and *B* alone? Smith might say that *A* has a

[8] A recent account is S Steel and R Stevens, 'The secondary legal duty to pay damages' (2020) 136 *LQR* 283. Ripstein and Swadling examine such arguments in chs 6 and 11 of this volume, respectively.

[9] See WN Hohfeld, 'Nature of Stockholders' Individual Liability for Corporation Debts' (1909) 9 *Columbia Law Review* 285, 293–94.

[10] The earliest clear account of this claim I know is B Zipursky, 'Civil Recourse, Not Corrective Justice' (2003) 91 *Georgetown Law Journal* 695, 718–21. Smith's key contributions are SA Smith, 'Why Courts Make Orders (and What this Tells Us About Damages)' (2011) 64 *Current Legal Problems* 51; SA Smith, 'Duties, Liabilities and Damages' (2012) 125 *Harvard Law Review* 1727; SA Smith, 'The Restatement of Liabilities in Restitution' in C Mitchell and W Swadling (eds), *The Restatement Third, Restitution and Unjust Enrichment: Comparative and Critical Essays* (Oxford, Hart Publishing, 2013); and SA Smith, 'A Duty to Make Restitution' (2013) 26 *Canadian Journal of Law and Jurisprudence* 157.

[11] Compare Smith (n 2) 75, 192, fn 26.

[12] AL Corbin, 'Legal Analysis and Terminology' (1919) 29 *Yale Law Journal* 163, 165.

[13] If individuals were liable to be placed under remedial duties, the repackaging of the duty as a liability would not make much of a difference: see SA Smith, 'Strict Duties and the Rule of Law' in LM Austin and D Klimchuk (eds), *Private Law and the Rule of Law* (Oxford, Oxford University Press, 2014) 189, fn 15.

[14] To ward off the concern that everyone is under this form of liability – since process can be started even if unjustified – a complete account would have to say something more about how the power features in a causal story leading to a *justified* order. Although I do not mean to minimise the explanatory burdens such an account faces, it is not my main concern here.

'cause of action' or 'action right' against *B*.[15] But this seems merely elliptical for a more complicated account of the powers and liabilities each party has or is under as against the court.[16] A test is: if all courts were abolished, what (if anything) would the law say *B* owed to *A* after a breach of duty (or receipt of an unjust enrichment)? So far as I can see, Smith's answer was: nothing.[17] This, as will become clear, is an important fact when trying to develop his unknowability objection.

III. The 'Unknowability Objection'

Smith raised numerous objections to the view that there is a duty to pay damages or make restitution following a wrong of an unjust enrichment.[18] Some focus closely on the positive law; I will not consider those. A theoretical argument – which, although said to be his 'main objection',[19] has received limited attention – is the 'unknowability objection'.[20]

Before considering that argument in more detail, a brief note on terminology. Smith's argument is formally raised to defend a doctrinal claim that the law does not contain remedial duties. But we can assess the theoretical argument without taking a view on the doctrine: if the argument is sound, and the law contains remedial duties, the argument is an objection *to* those duties. For ease of exposition – and, in particular, to avoid a distracting reference in every other sentence to a 'putative' duty – I will simply assume that the law does in fact contain strict duties (including remedial duties) and that Smith's argument is raised to criticise the law.

Here is how Smith presents his concern: 'if a substantive duty to pay damages existed, it would be an unknowable duty';[21] 'a substantive duty to make restitution would be unknowable'.[22] This means, Smith claims, that 'it would normally be impossible for wrongdoers to satisfy [a duty to pay damages] … because the duty's content could not be determined prior to a judicial decision'.[23]

Although helpful enough to start the inquiry, these statements are imprecise. They refer, in particular, to two distracting ideas that we should set to one side. The first is the reference to it being the *duty* that is unknowable. That is a little loose. Smith has no interest in ignorance of the law, or even, strictly, of legal norms in their particular application to individuals. Duties are 'unknowable', on the analysis he pursues, if and only to the extent that (in the manner examined below) the facts that constitute the duty are unknowable. So we should concentrate on that ignorance, not ignorance of

[15] Smith (n 2) 75, 80–82.

[16] See, eg, J Penner and K Quek, 'The Law's Remedial Norms' (2016) 29 *Singapore Academic Law Journal* 768, 781–86.

[17] It seems in principle open to Smith to say that if courts were abolished, the law should change; but whether that argument is open to him depends upon the structure of the unknowability objection.

[18] John Gardner finds 'at least five', and terms the objection I am considering the 'indeterminacy' objection: J Gardner, 'Damages Without Duty' (2019) 69 *University of Toronto Law Journal* 412, 413–14.

[19] Smith (n 2) 243.

[20] ibid 197–200 (compensation) and 243–45 (restitution).

[21] ibid 197.

[22] ibid 243.

[23] Smith, 'Duties, Liabilities and Damages' (n 10) 1743. See, too, Smith (n 2) 243 for a reference to the (im)possibility of compliance.

the duty itself. The second distraction is the reference to the possibility of compliance with the duty. The duty in question is difficult to comply with just in case its content is difficult to ascertain; once the content of the duty is known, there is no special difficulty of compliance.

These are true distractions rather than semantic quibbles because they both point to genuine but distinct problems one might have with a legal arrangement. As to the first, think of the objections one might make to a legal regime where the nature of one's duty is a function of a byzantine statutory regime, a regime impenetrable to all but the most brilliant lawyers. That duty might be unknowable, even when all the facts are known. As to the second, think of a duty that is strict in respect of compliance. This might be impossible for certain duty-bearers to meet, if (say) they lack the necessary capacities. These situations give rise to interesting and difficult concerns – but they are not Smith's concerns here, so we should set them to one side.

Thus clarified, we can focus on the key idea: ignorance of the facts. Smith distinguishes two types of facts of which the duty-bearer might be ignorant. The first are facts that part-constitute the existence of duty. For example, 'Vendors who sell defective goods may not know that their goods are defective. Similarly, manufacturers will often be unaware that their products have caused an injury.'[24] They will therefore be ignorant of breach and so of any remedial duty. Equally, the recipient of a mistaken payment might be ignorant of the fact of the payment or the fact of the mistake.[25] Such a person is ignorant of facts that part-constitute their remedial legal duty. The second type of facts are those that determine the scope of the duty. For example, a wrongdoer might be ignorant of 'the extent of the damage caused',[26] whether the victim was contributorily negligent or whether the victim has failed to mitigate their loss.

A duty-bearer might be ignorant of the facts because they have no relevant belief about them. If someone pays another money, and the payee is canoeing in the wilds of Canada, the payee may have no belief about their bank balance, and no means of learning any of the facts that constitute their duty. Yet what troubles Smith is that duty-bearers might find that the truth of their beliefs comes to depend upon the plaintiff's testimony, and he doubts that this can justifiably be relied upon. The root concern is not easy to isolate. It is hard to think it is really about knowledge: it is possible to acquire knowledge from another; and, anyway, the facts are what they are (with plaintiff testimony one way a defendant might acquire knowledge of them). The concern may instead be about power and our entitlement to public adjudication of disputes. Such concerns are – importantly, as revealed in section V – really concerns about legal ideals.

What, then, is the precise objection to the imposition of legal duties grounded on facts that are unknowable? Two types of objection are possible. The first asks how an individual's ignorance might make it the case that they have no moral duty to comply with the norm; the second (which Smith seemed to prefer) considers how the imposition of a duty in the teeth of individuals' ignorance might undermine systemic values (and, in particular, the rule of law). I start with the first.

[24] Smith (n 2) 197.
[25] Smith, 'A Duty to Make Restitution' (n 10) 174.
[26] Smith (n 2) 197.

IV. Moral Readings

A. Ought Implies Can

In early work, Smith invoked the moral maxim that 'ought implies can' ('OIC') to ground his unknowability objection.[27] Let me develop that thought, before saying why Smith was right to abandon it – there is no mention of OIC in his later analysis.

As generally understood, OIC holds that *A* ought to ϕ only if they are able to do so. The maxim is complex and deserves close attention.[28] For the purposes of Smith's unknowability objection, the important component of the maxim is 'can'.

Following most leading discussions, let us stipulate that 'can' concerns the ability of a particular individual, such that an agent is 'able' to ϕ only if they are physically and psychologically able to do so and have the relevant opportunity. If an individual is unable, in that sense, to ϕ, it is (OIC claims) not the case that the agent ought to ϕ. If it is not the case that the agent ought to ϕ (either independently of there being a legal duty to ϕ, or as a consequence of the imposition of a legal duty), there is a good argument that it is wrong for the law to make it the case that they have a legal duty to do so.[29] The OIC analysis of the unknowability objection holds, therefore, that duty-bearers are unable to satisfy the duties in question because of their ignorance of the facts constituting and shaping their duties; and that, therefore, the law should not place them under those duties.

There are two problems with this analysis. First, it unhelpfully conflates cases where the duty-bearer knows what is required (but cannot do it) and those where the duty-bearer does not know what the content of the duty is. Cases of the latter kind are not best understood in terms of inability. To see the distinction, notice that Smith's concern is not with ignorance of *how* to perform an action – where it can seem plausible that ignorance vitiates ability.[30] Duty-bearers know how to pay money to claimants. They are ignorant, instead, of (at least some of) the facts that determine the precise content of their duty. If OIC is to be a fruitful maxim with which to develop the unknowability objection, the challenge is to formulate an account of 'can' that overcomes the obvious thought: that the wrongdoer is *able* to pay the sum of money owed; they just do not know what precise act to perform.[31]

The second problem with the OIC account to explain the unknowability objection is that it proves too much. Canonically, OIC is a maxim about moral duties or reasons. Consistency requires that if one relies upon OIC to defend the unknowability objection, one must hold that underlying moral duties evaporate at the same time

[27] Smith, 'Duties, Liabilities and Damages' (n 10) 1744.

[28] For helpful accounts, see PBM Vranas, 'I Ought, Therefore I Can' (2007) 136 *Philosophical Studies* 167; and A King, *What We Ought And What We Can* (Abingdon, Routledge, 2019).

[29] I consider such an argument, and its complexities, in F Wilmot-Smith, 'Law, "Ought" and "Can"' (2023) 133 *Ethics* 529.

[30] Vranas (n 28) 170. Compare, though, PBM Vranas, '"Ought" Implies "Can" but Does Not Imply "Must": An Asymmetry Between Becoming Infeasible and Becoming Overridden' (2018) 127 *Philosophical Review* 487, 505 and fn 37.

[31] Gardner (n 18) 416–17. Compare, however, F Howard-Snyder, 'The Rejection of Objective Consequentialism' (1997) 9 *Utilitas* 241, 242; Vranas, 'An Asymmetry' (n 30) 505–07.

as legal ones. Relying upon the maxim to ground the unknowability objection thus commits one to the view that a wrongdoer has no *moral* duty where the precise content of that duty is indeterminate because the wrongdoer lacks knowledge of the facts. For Smith, strictly, the wrongdoer owes the victim nothing as a matter of law because of the unknowability objection. But this is an unintuitive account of their moral position. A wrongdoer can owe corrective moral duties even when the precise content of those duties is unclear or vague.

From this I conclude that OIC is not a profitable maxim on which to construct the unknowability objection, and Smith was right to drop it. There is, however, a more promising line in the philosophical literature, which Smith did not consider. Although I do not think it ultimately fruitful, it may be helpful to set it out briefly, lest others are more tempted by the moral readings than I.

B. Objectivism, Subjectivism, Prospectivism

Smith's principal interest was how an agent's epistemic circumstance affects what duties they can legitimately be placed under. There is a substantial literature considering this question. In Elizabeth Anscombe's vivid example:

> Suppose … that someone leaves a baby on a doorstep in the winter … [Does] this mean that I am obliged to rescue the baby, and am guilty if I do not take the care that would result in my realising that it was there? This would be an absurdity; this is precisely the sort of situation in which my obligation is conditional on my realising the situation.[32]

If Anscombe knew the baby was there, she would have a duty to save it. But many will share Anscombe's view that the existence of an obligation (and even a reason?) to save the child depends upon her knowledge (or, at least, the possibility thereof) that the baby is on her doorstep.

Examples like these – usually in the form of more complicated examples involving miners and doctors[33] – now proliferate in the philosophical literature. Some argue that our obligations are invariant to our knowledge of the facts.[34] Others say, with Anscombe, that obligations depend (in various ways) on our beliefs about or knowledge of the facts.[35] An important line of analysis – which, to my knowledge, has never been pursued[36] – should consider how the puzzles of that literature should be applied

[32] GEM Anscombe, 'On Being in Good Faith' in M Geach and L Gormally (eds), *Faith in a Hard Ground: Essays on Religion, Philosophy and Ethics* (Exeter, Imprint Academic, 2008) 120, 130.

[33] Miners: D Parfit, 'What We Together Do' [1988] unpublished, 1–2. Parfit attributes the case to D Regan, *Utilitarianism and Co-Operation* (Oxford, Oxford University Press, 1980) 265. Doctors: F Jackson, 'Decision-Theoretic Consequentialism and the Nearest and Dearest Objection' (1991) 101 *Ethics* 461, 462–63.

[34] eg GE Moore, *Ethics* (Oxford, Oxford University Press, 1912) 80–82; J Jarvis Thomson, *The Realm of Rights* (Cambridge, MA, Harvard University Press, 1990) 229–34; PA Graham, 'In Defense of Objectivism About Moral Obligation' (2010) 121 *Ethics* 88.

[35] eg HA Prichard, 'Duty and Ignorance of Fact' in J MacAdam (ed), *Moral Writings* (Oxford, Oxford University Press, 2002) 88; Sir David Ross, *Foundations of Ethics* (Oxford, Oxford University Press, 1939) 146–47; Anscombe (n 32) 108–09; TM Scanlon, *Moral Dimensions: Permissibility, Meaning, Blame* (Cambridge, MA, Belknap Press, 2008) 47–52.

[36] See, however, *Estate of Short v Brookville Crossing*, 972 NE 2d 897 (Ind App 2012), discussed by J Goldberg and B Zipursky, 'A Precedent-Based Critique of Legal Positivism' in T Endicott, HD Kristjansson and S Lewis (eds), *Philosophical Foundations of Precedent* (Oxford, Oxford University Press, 2022) 296, 306.

to the law. It also seems a promising basis from which to build Smith's unknowability objection.

Although this kind of analysis avoids the first reason to reject OIC as the basis of the unknowability objection, the second reason is also on its face dispositive. If the unknowability objection is founded upon a moral maxim, the objection depends upon the claim that there is no moral duty to compensate for wrongs. Yet, once more, this is unintuitive: wrongdoers owe victims *something* in virtue of their wrongs, and that is so irrespective of their ignorance of facts such as the amount of loss incurred from the wrong.[37]

C. Conclusion on Moral Reading

Smith ought to have (and, I think, if pressed, would have) conceded that it was wrong to construct the unknowability objection from moral maxims.[38] Consider his claim that the recipient of a mistaken payment has a 'reason to return the money'; his objection, instead, was 'to elevating this reason to a legal duty'.[39] This accepts that there were (or could be) moral reasons binding the beneficiary or the wrongdoer; the concern was that distinctively legal considerations precluded their elevation to a legal duty. What kind of considerations?

V. Legal Ideals

A. The Ideal of Legality

The rule of law is, Joseph Raz once claimed, the ideal '(1) that people should be ruled by the law and obey it, and (2) that the law should be such that people will be able to be guided by it.'[40] That law should be capable of guiding its subjects was central to his account. Laws should be prospective, open and clear, he claims, because '[o]ne cannot be guided by a retroactive law';[41] '[s]tability is essential if people are to be guided by law in their long-term decisions';[42] and the judiciary must be independent, because 'it is futile to guide one's action on the basis of the law if when the matter comes to adjudication the courts will not apply the law and will act for some other reasons'.[43]

[37] John Goldberg has rightly pointed out to me that '*something*' here may be quite limited, such as an apology, and that one does not need to know how best to apologise to be able *to* apologise. True enough. Even this, though, shows that Smith's case is put too high.

[38] In one of his last emails to me, in a discussion of the unknowability objection, Smith wrote that 'It is possible that my argument only applies to legal duties.'

[39] Smith, 'A Duty to Make Restitution' (n 10) 173.

[40] J Raz, 'The Rule of Law and its Virtue' in J Raz, *The Authority of Law: Essays on Law and Morality* (Oxford, Oxford University Press, 1979) 213. For his last word on the topic, see J Raz, 'The Law's Own Virtue' (2019) 39 *OJLS* 1.

[41] Raz, 'The Rule of Law and its Virtue' (n 40) 214.

[42] ibid 215.

[43] ibid 217.

This feature – that the law should be capable of guiding individuals – has featured prominently in many contemporary discussions of the rule of law.[44] Smith endorsed it.[45] And he presupposed that vast body of literature when he objected that an unknowable duty would 'be incapable of fulfilling the most basic role of legal rules – and the most basic requirement of the rule of law – namely, to guide behaviour'.[46]

Legality is a more fruitful avenue for analysis of Smith's objection than morality. That is because the objection can be developed without claims being held hostage to the right answers to debates in moral philosophy. Smith can, in particular, coherently claim that there should be no remedial duties because such duties violate the rule of law, without thereby committing himself to the implausible view that there are no remedial duties in morality. In what follows, I set out Smith's arguments for why remedial duties would violate the rule of law; finding them lacking, I argue that his own approach is objectionable for rule-of-law reasons.

B. Smith's Two Claims

Smith makes two separate claims that we should disambiguate.

i. *The Wrong Guidance?*

One line of argument he pursues is that remedial duties provide the wrong kind of guidance to their subjects. Thus he writes:

> If there is a duty to make restitution, then I should take whatever steps are necessary to ensure, as far as possible, that I comply with the duty, which means regularly checking my bank account, authorizing a third party to return mistaken payments, and so on. It is absurd to suppose that the law wants me to take such steps.[47]

He repeated that argument in his book.[48]

It is indeed absurd to suppose that the law wanted Smith to take those steps. The question is whether he was right that remedial duties enjoin their subjects to act in these ways. Smith claims that if we have to do whatever is necessary in order to comply with a duty, and the duty is conditional, we have to do whatever we can to know whether the conditions of the duty obtain. The answer therefore rests on the following claim: if one has a duty to ϕ if C, one also has a duty to ascertain whether it is the case that C. (The argument is then: since one has no duty to ascertain whether C obtains, it is not the case that the conditional duty exists.)

We should here distinguish reasons from duties. A reason is a fact that counts in favour of some act (or belief, etc). A duty is more stringent than a mere *pro tanto* reason.

[44] I discuss the requirement in more detail F Wilmot-Smith, 'Legality and Capacity' in H Psarras and S Steel (eds), *Private Law and Practical Reason: Essays on John Gardner's Private Law Theory* (Oxford, Oxford University Press, 2023).

[45] Smith (n 13) 198.

[46] Smith (n 2) 243.

[47] Smith, 'A Duty to Make Restitution' (n 10) 173.

[48] Smith (n 2) 243.

In Razian terms – which Smith would have endorsed – we can say that a duty is a reason which '(i) does not depend for its existence on one's goals at the time, and (ii) is also a reason not to act for certain conflicting reasons'.[49] A duty is, on this view, (i) a categorical reason; and (ii) protected (ie the same fact that counts in favour of some act also constitutes a reason not to act for countervailing reasons).

If I have a duty to ϕ, I may have a derivative duty to take various steps towards ϕing. This may involve a duty to ascertain facts that will allow me to maximise the value of ϕing (or to ascertain precisely which of various possible acts is best to perform). Consider a judge with a duty to decide a case: they have a duty to read the submissions, listen to the arguments and so on; those duties are derived from the practical duty. But such examples presuppose a duty, and the difficulty in Smith's case arises precisely when it is an open question whether the duty obtains. What then?

Recall Anscombe's example of the baby on the doorstep. The duty to rescue the infant was conditional upon knowledge: if there is a baby on the doorstep *and you know about it*, you have a duty to rescue the child. Anyone with a front door is under the generic conditional duty. But are we all under duties to do whatever it takes to ascertain whether a child is on our front doorstep? Surely not.

It is, however, implausible that we are permitted to insulate ourselves from any such facts. Conditional duties do give us reasons to ascertain whether the conditions of the duty have obtained. Yet the strength of such reasons will be context-sensitive. Absent anything to suggest the condition is triggered, for example, we need not investigate. (Have you checked your front doorstep for babies recently?) But if there is some suggestion that the condition has been met, the reason will be stronger. It will depend on the facts. If this is the right analysis, the wind goes out of Smith's dialectic sails. The reasons to investigate the facts will not be very strong and will be readily outweighed: our reasons to live autonomous lives, and to pursue the ends of an autonomous life, will mean we have no duty to engage in the neurotic means Smith envisages of ensuring compliance with some possible duty.

ii. No Guidance?

Smith's second and strongest claim is that remedial duties are 'incapable, even in theory, of guiding … behaviour'.[50] This claim is not easy to reconcile with the first argument, that remedial duties give improper guidance; for that reason, I consider it separately.

If it is impossible to know some fact, we cannot be guided by it. Thus if Smith is right that the facts that constitute our remedial duties are ones we cannot know (or even ones we 'cannot reasonably be expected to know'[51]), he must also be right that there is a rule-of-law objection to remedial duties. Let us therefore consider the two kinds of facts highlighted in section III. The first are those facts that part-constitute a duty. While it might be true that 'wrongdoers will often be unaware that they have

[49] J Gardner and T Macklem, 'Reasons' in J Coleman and S Shapiro (eds), *The Oxford Handbook of Jurisprudence and Philosophy of Law* (Oxford, Oxford University Press, 2004) 465. Raz developed this account in J Raz, *Practical Reason and Norms* (London, Hutchinson, 1975) ch 1.

[50] Smith (n 2) 243.

[51] ibid 197.

even committed a wrong'[52] – it is a matter for empirical speculation – it is not *always* true. Further, such facts are not impossible to know, at least as a general rule.

The second kind of facts are those that determine the scope of a remedial duty. For some of these, such as the extent of the damage caused, there is a fact of the matter – albeit that the fact might be very hard to ascertain. Perhaps Smith's best cases are those where there is no fact of the matter about what the duty requires, as is plausibly the case where there is a credible argument that certain consequential losses are too remote.[53] We should here accept Smith's basic point: it might be legally uncertain exactly what is required of a duty-bearer. This means that at least certain remedial duties are 'inchoate'.[54]

Does this mean the unknowability objection is right after all? I think not. Smith's analysis rests upon the view that it is a rule-of-law concern if duties do not specify the precise acts that would constitute compliance. And that is a mistake. To see this, consider a case where the payee receives a notification on their phone, stating that the funds were received and the payor's description of the payment as 'payment for plumbing work'. The payee then knows the fact of receipt and also would seem to know the reason for the payment. They know they should return the funds. This means that remedial duties can guide in some cases. In response to such cases, Smith seeks to confess and avoid. He writes that although such a person would know they have received money by mistake, this is not enough, because 'the unknowability objection is conceptual: it is sufficient, for this objection, that there could be circumstances in which it is not possible for individuals bound by the alleged duty to know they are bound'.[55]

I am not sure what he meant to claim by characterising the objection as 'conceptual'.[56] Perhaps he meant to claim that it is part of the concept of a legal norm that there are never any circumstances in which an individual bound by the norm cannot know they are bound. But that is surely not true. Even a 'moral impact' theory of law rules out only 'truly evil legal norms'.[57] And it is not 'truly evil' to have norms that might be unclear in their application in all circumstances.

More interesting is the claim that a norm objectionably and unanswerably violates the rule of law if there 'could be circumstances' where it cannot guide because the constitutive facts cannot be known. This does not fit the leading accounts of the rule of law, including the one Smith purports to endorse. Raz's claim was that 'the law should be such that *people* will be able to be guided by it'.[58] He does not say that *each person* must be capable of being guided by *each norm* at *every possible moment*. Smith seemed

[52] ibid.

[53] A simple example, which I owe to John Goldberg, is compensation for pain and suffering in a personal injury case. And another example is the availability of 'cost of cure' damages which, following *Ruxley Electronics v Forsyth* [1996] AC 344 (HL), are not available where the cost of cure is out of all proportion to the cure's value. I am grateful to Josh Getzler for the suggestion, though do not pursue it in detail because it gives rise to intricate puzzles around the best interpretation of that case and the cost-of-cure award.

[54] Smith, 'Duties, Liabilities and Damages' (n 10) 1728.

[55] Smith (n 2) 244.

[56] The language was carefully chosen: cf Smith, 'A Duty to Make Restitution' (n 10) 173.

[57] M Greenberg, 'The Moral Impact Theory of Law' (2014) 123 *Yale Law Journal* 1118, 1337.

[58] Raz, 'The Rule of Law and its Virtue' (n 40) 213 (emphasis added). See too MH Kramer, *Objectivity and the Rule of Law* (Cambridge, Cambridge University Press, 2007) 169.

to agree: recall his claim that 'Duties should be able to guide those subject to them.'[59] And was right to do so.[60] Very many legal duties, including primary legal duties, are often inchoate in the same way as remedial duties. Consider: the precise contractual performance required by a vague duty; whether some act will constitute 'assistance' of a breach of fiduciary duty; whether a restrictive covenant is enforceable. In all these cases, the legal standards and their application to the facts of a case are indeterminate and can only be fixed by a court; there will be no fact of the matter until such a determination is made. But this does not render the underlying duties deficient by the lights of the rule of law, much less conceptually incoherent.

To the extent, then, that the unknowability objection rests upon this conception of the rule of law, it rests on a mistake (and an inconsistency in Smith's own analysis). Once that mistake is cleared away, an obvious point can be made. One can be guided by a duty to ϕ even if one does not know the precise act required to constitute ϕing. Knowledge, for example, that one is under a duty to pay an unliquidated sum to a claimant guides us: to inquire of the claimant what damage was done, to assess their claim, to seek a settlement. By contrast, if the only legal consequence of a wrong is that the liabilities Smith anticipated arose, wrongdoers are given no direct legal guidance; the liability enjoins nothing. That is a feature of Smith's argument – but it, surely, is a bug by the standards of the rule of law.

VI. Conclusion

Smith believed that the unknowability objection was his most important against the duty view. For that reason alone, the claim deserves our attention. His claims are incautious and the objection does not succeed. But the underlying issue, ignorance of fact, is important, and its application to the duty to pay damages raises delicate and difficult issues.

Any complete analysis of these issues would have to distinguish between how knowledge – or the possibility of some actor's having knowledge – interacts with conditions of (i) duty; (ii) enforceability; and (iii) blame. It should also consider how any system that aspires to create duties of reciprocal freedom can condition duties upon knowledge (since whether an agent has knowledge is classically a private and unilateral matter).

Steve was unique in noticing that this is an issue worthy of closer investigation. Bravo – and *vale*.

[59] Smith (n 2) 199.

[60] For discussion on this point and a contrast with Raz's account of reasons, see Wilmot-Smith (n 44) 86.

21

The Cough Drops on Loyalty

LIONEL SMITH*

I. Introduction

I begin with a word about the title of my chapter, or two words perhaps. The first is that one day at McGill, our then-colleague Rod Macdonald came upon Steve Smith and me, deep in debate about one thing or another. 'Ah,' he said, 'the cough drops!' This allusion was obscure to me, but it turns out that for much of the twentieth century, 'Smith Brothers' cough drops were the leading brand in the United States.[1] The apparently iconic logo of the two bearded brothers has been revived.[2] So that is the cough drops; what about loyalty? In 2003, I published an article entitled 'The Motive, Not the Deed'.[3] The title was borrowed from a passage in a play by WB Yeats, and I chose it because the principal argument of the text was that it is a distinctive feature of fiduciary law that significant legal consequences are attached to the motive with which a fiduciary power-holder acts. Those who know Steve's mischievous nature will not be surprised to learn that when he turned to this field and concluded that motive is *not* relevant to it, he published his article under the title 'The Deed, Not the Motive'.[4]

When the present volume was being planned, Steve expressed the wish that contributors would engage with arguments that he had made. In this spirit, I will aim to show that the law does routinely pay attention to motive in this field, and that it needs to do so for reasons that are particular to the law of fiduciary relationships and to similar relationships in civil law and public law.[5] I will lean heavily on Steve's well-known

* I thank John Goldberg for insightful comments on an earlier draft.

[1] A Wikipedia page tells the story of the eventual sale of the business, and of more recent attempts to re-establish it: see at https://en.wikipedia.org/wiki/Smith_Brothers.

[2] The drops are currently available for direct sale at https://smithbrothers.co.

[3] L Smith, 'The Motive, Not the Deed' in J Getzler (ed), *Rationalizing Property, Equity and Trusts: Essays in Honour of Edward Burn* (London, LexisNexis Butterworths, 2003) 53; repr Oxford University Press (2005) and also available on SSRN, https://ssrn.com/abstract=382341.

[4] SA Smith, 'The Deed, Not the Motive: Fiduciary Law Without Loyalty' in PB Miller and AS Gold (eds), *Contract, Status and Fiduciary Law* (Oxford, Oxford University Press, 2016) 213.

[5] In this chapter I will hereafter generally use 'fiduciary relationships' to refer to situations, whether in private or public law and whether in common law or civil law, that have the characteristics that I identify in section III.A.

articulation of the ambitions of 'interpretive' theories of law,[6] which can be tested, among other ways, by how well they fit the actual law. The positive law clearly requires fiduciaries to act with loyalty.

This chapter proceeds as follows. Section II discusses Steve's arguments as to why fiduciary law cannot be about loyalty. It is mainly preoccupied with the meaning, or meanings, of loyalty. I will agree with Steve that the law is not concerned with loyalty as Steve defined it in his text. But 'loyalty' has many meanings, and just because the law does not require the loyalty that Steve discussed, it does not follow that the law does not require loyalty.

In section III, I will explain why the law *must* require a legal version of loyalty that is measured subjectively, through an inquiry into motive. This is because the core of fiduciary law is the holding of powers that one holds for some other-regarding mission. Where these powers are discretionary, the law does not dictate exactly how they must be used; it is the holder of the power who holds the discretion. But such other-regarding powers can only rightly be used in the pursuit of the mission for which they were granted. Thus, to know whether the power has been rightly used, we must go beyond the objective results and have regard to what the power-holder was trying to accomplish. Acting with the proper motive is a particular kind of loyalty: loyalty in the exercise of other-regarding authority.

Section IV suggests that fiduciary law will always be misunderstood by those who fail to see that its defining characteristic is action in law not for oneself but for others. That is because this characteristic, which is not found in other fields of private law, brings into play a range of principles that are unique to fiduciary law.

II. What Does 'Loyalty' Mean in this Context?

In relation to the meaning of loyalty, Steve made two arguments as to why fiduciary law cannot be about loyalty, or cannot involve duties of loyalty.[7] First, 'there is no such thing as instant loyalty'[8] and so it is actually not possible for a duty of loyalty to attach, automatically, to fiduciary relationships at the moment they arise. Second, and here in agreement with my own earlier text, he said that 'acting loyally always involves acting for a particular kind of motive'.[9] Since what he saw as the core of legal fiduciary duty does not involve any inquiry into motive, this showed for him that fiduciary law is not concerned with loyalty. It is impossible to take a position on these arguments without taking a position on what loyalty means in law.

A. Can there be 'Instant Loyalty'?

The first argument is perhaps the more surprising, when we see 'duties of loyalty' everywhere in the law. Steve argued that acting loyally is only possible in a 'meaningful

[6] SA Smith, *Contract Theory* (Oxford, Oxford University Press, 2004) ch 1.
[7] SA Smith (n 4) 214–17.
[8] ibid 214.
[9] ibid 215.

relationship' involving commitment,[10] because part of what loyalty means is that one is motivated by that commitment. He took it as obvious that this meant that the relevant relationship must have existed over some non-trivial period of time. Since fiduciary relationships, like contracts, can arise instantly – as where a trustee takes on the trusteeship of a trust – he said it was literally impossible that loyalty could be required in all such relationships.

While I agree that loyalty and disloyalty can only arise in respect of certain relationships, I disagree that any such relationship must have some minimum temporal duration before those considerations can come into play. My agreement with Steve on this point can be put in this way: we can only talk meaningfully about loyalty in relationships where the *relationship itself* demands loyalty; that is, where it demands decision-making that pays attention to the interests of the object of loyalty, being someone or something other than the decision-maker.[11] Thus I agree with Steve that you can comply with most contractual obligations while considering only your own selfish interests, and that this compliance is not usefully called 'loyalty'.

There is a passage in which Steve aims to show the difference between loyalty and contract, which is important for him since contracts create duties instantly. Acting loyally, he says, requires a particular kind of motive; and so '[i]t is not possible,' he says, 'to act loyally – or disloyally – by accident or when one is sleep-walking'.[12] This, he says, is a crucial difference between promise-keeping and loyalty. You *can* perform a promise by accident, whereas conduct is only properly seen as loyal if it is 'performed at least in part because of that [loyalty-demanding] relationship'.[13]

Since I agree with Steve that loyalty requires other-regarding reasoning, I also agree that we cannot be loyal accidentally. But if loyalty is defined only by its content – by what it requires a person to do, or not to do – then 'promise' (or 'contract') cannot be systematically *opposed* to loyalty. After all, whatever loyalty requires could be the subject of a promise (or a contract), as is evidenced by the ubiquity of legally binding oaths of loyalty. For office-holders, these oaths typically use the language of 'faithful' or 'loyal' service. A judge of the Supreme Court of Canada must swear to 'duly and faithfully, and to the best of my skill and knowledge, execute the powers and trusts reposed in me'.[14]

[10] ibid 214–15.

[11] In summarising in this way *what* loyalty requires, I believe I am in agreement with Steve (ibid 215–16). As far as the link to relationships, I have called certain approaches to fiduciary law (including my own approach) 'relational': L Smith, 'Parenthood is a Fiduciary Relationship' (2020) 70 *University of Toronto Law Journal* 395, 413–18. I note that I am not the first person to disagree with Steve about 'instant loyalty': see AS Gold, 'The Reasonably Loyal Person' in H Psarras and S Steel (eds), *Private Law and Practical Reason: Essays on John Gardner's Private Law Theory* (Oxford, Oxford University Press, 2023) 330. Gold's response to Steve is different from mine inasmuch as I argue that 'loyalty' has a special meaning in law, while Gold argues that there can be instant loyalty even when we are using 'loyalty' in an 'ordinary' sense. A more fundamental difference between my position and Gold's is that my argument in this paper, and in L Smith, *The Law of Loyalty* (Oxford, Oxford University Press, 2023) esp 87–93, is that legal loyalty is always measured subjectively (albeit sometimes subject to objective requirements), which is why courts have never used, and should not use, a standard of the 'reasonably loyal person'.

[12] SA Smith (n 4) 215, here citing S Galoob and EJ Leib, 'Intentions, Compliance, and Fiduciary Obligations' (2014) 20 *Legal Theory* 106.

[13] SA Smith (n 4) 215.

[14] Supreme Court Act, RSC 1985, c S-26, s 10. Gold (n 11) also invokes loyalty oaths in response to Steve's argument (at 338).

The law treats the oath as immediately effective; its most obvious legal effect is that it instantly capacitates the person to take up the office. Similarly, a person who becomes a citizen via an oath of loyalty immediately acquires new capacities and rights. Crucially, both types of oath may instantly create legal obligations of loyal service that did not exist before.[15] Marriage vows may be another example.

Again, if loyalty is defined by its content – by what loyalty *requires* of a person – then a requirement to be loyal could have multiple sources. One of them could be promising or contracting, and this would make room for instant loyalty. Steve, however, took loyalty to be defined not only by its content but also by its source. The content, as we have seen, relates to a requirement to reason and act in an other-regarding way. But for Steve, loyalty, quite apart from *what* it requires, can *by definition* only arise in a relationship not just of commitment but of *affective* commitment.[16] That is why he thought there cannot be instant loyalty, and this would hold true regardless of what it is that loyalty requires of a person. If loyalty can only arise from affective commitment then it is unlikely to be relevant to fiduciary law or to any kind of law, since affective commitment is not relevant to the operation of legal rules.[17] 'My dog is loyal to a fault, but I would not want him managing my assets.'[18] Steve took this affective aspect of loyalty to be self-evident.[19]

The reason I disagree with Steve here is that I do not think that loyalty *in law* has the definition that he was using. It may be that loyalty, as it is understood outside of the law, can only arise out of a relationship of affective commitment. Legal relationships have, in principle, a defined beginning and a defined end point; and there are very good reasons for this. If there is such a thing as a legal duty or requirement of loyalty, it must follow that it *can* arise instantly, when the kind of relationship that demands loyalty arises.

B. Legal Loyalty

Given that legal terms often carry meanings distinct from their non-legal counterparts (think of 'estate' or 'nuisance'), we should not be surprised that 'loyalty' might have

[15] For example, a violation by a judge of the oath of office would be grounds for impeachment. Violation of an oath of office may also be a criminal offence (see *Gaskins v State* 318 Ga App 8, 733 SE2d 338 (2012, CA)). Furthermore, a person who swears loyalty on becoming a new citizen may be obliged to perform military or other public service, and may be subject to penalties for disloyalty (such as treason) that would not apply to a non-citizen.

[16] Here I use 'affective' in the primary sense given by the *Oxford English Dictionary* at www.oed.com: 'Of or relating to the affections or emotions, esp as contrasted with the intellect or rational faculty; emotional.'

[17] A possible exception might be in relation to disputes about child custody, although it is worth noting the limited role of affective commitment even here. All of the duties of parenthood can exist without any affective commitment, which is most clearly illustrated where some agency of the state is in the role of parent towards a child.

[18] SA Smith (n 4) 218.

[19] ibid 214: 'Loyalty … on any plausible account … has two features … The first is that ascriptions of loyal behaviour always have a temporal element: there is no such thing as instant loyalty.' My inference from Steve's otherwise unexplained insistence on a temporal element (and his reference to his dog) is that he thought that it goes without saying that loyalty requires an affective element. Steve cited the similar argument made in J Penner, 'Is Loyalty a Virtue, and Even If It Is, Does It Really Help Explain Fiduciary Liability?' in AS Gold

acquired a special meaning in law. Indeed, it now has more than one technical legal meaning. Although 'loyalty' is required of a fiduciary, a *different* kind of (legal) loyalty is required of a non-fiduciary employee.[20] There is still another legal duty (or principle) of loyalty in the institutional law of the European Union.[21]

Loyalty has a meaning in law that is related to, but not necessarily the same as, what loyalty means between, for example, spouses or friends. On my understanding of a fiduciary relationship, the fiduciary always acquires (in one way or another) legal or factual powers, and acquires them not for the fiduciary's own benefit but in order to use them to pursue some other-regarding mission (which is often to advance the interests of a beneficiary).[22] If the powers are bestowed upon the fiduciary *only* to allow them better to achieve an other-regarding mission, like advancing the interests of another person, then it would be improper to use them in any other way. In this sense, the fiduciary who accepts such other-regarding powers makes a commitment to pursue that mission. If the mission is the pursuit of the interests of a beneficiary, then the fiduciary enters (instantly) a relationship of commitment to that person and their interests. And if (as both Steve and I agree) the rightful or loyal use of these powers depends upon the motive with which they are used – it must be a motive that respects the relationship of commitment – then we can easily construct a legal understanding of fiduciary loyalty that is consonant with at least some of Steve's own arguments. Fiduciary loyalty is loyalty in the exercise of one's judgement with respect to one's other-regarding powers.[23] It is loyalty in the exercise of other-regarding legal authority. It is not surprising that this conception differs from the conception of loyalty, for example, between friends or spouses, who do not hold other-regarding legal powers but who, similarly, should (if acting loyally) be motivated in other-regarding ways.

Steve was naturally aware of the possibility that loyalty in law might mean something different from what it means outside of law.[24] But he argued that its use in law could only be justifiable if its legal meaning was close to its 'ordinary' meaning; and he claimed that 'fiduciary law has nothing to do with loyalty in the ordinary sense of the word'.[25] I will aim to show that fiduciary law does indeed have a great deal to do with loyalty in what Steve called the ordinary sense of the word: a requirement that one make decisions for other-regarding reasons, based on a relationship of commitment. Legal loyalty, however, does not require *affective* commitment.

and PB Miller (eds), *Philosophical Foundations of Fiduciary Law* (Oxford, Oxford University Press, 2014) 159, 162: 'Loyalty is a form of emotional commitment.' Penner is there agreeing with S Keller, *The Limits of Loyalty* (Cambridge, Cambridge University Press, 2007), whom Steve also cited (SA Smith (n 4) 214, fn 4).

[20] This is true in the common law (A Frazer, 'The Employee's Contractual Duty of Fidelity' (2015) 131 *LQR* 53) and in the civil law of Quebec (M Cantin Cumyn, 'L'obligation de loyauté dans les services de placement' (2012) 3 *Bulletin de droit économique* 19). US law is different inasmuch as it holds that all employees are agents; and since all agents are fiduciaries, this distinction between employees and fiduciaries does not arise (American Law Institute, *Restatement of the Law Third: Agency*, vol 1 (Philadelphia, PA, ALI, 2006) § 1.01, comment *c*).

[21] M Klamert, *The Principle of Loyalty in EU Law* (Oxford, Oxford University Press, 2014).

[22] The formulation aims to be general enough to include relationships that oblige the fiduciary to advance an abstract purpose rather than the interests of a beneficiary.

[23] L Smith, *The Law of Loyalty* (n 11) 30–32.

[24] SA Smith (n 4) 220–21.

[25] ibid 220.

C. Loyalty and the Rules about Conflicts and Unauthorised Profits

This brings us to Steve's second argument against loyalty in fiduciary flaw. He said that 'acting loyally always involves acting for a particular kind of motive'.[26] I agree.[27] He also said that the rules governing fiduciaries that apply to acting in conflict situations and to the extraction of unauthorised profits do *not* look to motive.[28] Again, I agree.[29] For Steve, '[l]oyalty's dependence on motive is fatal to any attempt to explain fiduciary law in those terms because the core rule of fiduciary law – the no-conflict rule – is unconcerned with motive'.[30] Our disagreement here is thus simple to explain. For me, the rules about conflicts (and the rules about unauthorised profits) are *not* the core of fiduciary law. They are, rather, an important protection of that core. It is the concern with motive, which Steve rightly saw to be crucial to loyalty, that forms the core of fiduciary law.

III. The Core Concern of Fiduciary Law is the Loyal Use of Fiduciary Powers

A. The Requirement of Loyalty in Fiduciary Powers

Following the interpretive tradition of whose methodology Steve was a trailblazer, his great book on remedies starts from the positive law.[31] In our many conversations leading up to its publication, I was repeatedly impressed and sometimes astonished by his mastery of many very fine details of positive remedial law. I will try to make my own case here by moving in the same direction: not starting from theory, but from the law, and indeed from remedies.

The first sentence of the unanimous advice of the Privy Council in a 2022 decision is this: 'It is a fundamental principle of equity that a fiduciary power may be exercised only for a purpose for which the power has been conferred.'[32] This is a venerable principle in the common law tradition.[33] Nor is this some *recherché* principle of trust law; it is a general principle of all fiduciary relationships. It applies, for example, to the fiduciary powers of corporate directors and may be invoked in disputes over the use of

[26] ibid 215.

[27] L Smith (n 3); L Smith, *The Law of Loyalty* (n 11) ch 3. I am not here distinguishing between 'purpose' and 'motive'; for discussion, see ibid 82–84.

[28] SA Smith (n 4) 216.

[29] L Smith (n 3); L Smith, *The Law of Loyalty* (n 11) chs 4–5.

[30] SA Smith (n 4) 216.

[31] SA Smith, *Rights, Wrongs, and Injustices: The Structure of Remedial Law* (Oxford, Oxford University Press, 2019).

[32] *Grand View Private Trust Co v Wong (No 2)* [2022] UKPC 47 [1]. See also *Wong v Burt* [2004] NZCA 174, [2005] 1 NZLR 91 [27] and *Lehtimäki v Cooper* [2020] UKSC 33, [2022] AC 155 [44]–[45].

[33] In *Eclairs Group Ltd v JKX Oil & Gas plc* [2015] UKSC 71, the roots of the principle in private law are identified in 18th-century Chancery case law.

such powers, often in contests for corporate control.[34] It is easy to find also in the civil law,[35] and in the law governing the exercise of public powers.[36] Powers that are granted not for the benefit of the grantee but in order to equip her to accomplish some other-regarding mission, can only be rightly used in the furtherance of that mission; that is, in the pursuit of the purposes for which the power was conferred.

As a result, the exercise of a fiduciary power is liable to be set aside if the power-holder acted with an improper motive. Such an improper exercise creates a Hohfeldian liability, but not a liability to be ordered to pay damages. The problem relates to the exercise of a legal power, and the remedy is that the exercise of the power is liable to be set aside.[37] Hart showed us that not every legal rule imposes a duty. Some rules tell us how to exercise powers, and a failure to follow the rule does not necessarily mean that we have done anything wrong; it may mean that we have not properly exercised the power.[38] When we are considering the supervision of those who hold powers for others, liability in damages is the ambulance at the bottom of the cliff, for when there is nothing else to be done; a fence at the top is the first solution. In this case, that means review of how the powers have been used.

B. This Requirement of Loyalty is at the Heart of Fiduciary Law

The defining feature of the fiduciary relationship is the holding of powers that one does not hold for one's own benefit but for the benefit of others, or for the accomplishment of an other-regarding mission. In this sense, the judicial surveillance of the loyal exercise of those powers is at the very heart of fiduciary law.

The easiest way to show this is, again, through the positive law. The rules about conflicts and unauthorised profits, to which we will return, can be disapplied in various ways; although presumptively present in fiduciary relationships, they can be modified and even effectively removed without changing the nature of the relationship as fiduciary. But if a person holds legal powers and holds them *not* to pursue an other-regarding mission but rather for their own benefit to use as they wish, then those are not fiduciary

[34] *Hogg v Cramphorn Ltd* [1967] Ch 254; *Schnell v Chris-Craft Industries Inc* 285 A2d 437 (1971, Del); *Teck Corp v Millar* (1972) 22 DLR (3d) 288 (BCSC); *Howard Smith Ltd v Ampol Petroleum Ltd* [1974] AC 821 (PC); *Whitehouse v Carlton Hotel Pty Ltd* (1987) 162 CLR 285; *Eclairs Group* (n 33); *Coster v UIP Companies Inc* 255 A3d 952 (2021, Del). For more on the Delaware corporate law aspects, see LE Strine Jr et al., 'Loyalty's Core Demand: The Defining Role of Good Faith in Corporation Law' (2010) 98 *Georgetown LJ* 629, 641–44.

[35] L Smith, *The Law of Loyalty* (n 11), 8, 81.

[36] For example *R v Tower Hamlets London Borough Council, Ex p Chetnik Developments Ltd* [1988] AC 858 (HL), 872 and *Porter v Magill* [2002] 2 AC 357 (CA, HL), 463; see also L Smith, *The Law of Loyalty* (n 11), 382–84, 397–98, 408.

[37] It is possible, of course, that the fiduciary is *also* liable to some money award, depending on other aspects of the facts, which may be called a liability in damages or may rather be framed in terms, for example, of 'accounting' or 'equitable compensation'; but this is conceptually separate from the liability to have the exercise of the fiduciary power set aside.

[38] HLA Hart, *The Concept of Law*, ed L Green (3rd edn, Oxford, Oxford University Press, 2012) 27–35. In the case law of England and Wales, there is uncertainty about whether an exercise of a fiduciary power for an improper purpose is void (at least 'in Equity') or (as I would argue) only voidable; see *Pitt v Holt* [2013] UKSC 26, [2013] 2 AC 108 [93]–[94]. This rarely makes any practical difference, which is probably why the issue lingers unresolved.

powers and the relationship is not a fiduciary relationship. This is why fiduciary powers are and must be found in all fiduciary relationships.[39] Conversely, if there are no powers, or the only powers are held in a non-fiduciary capacity, then the relationship is not fiduciary.[40] Thus Lady Arden recently said, in the Supreme Court of the United Kingdom:

> [T]he key principle is that a fiduciary acts for and only for another. He owes essentially the duty of single-minded loyalty to his beneficiary, meaning that he cannot exercise any power so as to benefit himself … So 'the distinguishing obligation' of a fiduciary is that he must act only for the benefit of another in matters covered by his fiduciary duty.[41]

The core of fiduciary law, then, is the proper use of powers that are held for other-regarding purposes; the loyal use of them, as I have defined 'loyalty'.[42] The cases on 'proper purposes' (and on some other rules as well) understand themselves as being entirely concerned with the rules that govern the proper exercise of *fiduciary* powers.[43] It is true that the phrase 'proper purposes' is sometimes used in the context of powers held by persons who are not fiduciaries.[44] Some have claimed that this demonstrates that the fiduciary 'proper purposes' doctrine is not particularly part of fiduciary law but is more general.[45] But it is clearly a mistake to think that because non-fiduciary power-holders may be said to be subject to *some* rules about 'proper purposes', therefore *no*

[39] This account easily makes room for what we see in the positive law: that fiduciary powers may be granted by law or by court order. The source of the power is not germane to its characterisation as fiduciary or not. This is contrary to the approach of those (arguably including Steve: SA Smith (n 4) 214, fn 3, 232–34; but see his careful analysis of possible counter-examples: ibid 234–37) who view fiduciary relationships as always arising from agreement.

[40] A difficult case is that of the fiduciary advisor, like a lawyer or real estate agent, whose only power may be factual, in relation to the giving of advice. As a matter of positive law, such people can clearly be fiduciaries, and so in this case of advisors, an other-regarding *factual* power may be treated by the legal system as equipollent to a legal power. For one apparent judicial acceptance of my argument on this point, which has been cited many times in subsequent cases, see Leggatt LJ (as he then was) in *Sheikh Tahnoon Bin Saeed Bin Shakhboot Al Nehayan v Kent* [2018] EWHC 333 (Comm) [159]. This assimilation of advice to legal power arguably is necessitated by the impossibility of systematically unpacking and isolating the reasons that go into human decision-making. See L Smith, *The Law of Loyalty* (n 11) 264–72.

[41] *Lehtimäki v Cooper* [2020] UKSC 33, [2022] AC 155 [44]–[45]. See also *Al Nehayan v Kent* (n 40): '[F]iduciary duties typically arise where one person undertakes and is entrusted with authority to manage the property or affairs of another and to make discretionary decisions on behalf of that person. … The essential idea is that a person in such a position is not permitted to use their position for their own private advantage but is required to act unselfishly in what they perceive to be the best interests of their principal. This is the core of the obligation of loyalty which Millett LJ in the *Mothew* case [1998] Ch 1 at 18, described as the "distinguishing obligation of a fiduciary".'

[42] Text at n 23.

[43] These other rules that govern the exercise of powers by fiduciaries of their fiduciary powers include rules against considering irrelevant matters or failing to consider relevant matters (see *Pitt* (n 38)); rules against delegation and fettering of discretion (*Re Hay's Settlement Trusts* [1982] 1 WLR 202 (ChD)); and rules requiring periodic consideration of the exercise of the power (*Re Gulbenkian's Settlement* [1970] 1 AC 508 (HL); *McPhail v Doulton* [1971] AC 424 (HL)). These rules are obviously part of fiduciary law because they presumptively apply to fiduciary power-holders but not to non-fiduciary power-holders. They are triggered, in other words, by the bare consideration that the power is held in a fiduciary capacity. In my view they are all aspects of loyalty in the sense of the proper use of the fiduciary power.

[44] eg *Vatcher v Paull* [1915] AC 372 (PC).

[45] M Conaglen, *Fiduciary Loyalty: Protecting the Due Performance of Non-Fiduciary Duties* (Oxford, Hart Publishing, 2010) 44–50. Steve followed this line: SA Smith (n 4) 217, fn 18.

such rule is properly considered part of fiduciary law. The non-fiduciary power-holder is basically required to act in good faith; they are not, however, required to use the power to advance some interest other than their own.[46] And again, the cases dealing with the restrictions on the use by fiduciaries of their fiduciary powers *always* describe this as part of fiduciary law.[47] The restrictions on fiduciaries are much more demanding than those that may apply to non-fiduciaries.

A liability to have one's exercise of a fiduciary power set aside, therefore, relates to the judicial supervision of the core feature of the relationship, and thus to what makes a relationship a fiduciary relationship. In Steve's book on remedies, there is not much discussion of this kind of remedial order. There is a passage on judicial orders that are 'constitutive' of legal relationships, and this seems to include an order that an exercise of a power is voidable and has been avoided.[48] But the focus of his study is elsewhere, and it is possible to wonder whether Steve's understanding of fiduciary law would have been different if I had persuaded him of the centrality of the judicial review of the exercise of fiduciary powers. Why such exercises should be voidable rather than void is a matter that deserves attention, but the short answer seems to be that they involve not an *absence* of authority but a *misuse* of authority.[49]

C. This Requirement of Loyalty, which is at the Core of Fiduciary Law, Must Usually be Subjective

Steve and I agreed that an inquiry into whether someone has been loyal requires an investigation of their subjective motivations.[50] He thought that any such inquiry was unrelated to loyalty, and was not part of fiduciary law.[51] But the positive law treats it as central to fiduciary law.[52] In one recent and widely cited case, it was said that '[l]oyalty in this context [of fiduciary relationships] means being guided solely by the interests of the principal and not by any consideration of the fiduciary's own interests'.[53] Whether or not one was guided by certain interests and not by others can only be a subjective inquiry into the decision-maker's reasoning process. In the most recent leading case, it was explicitly held (on the basis of a long line authority) that *what are the proper purposes*

[46] See also L Smith, *The Law of Loyalty* (n 11) 102–06. In *Vatcher* (n 44), for example, the Privy Council stated (at 378) that there would be 'fraud on a power' held by a non-fiduciary where, via a prior agreement or otherwise, the power was exercised so as to benefit someone who was not an object of the power (ie not entitled to benefit). This is not really a principle about purposes but about objectively unauthorised outcomes.

[47] See the cases in nn 32–34 and 40–43, and L Smith, *The Law of Loyalty* (n 11) ch 3.

[48] SA Smith (n 31) 15.

[49] L Smith, *The Law of Loyalty* (n 11) 126–38.

[50] Text above at n 9.

[51] SA Smith (n 4) 217, fn 18. It is interesting to note, however, that in his explanation of the evolution of Equity in the common law tradition, Steve observed that a key difference between Equity and the common law was that Equity was concerned with the defendant's motives: SA Smith (n 31) 38.

[52] See the cases in nn 32–34 and 40–43. At one point Steve referred not to motive but to 'disposition' (SA Smith (n 4) 219). I agree with him that the law does not inquire into whether a fiduciary is, or is not, well-disposed towards their beneficiary; legal loyalty looks at motivation in the sense of the goals that a decision aims to achieve. His discussion of disposition seems to reflect Steve's view, discussed in section II.A, that loyalty can only arise in relationships of affective commitment.

[53] *Al Nehayan v Kent* (n 40) [159].

for which a fiduciary power may properly be used is a question of objective interpretation of the instrument granting the power;[54] but *whether the power was used properly* requires investigation of the subjective reasons for decision of the power-holder.[55]

According to Steve, fiduciary law is concerned only with whether the fiduciary has (objectively) performed their mission or 'mandate'.[56] Fiduciary law, on this view, then adds additional objective rules to make it more likely that fiduciaries do perform their mandates. On this vision, all the rules are objective. But as we have seen, the positive law does not look like this; the reason it does not, and cannot, arises out of the consideration that most fiduciary powers are discretionary.[57] In such a case, the fiduciary must not 'exceed' the power; this applies also to a non-fiduciary, and means that the power can only be used to do that which it objectively authorises. But the law governing *fiduciary* power-holders is stricter than this. Following the inquiry into whether the fiduciary acted within their authority, there is a separate and independent inquiry into whether they *misused* their authority; meaning, the authority that they objectively held. And this inquiry is necessarily subjective.

This means that two different fiduciaries holding the same power (and acting within its objective scope) could use the power in the same way, objectively speaking; but one could find that their exercise of the power is unimpeachable, while the other could find that their exercise is liable to be set aside because the fiduciary was improperly motivated. The fiduciary holds the power, and therefore exercises their own judgement as to how and whether to use it; but they must always satisfy the inquiry into their subjective motivation. For example, most of the relevant corporate law cases are about the power to issue new shares. In these cases, the board clearly had the power to issue new shares, and exercised it; the focus is on the separate question whether the board acted for a proper purpose.[58] That inquiry can only possibly proceed at a subjective level. If the inquiry into 'proper purpose' were objective, it would just be part of the inquiry into what was the objective scope of the power. Likewise, a recent leading trust law case involved a discretionary power to add anyone in the world as a beneficiary of a trust. The corporate trustee added a person. Obviously, it had the power to do this. But based on an objective inquiry into the proper purposes for which this power could be used, and a *subjective* inquiry into what actually motivated the power-holder, it was held that the trustee misused its power; it used it for an improper purpose.[59]

What this means is that where a fiduciary holds *discretionary* powers – which is almost always the case – there is no entirely objective answer to whether they have fulfilled their 'mandate'.[60] Different fiduciaries can rightly use their powers differently.

[54] *Grand View Private Trust Co* (n 32) [61].

[55] ibid [72].

[56] SA Smith (n 4) 217.

[57] For an argument that they are not *necessarily always* discretionary, see L Smith, *The Law of Loyalty* (n 11) 23–25, 106–09.

[58] *Hogg* (n 34); *Teck* (n 34); *Howard Smith Ltd* (n 34); *Whitehouse* (n 34); *Coster* (n 34). *Eclairs Group* (n 33) was not about share issues, but states clearly the subjective nature of the inquiry (see ibid [15]).

[59] *Grand View Private Trust Co* (n 32).

[60] In L Smith, *The Law of Loyalty* (n 11) 89, fn 41; 98, fn 80, this is called the 'one right answer fallacy'. Of course, an objective standard of reasonableness leaves room for a *range* of lawful conduct as well as a range of unlawful conduct, rather than dictating a single course of action. But if the only inquiry was objective, there would be no inquiry into proper purposes. Steve suggested (SA Smith (n 4) 217) that a duty of loyalty

Conversely, the *same* use of a power, viewed objectively, could be proper by one fiduciary (who acted for a proper purpose) and improper and voidable by another (who acted for an improper purpose). The subjective inquiry into the motivations of a fiduciary power-holder is not exceptional but rather fundamental to the supervision of the proper use of those powers.[61]

D. The Rules about Conflicts and Profits are not the Core of Fiduciary Law

Steve, following some authors, took the view that the core of fiduciary law – the only fiduciary duties in need of justification for a sound understanding of the field – lies in the rules about conflicts and unauthorised profits; and, indeed, that these two things are interrelated inasmuch as the rule about unauthorised profits is a sanction or remedy for a breach of the rules about conflicts. He accepted that, viewed this way, it would be an 'odd' remedy,[62] but aimed to explain it as appropriate to what he took to be the core fiduciary duty against (being in) conflicts, a duty that was seen as no more than a way to reduce the likelihood that some other non-fiduciary duties might be breached.[63] This position does not fit the reasoning in the cases; while they do (rarely) refer to 'temptation' and 'prophylactic' duties, this is in the context of aiming to secure fiduciary loyalty itself – that is, the loyal use of fiduciary powers – not to secure the performance of other obligations.[64]

The view that Steve took here is of quite recent vintage. Paul Finn articulated a version of it in 1989,[65] although this was inconsistent with his earlier work[66] and he later

might conflict with the fiduciary's duty to act with care, skill and diligence in the sense that the fiduciary might act loyally but unreasonably. In fact, the law requires the fiduciary to comply with both duties, and others as well.

[61] As Steve noted (SA Smith (n 4) 222), I have argued that this part of fiduciary law is not about 'duties' in the strictest sense: when a fiduciary power is exercised for an improper purpose, the fiduciary is not (for that reason alone) liable in damages (see text at n 37 and L Smith, *The Law of Loyalty* (n 11) 136–38). Rather, they are liable to have the exercise of the power set aside. In *Grand View Private Trust Co* (n 32), the Privy Council referred ([51], [52]) to the 'duties and restrictions' on a fiduciary power-holder.

[62] SA Smith (n 4) 222.

[63] ibid 213, fn 2 and *passim;* in this he followed Conaglen (n 45).

[64] In *Al Nehayan v Kent* (n 40) [159], Leggat LJ said (emphasis added): 'Loyalty in this context means being guided solely by the interests of the principal and not by any consideration of the fiduciary's own interests. *To promote such decision-making*, fiduciaries are required to act openly and honestly and must not (without the informed consent of their principal) place themselves in a position where their own interests or their duty to another party may conflict with their duty to pursue the interests of their principal.' Similarly, the High Court of Australia has spoken of the rules about conflicts as forbidding conflicts between the fiduciary's self-interest and their *fiduciary* duties: *Chan v Zacharia* (1984) 154 CLR 178, 198; *Warman International Ltd v Dwyer* (1995) 182 CLR 544, 557; *Howard v Federal Commissioner of Taxation* [2014] HCA 21, 253 CLR 83 [33], [108]. See also *Guinness plc v Saunders* [1990] 2 AC 663 (HL) 700 (Lord Goff): '[T]he directors of a company, like other fiduciaries, must not put themselves in a position where there is a conflict between their personal interests and their duties as fiduciaries …' All of these pronouncements are inconsistent with a view that the conflict rules exist to reduce the likelihood of the breach of *non*-fiduciary duties.

[65] PD Finn, 'The Fiduciary Principle' in TG Youdan (ed), *Equity, Fiduciaries and Trusts* (Toronto, Carswell, 1989) 1.

[66] PD Finn, *Fiduciary Obligations* (Sydney, Law Book Co, 1977); repr P Finn, *Fiduciary Obligations: 40th Anniversary Republication with Additional Essays* (Annandale, NSW, Federation Press, 2016).

revised it to bring the control of fiduciary powers back into view.[67] Meanwhile, however, it was adopted by the High Court of Australia and has become the dominant (but not universally held) view in that country.[68] Starting in the 1990s, some US scholars focused on making sense of the rules about conflicts and unauthorised profits, which are clearly in need of some particular justification.[69] Both the Australian and the US approaches led, unfortunately, to a situation in which scholars paid insufficient attention to the other legal elements of fiduciary relationships, elements which are well-established and have been refined in case law going back to the eighteenth century.

Not everything can be at the core of something. I have argued that the core of fiduciary law is the judicial supervision of the proper use of fiduciary powers. Although the rules on conflicts and unauthorised profits are a very important part of fiduciary law, they are not the core, nor are they so closely related to one another that one of them is part of the other. In fact, the remedy for exercising a fiduciary power while in a conflict is the setting aside of the exercise, which is available without inquiry as to whether there was a profit (or a loss).[70] This is the same remedy that is available for an exercise of a fiduciary power for a proven improper purpose. The inference is unavoidable that there is a link. The link is simply this: that when a power is exercised in a conflict, it is impossible (even for the good faith power-holder) to know whether it was exercised for a proper or an improper purpose.[71] The law protects the beneficiary by allowing them to set the exercise aside just as if an improper purpose had been proved.[72]

As for the rule on unauthorised profits, it is not a sanction for a violation of the rules about conflicts. One proof of this is that the rule about unauthorised profits does not require proof of a conflict or indeed of any wrongful conduct.[73] It only requires that the fiduciary extracted an unauthorised profit from acting in that role.[74] One implication of this, also found in the positive law, is as follows: profiting fiduciaries are not allowed to argue that they should be allowed to keep their unauthorised profit because there is no causal link to any conflict or other problematic conduct.[75] They *would* be able to argue that, *if* the rule provided a remedy for wrongdoing. But the rule about unauthorised profits is simply a rule that when you are acting *for and on behalf* of someone, any profit that you extract is treated by the law is attributable to them, just

[67] PD Finn, 'Fiduciary Reflections' (2014) 88 *Australian Law Journal* 127, 131, fn 41.

[68] For citations and an attempt to rebut this view, see L Smith, 'Prescriptive Fiduciary Duties' (2018) 37 *University of Queensland Law Journal* 261.

[69] R Cooter and BJ Freedman, 'An Economic Model of the Fiduciary's Duty of Loyalty' (1990) 10 *Tel Aviv University Studies in Law* 297; FH Easterbrook and DR Fischel, 'Contract and Fiduciary Duty' (1993) 36 *Journal of Law and Economics* 425.

[70] Steve referred to this kind of rescission but set it aside as 'not easy to explain': SA Smith (n 4) 224, fn 29. Since (as I will argue) the rule against unauthorised profits is quite separate from the rules about conflicts, rescission is actually the *only* thing that needs to be explained about the rules on conflicts.

[71] See eg *Parker v McKenna* (1874) LR 10 Ch App 96 (DC) 118; *Re Lamb* [1894] 2 QB 805 (CA) 820; *Canadian National Railway Co v McKercher LLP* [2013] 2 SCR 649, 2013 SCC 39 [38]. This is another example (see also n 40) of the law's recognising that it is not always possible to unpack human reasoning.

[72] See L Smith, *The Law of Loyalty* (n 11) ch 4. As discussed there, third parties in good faith (eg who have contracted with the conflicted fiduciary) are, of course, protected as appropriate.

[73] *Regal (Hastings) Ltd v Gulliver* (1942) [1967] 2 AC 134 (HL).

[74] L Smith, *The Law of Loyalty* (n 11) ch 5.

[75] ibid 195–96.

as any cost properly incurred by you is attributable to them.[76] The rule is not about wrongdoing at all.

The view that the only fiduciary duties are those specified by the rules about conflicts and unauthorised profits is sometimes based on the view that these are the only 'peculiarly' fiduciary duties, when judged by the content of the duties.[77] Even on this approach, the rules that govern fiduciaries (but that do not apply to non-fiduciaries) in the exercise of their fiduciary powers should surely be part of fiduciary law. Those are the rules that enforce the loyal use of such powers. I have argued elsewhere, however, that it is a mistake to try to decide which duties are 'fiduciary' by looking at the content of the duty, if only because (as mentioned above, in section II.A) a duty of any content can be replicated by contractual promise. The better view, and one that reflects the positive law, at least outside of post-1992 Australia, is that fiduciary duties (and other legal relations, such as required modalities for the valid exercise of powers) are those that arise, or arise presumptively, from a fiduciary relationship, as I have defined it.[78]

IV. Conclusion

My disagreement with Steve is a variant of one that I have also had with other scholars. Speaking very generally, it seems to me that it arises in this way. Many scholars seek to understand fiduciary law using the same analytical tools that they use in other fields of private law. For example, when they see a defendant who is required to give up a gain, they assume that this must be a sanction for some kind of wrongdoing, and they turn to trying to work out what the wrong is that supports this gain-based remedy.[79]

In my view, this approach cannot succeed, because there is a fundamental difference between fiduciary law and non-fiduciary law: in the former, people are required to be guided by interests other than their own. All of the peculiar, interesting and difficult features of fiduciary law are outgrowths of this basic consideration, which fundamentally divides fiduciary law from the rest of private law. This means that fiduciary law is governed by principles that do not otherwise apply in private law, and this makes it impossible to understand fiduciary law using only the tools that apply elsewhere.

In one of his most important contributions, Steve argued that we should try to understand the law through 'intermediate justifications' rather than 'comprehensive moral theories'.[80] In these terms, fiduciary law has its own intermediate justifications growing out of the fundamental nature of the fiduciary relationship. Let me give two examples.

[76] *Jennings v Mather* [1902] 1 KB 1 (CA), 6–7: 'A trustee is prohibited by law from making any profit for himself out of the trust estate, a rule which is enforced with great stringency; it is only just that, on the other hand, he should be legally protected against all liabilities properly incurred by him in the administration of the trust estate.'

[77] Conaglen (n 45) ch 3.

[78] See L Smith (n 68).

[79] Even if it might be an 'odd' remedy: text at n 62.

[80] SA Smith, 'Intermediate and Comprehensive Justifications' in S Degeling, M Crawford and N Tiverios (eds), *Justifying Private Rights* (Oxford, Hart Publishing, 2020) 63. In my own study I deploy the idea of 'justificatory principles', which I believe is similar to Steve's 'intermediate justifications': L Smith, *The Law of Loyalty* (n 11) 14–16.

First, as we have seen, when one person A is acting for and on behalf of another person B, both the costs and benefits of so acting are attributed to B. That explains the rule against unauthorised profits without reference to wrongdoing, reflecting the positive law. Second, when one person A holds powers that equip A to act for and on behalf of another person B, those powers of A can always be taken away from A.[81] This is because A does not hold those powers as assets; and this is fundamentally different from, for example, powers acquired in a non-fiduciary contractual context.

I think that if I could have better explained my understanding of legal loyalty to Steve, he would have liked it, because although it does not correspond exactly to his notion of affective loyalty, it has a lot in common with it. It is all about reasoning that is guided by the interests of another. It would perhaps have been a bigger job to convince him that fiduciary law has its own intermediate justifications; but since it was Steve who taught us that a good interpretive theory must fit the law that it is interpreting, I think I would have got a sympathetic hearing.

[81] L Smith, *The Law of Loyalty* (n 11) 75.

22

Free-standing Liabilities

NICHOLAS J McBRIDE*

When Steve and I were both at Oxford (1991–97), it was customary to think of private law as coterminous with the law of obligations – indeed, it was quite the fashion then to propose that courses on Contract Law and Tort could be replaced with courses on Obligations. That we now think of the law of obligations as only being part of private law is, in large part, due to Steve's work, which forcibly reminded us all that – in Hohfeldian terms – the law ties private individuals together not just through claim-rights and corresponding duties, but also through powers and corresponding liabilities. The subject of this chapter is the set of liabilities that – as we shall see – are the most independent of the private law obligations that we owe each other. It is no exaggeration to say that this chapter could not have been written were it not able to rest on the broad shoulders provided by the giant advances in thinking about private law triggered by Steve's work.

I. Definitions

A. Liabilities

Steve made sense of the concept of a liability as follows:

> A liability is different from a duty. Duties describe things that we must do; liabilities describe things that may be done to us. To say that we have legal duties to do X means that, from the law's perspective, we must do X. In contrast, to say that we have liabilities to X, means that X may be done or imposed upon us by another person or institution.[1]

Such a seemingly simple definition in fact leads us into a thicket of difficulties:

1. *Liabilities, powers and no-duties.* In the Hohfeldian scheme, liabilities are the flip-side of powers, where A has a power in relation to B if they have the ability to alter

* My thanks to John Goldberg and Jason Neyers for comments on an earlier draft of this chapter.

[1] SA Smith, *Rights, Wrongs, and Injustices: The Structure of Remedial Law* (Oxford, Oxford University Press, 2019) 192.

B's *legal* position in some way. In such a case, B is said to be liable to have their legal position altered by A in that way. Steve's definition is not so limited. On the face of it, Steve's 'liability' also covers the situation where A has no duty not to alter B's *factual* position in some way. (In alternative Hohfeldian language, A has a privilege or a liberty to alter B's factual position in some way.) An example would be A's being free – as a member of Parliament speaking in the House – to tarnish B's reputation by calling her out as being a drug dealer. On Steve's definition, B could be said to be liable to have her reputation tarnished by A, as that is something that 'may be done to' her. In what follows, I will follow the Hohfeldian tradition and only use the term 'liability' to describe the flipside of a legal power to alter someone else's legal position.

2. *Done or imposed upon us.* In another respect, Steve's definition of a liability is narrower than the Hohfeldian one. If A offers to sell B his car for £500, and places no limit on how B might accept that offer, B can alter A's legal position by posting a letter to A, accepting the offer: at that point A will come under a contractual duty to sell B his car for £500. So having made an offer to B, A is liable in a Hohfeldian sense to incur a contractual duty to sell B his car for £500. But it would be odd to talk about that contractual duty's being 'done or imposed upon' A when A *wants* to incur a duty to sell his car to B. Steve's definition suggests that a liability only exists where A's position might be changed by B in a way that would be unwelcome to A, or – at least – in a way that A did not ask for or invite. In what follows, I will follow Steve's example and only use the term 'liability' to describe the flipside of a legal power to alter someone's legal position in a way that they did not ask for or invite.
3. *Liabilities and duties.* The fact that liabilities are different from duties does not mean that a given defendant will be subject either to a liability or a duty: they may well be subject to both. For example, if D has a legal duty to pay £100 to C, D will usually be subject to a liability to be made to pay that £100 to C.[2] We can call a liability that is intended to make a legal duty enforceable 'replicative'[3] or 'duty-supporting'.[4] I have argued elsewhere, in commenting on Steve's work, that if D is subject to a liability to be made to pay £100 to C, the law might well, and frequently does, impose duties on D, requiring D not to get in the way of C's being able to exercise the power they have to make D pay that money to C.[5] Unlike the previous example, here the liability comes first and the duty is intended to shore up the liability – not the other way round. So we can call these kinds of duties 'liability-supporting'. More complex structures are possible. D could have a duty to pay £100 to C, which is supported by a liability to be made to pay that £100 to C, which liability is in turn supported by a duty on D not to get in the way of C's exercising their power to make D pay them £100, which duty is in its turn supported by a liability to be made to pay C non-compensatory damages should D get in C's way.

[2] 'Usually' because the two things do not always go together. If C is a prostitute, and D her client, D will have a legal duty to pay C for her services, but will not be subject to a liability to be made to pay that money to C: his duty to pay will be unenforceable.

[3] Following R Zakrzewski, *Remedies Reclassified* (Oxford, Oxford University Press, 2005) 55 (who was himself following Kit Barker in this regard).

[4] Following NJ McBride, *The Humanity of Private Law*, Part I: *Explanation* (Oxford, Hart Publishing, 2019) 55.

[5] N McBride, 'Stephen A Smith on Duties and Liabilities' at https://ssrn.com/abstract=2668742, 11–13.

B. Liability or Duty?

The fact that liabilities and duties – though wholly distinct as concepts – often come nested within each other can make it difficult to know whether in a given case, the law's *first* response to something the defendant has done is to impose a liability or a duty on the defendant. Consider:

> *Jagger*. Penner carelessly runs over what seems to be a shambling, decrepit tramp. The 'tramp' turns out to be Mick Jagger, and his injuries cause him to cancel a Rolling Stones tour that would have netted him £2 million.[6]

There is no doubt here that the law will intervene to help ensure that £2m is transferred from Penner (or Penner's insurer) to Jagger. But how does it do this? Does it (i) make Penner liable to be made to pay Jagger £2m (with a duty to pay that money to Jagger arising later on down the line, if Penner and Jagger enter a settlement, or Jagger obtains judgment against Penner); or (ii) does it impose a duty on Penner to pay Jagger £2m (with a liability to be made to pay that sum arising to support or replicate that duty)? The question has, of course, sharply divided tort law theorists. Steve joined John Goldberg and Benjamin Zipursky in arguing that (i) is the correct analysis.[7] Arthur Ripstein, John Gardner, and Sandy Steel and Robert Stevens all think that (ii) is the better view.[8]

The debate on this matter has been inconclusive, for two reasons. The first is that people's positions in this debate have tended to be driven by wider positions that they have taken on the nature of tort law and private law.[9] The second is that when they have sought for some neutral ground on which we could determine whether (i) or (ii) is correct, participants in this debate have tended to locate that ground in the case law – and the case law is signally inconclusive on the matter.[10]

[6] See J Penner, 'Don't Crash Into Mick Jagger When He is Driving His Rolls Royce: Liability in Damages for Economic Loss Consequent Upon a Personal Injury' in P Miller and J Oberdiek (eds), *Civil Wrongs and Justice in Private Law* (Oxford, Oxford University Press, 2020) 253.

[7] Smith (n 1) 191–201; SA Smith, 'The Significance of a Civil Wrong' in Miller and Oberdiek (eds) (n 6) 157; J Goldberg and B Zipursky, *Recognizing Wrongs* (Cambridge, MA, Harvard University Press, 2020) chs 4 and 5.

[8] A Ripstein, *Private Wrongs* (Cambridge, MA, Harvard University Press, 2016) ch 9; J Gardner, *Torts and Other Wrongs* (Oxford, Oxford University Press, 2019) ch 2, 99–100; S Steel and R Stevens, 'The Secondary Legal Duty to Pay Damages' (2020) 136 *LQR* 283.

[9] Even Steve's position – which could have been expected to be least affected by wider debates about the foundations of tort law, and most concerned with finding out 'Just the facts, ma'am' – was affected by his view that legal duty-imposing rules actually tell us what '"all-things-considered" (or "moral" or "unqualified")' duties we have: Smith (n 1) 116. For criticisms of this view, see NJ McBride, 'Are There Any Moral Duties?' in H Psarras and S Steel (eds), *Private Law and Practical Reason: Essays on John Gardner's Private Law Theory* (Oxford, Oxford University Press, 2023) 43.

[10] For example, Steel and Stevens argue that the existence of the remedy of distress damage feasant – entitling A to detain a chattel of B's that has come onto A's land and done damage until B makes a satisfactory offer to compensate A for the damage – shows that a tortfeasor has a legal duty to pay compensation to the victim of his tort: 'It would be odd if A were entitled to keep B's property without B's consent in order to obtain compensation from B, if B were under no legal duty to pay such compensation.' (Steel and Stevens (n 8) 288.) But it is not clear that B needs to have committed a *tort* for the remedy of distress damage feasant to apply – all that is required is that B's chattel was 'trespassing' in the sense that it was on A's land without A's consent. So before the Animals Act 1971, a straying animal belonging to B that caused damage to A's land could be detained by A, but B will not have committed the tort of trespass to land merely because his animal strayed onto A's land: *Buckle v Holmes* [1926] 2 KB 125 (CA).

A more promising basis for resolving this debate is to reflect on what a *law-abiding* person would regard themselves as bound to do in situations like *Jagger*.[11] Could Penner wait and see what Jagger did by way of suing him for compensation, without thinking that by doing so he was flouting the law? I think he could – and I cannot imagine that the defenders of (ii) would try to contend that he could not.[12] If this is right, then the defenders of (ii) would have to concede that there is something wrong with their position, and that (i) better captures the reality of Penner's situation. Contrast:

> *Car*. Fred promises to pay Rob £100 if Rob washes his car. Rob does so, and Fred is satisfied with the job that has been done.

In this situation, I do not think that Fred could think of himself as being law-abiding if he were to sit back and wait to be sued by Rob for the money that he had promised to pay Rob. This indicates that, unlike in *Jagger*, Fred is under a legal duty to pay Rob the promised £100 and not just subject to a liability to be made to pay Rob £100. Similarly:

> *Hire*. Bill arranges for his car to be repaired by Josh. Josh promises to provide Bill with a courtesy car that he can use while his car is being repaired. When Bill delivers his car to Josh's garage, no courtesy car is available and Bill has to spend £500 on hiring a car.

Again, I do not think Josh can sit back and wait to see if Bill sues him for the expense he has incurred because of Josh's failure to provide him with a courtesy car and still think of himself as being a law-abiding citizen. In order to preserve that image of himself, he has to be more proactive and reach out to Bill and offer to make him whole. *Hire* and *Jagger*, together, indicate that there is something radically different about compensatory remedies in contract and tort – the first give effect to duties, the second to liabilities. Why this should be is beyond the scope of this chapter.[13] More pertinent to defining its scope is:

> *Salary*. Due to a computer glitch, Lionel's salary is paid twice over into his bank account by his employer.

Suppose Lionel is aware of the overpayment. If his friends asked him, 'What are you going to do?', could they think that he was law-abiding if he responded 'Nothing – I'll wait to see if my employer comes after me and demands their money back. I think it's likely they won't even notice what's happened'? I do not think they could, and English law agrees – its consistent view has been that Lionel's taking such a stance is tantamount to theft.[14] Steve disagreed, arguing that Lionel was not under a duty to pay back

[11] That legal duties are centrally addressed to those who are willing to abide by the law was, of course, a central claim of HLA Hart, *The Concept of Law* (Oxford, Clarendon Press, 1961) 6–13, ch 2, 38–42.

[12] It should be noted that just as there is a difference between what the law requires us to do and what morality requires us to do, there is a difference between what a law-abiding person would do and what a morally righteous person would do. The test in the text focuses on what someone who is simply concerned to obey the law would do.

[13] The basis of an answer is provided by NJ McBride, *Key Ideas in Contract Law* (Oxford, Hart Publishing, 2017) 3–10; McBride (n 4) 166–67, 204–12.

[14] *Moynes v Coopper* [1956] 1 QB 439 (CA) (acquitting Lionel of theft (larceny), but reluctantly); R Cross, 'Stealing Through a Mistake' (1956) 72 *LQR* 181, 183 (condemning the decision in *Moynes* as a 'public scandal'); Theft Act 1968, s 5(4) (reversing *Moynes*); *R v Gilks* [1972] 1 WLR 1341 (CA) (applying s 5(4)); *Westdeutsche Landesbank v Islington LBC* [1996] AC 669 (HL) 715 (retaining money paid by mistake, being

the money that was paid him by mistake.[15] However, reflection on what a law-abiding individual would have done indicates that *Salary* is more like *Hire* than *Jagger*.[16]

C. Free-standing

Steve defined a 'free-standing' order as follows:

> Free-standing orders are neither replicates nor substitutes for substantive duties; nor is their content a response to the breach of such duties.[17]

Building on this definition, we can say that *a free-standing liability is not 'duty-supporting' and it does not arise as a result of the breach of a duty*. It stands on its own two feet, outside the world of duties that we owe each other. Free-standing liabilities belong to what Ian Ayres calls 'optional law'.[18] Where A is subject to a free-standing liability to B: (i) B has the option of altering A's legal position in a way that A did not ask for or invite, while (ii) at the same time, A has the option of waiting to see whether B will alter his (A's) legal position in that way, and (iii) B is given that option even though A has not done anything legally wrong in relation to B.

None of the liabilities we have looked at so far are free-standing in this sense. In *Car*, *Hire* and *Salary*, (ii) is not satisfied – the subject of the liability in those cases does not have the option of sitting back and waiting to see whether their legal position will be altered by their counterpart: they are under a duty to be proactive and alter their legal position themselves. In *Jagger*, (ii) is satisfied, but (iii) is not – Penner has done something legally wrong in relation to Jagger.

It should be noted that Steve argued that Penner's liability in *Jagger* is free-standing (on *his* definition of what 'free-standing' means) because Penner's liability is not duty-supporting *and* is *not a response to* the fact that Penner has *breached* a legal duty (of care) owed to Jagger. In Steve's view, 'while a standard compensatory award (eg damages for negligence) is conditional on proof of a wrong, the wrong is a condition, not the reason, for the award. The reason for an ordinary compensatory award is … an injustice',[19] where Steve defined 'an injustice' as 'an unfair loss or gain that has arisen from a transaction between the claimant and defendant'.[20]

It is beyond the scope of this chapter to get into debates over whether Penner's liability to Jagger arises because he wronged Jagger through his careless driving, or whether

aware of the mistake, will create a constructive trust over the money paid over, in the same way as a thief holds stolen money on trust for the owner (ibid, 716)).

[15] SA Smith, 'A Duty to Make Restitution' (2013) 26 *Canadian Journal of Law and Jurisprudence* 157; SA Smith, 'The Restatement of Liabilities in Restitution' in C Mitchell and W Swadling (eds), *The Restatement Third: Restitution and Unjust Enrichment – Critical and Comparative Essays* (Oxford, Hart Publishing, 2013) 227.

[16] *Contra*, SA Smith, 'Unjust Enrichment: Nearer to Tort than Contract' in R Chambers, C Mitchell and J Penner (eds), *Philosophical Foundations of the Law of Unjust Enrichment* (Oxford, Oxford University Press, 2009) 181.

[17] Smith (n 1) 101.

[18] I Ayres, *Optional Law: The Structure of Legal Entitlements* (Chicago, IL, University of Chicago Press, 2005).

[19] Smith (n 1) 101. See also Smith (n 7).

[20] Smith (n 1) 223.

it arises because (Steve's view) it is sometimes fair to hold people liable for the losses they have caused others, and one of the situations where it is fair to do this is where the losses are a result of the loss-causers' doing something that they should not have done.[21] My definition of a free-standing liability conveniently bypasses such debates by stipulating that a liability that A has incurred to B can only count as free-standing if it arises even though A has not done anything legally wrong to B. On *that* definition, Penner's liability to Jagger does not count as free-standing.

II. Examples

With these definitions in mind, what examples can we give of the law's recognising a free-standing liability? We can begin with a list of such examples that can be gleaned from the *summa* of Steve's thought: his book *Rights, Wrongs, and Injustices*.

A. Steve's List

Taking pride of place in Steve's list of free-standing liabilities was (i) the liability of a defendant in restitution to account for the value of a benefit they had received from a claimant; and (ii) the liability of a tortfeasor to pay compensatory damages to the victim of their tort. For the reasons explained in section I, I do not think either of these liabilities counts as free-standing, on my definition of a free-standing liability: (i) is not free-standing because it is duty-supporting; (ii) is not free-standing because, while it is not duty-supporting, its existence is conditional on the breach of a duty.

So what else was on Steve's list? The following:

(1) Financial orders on divorce.[22]
(2) Liabilities to be made to allow one's neighbour access to one's land.[23]
(3) Liabilities to have a consumer credit agreement altered if it is unfair.[24]
(4) Vicarious liabilities.[25]
(5) Liabilities arising under the rule in *Rylands v Fletcher*.[26]
(6) Liabilities to be made to compensate owners whose property the defendant has lawfully damaged in circumstances of necessity.[27]
(7) Liabilities to be made to pay damages in lieu of an injunction where an injunction is refused because of the desirability of the defendant's behaving in the way the claimant seeks an injunction against.[28]

[21] ibid 267.
[22] ibid 101.
[23] ibid 102, fn 27.
[24] ibid.
[25] ibid 259.
[26] ibid 259–60.
[27] ibid 261.
[28] ibid 261–63.

(8) Liabilities to be made to pay damages in lieu of a contract's being rescinded for innocent misrepresentation.[29]
(9) Liabilities to be made to pay compensation to a claimant where you have committed a wrong to a third party and the claimant has suffered loss as a result.[30]

Are all of these genuine examples of free-standing liabilities? Recall that a free standing liability is (i) not replicative of a duty or duty-supporting, and (ii) arises regardless of whether the subject of the liability did anything legally wrong to the person who is able to exercise the power corresponding to that liability.

If it is right to say – as Steve did, and I agree – that the liability to pay compensatory damages in *Jagger* is not duty-supporting, then (i) is automatically satisfied in (4) above – if Penner happened to be acting in the course of his employment in running down Jagger, it could hardly be said that his employer's vicarious liability to pay compensatory damages to Jagger is duty-supporting when Penner's liability is not. And (ii) is also satisfied in (4) above, provided one does not accept the 'master's tort' theory of vicarious liability, as arising out of the defendant's having done something wrong to the claimant by virtue of the act of one of the defendant's subordinates. If one rejects this theory then (4) seems to be a free-standing liability.

The same is true of (5) above: (i) is satisfied because if careless Penner's liability to pay damages in *Jagger* is not duty-supporting, it is hard to see how a careful defendant could be said to have a duty to pay the damages that he is made to pay under *Rylands v Fletcher*; (ii) is also satisfied: the (at the time) controversial position taken by McBride and Bagshaw back in 2001 that a defendant who is held liable under *Rylands* has not (necessarily) done anything legally wrong, and should not therefore be regarded as having committed a tort, is now orthodoxy.[31]

Liabilities (4) and (5) are therefore central cases of free-standing liabilities. Liability (2) is also obviously free-standing if D's liability to be made to allow D's neighbour, N, access to D's land applies in cases where D has done nothing wrong to N and where D has no duty to allow N to access D's land. This seems to be the case under the Access to Neighbouring Land Act 1992: the only conditions on N's being able to gain access to do work on D's land are where it is necessary to do so to prevent damage to N's land and N's gaining access to D's land to do that work would not disturb D's use and enjoyment of their land. In such cases, D's refusing to allow N access to D's land might be unneighbourly, but it could hardly be said to be illegal.

Liability (3) also seems to be free-standing for the interesting reason that where B has loaned money to C on terms that are judged to be unfair, B cannot be said to have a duty to alter the loan agreement between B and C because that is not something that B can do unilaterally: it has to be done by B *and* C; and if not by them, by a court. So B's liability to have the terms of the B–C agreement altered to B's disadvantage – in England, under section 140A of the Consumer Credit Act 1974 – is not duty-supporting. It also does not seem to arise out of B's having done anything wrong to C: it is difficult to argue that there is a duty not to lend money to someone else on unfair terms.

[29] ibid 264.
[30] ibid 264–65.
[31] ibid 259–60; D Nolan, 'The Distinctiveness of *Rylands v Fletcher*' (2005) 121 *LQR* 421, 437–38; P Jaffey, 'Liabilities in Private Law' (2008) 41 *Legal Theory* 233, 240; Goldberg and Zipursky (n 7) 191.

Other examples are more problematic. It is strongly arguable that liabilities (1), (6), (7) and (8) are duty-supporting and therefore not free-standing. Taking liability (6) first, and considering the classic example of a mountaineer who – in order to escape an impending and life-threatening storm on the mountain he has been climbing – breaks into a hut and takes advantage of some of the provisions stored there, most law-abiding people would look askance at the mountaineer were he to walk away and not make any attempt to compensate the hut owner for the damage done in using the hut.

A good case can be made for thinking that a defendant has a *duty* to pay damages in lieu of a remedy such as an injunction or rescission: it is only fair that if such a remedy would normally be granted against them, but they are asking a court not to do so, then they should pay the claimant the monetary equivalent of what they are asking the court to deprive the claimant of. If this is right, then (7) and (8) are not free-standing but duty-supporting.

Turning to liability (1), it is hard to see why a court has jurisdiction to make financial orders on divorce if there is not some sense in which a married couple, even after divorce, are subject to ongoing duties owed to each other to support the other. If this is right then (1) is, like (6), (7) and (8), duty-supporting.

This leaves liability (9), under which Steve grouped a number of different liabilities: (i) claims for contribution against a co-tortfeasor under the Civil Liability (Contribution) Act 1978; (ii) claims for compensation under the Fatal Accidents Act 1976; (iii) claims for compensation under the Contracts (Rights of Third Parties) Act 1999; and (iv) claims for compensation under the Congenital Disabilities (Civil Liability) Act 1976 and the Latent Damage Act 1986.[32] All but (iii) pass muster as free-standing in nature. For example, if Penner's liability to pay compensatory damages to Jagger is not duty-supporting, it is hard to see how any potential claim for contribution that he has against a co-tortfeasor (such as Jagger's bodyguard, who carelessly failed to save Jagger from being run over) could be duty-supporting. And, of course, the co-tortfeasor is held liable to Penner even though he has not done anything wrong to Penner. Class (iii) is more doubtful: if the liabilities in *Car* and *Hire* are duty-supporting and not free-standing, then it is arguable that liabilities to a third party to the contract in such cases are also duty-supporting.

So, of Steve's suggested list of free-standing liabilities, we end up with (2), (3), (4) and (5), and most examples under (9), as genuinely free-standing. However, there are some omissions from the list that we can add to replace the deleted items.

B. Other Examples

The following examples might be added to the list in section II.A:

(10) *Strict product liability*. Given Steve's willingness to regard liability under the rule in *Rylands v Fletcher* as free-standing, it is puzzling that he did not similarly classify a manufacturer's strict liability to compensate those physically harmed by a dangerously defective product produced by the manufacturer, and indeed did not

[32] Smith (n 1) 264.

mention that liability in his book. It may be that such a classification would have set off some North American sensitivities: if we say that strict product liability is not (strictly speaking) based on the manufacturer's having committed a tort, then tort law becomes very small in North-American eyes.[33] However, anyone not labouring under the influence of such sensitivities will readily acknowledge that strict product liability arising under, for example, the Consumer Protection Act 1987 is free-standing.[34]

(11) *Rescission for innocent misrepresentation.* If Steve was willing to think of a liability to pay damages in lieu of rescission for innocent misrepresentation as free-standing, then he surely would have accepted that the liability to have a contract procured by innocent misrepresentation rescinded was free-standing.[35] A doubt over whether this liability is free-standing is created by Tony Weir's arguing that the liability arises in response to the fact that 'if you … make an honest mistake in what you say and the other party believes you and contracts on that basis, it would be very bad of you to try to take advantage of the mistake you innocently caused, and equity will not allow you to do it. Although there is no fraud in the transaction, there is fraud in the action …'[36] This suggests that this kind of liability is duty-supporting: it corresponds to a duty on the part of the misrepresentor not to enforce the contract that has resulted from his misrepresentation. However, the liability to have a contract procured by innocent misrepresentation rescinded will still count as free-standing if – as with liability (2) in section II.A – the misrepresentor would not be acting illegally but merely *unvirtuously* by attempting to enforce a contract that resulted from his innocent misrepresentation.

(12) *Rescission of unfair salvage agreements.* It is well established that an agreement to save a ship from sinking by towing it to safe harbour is liable to be set aside if the price agreed on for salvaging the ship is unfair.[37] It might be thought that this liability is not free-standing, as it arises out of the wrong of taking unfair advantage of a ship owner's plight to gouge the owner for an excessive fee to rescue his ship. However, this explanation is made untenable by the fact that a salvage agreement is liable to be set aside if the price agreed on for saving a ship is *too low*, as well as too high.[38] The liability is not therefore conditional on any kind of wrongdoing by the salvager and therefore must be free-standing.

[33] See NJ McBride, 'Review of Goldberg and Zipursky, *Recognizing Wrongs*' (2020) 83 *MLR* 1124, 1125–26 for the same diagnosis of Goldberg and Zipursky's attempts to argue that strict product liability is based on the manufacturer's having committed a tort.

[34] Liability under the 1987 Act is so obviously free-standing that the law has to engage in a fiction to allow claims to be brought under the Fatal Accidents Act 1976 where a dangerously defective product has killed someone: s 6(1)(a) of the 1987 Act provides that in such a case, the death will be '*deemed* to have been caused … by [the manufacturer's] *wrongful* act, neglect or default' (emphasis added).

[35] That it did not figure in Steve's list of free-standing liabilities is because he was mainly concerned with discussing free-standing liabilities that were designed to remedy an injustice – an unfair loss or gain arising between the claimant and defendant.

[36] T Weir, 'Contracts in Rome and England' (1992) 66 *Tulane Law Review* 1615, 1624. See also *Redgrave v Hurd* (1881) 20 ChD 1 (CA), 12–13.

[37] *The Port Caledonia and The Anna* [1903] P 184.

[38] *The Theodore* (1858) Swab 351, 352; *The Phantom* (1866) LR 1 A & E 58; *The Westbourne* (1899) 14 PD 132. See also the International Convention on Salvage (London, 28 April 1989), Art 7(b).

(13) *Building Safety Act 2022*.[39] This Act was introduced in the aftermath of the 2017 Grenfell Tower fire and sought to come to grips with the issue of who was going to pay for the costs of remedying the hundreds of high-rise buildings that were made with the same flammable cladding that was responsible for the Grenfell Tower fire. Section 130 gives the courts the power to make Company A vicariously liable for Company B's liabilities in respect of building defects if A is 'associated' with B by virtue of the fact that one controls the other or they are both controlled by a third company (section 131) and it would be 'just and equitable' to make A liable in respect of B's liabilities. Whether or not *B*'s liabilities are appropriately analysed as free-standing, any liabilities that *A* incurs under section 131 will be free-standing. Just as with liability (4) in section II.A, it will not be possible to argue that A's liability arises out of anything wrong that A has done, or gives effect to a prior duty to which A is subject.

C. The List

The above reflections allow us to produce the following list of free-standing liabilities:

(1) Liabilities to be made to allow one's neighbour access to one's land.
(2) Liabilities to have a consumer credit agreement altered if it is unfair.
(3) Vicarious liabilities.
(4) Liabilities arising under the rule in *Rylands v Fletcher*.
(5) Liabilities to be made to pay compensation to a claimant where you have committed a wrong to a third party and the claimant has suffered loss as a result.
(6) Strict product liability.
(7) Rescission for innocent misrepresentation.
(8) Rescission of unfair salvage agreements.
(9) Liabilities arising under section 130 of the Building Safety Act 2022.

III. Explanations

The above examples of free-standing liabilities seem to fall into three groups, corresponding to three distinct roles that they play.

A. Liabilities Promoting Social Goods

The first group exists in order to achieve some social good. A defendant who is affixed with one of these (what we can call) 'type 1' free-standing liabilities has no duty to promote that good, but other people are empowered to make the defendant serve that

[39] My discussion here is indebted to the pioneering work of Sue Bright and Ben McFarlane: see their chapter 'Private Law Failings and Policy Development Following the Grenfell Tower Fire' in J Gardner et al (eds), *Politics, Policy and Private Law*, vol 1 (Oxford, Hart Publishing, 2023), 127.

good if they wish to make the defendant do this. Concerns that imposing a type 1 free-standing liability on a defendant amounts to using the defendant as a mere means to an end are allayed by pointing to some aspect of the defendant that means that it is 'not unfair' to call on them to serve a particular good. Examples of type 1 free-standing liabilities in the list in section II.C are (4), (8) and (9).

The social good served by (4) is allaying anxiety – providing people living in the shadow of some new, dangerous and unpredictable technology that is being developed on someone else's land with the assurance that, should things go wrong and they be harmed as a result, they will be able to call on the person operating the novel technology to compensate them for that harm.[40] It is not unfair to make the operator so liable, as they will reap the benefits of that technology should things go right.[41]

The social good served by (8) in the list is the maintenance of a large shipping fleet – an important good for a maritime nation, and one that was most poignantly illustrated by the rescue of the British Army from the beaches at Dunkirk in 1940. As Dr Lushington observed in *The Henry*, 'It is very desirable that agreements [to salvage ships in peril] should exist.'[42] The courts promote the making of such agreements by making it clear to the parties that there is no point dickering over the terms on the high seas: should the terms so arrived at strike the courts back in port as unjust or unfair, those terms are liable to be set aside. Doing so is not unfair to either party – the owner of the ship in peril gets to keep his ship and is made to pay a fair price for doing so, and the salvagor of the ship is fairly remunerated for their efforts.

The social good served by (9) in the list is the removal of a dangerous substance from the outside of blocks of flats without those least able to pay for that removal – the tenants of the flats – being made to pay for this. It is not unfair to make a company liable under section 130 of the Building Safety Act 2022 to pay for that remediation work as, being associated with a company that *is* liable for that work, it will have benefited in some way financially from that other company's activities in creating the danger that now has to be cleared up.

B. Liabilities Promoting the Legitimacy of Private Law

The second group of free-standing liabilities does not seek to promote any external social good, but instead exists to preserve the legitimacy of the legal system. Examples of these type 2 liabilities are (3), (5) and (6) in the list in section II.C. Once again, the defendant who is subject to this kind of free-standing liability is under no duty proactively to take steps to shore up the legal system's legitimacy. But he can be made to do so where doing so would not be unfair on the defendant given the defendant's position or conduct.

Liabilities (3) and (6) exist to ensure that a claimant (C) does not hit an insuperable wall when seeking to make a claim against a defendant (D). In (3), C wants to sue

[40] See McBride (n 4) 72.

[41] The locus classicus of all such arguments is AM Honoré, 'Responsibility and luck: the moral basis of strict liability' (1988) 104 *LQR* 530.

[42] *The Henry* (1851) 14 Jur 183, 183.

D for compensation in respect of harm that C has suffered as a result of being wronged by (let us suppose) D's employee (E). If D had ordered E to commit the wrong then C could easily sue D as an accessory to E's wrong. There is suspicion that E *was* ordered to commit the wrong as E was acting 'in the course of his employment' by D in committing that wrong; but D denies that he ordered E to commit that wrong, and can point to instructions issued to E telling E not to commit such wrongs in doing his job. In light of this, C's claim will fail, as C cannot get access to the truth about what actually transpired between D and E. In order that C not be left with the feeling that the legal system is 'all mouth and no trousers' when it comes to doing justice in C's case, the courts ride roughshod over D's denials and hold him liable anyway, merely because E was acting in the course of his employment by D in committing the tort.[43] Doing so is not unfair for a number of reasons:[44] D can easily afford to pay for E's wrong; D will have benefited financially from all the times E carried out his functions without wronging anyone; D probably could have done more to control E and prevent E from committing his wrong.

Similar reasoning underlies liability (6), where C has been injured by a dangerously defective product manufactured by D. C would have a good claim against D if D had been negligent in manufacturing the product, but proving negligence will ordinarily be impossible for C. So the law holds D liable anyway, reasoning that it is not unfair to do so given the financial rewards D will reap from all the products manufactured by D that prove not to be dangerously defective.[45]

The sort of liabilities gathered under (5) in the list exist to ensure that the legal system does not operate in an arbitrary way in distributing the burdens of compensating or indemnifying those who have suffered loss.[46] So where C and D are both liable to X in respect of some harm X has suffered at their hands, and X sues C for full compensation in respect of that harm, C is allowed to seek a 'just and equitable' contribution from D so that X's choice does not saddle C with the full burden of compensating X. Similarly, if C and D are co-guarantors of a debt owed to X which is not paid, and X seeks to sue C in respect of that debt, C can seek to make D pay her back 50 per cent of the monies she was made to pay X. And C and D can then seek a full indemnity from X's debtor, who was the one who should have paid in the first place.

C. Liabilities Promoting Virtuous Behaviour

Finally, the third group of free-standing liabilities exists to empower others to compel a right-holder to act virtuously in exercising that right. Examples of these type 3

[43] See McBride (n 4) 248–49.

[44] See *Various Claimants v Catholic Child Welfare Society* [2012] UKSC 56, [2013] 2 AC 1 [35] (per Lord Phillips).

[45] It might be argued that these arguments merely support *presuming* that D is liable to C, and putting the onus on D to show that he did not order E to commit his tort/was not at fault for the defect in the product that harmed C. However, taking such a position would still put C under a fundamental disadvantage given how easy it would be for D to manufacture evidence to put the burden of proof back on C, and how difficult it would be for C to show that that evidence was manufactured.

[46] See McBride (n 4) 212–16; R Stevens, *The Laws of Restitution* (Oxford, Oxford University Press, 2023) ch 9.

free-standing liabilities are (1), (2) and (7) in the list in section II.C. In James Penner's terminology, these liabilities force a right-holder not to act like a 'jerk'.[47] But why in these situations is the right-holder merely *liable* to be made not to act like a jerk? Why is the right-holder not put under a *duty* not to act like a jerk? After all, we could say that a trustee is a right-holder who is under a duty not to act like a jerk – or, in more technical language, 'not to be a stickler for his rights in a bad way'.[48] We have already seen that with liability (2), the right-holder is only under a liability because he needs the court's help not to act like a jerk. But that is not true of (1) or (7). The choice between employing a liability or a duty in (1) or (7) seems to come down to whether (i) we want the right-holder to be allowed to act like a jerk in exercising his rights in relation to C unless and until C objects, or (ii) we want the right-holder not to act like a jerk in exercising his rights in relation to C unless and until C permits him to do so. The law has evidently taken position (i) when subjecting the right-holder in (1) and (7) to a free-standing liability not to act like a jerk. Its doing so should come as no surprise given the importance attached by the law to allowing landowners and contractors maximal freedom in exercising their respective rights.

IV. The New World

Steve's work shows us that the premier biennial conference on private law is misnamed in being called 'Obligations'. We live in a new world where private law must be understood not just in terms of the rights and obligations it recognises that parties owe each other, but also in terms of the powers and liabilities that exist between people. Free-standing liabilities show that those powers and liabilities are not always subsidiary offshoots of the rights and obligations we owe each other but perform distinctive and independent roles within private law. It follows that any account or theory of private law that simply sees it as giving effect to certain rights and obligations will be radically defective. We are all greatly in Steve's debt for reminding us of this fact.

[47] J Penner, 'We All Make Mistakes: a 'Duty of Virtue' Theory of Restitutionary Liability for Mistaken Payments' (2018) 81 *MLR* 222, 225.

[48] Aristotle, *Nicomachean Ethics* 1138a1.

23

Is Private Law Normatively Distinctive?

PAUL B MILLER

I. Introduction

With the recent passing of Stephen Smith, we in private law theory have lost one of our best. In person, Smith was luminescent in multiple ways: brilliant, obviously, but also warm, genial and mischievously funny. On the page, Smith illuminates still through contributions that will continue to shape scholarship in the field.

Stephen Smith wrote so insightfully about so many topics that it is difficult to focus on a single work or theme in memorialising him. There is his groundbreaking monograph on contract theory,[1] as well as his more recent opus on remedies.[2] But there is also a formidable body of work on general private law theory and the nature of the common law, as well as incisive analysis of a medley of topics in tort, unjust enrichment and fiduciary law. One is spoiled for choice in reflecting on ways in which Smith helps us to better understand private law. Nevertheless, a choice having to be made, I decided upon an essay that elaborates some of his methodological convictions and shows how his general jurisprudential views shaped his work on private law. In 'The Normativity of Private Law',[3] Smith argues that leading accounts by utilitarians and their ilk betray a fundamental misunderstanding of private law. The misunderstanding is rooted in their failure to acknowledge or to grapple properly with the normativity of private law. Blinkered by commitments characteristic of legal nihilism, nominalism and/or a narrow behaviourism, they fail to consider that private law is what it appears to be: a normative system that presents itself as morally authoritative (ie, as a binding, but also reliable, source of guidance about what we may or ought to do[4]). In the essay,

[1] SA Smith, *Contract Theory* (Oxford, Oxford University Press, 2004).

[2] SA Smith, *Rights, Wrongs, and Injustices: The Structure of Remedial Law* (Oxford, Oxford University Press, 2019).

[3] SA Smith, 'The Normativity of Private Law' (2011) 31 *OJLS* 215.

[4] This account also draws on my own views developed in PB Miller, 'Juridical Justification of Private Rights' in M Crawford, S Degeling and N Tivieros (eds), *Justifying Private Rights* (Oxford, Hart Publishing, 2020) 105; PB Miller, 'The New Formalism in Private Law' (2021) 66(2) *American Journal of Jurisprudence* 175; and PB Miller, 'Formalism, Legality, and the Rule of Law' in T Kuntz and PB Miller (eds), *Methodology in Private Law Theory: Between New Private Law and Rechtsdogmatik* (Oxford, Oxford University Press, 2024) 205.

Smith forcefully asserts the normativity of private law, establishing lodestars that would inspire subsequent developments in the New Private Law.[5]

My engagement with Smith's work will unfold as follows. Section II offers a selective summary of Smith's views on the normativity of private law, noting the indicia he isolates and situating his views relative to those of his antagonists. It also holds that Smith's arguments succeed on his terms: Smith is right to say that one cannot understand private law without recognising and engaging with its normativity. In section III, I reorient Smith's project, asking what it might have to teach about a question that has been a bugbear in private law theory for decades: whether there is anything genuinely distinctive about what is conventionally denominated 'private law'. I argue that one can find within Smith's work resources for a productive reframing of the question whether private law is normatively distinctive. The reframing allows for nuance absent in sweeping affirmative answers to this question in older work of private law theory, while at the same time making the question more tractable and interesting. Section IV concludes.

II. Smith on the Normativity of Private Law

In 'The Normativity of Private Law', Smith suggests that broad swathes of private law theory, mostly of American extraction, betray a deep and decisive misunderstanding of private law. This work – which Smith associates with utilitarianism and Holmes' sanction theory of law – combines elements of moral antirealism, legal realism, functionalism and behaviourism. It reduces law to a mechanism of social control and considers its effectiveness exclusively in terms of its empirically verifiable impact on social behaviour; namely, whether the law's threat of sanction successfully induces obedience. Law is said to provide effective stimulus only through a credible threat of coercive force, with the supposition that the representative person in a political community governed by law will be motivated to obey only on the basis of fear of sanction. Thus, the view tends to equate law with sanctions, or to claim that the only practically important element in the public theatrics of law is a credible threat of coercive imposition of sanctions. Falling out of the picture are law's substantive norms: the rights and duties, powers and liabilities, and other constructs that lawyers know prefigure and mediate the application of sanctions.

As Smith recognised, this way of thinking about law has held enduring appeal despite having been pilloried in general jurisprudence.[6] And it continues to permeate American legal thought, with its influence partly explaining persistent disinterest

[5] Smith supported the founding of this movement by contributing to an inaugural symposium published by the Harvard Law School – SA Smith, 'Duties, Liabilities, and Damages' (2012) 125 *Harvard Law Review* 1727 – and by initiating (with Andrew Gold, John Goldberg, Henry Smith and me) the annual North American Workshop on Private Law Theory.

[6] Most influentially, in HLA Hart's criticisms of the work John Austin. See HLA Hart, *The Concept of Law*, 3rd edn (Oxford, Oxford University Press, 2012).

in private law doctrine, procedures and institutions.[7] Indeed, its allure is much wider than Smith suggests. While its lineage may be traced to select strands of positivism and consequentialism, its endurance reflects mutually reinforcing tendencies of other domestic intellectual movements, especially American legal realism and neoclassical law and economics. The combination of functionalism and behaviourism, and concomitant emphases on coercion, sanctions and outcomes have been appealing to a cast as varied as certain positivists sceptical of strong claims about the normativity of law,[8] the brass-tacks pragmatist concerned only with the law's consequences,[9] the legal realist sceptical whether substantive law can bind,[10] the critical legal studies scholar who sees law primarily as an instrument of control and oppression,[11] the utilitarian who thinks that what matters morally is not what the law says but what it does,[12] and the legal economist interested in the law's efficiency and impact on social costs.[13]

Smith is not one to deny the importance of the law's social consequences. Quite the opposite: he tries to persuade utilitarians that they ought to take substantive law seriously because it demonstrably shapes social behaviour in ways that impact social welfare.[14] Nevertheless, Smith claims that loosely utilitarian/Holmesian perspectives fundamentally misunderstand private law. The root problem is their refusal to take private law at face value, that is, to consider that private law *is* what it *appears* to be. Against those who 'regard legal norms as shams',[15] Smith insists that private law is a complex normative system: a finely woven framework of bona fide norms (legal rules) and the normative social practices through which these norms are developed, relied upon as guides to right conduct and, where apt, enforced on the presumed basis that they are morally authoritative. Smith's suggestion is that the appearance of normativity that lies plain for all to see on the surface of private law is meant to be, and is typically taken to be, real. Hence his claim that one cannot understand private law, including behaviour responsive to the substantive norms found in doctrine, if one abstracts from the law's normativity.

But what does it mean, exactly, to take private law at face value, and to see in it evidence of the law's normativity? For Smith, it means recognising and engaging directly with the *language* in which law is given and associated linguistic practices (*social behaviour*) through which law is received and taken up in daily life, in and out of court.

[7] For discussion, see JCP Goldberg, 'Pragmatism and Private Law' (2012) 125 *Harvard Law Review* 1640.

[8] See generally B Leiter, 'Legal Realism and Legal Positivism Reconsidered' (2001) 111 *Ethics* 278.

[9] Goldberg (n 7).

[10] See, eg, E Sherwin, 'Formalism and Realism in Private Law' in AS Gold et al (eds), *The Oxford Handbook of the New Private Law* (Oxford, Oxford University Press 2020) 465.

[11] See, eg, D Kennedy, 'The Critique of Rights in Critical Legal Studies' in W Brown and J Halley (eds), *Left Liberalism/Left Critique* (Durham, NC, Duke University Press, 2002) 178.

[12] As exemplified in L Kaplow and S Shavell, *Fairness versus Welfare* (Cambridge, MA, Harvard University Press, 2002).

[13] See, eg, R Coase, 'The Problem of Social Cost' (1960) 3 *Journal of Law & Economics* 1; L Kaplow, 'Private Versus Social Costs in Bringing Suit' (1986) 15 *Journal of Legal Studies* 371; and R Posner, *Economic Analysis of Law*, 9th edn (Boston, MA, Aspen Publishing, 2014).

[14] Smith (n 3) 227 (observing that 'legal norms are low-cost tools for influencing behaviour').

[15] ibid 216.

In turn, that means recognising that law makes pervasive and intentional use of *normative language*[16] and that social practices up- and down-stream of posited law are treated by participants as *normative social practices*.[17] In respect of the latter, one might say that normative social practices central to law feature behaviour by participants that is intelligible as normative partly in so far as it involves deliberate or witting interactions governed by a shared economy of norms (eg, the assertion of a right, demand for a remedy and so on).[18] As Hart recognised in his criticisms of Austin, it is certainly possible to theorise law without recognising its normativity from a posture detached from the social practices constitutive of it.[19] But from that vantagepoint, one cannot see and so one is apt to misjudge what motivates behaviour and how pertinent social practices are understood by those who engage in them.

To truly understand law, Hart taught, one must understand it from the internal vantagepoint of participants in social practices constitutive of law, viewing legal rules as they typically do, privileging their understanding of the language in which law is given and received as well as their understanding of the behaviour it elicits.[20] So, too, Smith says, to understand private law one must view its normative language and social practices in a way true to the shared understandings of legal officials and citizens. Of the former, echoing Raz on the law's implicit assertion of moral authority,[21] Smith says 'judges and lawmakers who present and explain law in normative language presumably assume that this language means something to the citizens to whom it is directed. Why else use it?'[22] Of citizens, he observes that we tend to see in law a claim of moral authority and to accept it: 'empirical studies have shown that many citizens believe that there is a moral obligation to obey the law and, further, that they often act on this belief'.[23] By ignoring these perspectives, one fails to see that the law guides through general rules and judicial rulings before it imposes sanctions, and that people ordinarily comply with rules and rulings, relying on them as a guide to right conduct, irrespective of whether there is a real prospect of their being sanctioned.

[16] Thus, Smith (ibid 215) emphasises that 'Private law presents itself in normative language. Judicial decisions in private law cases are replete with references to "duties", "obligations", "rights", "wrongs" and so on.'

[17] In Smith's words (ibid 221), '[T]he law presents itself as a normative institution … the most obvious way the law does this is by enacting rules that specify how citizens should behave. There are legal rules specifying that contracts should be performed, that no one should enter another's land without permission, that money paid by mistake should be returned and so on. The normativity of these "private law" rules is typically apparent on their face: most private law rules are framed in terms of duties to do or not do something … More specifically, private law duties are presented as setting out moral duties – as specifying things that ought, morally, to be done.'

[18] See Miller, 'The New Formalism in Private Law' (n 4).

[19] Hart (n 6) chs 1 and 2.

[20] ibid. On this and other conceptions of the internal point of view, see PB Miller and JA Pojanowski, 'The Internal Point of View in Private Law' (2022) *American Journal of Jurisprudence* 247. See also J Finnis, 'On Hart's Ways: Law as Reason and as Fact' (2007) 52 *American Journal of Jurisprudence* 25; and JCP Goldberg and BC Zipursky, 'Seeing Tort Law from the Internal Point of View: Holmes and Hart on Legal Duties' (2006) 75 *Fordham Law Review* 1563.

[21] J Raz, 'Hart on Moral Rights and Legal Duties' (1984) 4 *OJLS* 123, 131 ('No system is a system of law unless it includes a claim of legitimacy, of moral authority.').

[22] Smith (n 3) 222.

[23] ibid 223. See also Smith's observation that 'citizens sometimes do what legal rules stipulate simply because they are legal rules and not because of the incentives that the law offers for compliance': ibid 216.

III. Is Private Law Normatively Distinctive?

Smith's 'The Normativity of Private Law' convincingly makes the case for, well, the normativity of private law. That is, Smith convincingly shows that private law presents itself as a normative system, constituted and sustained by normative practices; practices of norm-generation and norm-reliance in which substantive norms are prominent. Smith also convincingly argues that the normativity of private law is essential to its nature, such that one cannot understand private law without understanding that, how and by what mechanisms it asserts or otherwise evinces normativity linguistically (ie, in its characteristic modes of expression) and behaviourally (ie, in its characteristic modes of being posited, applied, or enforced and in being relied upon directly as guide to right conduct). For reasons of my own, elaborated elsewhere, I shall take it that Smith's arguments, constructive and critical, are sound.[24]

Smith's case is decisive against those who ignore the normativity of law as manifested in the social practices in which private law's norms figure, or who treat those practices and norms as immaterial. It also stands, if not as a refutation, as a provocation to those who recognise private law's normativity but take it as either reflecting collective self-delusion marked by semi-conscious avoidance of law's indeterminacy or as a charade involving deliberate concealment of political will to power. Here, as elsewhere,[25] Smith rejects legal nihilism, as well as nominalistic indictments of doctrine, doctrinal knowledge and legal conceptual analysis.

Smith thus succeeded in the project he set for himself. And he succeeded in a way that should, if I may be excused for considering only the philosophers in his audience, be compelling to the positivist, the natural law theorist and to jurisprudes within neither tradition. Smith suggests that our collective experience of private law, oriented by the vantagepoint of participants, indicates a normativity that is recognised and accepted by officials and citizens alike. Whether acting as legislator, judge, political representative, bureaucrat or citizen, most of us treat law as a practically authoritative source of normative guidance in various social practices that belong to law or that fall within its sway.[26] In doing so, we generate social conditions of legality that turn on the practical efficacy of law as an authoritative guide to conduct.[27] Again, I stress that this does not commit Smith to the apologetic view that law is an unerring guide. As Raz would have it, the law necessarily *claims* moral authority or, as Green puts it, the law is necessarily *apt* for the realisation of justice and acts with moral pretence.[28]

[24] Miller, 'The New Formalism in Private Law' (n 4). On similarities and dissimilarities between our views, see Miller, 'Juridical Justification of Private Rights' (n 4) fn 3; and SA Smith, 'Intermediate and Comprehensive Justifications for Legal Rules' in S Degeling et al (eds) *Justifying Private Rights* (Oxford, Hart Publishing, 2020) 75, 75, fn 1.

[25] Smith (n 1) ch 1.

[26] Which is simpatico with Smith's claim that 'private law rules are presented as setting out moral duties' and his observation that 'from the law's perspective a legal duty is necessarily a moral duty'. Smith (n 3) 221.

[27] See Miller, 'Formalism, Legality, and the Rule of Law' (n 4).

[28] Raz (n 21); L Green, 'Positivism and the Inseparability of Law and Morals' (2008) 83 *New York University Law Review* 1035, 1050. See also Smith (n 2) 117, fn 22: 'I refer to the courts' "claims" to declaratory and directive authority to make clear that I do not assume that courts actually possess either kind of authority … to explain the practice of issuing orders … it is sufficient to show … that the practice might plausibly be thought to be justified. It is not necessary that the practice actually be justified.'

I think Smith would agree and hence would say that we can and ought to recognise the normativity of private law while holding open the question whether, where and how the law delivers on its claim to moral authority.[29]

Smith's reclamation of the normativity of private law, though, naturally raises another set of questions. They spring to mind because they have been put to private law, and to private law theorists, for decades, having germinated in the same milieu that fostered doubts about or indifference to the normativity of private law (ie, twentieth-century American legal thought). The questions: What is distinctively private about private law? And what are the relationship(s) between private and public law?

These questions present wide vistas of inquiry. To address them in a way responsive to the milieu in which they have flourished, one would need to unearth factors that have shaped the motivation(s) with which the questions have been pressed and the prejudice that sometimes accompanies them (eg, a presumption that there is nothing distinctively private about private law, or that boundaries between private and public law, even if meaningful in practice, have been deliberately constructed and are policed for suspect reasons). It is tempting to say something in an aperture that matches the breadth of the questions, given the bewitching spectre they have cast over late twentieth- and early twenty-first-century private law theory.[30] But I could not hope to make much progress here. And, so, I will consider a narrower question directly suggested by Smith's project: What (if anything) is *normatively* distinctive about private law?

I say that this question is suggested by Smith's project for two related reasons. First, Smith makes repeated reference to 'legal normativity', which implies that private law is a source of or manifests something other than moral or extra-legal normativity, but raises the question what 'legal normativity' consists in and whether the 'legal normativity' found in private law differs from that found elsewhere. Second, Smith makes repeated reference to 'private law' rather than 'law' generically, and examples meant to illustrate 'legal normativity' are drawn from fields conventionally thought to fall within private law, including norms and structural features usually thought to be, or to reflect, distinguishing marks of 'private law' (eg, correlative primary rights and duties, remedies that effectuate interpersonal redress, and orders that compel behaviour between private citizens interpersonally).

In what follows, I aim to show how the question about the normative distinctiveness of private law might be made tractable by being given a Smithian framing. The framing adds nuance, allowing one to see complexities often neglected in work that asserts normative distinctiveness for private law. But before I present the Smithian framing, it should first be noted that *none* of the evidence that Smith presents to establish the normativity of private law is suggestive of its normative distinctiveness. Rather, each reflects Smith's learning in general jurisprudence. The result is an account that is as illuminating of the normativity of public law as of private law.

[29] See Smith (n 5) 1746: '[L]egal rules are normative propositions … it is part of the very meaning of a legal rule that it is meant to reflect reasons – moral reasons – that already apply to those subject to it. When a court or legislature says that "there is a duty to do X," it is saying that citizens are morally obliged to do X. This understanding does not mean that citizens are in fact morally obliged to do X (the law may be mistaken).'

[30] Consider EJ Weinrib, *The Idea of Private Law* (Cambridge, MA, Harvard University Press, 1995); EJ Weinrib, 'Private Law and Public Right' (2011) 61 *University of Toronto Law Journal* 191; and H Dagan and BC Zipursky, 'The Distinction Between Private Law and Public Law' in H Dagan and BC Zipursky (eds), *Research Handbook on Private Law Theories* (Cheltenham, Edward Elgar, 2020).

Consider first Smith's emphasis on the normative language in which law is expressed: the language of right and duty, wrong and remedy. This language pervades public law,[31] much as it does private law, and so while it exemplifies the normativity of private law, it does not establish that private law is normatively distinctive. If one wanted to show that, for example, the deontic structure of civil liability reveals something normatively distinctive about private law, one would need to point to something further (perhaps considerations emphasised by corrective justice theorists[32]).

Second, reflect for a moment on Smith's emphasis on the vantagepoint of participants in the normative social practices constitutive of private law, especially behaviour whereby legislators, lawyers, judges and ordinary citizens treat law as an authoritative guide to right conduct. Again, these are observations about the nature of law as such, drawing on features of social rules, practices and behaviour that are consistent across public and private law. It is commonly claimed that the distinctiveness of private law can only be appreciated through adoption of an internal point of view, and further that from this vantagepoint one can see that private law has an immanent and autonomous moral logic.[33] But this claim is poorly supported and differs from Smith's more modest Hartian methodological point that one should investigate social rules from the perspective of participants in rule-governed social practices.[34]

Third, I would point to Smith's argument that court orders reflect the normativity of private law in so far as they are a unique kind of norm-giving practice (one in which courts give personalised normative directives to defendants about how to behave rightfully in specific circumstances). As far as I am aware, no one has attempted to show that private law is normatively distinctive in virtue of the kinds of orders made in the context of civil litigation. And that is well and good, for here, too, we have evidence of the normativity of law that applies equally to public as to private law (public law, too, features orders properly characterised as personalised normative directives that function as orders in civil suits do, rendering the general guidance supplied by law determinate and making it specifically actionable by those subject to the order).[35]

Finally, in reply to those who allow the normativity of law but insist that 'legal normativity' is just a form of moral normativity, Smith says – echoing Finnis on law as 'salient coordinator'[36] – that law resolves normative problems that could not be as effectively or decisively resolved otherwise.[37] Here again we have an important observation about the normativity of law, and one that is concerned with its distinctiveness. But the concern is with the distinctiveness of 'legal normativity' broadly. Thus, once more

[31] See H Lauterpacht, 'Kelsen's Pure Science of Law' in H Lauterpacht (ed), *International Law: Collected Papers*, vol II (Cambridge, Cambridge University Press, 2009).

[32] See, eg, J Coleman, *Risks and Wrongs* (Cambridge, Cambridge University Press, 1992); Weinrib, *The Idea of Private Law* (n 30); EJ Weinrib, *Corrective Justice* (Oxford, Oxford University Press 2012); and J Gardner, 'What is Tort Law For? Part 1. The Place of Corrective Justice' (2011) 30 *Law & Philosophy* 1.

[33] Weinrib, *The Idea of Private Law* (n 32); EJ Weinrib, 'The Jurisprudence of Legal Formalism' (1993) 16 *Harvard Journal of Law & Public Policy* 583.

[34] For more, see Miller and Pojanowski (n 20).

[35] As Smith emphasised. See Smith (n 2) 16.

[36] J Finnis, *Natural Law and Natural Rights* (Oxford, Oxford University Press 1980) 231–32. See also J Finnis, 'Law as Co-ordination' (1989) 2 *Ratio Juris* 97. For discussion of wider questions of political philosophy raised by Finnis' analysis, see L Green, 'The Duty to Govern' (2007) 13 *Legal Theory* 165.

[37] In Smith's words, 'Legal norms are sometimes introduced to address situations for which conventional moral norms provide no solution (eg, a co-ordination problem) or where conventional morality is unclear.' Smith (n 3) 228.

we appear to be bereft in isolating something normatively distinctive about private law, save for the possibility that private law provides effective and decisive resolution of a distinctive subset of conflict and coordination issues (a possibility about which I shall have more to say below).

It might seem that, given that the evidence Smith provides of the normativity of private law applies equally to public law, one will not find in his account resources with which to address the question whether private law is normatively distinctive. Quite the opposite. The resources needed are the more basic materials with which Smith constructs his arguments, notably: (i) his suggestion that there is such a thing as 'legal normativity'; (ii) his recognition that 'legal normativity' might be grounded in, and yet might also come apart from, moral, conventional and other sources of normativity; (iii) his suggestion that serious reflection on 'legal normativity' commends attention to particular legal norms in private law (ie, specific substantive, procedural and remedial norms), including attention to their content and the context(s) in which they are to guide conduct; and (iv) his recognition that 'legal normativity' encompasses norm-giving practices other than the positing and enforcement of general laws (eg, the giving of orders but also, I would add, less-commented-upon things like the exercise of supervisory jurisdiction and the issuance of advisory opinions).

As I have said, I mean to draw upon Smith for a Smithian framing of the question of the normative distinctiveness of law. My aim is not to try to answer that question, even in outline, for reasons that will soon become obvious: the question, properly unpacked, is far more complex than is acknowledged in responses to it in the literature thus far. So, in turn, the task of answering it will be burdensome. With this in mind, I present the Smithian framing in three steps, focusing first on the *nature and scope* of normativity; second, on *dimensions* of normativity; and, third, on the question whether distinctive features of the normativity of private law (supposing there are any) reflect an *inherent* or merely *accidental* distinctiveness. In my view, an adequate answer to the beguilingly simple question of the normative distinctiveness of private law will need to address, in detail, each of these elements.

Let us first consider how the question, put in terms of the *scope* of normative distinctiveness, might be understood. There are at least four possibilities: first, that law generally (and hence, *ipso facto*, private law) is not normatively distinctive but rather partakes of other, primary, forms and sources of normativity (eg, of morality or convention); second, that law generally is normatively distinctive relative to other forms and sources of normativity, but private law is not (ie, that private law manifests a general legal normativity); third, that private law is normatively distinctive relative to other bodies of law, especially public law, in its strain of legal normativity or in the ways in which it proves responsive to other forms and sources of normativity; and, fourth, that private law is not normatively distinctive per se, taken as a whole, but particular subfields conventionally viewed as being within private law are.

I take Smith to have rejected the first possibility, but not out of hand. He allows that legal normativity might draw from other sources of normativity (eg, in so far as the law incorporates moral norms or responds to practical reasons generated by them), but Smith maintains that 'legal normativity' is distinctive. The distinctiveness is put by him in Razian and Finnisian terms (ie, in terms of the peremptoriness of the moral authority claimed by law, and our need for decisive resolution of conflict and coordination issues).

One could imagine further elaboration of the same point along different lines (eg, in terms of rule-of-law values). As for the second, third and fourth options, I take them to be left open by Smith's account.

We may now consider the *dimensions* in respect of which private law might, or might not, prove normatively distinctive. It is important to recognise first and foremost that there *are* multiple dimensions to the law's normativity. Thus, there is a real risk of distortion – one amply borne out in the literature – in sweeping claims of normative distinctiveness for private law.[38] It is not that these claims miss their mark entirely (ie, that they fail to reveal *anything* that is normatively salient to, and possibly distinctive about, private law) but rather that they grossly oversimplify. There are likely to be no sound, sweeping generalisations to be made on this score. Thus, I offer a Smithian reframing meant to elicit specific dimensions of the normativity of private law in respect of which there are live questions about private law's distinctiveness.

There are at least five dimensions worth considering: *first*, the substantive, remedial and/or procedural norms of private law (generally, or by subfield) might prove normatively distinctive in their *justification* (ie, in their aim(s), in the value(s) that lend those aims moral force, and in the moral intelligibility of the relationship between the aim, mode of formal expression, content and moral impact of a given norm); *second*, the *formal relational structure* of substantive, remedial and/or procedural norms of private law (again, generally, or by subfield) might prove normatively distinctive (eg, in so far as they establish guidance and/or provide for accountability, answerability and redress on a bilateral, multilateral or omnilateral basis); *third*, private law's substantive, remedial and/or procedural norms (generally, or in specific subfield(s)) might prove normatively distinctive in their *content* (ie, in their characteristic exhortations, facilities and demands) and in what they require by way of *compliance*; *fourth*, the substantive, remedial and/or procedural norms of private law might turn out to be normatively distinctive in respect of the *identity of their addressees* and/or the capacities or roles in which these persons are addressed (eg, as subject, citizen, judge, legislator or bureaucrat); *fifth*, the substantive norms of private law may prove normatively distinctive in respect of the *spheres of social life* upon which they touch; *sixth*, the substantive, remedial and/or procedural norms of private law might prove distinctive in their *institutional mode of administration* (eg, in respect of the role of non-judicial officials in initiating and terminating proceedings, whether they admit of informal dispute resolution, characteristic rules of evidence and procedure, modes of decision-making and reason-giving, and so on); and *seventh* and finally, private law might prove normatively distinctive in respect of the *kind(s) of remedies, orders and other modes of officially sanctioned redress* deemed suitable as a judicial response to proven legal causes of action and accepted petitions for equitable relief.

Finally, one might ask about the *nature* of normative distinctiveness claimed for private law. Is it *inherent*, such that it indicates something essential to and unique about private law (or its subfield(s)), reflecting the universal moral salience to law of

[38] For an argument that this risk is realised in work emphasising correlativity or bilaterality as a structural feature of private law, see A Dorfman, 'Private Law Exceptionalism? Part I: A Basic Difficulty with the Structural Arguments from Bilaterality and Civil Recourse' (2016) 35 *Law & Philosophy* 165.

facets of the human condition? Or is it *contingent*, reflecting the variable moral salience of facets of the human condition that reflect dynamic features of our circumstances (eg, prevailing conventions, customs, cultural understandings, background posited law, socioeconomic and environmental conditions)? Of course, the correct answer might well be 'both': private law might be inherently *and* contingently normatively distinctive.

I read Smith as standing with other modern positivists in conceding some necessary connections between posited law and morality. For instance, Smith says that legal duties are necessarily presented as moral duties, and, following Raz, he thinks that the law necessarily claims moral authority.[39] But, with Raz, Green[40] and other modern positivists, Smith emphasises that whether the law lives up to its claims is a contingent thing. Unfortunately, none of this tells us his views on whether private law is inherently normatively distinctive, or contingently distinctive or both. I gather that if he had been asked, Smith's answer might well have been 'It depends.' More specifically, it depends on specifics about the moral work that private law performs or promises to perform.

IV. Conclusion

Stephen Smith's contributions to private law theory are immense and will be enduring. Many antedated the New Private Law but have inspired and motivated many of us who would, with Smith, with time come to be associated with the movement. As I have argued in other work, the New Private Law takes the normativity of private law seriously, but in a non-dogmatic way. Smith laid cornerstones for this way of thinking about private law in 'The Normativity of Private Law', inviting his readers to grapple with private law as it presents itself to us: as a system of authoritative normative guidance that must be understood from the vantagepoint of participants who treat it as such. Smith's suggestion that one ought to take the normativity of private law seriously would embolden those in and beyond the New Private Law who shared his scepticism of different strains of legal nihilism and nominalism circulating in twentieth- and twenty-first-century American legal thought.

But now, in Smith's absence, private law theory continues to labour under other burdens, some rooted in the lingering suspicion, sometimes voiced as accusation, that private law is just public law in another form. Smith did not respond to these views other than by ignoring them (as most theorists outside the United States have done). But I have suggested here that some of the scaffolding of Smith's arguments establishing the normativity of private law might be repurposed in support of a response to those sceptical of the distinctiveness of private law. This work, if it is to be truly Smithian in spirit, will be at once open to the possibility of being proved wrong and analytically rigorous. Consistent with those hallmarks, one must first consider different ways in which private law might prove distinctive. It might, for instance, be historically,

[39] Raz (n 21). See also J Raz, *The Authority of Law: Essays on Law and Morality* (Oxford, Oxford University Press 2009).

[40] Green (n 28).

institutionally, politically or socioeconomically distinctive. Smith's work may not shed light on these inquiries, but it does prove useful in reframing a different question: whether private law is normatively distinctive.

On the latter question, I have suggested that the Smithian spirit of open-mindedness and rigour require that we avoid the temptations of clever but superficial answers: simple moral stories with which we might content ourselves but convince no one. Arguably, some older work of private law theory spins simple narratives of this sort, conflating different dimensions of private law and of its normativity (eg, running together claims about the moral aims of substantive, remedial and procedural norms by asserting implausibly tight moral continuity between them) and by asserting that all of private law manifests a singular inherent normative logic. In a Smithian spirit, I think we would do better to step back and take stock: to examine the ways in which private law might partake of a general legal normativity or constitute a legal normativity of its own, to examine the various possible connections between legal and non-legal sources of normativity, to consider the various dimensions of normativity that need to be isolated for the inquiry to be tractable, and to consider that private law might be inherently and/or contingently normatively distinctive along any of these dimensions, if it proves distinctive at all. This conclusion leaves us without answers but instead with a reframing that makes a seemingly simple question more difficult to answer. This might seem a poor return. However, Smith was not afraid of taking a long time to develop intricate answers to hard questions, unafraid of their complexity. His example should encourage us to do the same.

APPENDIX

List of Publications 1994–2022

STEPHEN ALEXANDER SMITH

Books

Rights, Wrongs, and Injustices: The Structure of Remedial Law (Oxford, Oxford University Press, 2019). 368 pp.
Atiyah's Introduction to the Law of Contract, 6th edn (Oxford, Oxford University Press, 2005). 441 pp.
Contract Theory (Oxford, Oxford University Press, 2004). 450 pp.
Introducing Common Law Concepts (The Hague, Asser Press, 2001). 290 pp.

Contributions to Edited Volumes

'Intermediate and Comprehensive Justifications' in S Degeling, M Crawford and N Tiverios (eds), *Justifying Private Law Rights* (Oxford, Hart Publishing, 2021) 63–83.

'The Significance of a Civil Wrong' in P Miller and J Oberdiek (eds), *Civil Wrongs and Justice in Private Law* (Oxford, Oxford University Press, 2020) 157–83.

'The Structure of Remedial Law: Four Questions' in D Campbell and R Halson (eds), *Research Handbook on Private Law Remedies* (Cheltenham, Edward Elgar, 2019) 458–75.

'The Deed Not the Motive: Fiduciary Law Without Loyalty' in A Gold and P Miller (eds), *Contract, Status and Fiduciary Law* (Oxford, Oxford University Press, 2016) 213–39.

'Form and Substance in Equitable Remedies' in A Robertson and M Tilbury (eds), *Divergences in Private Law* (Oxford, Hart Publishing, 2016) 321–42.

'Duties to Try and Duties to Succeed' in A Dyson, J Goudkamp and F Wilmot-Smith (eds), *Defences in Tort* (Oxford, Hart Publishing, 2015) 63–83.

'Strict Duties and the Rule of Law' in L Austin and D Klimchuk (eds), *Private Law and the Rule of Law* (Oxford, Oxford University Press, 2015) 189–206.

'Remedies for Breach of Contract: One Principle or Two?' in G Klass, G Letsas and P Saprai (eds), Philosophical Foundations of Contract Law (Oxford, Oxford University Press, 2014) 341–61.

'The Restatement of Liabilities in Restitution' in C Mitchell and W Swadling (eds), *The Restatement Third, Restitution and Unjust Enrichment: Comparative and Critical Essays* (Oxford, Hart Publishing, 2013) 227–50.

'Rule-Based Rights and Court-Ordered Rights' in A Robertson and D Nolan (eds), *Rights and Private Law* (Oxford, Hart Publishing, 2011) 221–50.

'Rights and Remedies: A Complex Relationship' in K Roach and R Sharpe (eds), *Taking Remedies Seriously* (Ottawa, CIAJ, 2010) 31–62.

'The Rights of Private Law' in A Robertson and HW Tang (eds), *The Goals of Private Law* (Oxford, Hart Publishing, 2009) 113–38.

'Unjust Enrichment: Nearer to Tort than Contract' in R Chambers, C Mitchell and J Penner (eds), *The Philosophical Foundations of Unjust Enrichment Law* (Oxford, Oxford University Press, 2009) 181–208.

'The Limits of Contract' in J Neyers, R Bronaugh and S Pitel (eds), *Exploring Contract Law* (Oxford, Hart Publishing, 2009) 1–24.

'Hayek' in P Cane and J Conaghan (eds), *The New Oxford Companion to Law* (Oxford, Oxford University Press, 2008) 521–22.

'Substitutionary Damages' in C Rickett (ed), *Justifying Private Law Remedies* (Oxford, Hart Publishing, 2008) 93–114.

'The Law of Damages: Rules for Citizens or Rules for Courts?' in D Saidov and R Cunnington (eds), *Contract Damages: Domestic and International Perspectives* (Oxford, Hart Publishing, 2008) 33–64.

'Rights, Remedies, and Causes of Action' in C Rickett and R Grantham (eds), *Structure and Justification in Private Law: Essays for Peter Birks* (Oxford, Hart Publishing, 2008) 405–21.

'Contract, Doctrinal Issues in' in D Clark (ed), *Encyclopedia of Law and Society: American and Global Perspectives*, vol 1 (Thousand Oaks, CA, Sage Publishing, 2007) 290–95.

'The Enforceability of a Promise: English Report' in J Gordley (ed), *The Enforceability of Promises in European Contract Law* (Cambridge, Cambridge University Press, 2001) [approx 40 pp, broken up across multiple case studies].

'In Defence of the Third-Party Rule' in P Kincaid (ed), *Privity: Private Justice or Public Regulation* (Aldershot, Ashgate, 2001) 147–71 [reprinted from (1997) 17 *Oxford Journal of Legal Studies* 643–63].

'Towards a Theory of Contract' in J Horder (ed), *Oxford Essays in Jurisprudence: Fourth Series* (Oxford: Oxford University Press, 2000) 107–29.

'Freedom, Capacity in Contract' in C Gray (ed), *The Philosophy of Law: An Encyclopedia* (New York, Garland Publishing, 1999) 318–20.

'Contract' in A Lewis (ed), *Current Legal Problems: Annual Review - Volume 48 Part 1* (Oxford, Oxford University Press, 1995) 4–32.

'Contract' in A Lewis (ed), *Current Legal Problems: Annual Review - Volume 47 Part 1* (Oxford, Oxford University Press, 1994) 5–38.

Journal Articles

'Rights-Threats, Wrongs, & Injustices: The Common Law's Causes of Action' (2017) 27 *New Zealand Universities Law Review* 1033–59.

'A Duty to Make Restitution?' (2013) 26 *Canadian Journal of Law and Jurisprudence* 157–79.

'Duties, Liabilities, and Damages' (2012) 125 *Harvard Law Review* 1727–56.

'Comparative Legal Scholarship as Ordinary Legal Scholarship' (2011) 5 *Journal of Comparative Law* 331–55.

'Why Courts Make Orders (And What This Tells Us About Damages)' (2011) 64 *Current Legal Problems* 51–87.

'The Normativity of Private Law' (2011) 31 *OJLS* 215–42.

'"The Reasonable Expectations of the Parties": An Unhelpful Concept' (2010) 48 *Canadian Business Law Journal* 366–88.

'The General Provisions on Contract in the Civil Code of the Russian Federation' (2004) 30 *Review of Central and East European Law* 49–75.

'The Provisions on Gift in the Civil Code of the Russian Federation' (2004) 30 *Review of Central and East European Law* 77–100.

'The General Provisions on Purchase and Sale in the Civil Code of the Russian Federation' (2004) 30 *Review of Central and East European Law* 100–59.

'The Structure of Unjust Enrichment Law: Is Restitution a Right or a Remedy?' (2003) 36 *Loyola of Los Angeles Law Review* 1037–62.

'Justifying the Law of Unjust Enrichment' (2001) 79 *Texas Law Review* 2177–97.

'The Reliance Interests in Contract Damages and the Morality of Contract Law' (2001) 1 *Issues in Legal Scholarship: Article 1*, 1–38 [electronic journal].

'Concurrent Liability in Contract and Unjust Enrichment: The Fundamental Breach Requirement' (1999) 115 *LQR* 245–64.

'Contracts for the Benefit of Third Parties: In Defence of the Third-Party Rule' (1997) 17 *OJLS* 643–63.
'Performance, Punishment, and the Nature of Contractual Obligation' (1997) 60 *MLR* 360–77.
'Contracting Under Pressure: A Theory of Duress' (1997) 56 *CLJ* 343–73.
'Future Freedom and Freedom of Contract' (1996) 59 *MLR* 167–87.
'In Defence of Substantive Fairness' (1996) 112 *LQR* 138–58.
'Reconstructing Restraint of Trade' (1995) 15 *OJLS* 565–95.
'Of Remedies and Restrictive Covenants' (1994) 7 *Journal of Contract Law* 164–80.

Review Essays

'Are Tort Remedies "Civil Recourse"?' (2022) 41 *Law and Philosophy* 83–104.
'Taking Tort Seriously' (2020) 71 *University of Toronto Law Journal* 415–42.
'Troubled Foundations for Private Law' (2008) 21 *Canadian Journal of Law and Jurisprudence* 459–76.
'A Map of the Common Law?' (2004) 40 *Canadian Business Law Journal* 364–83.
'Taking Law Seriously' (2000) 50 *University of Toronto Law Journal* 241–59.

Shorter Articles/Comments in Journals

'The Law Commission's Proposals on Privity: Which Duty? Whose Right?' (1997) 1 *Amicus Curiae* 13–14.
'Rights, Remedies, and Normal Expectancies in Tort and Contract' (1997) 113 *LQR* 426–32.

Book Reviews

Review of R Zakrzewski, *Remedies Reclassified* (2006) 122 *LQR* 164–70.
Review of D Patterson, ed, *A Companion to the Philosophy of Law and Legal Theory* (1998) 114 *LQR* 322–24.
Review of E Weinrib, *The Idea of Private Law* (1996) 112 *LQR* 363–68.
Review of D Owen, ed, *Philosophical Foundations of Tort Law* (1996) 112 *LQR* 694–96.
Review of J Beatson & D Friedmann (eds), *Good Faith and Fault in Contract Law* [1996] *Restitution Law Review* 261–65.

Other Research

'The Provisions on Sale and Purchase in the Russian Civil Code' (2000), paper prepared for the McGill–Russia Legal Collaboration Project, translated into Russian (funded by CIDA). 99 pp.
'The Provisions on Gift in the Russian Civil Code' (2000), paper prepared for the McGill–Russia Legal Collaboration Project, translated into Russian (funded by CIDA). 49 pp.
'The General Provisions on Contract in the Russian Civil Code' (1999), paper prepared for the McGill–Russia Legal Collaboration Project, translated into Russian (funded by CIDA). 24 pp.
'The Domain of Contract and the Contract Law of the People's Republic of China', paper prepared for and presented at the Canada–China Senior Judges Training Project, 3rd Joint Seminar, Beijing, 14–18 June 1999. Paper translated into Chinese and published privately. 21 pp.
'Remedies for Breach of Contract and the Contract Law of the People's Republic of China', paper prepared for and presented at the Canada–China Senior Judges Training Project, 3rd Joint Seminar, Beijing, 14–18 June 1999. Paper translated into Chinese and published privately. 23 pp.

INDEX

www.ingramcontent.com/pod-product-compliance
Lightning Source LLC
LaVergne TN
LVHW010559310126
830691LV00003B/94
* 9 7 8 1 5 0 9 9 7 1 1 5 2 *